Common roots
–separate branches

Railway history and preservation

*Proceedings of an international symposium
held at the National Railway Museum, York
from 8 to 12 October 1993*

edited by Rob Shorland-Ball

Science Museum for the
National Railway Museum, York

Published 1994

British Library Cataloguing-in-Publication Data
A catalogue record for this publication is available
from the British Library

Set from Pagemaker in Postscript Monotype Plantin Light.
Printed in England by Hobbs the Printers, Southampton, UK.

ISBN 0 901805 77 7

Science Museum, Exhibition Road, London SW7 2DD, UK
National Railway Museum, Leeman Road, York YO2 4XJ, UK

Common roots – separate branches

Contents

List of contributors

Philip Atkins	Librarian, National Railway Museum, York, UK
Peter D Barton	Director, Railroaders Memorial Museum, Altoona, Pennsylvania, US
Gordon Biddle	Writer and Lecturer on Transport History, UK
Neil Cossons	Director, National Museum of Science & Industry, UK
Stephen E Drew	Senior Curator, California State Railroad Museum, Sacramento, California, US
Kilian T Elsasser	Curator and Project Manager, Verkehrshaus der Schweiz, Luzern, Switzerland
Robert Emerson	Director, Railroad Museum of Pennsylvania, US
Alfred Gottwaldt	Senior Curator, Museum für Verkehr und Technik, Berlin, Germany
H Roger Grant	Professor of History, University of Akron, Akron, Ohio, US
Walter P Gray III	Director, California State Railroad Museum, Sacramento, California, US
J Patrick Greene	Director, Museum of Science & Industry in Manchester, Manchester, UK
John P Hankey	(Formerly) Senior Curator, B&O Railroad Museum, Baltimore, Maryland, US
Herbert H Harwood, Jr	(Formerly) Director, Commerical Administration, CSX Transportation, Baltimore, Maryland, US
Christine J Heap	Curator, Research, Scholarship and Publication, National Railway Museum, York, UK
Dieter Hopkin	Head of Library and Archive Collections, National Railway Museum, York, UK
Stephen Joseph	Director, Transport 2000, UK
Lars Olov Karlsson	Director, Sveriges Järnvägsmuseum, Gävle, Sweden
John A Latschar	Superintendent, Steamtown National Historic Site, Scranton, Pennsylvania, US
Linn Moedinger	Vice President and Chief Mechnanical Officer, Strasburg Rail Road Company, Strasburg, Pennsylvania, US
David Morgan	Chairman, Association of Railway Preservation Societies, UK
J Allan Patmore	Professor Emeritus, University of Hull, Hull, UK
Rob Shorland-Ball	(Formerly) Deputy Head, National Railway Museum, York, UK
Jack Simmons	Professor Emeritus, University of Leicester, Leicester, UK
L J Soane	Executive Director, Railway Heritage Trust, Watford, UK
Paul van Vlijmen	Director, Nederlands Spoorwegmuseum, Utrecht
Peter van Zeller	Driver and Museum Curator, Ravenglass & Eskdale Railway, Ravenglass, UK
James A Ward	Professor of History, University of Tennessee, Chattanooga, Tennessee, US
John H White, Jr	Senior Historian Emeritus, Museum of American History, Smithsonian Institution, Washington DC, US
William Withuhn	Curator (Transportation), Museum of American History, Smithsonian Institution, Washington DC, US

Foreword

Neil Cossons

It is a matter of great pleasure that the National Railway Museum, one of the group of museums that form the National Museum of Science & Industry, should have arranged and hosted the first international symposium on railway history and preservation. Notwithstanding the work of the International Association of Transport Museums, I believe that such a gathering of museum curators and directors, academics and railway operators to be unprecedented. The symposium, and these proceedings, will, we hope, act rather as pebbles in a pool sending out ripples which, in due course, will create waves.

The wisdom of a museum derives from its collections. And the value of those collections, in the wider cultural sense, derives from our knowledge and understanding of them. This is no less true when it comes to the preservation of an historic building or, for that matter, a branch line. It is essential, therefore, that we develop the knowledge and understanding of the material that it is our privilege to hold. That means serious research, carried out by competent people and to the standards accepted in the wider world of scholarship. Only with that knowledge and understanding will we be able to develop our collecting and conservation policies, and advance the broader understanding of the railway, its history, its technology, and its place in society.

But preservation, despite what some of us might like to think, is not an end in itself. We preserve our past in order that the public at large may gain some broader understanding. Our purpose therefore is education, enlightenment and inspiration. It is that, and that alone, that justifies the charitable non-profit status that museums and preservation societies enjoy.

I have been concerned for some time about the lack, in Britain at least, of new and original research on railways which is so essential to underpin the physical preservation work which is carried out with such vigour and enthusiasm. Although the number of books and pamphlets published about railways is enormous, the number of analytical or synoptic studies that consider railways in the wider context is relatively small. Not only do we lack major definitive studies on some of our most important railways but the economic and social history of the railway has, to a large extent, been neglected. By the same token, much of what is written lacks a breadth of vision and broad historical understanding; as a result the effort is often wasted.

I welcome the publication of these proceedings and hope that the symposium will be the first of a regular series of such international meetings. But meeting in itself is not enough. We need to establish a debate and, more importantly, to promote research and scholarship in order to inform our policies for preservation, the quality of our presentation, but, above all, the wider understanding, on the part of the public at large, of the importance of the railway. To this end we have formed a link between the National Railway Museum and the University of York which will take the form of an Institute of Railway Studies. This will be headed by a Professor of Railway Studies who, besides holding an academic position in the University, will be Head of Research at the National Railway Museum. Out of this will come, we intend, a growth in the quality and quantity of serious study and research on the railway. I hope that by the time of the next symposium we will be in a position to demonstrate some of the first fruits of this liaison. If others felt compelled to follow suit we should be delighted.

Preface

William Withuhn

Rob Shorland-Ball began planning *Common Roots – Separate Branches* in 1991. His proposal was to convene the first-ever international symposium of railway historians and preservationists. It was a path-breaking proposal, one that sought both to capitalise on the growing worldwide maturity in railway preservation activities and to help push that maturity to a new level.

I believe that the success of the York symposium has now set a new standard for our field. In the quality of its papers and discussions, and particularly in the honest grappling with issues of meaningful interpretation of railway history for the general public, the reader will find gold in these proceedings.

The international perspective is crucial for all of us, in my estimation. Only by the widest sharing of ideas and experience in historical research, in preservation, in exhibit approaches and in interpretative modes can we grow as a field. Our historical field is embedded in the larger contexts of industrial and social history, and those contexts are fundamentally international.

Our efforts at public interpretation also have an international context. Symposium participants were united in the view that our days of internalist approaches to interpretation are over. Museums and preservation groups around the world know that meaningful interpretation for the non-specialist, general audience is the *sine qua non*. Without reaching – explicitly and effectively – the general public, our field cannot be widely perceived as a vital part of our broader cultural heritage, nor can we gain the long-lasting private or public support that we require for our preservation activities. The fact is that our field is rapidly improving in the quality of its interpretative approaches for the general public. The York symposium was, to me, most exciting in showing how much we each have to gain from international comparisons of our work.

The Smithsonian Institution was delighted to assist by lining up the American contingent of participants and by serving as one of the event's co-sponsors. We hope that there will be a second international railway preservation symposium, and, indeed, a continuing series, with an international sponsorship.

Introduction

Rob Shorland-Ball

The papers published in this volume are the proceedings of an international symposium on railway preservation and interpretation which took place at the National Railway Museum (NRM), York, in October 1993.

In the course of preparing and refining the programme I received a very helpful letter from John Hankey, formerly the Senior Curator at the B&O Railroad Museum in Baltimore. He wrote (inter alia):

... I do not suggest that we get too abstract or introduce needlessly complex ideas. We do, however, have a marvellous opportunity to weave the interests and experiences of this unprecedented gathering of railway preservationists into a useful fabric.

It was apparent to those who attended the symposium that the weaving of such a fabric had indeed taken place, albeit that we were not immediately able to distinguish the colour or the texture of what had been woven. I hope that the publication of the symposium papers will give substance to the fabric and provide the means to make it up into something useful, long-lasting and hard-wearing.

The basic framework for the meeting was determined in a series of detailed discussions with William Withuhn, Curator (Transportation), at the Smithsonian. Subsequently Neil Cossons, Director of the National Museum of Science & Industry, of which the NRM is a part, emphasised that a concern for the relative lack of scholarship in the field of railway preservation should underpin our planning and be discussed during the symposium. With that in mind we planned a gathering which would bring together contributions from a wide range of disciplines – historians, museum curators, archaeologists, geographers, railway operators – to examine and critically evaluate the significance of railways and railway preservation in the context of their own subject experience and interest.

The table of contents for these proceedings follows the structure and the intellectual framework of the symposium programme. After an introductory paper by Ward, we begin with the physical infrastructure of the railway; the first papers review railway buildings and structures in Britain and the US and then, more specifically, in Altoona, Pennsylvania, and Berlin in Germany. Harwood's paper on the B&O Railroad in the US concludes the section. It provides an illustration of academic research and practical fieldwork combining to uncover the remaining early structures of a pioneering American railway.

Mechanical engineering made the railways work; White's encylopaedic paper on early locomotive developments in the US, studies of locomotives in Britain and research on British locomotives in Sweden all relate to the theme of common roots which grew and separated in different areas and countries.

The two papers on historical context give a holistic view of railways and social history, and railways and geography, by Simmons and Patmore. Those on research are more specific and reflect our concern in planning the programme to cover railway-related work in other disciplines. Grant, an American historian, provides an interesting perspective on railway-influenced urban development in the US which counterpoints Simmons' review of British towns and the coming of the railway. Greene, an archaeologist, illustrates the application of archaeological techniques to the study and understanding of an important early railway building: the 1830 warehouse at Liverpool Road station in Manchester.

The preservation and interpretation of the railway heritage occupied two days of the symposium and included a visit to a preserved railway. The published papers indicate the variety of work being undertaken and the varying but related philosophies employed.

The symposium had several aims: to bring together in an international gathering a variety of practitioners for whom the study of railways is significant; to hear papers, to encourage discussion and debate and to establish links between those whose work or interest in railways can contribute to the sum of knowledge of the subject; to break down the barriers between those who count rivets and those whose concern is an academic study of railways so that each may draw on the knowledge of the other; and, probably most importantly, to create an awareness – especially in the UK – that railway studies and railway museology has an academic and scholarly respectability and is not merely people 'playing with trains'.

The issue of railway scholarship was taken up in characteristically vigorous fashion by Neil Cossons in an after-dinner speech during the symposium. His concern was that the generation of railway scholars such as Michael Robbins and Jack Simmons – both of whom contributed to the symposium – was not being followed by younger researchers and writers. Cossons noted the enormous physical vitality of the railway preservation movement of the last 40 years but deplored the fact that so little academic research was being undertaken, in parallel with and complementing the work of

railway restoration and operation. These trenchant views provoked widespread debate, a debate which is apparent, explicitly or implicitly, in several of the papers published in these proceedings. Indeed, the symposium itself and the quality and breadth of the papers go some way to answering Cossons' concern that railway studies should be pursued not just by specialists writing for specialists but with an academic rigour and breadth of vision reflecting the significance of the railway as an economic and social force which has changed the world.

Finally, may I thank all those friends and colleagues who contributed to the success of the symposium. I hope that these proceedings, which constitute the formal papers delivered during the four days of the meeting, will prove a valuable source of reference and will provoke discussion and debate in years to come.

Common roots–separate branches

James A Ward

A word of introduction is in order to put what follows in some perspective. Rob Shorland-Ball in his charge to me a few months ago asked that I should prepare a keynote address relating the preservation of our railways' heritages to 'the wider context of geographical, historical and archaeological understanding'. He warned that he did not want the gathering to become self-serving with 'the converted speaking to the converted'. Rob's request reminded me of Robert Hutchins' motto, 'Feel free', which hung over the door of his Presidential office at the University of Chicago. I, too, have taken some liberties in this paper. Rob wanted me to challenge what Neil Cossons, the Director of the National Museum of Science & Industry, believes to be the general assumption that 'railway preservation is a harmless and inconsequential activity carried out by consenting adults in private'.[1]

Allow me to start with a personal story. Last summer I wandered around the Colonial Williamsburg Museum with my family in 104 °F temperatures soaking up the American colonial experience. This beautiful, restored village probably looks 100 per cent better than it ever did in the colonial era. But while looking at colonial architecture, colonial wigmakers, colonial courtroom procedures, colonial firearms, colonial gardens, colonial lemonade, colonial food, colonial fashions and even colonial birdhouses, I experienced a rather vague feeling of unease, a sense that something was out of place. At the end of the day, we sat on a colonial bench in front of a colonial tavern waiting to eat and it suddenly occurred to me what was wrong. I turned to my colonial daughter, for she is studying colonial history at nearby William & Mary College, and exclaimed that I had a great deal of trouble putting all this in perspective because there were no colonial railways. I lacked a centre, an interpretative framework to bring together the disparate information my brain and senses had processed throughout the long day. As a man who makes his living trying to bring the nineteenth century alive for hormonal 20-year-olds, and who uses railroads as a focal point of departure for almost all facets of that wonderful century, I found myself quite out of my

element in graceful Williamsburg. It was not a world the railways had made, although, ironically, the restoration was financed by Rockefeller *largesse*, derived in part from the millions wrung by him from the eastern trunk railroads.

Allow me one more, much shorter, story. When I returned home I dropped my wristwatch on the floor, a timepiece awarded to me for the singular achievement of having graduated in good standing from high school. I took it to our local watch wizard who looked at it and exclaimed: 'a Ball, a railroad watch made when the trains ran on time'. The watchman looked at an artefact from the period and immediately made a connection between it and some other, less tangible, aspect of his own railway experience. And that is what we are about in this symposium: we are exploring ideas and techniques that will enable us to preserve and interpret railway artefacts – to demonstrate their essential contribution to the world in which we live. We are, however, more ambivalent than that; we want to accentuate the significance of the railroads' global contributions to culture, economics, politics and every other realm of life: *Common Roots – Separate Branches.*

Keynote addresses are usually stirring calls to action, affirmations that we are on a holy quest to uncover the great truths by which we live. The reality is that I bring both good news and bad news. The bad is that what we are attempting to do here is quite impossible, at least by any standards that we have set ourselves. The good news is that it does not make any difference because we will succeed in spite of ourselves. I do believe, however, that we should strive to achieve the impossible: to convey the full measure of the railways' importance to bygone eras through our artefacts and documents.

Our fundamental problem is that railroads appeal to us on several levels, and the most obvious, the real world of physical things, is often not the most important. It does have the distinct advantage, however, of illustrating the profound changes that everyone, even the dullest among us, can see. Buildings, structures, trackwork, locomotives, wagons and the like stand as monuments to the goals our forefathers set for themselves and mark their accomplishments. Their sheer size, technical complexities and ubiquity belie the popular notion that everything worthwhile has been invented since we were born. Even at rest, locomotives exude power which any bystander can sense. Depot architecture and building materials demonstrate the level of craftsmanship of their period and, if the observer is especially sharp, can suggest the variety of local businesses which supplied the contractors. Railroad uniforms (even down to their buttons), lanterns, oil cans and shovels all attest to the physical work long-dead men performed in the name of moving goods and people.

All that, however, is much like a stroll through Colonial Williamsburg: interesting but not very fulfilling. For the railroads unleashed a power and energy in the nineteenth century that led men everywhere to assault the brute forces of nature which had held them in thraldom for centuries. It was more than simply the arrival of steam power and the industrial revolutions that set workers in motion. Russia, after all, girded an entire landmass with iron rails without the benefit of a very energetic industrial base.

Railroads appealed to these people's subconscious and to their emotions, and those are the appeals which are so difficult to reproduce a century and a half later – or even the following day. The appeals are the most transitory of feelings, often barely understood, but that does not make them a whit less important to our agenda. Something more powerful than the promise of $1.25 a day prompted recent Irish immigrants to haul black powder into the Hoosac Tunnel's unfinished bore in western Massachusetts, drill holes in granite faces with hand drills and then blow their charges in the hope that they could gain a foot a day on the mountain's fastness. English stonemasons, who defied heights on rickety scaffolding to lay massive stones in the supporting piers of so many beautiful and durable railway bridges in the kingdom, risked life and limb for more than a few shillings. They were driven by vague notions of progress, and by the hope for material gain, to rearrange their physical landscapes to accord more nearly with their changed emotional ones, and in the process created the *Separate Branches* which we are investigating here. In their daily pursuit of tasks, they called forth a world in which their railroads altered every known human contour, from the sandwich business to the concept of the proper role of government in private enterprise. They redefined corruption and the concept of property holding, and engendered class conflict in the UK, while doing just the opposite in the US.

Even the most hard-bitten devotees of mechanical excellence among us, those of us who stand in admiration before well-tightened stay bolts and wax enthusiastic over roller bearings, derive our appreciations from some ill-understood, deep-seated emotional need for physical perfection. And we go even further: we give human personalities to our mechanical behemoths made of cast iron, steel, wood and dirt, and are able to utter with a straight face as a begrimed engineer of the Southern Railroad's 4501 steam engine once did in my hearing: 'she's steady on her feet at 50 miles per hour'. Nobody in the crowd expressed puzzlement that this most masculine of productions had assumed a feminine gender and feet. At an emotional level we knew exactly what the engineer was saying.

Many people with a love of railroads make their daily bread from their preservation, maintenance and interpretation. For certain folks it goes beyond mere love: some risk their lives to capture that perfect photograph or to tape the sounds of exhaust valves popping. In the US we call them 'foamers', but they do illustrate just how powerful the railways' attractions can be to the human spirit.

It is not the 'foamers', however, that we are trying to reach. In a very real sense it is ourselves. We seek to reproduce our own enthusiasms for the railroad world and its importance to our daily concerns. And that is what makes the task so very nearly impossible for all those of us who are trying to re-create with inadequate words, steel, architecture, archaeology and corporate records, something that, say, Norman Rockwell, an illustrator of emotions, did by artistic instinct. With only canvas, brushes and oils, he painted a station scene showing lovers and parents standing about awkwardly awaiting the train that would carry their boys, in the prime of their lives, off to war. Our own personal memories of parting and death often include trains, and the confusion, smells, and sounds of a working station. Rockwell did not paint those later trains that slipped into town at dawn quietly to off-load coffins full of war's carnage. He had already made the point that railways often created a sense of alienation and loss.

However, railroads also created a sense of hope and expectation, often fulfilling desires. Crowds gathered early at stations in all countries to greet relatives and friends and passed the time in social intercourse. Folks gravitated to train stations even when no trains were due, just to catch up on the latest gossip and await the news that broke over the new telegraph line. Likewise, lovers, looking as respectable as possible on the station platform, boarded the 2.10 local for a 20-minute ride to a safe trysting place. They never forgot the smell of coal smoke and the feel of cinder-laden wind in their faces as they rode towards passionate embrace. The railway became a lasting part of their intimate lives, and it is our challenge to replicate something of that emotional fervour in our present-day audiences.

For most of us, unfortunate enough to miss the 2.10, railroads more poignantly evoke our childhoods. Mingle with visitors at any railway museum and you will hear older folks telling tales of their youth as they pass on their personal histories against the tableaux of railroad artefacts. Somehow, we must strive to instill in others our own youthful rail experiences: like my own memories of being tucked up in a warm Pullman berth, somewhere out on the Illinois prairie, listening to the soporific music of the train passing over the rail joints; or even, almost 20 years later, standing between passenger cars on the New York Central's *Pacemaker*, somewhere south of Rochester, New York, in the dead of winter, the snow swirling past in the dark night, watching the conductor time telephone poles as they flashed past, and hearing him shout that the train was speeding me home from college at over 100 mph. There is a youth and innocence in all this that I fear may not be amenable to duplication at any level. Nevertheless, we have to try, because the personal elements of nostalgia are among the strongest weapons we have in our interpretative arsenal.

On a less intense level, we have to recognise and explain the fact that railroads have altered our conceptions of art and beauty. They wrench a mechanical intruder into the aesthetics of the art world, to paraphrase Leo Marx. They have expanded our definition of the natural world and the human condition to include the pleasing lines of brute mechanical contrivances and their supporting casts. The Starrucca viaduct in Pennsylvania, for instance, still draws photographers awed by its grace and immensity. Nineteenth-century painters draw the structure into its surrounding natural scene; theirs was a transitional phase which led eventually to works such as those by the late Grif

Teller, who relegated nature to the background as he caught the tension and power of the machines themselves.[2] The sight of 'clean' English steam locomotives, their working parts cleverly hidden, their exterior skins 'slippery' in their bright paint schemes, their huge driving wheels singing away the miles, is a beautiful one. By contrast, the huge Union Pacific Railroad 'Challengers' with all their appurtenances hanging helter-skelter on their exteriors, are bigger than some of the dinosaurs that once roamed their territory and speak to our appreciation of varieties of beauty.

We must remember that our sense of the beautiful arose, at least in part, from our fears of the railroad. We have an infinite capacity for self-deception and redefinition; we hastened acceptance of the 'iron horse' in our everyday worlds by hiding its noise, dirt, fearsome speeds and danger, and by disguising it in a metaphorical rural setting that made it normal and beautiful. By the twentieth century we no longer needed such artifices; Raymond Loewy could, with pride, take an ugly duckling electric locomotive and create a thing of intrinsic beauty. His Pennsylvania Railroad class GGI, examples of which are in the museums of Altoona and Strasburg, draw crowds daily, but do those crowds have any appreciation of how their sense of beauty has been forever altered or that there is an aesthetic synergy between the GGI and Andy Warhol's Campbell's soup can? But I digress.

Finally, at the emotional level of understanding, there is an important element of sophistication that envelops railways. Most of us intuitively comprehend the technical sophistication that made the industry possible. Those brave enough to venture into some of the more comprehensive railway histories learn that such mechanical ingenuity was accompanied by organisational and financial inventiveness as well. The politics that surrounded the invention, especially in France and Germany in the industry's infant years, where governments were more intimately involved, and in the US where railway magnates raised the practice of political corruption to a fine art, are central to the railroads' story, both to its roots and branches. But at a more personal level, the railroads displayed a sophisticated ambience as well. A peek into Queen Victoria's coach in the British National Railway Museum gives one the sense of the meaning of 'royal treatment'. We commoners, however, experienced the same feeling when we went into a dining car. The sight of white linen tablecloths with fresh flowers in heavy cut-glass vases, surrounded by real silverware and cloth napkins, lent a patina of grace and polish, especially after the cooks, squeezed into their tiny galley, had concocted their gastronomic delicacies on charcoal and coal stoves.

We still have dining trains in operation; the more energetic among us can browse in art museums which possess paintings that show railroads enhancing their natural surroundings; and we can, perhaps, with great efforts reproduce the sights, sounds and even smells of bygone railway worlds to evoke a sense of nostalgia. The sensory projections may be a bit more difficult for authors, archivists and architects to achieve, but we have all seen examples of our crafts that convey a sense of smell.

The fault line through all this though, as some railway preservationists have noted, is that most people have no nostalgic memories of the time when railways were central to their lives.[3] Those fighting in Vietnam, the Falklands and Iraq left on 747s from antiseptic airports. It is a little more difficult to feel an affinity for surroundings that are always painted eggshell white, carpeted and strewn with chrome ashtrays. Airports are too big; they lose the intimacy of the crowded platform. We face a much more difficult challenge to reach this younger generation, although they are already visually attuned and that is to our advantage for they cannot cut us off with their TV remote-control units. We have to show them the beauty inherent in railroads and pass on to them our own emotional attachments. We want to teach them to appreciate what we revere, but to do that we have to touch their souls – the most difficult thing in the world to do.

Compounding our problems is the fact that our separate branches represent the subcategories into which we have relegated our realities, perceptions and emotions. Our branches have all become so complex that we have come together here to make sense of them. For example, there are those of us who dedicate our lives to the location and preservation of railway artefacts; we can sometimes be rather smug in our assumption that they speak for themselves and that their simple existence is enough to justify our efforts. This is not to belittle preservation efforts; every edifice needs a secure foundation. Someone has to know how to resuscitate steam engines, fabricate parts and repair and replace costly veneers. But our very presence here indicates that we believe that such technical expertise is not an end in itself. Those artefacts, as random as their survival has been, must be mustered and presented against appropriate backdrops, as in good theatre, to illustrate their utility and draw forth the desired emotional response from viewers. Many of us make our livings exhibiting and interpreting railroad 'relics', and we have only to look about us here at the National Railway Museum to see a most successful example of our art.

Then there are those of us, poor scribes, who attempt to re-create the romance and power of the railways using a language inadequate to the task. Good historians bring a two-dimensional world, black print on white paper, alive, and create with words what Rockwell did with oils. Most of us simply describe. The ideal would be to create in the reader's mind the sights, sounds and smells that affected us so powerfully and give meaning to what we experienced. We historians all project our twentieth-century experiences and desires back into the nineteenth when we write of that world – that is what gives the discipline meaning and keeps us employed.

Of late there has been a surge of environmental interest in the world the railroads made; in other words, there is now another branch on our metaphorical tree. This approach has enabled us to look at the business from a fresh angle: that of the biological, animal and human ecosystems that developed between the fences that stretched along many rail lines.[4] From the human perspective, this was a new world with its own laws, morality, fashions, economic justification and even dietary standards. The degree to which that corporate environment impinged on the world that existed outside the fences determined the cultural and social differences observed on railroads around the world. These are the interfaces we are here to examine.

At the other end of the spectrum, economists spin their webs ever finer and create imaginary worlds without railways, full of 'forward and backward linkages' that engender more statistical tables than the Pennsylvania Railroad's annual reports.[5] Despite the fact that economists wrap their musings in some of the most unreadable prose in the English-speaking world, they have at least forced us to re-evaluate our basic assumptions about the importance of the railway, and especially its economic importance. Where there is so much smoke, however, there must be fire: most of us still think that there must be something to the old chestnut that railroads created our modern economic world.

Our problem, however, is not the branches that have budded in the last decades. On the contrary, they are perches that enable us to see new aspects of the industry and to look at old verities from new angles. Our problem lies in the roots. As individuals we view the world around us through different eyes and from our own cultural perspectives, and we carry this baggage back into railway history. I was struck recently – while working with BBC film makers struggling to make thematic sense of railways in four nations – by just how different our approaches to the subject were. They were much more visually orientated than I, and looked to the juxtaposition of railroad objects to deliver subtle and implicit messages. They chased sunsets, rail crossings and speeding trains, and filmed all three together to show power in the context of unchanging nature; I would have used 300 pages of text to evoke the same image and then would not have got it quite right.

Those of us with a mechanical bent lust in our hearts, to paraphrase President Jimmy Carter, at the sight of a rail artefact. We undress it in our minds, exposing its most complex intimate workings, seeking to understand the inventive genius of the age that enabled mankind to rearrange the earth. We conjoin mechanical sophistication and progress and equate both, perhaps subconsciously, with our eventual triumph over all the ills that beset us, from war to poor health. But this is proof positive that we of the late twentieth century are not as cynical as we sometimes fear, for the generation of the 1830s and 1840s on both sides of the Atlantic believed exactly the same thing. We are not disillusioned, just slow.

However, those of us who toil in corporate archives rooting through the dusty papers that railroad clerks neglected to throw away are optimistic that we can unravel the motivating forces behind the contagious railway movement in the nineteenth century to explain it to our contemporaries. We assume that the vital truth lies buried somewhere in front-office decisions to build or buy more locomotives, to bribe the right people to acquire feeder roads or to attempt to dampen labour's wage demands. People, organised in vast bureaucracies, made the railroads work. We can divine labouring conditions from weekly pay vouchers, the ethnicity of surnames and average ages. We re-create the world of the railway worker from such scraps, confident that somehow historians and exhibitors can bring the long-dead information to life and

make it vital to a reading and viewing public afflicted by ever-shorter attention spans.

Architectural historians have lately come to railroad studies on both sides of the Atlantic, operating upon Louis H Sullivan's *credo* that 'form follows function'. They have examined closely what most of us agree were the temples of their age, the great railway stations with their glass roofs and broad concourses, teeming with humanity much as medieval cathedrals. And we have found that the temples were full of money changers as well. The largest of the railway stations encompassed self-contained markets, day in, day out, offering for sale almost everything we need. These miniature societies were not confined to the great railway stations; on a smaller scale, rural stations everywhere, including two-storey ones, illustrated in their layouts the peculiar manifestations and demands of the emerging corporate world.[6] We eagerly brought our cultural and social baggage under their roofs and adapted, much like starlings in a city park, to environments the railways created – hence more separate branches.

All of us here, then, are much like the blindfolded men in the old fable, sent out to describe an elephant by touch. Each selected a different part of the beast and their reports, of course, were not only humorous, but bore absolutely no relationship to reality. Like the elephant touchers, we are not so much separated by geography as imprisoned by the ways we look at the animal. And overlaying our different viewpoints are the cultural and social differences that colour our interpretations. Our barriers though, are largely self-imposed and self-perpetuating. We eagerly entice apprentices, docents, graduate students, interns and assistants into our orbits to teach them the 'right' way to do things. We assign them some obscure part of the 'railephant's' anatomy and bid them to toil away at it until they have detailed it minutely. Many of them do, and enjoy themselves immensely because they are kindred souls, driven by the same demons that drew us here.

Those demons, often unrecognisable, are the reason I wrote earlier that I think what we are trying to do is probably impossible. We are all too chronologically removed from the 'railephant' ever to have a ghost of a chance of replicating it, for ourselves or others. That leaves us with the unpalatable option of deciding what portion of it we want to exhibit, examine, interpret or write about. And no matter how well we perform our tasks, we are always left unfulfilled, for we know there is more to the subject. On the one hand we rejoice, claiming that we have left that work for others, the future generation perhaps. On the other, with the finite time at our disposal, we would like to see what the rest of it looks like. We all have an inkling of its outline and maybe even know how it behaved, but the whole thing does not fit in our buildings, depots, parks, tourist lines and books. We cannot even get quite all of it in the camera's lens. But I do not think that that should upset us. Those who worked on the railroads in their heyday never had a clear overview of what the industry was all about either. I doubt that J Edgar Thomson, president of the Pennsylvania Railroad during the Civil War, knew what it was like for an engine driver to work a 36-hour stint in the primitive equipment of the day. But then that driver had no inkling of the pressures Thomson was under to keep his road open to deliver military supplies day and night to the Union armies. They were standing at opposite ends of the 'railephant'. If they were there and could not embrace the totality of the industry, why should we expect to be able to do so vicariously and to be able to pass our knowledge on to an interested public that has an even foggier notion of what the industry was all about?

Let us be honest and admit that we are most pleased when our exhibits, books and re-creations satisfy us personally. That is because we got into this business for self-satisfaction, to serve personal needs and interests that we all secretly harbour. Like all worthwhile undertakings, railroad history is an intensely personal vocation (just ask our partners and families), and if we understand that and serve our own intellectual and emotional hunger then, I suspect, we will do a much better job for our publics.

In all our exhibits, books, archives, restored buildings, collections of railway artefacts and working museums, we are seeking to re-create our *own* experiences, emotions and truths. And we surmise, with perfect logic, that if we can transmit them with any intensity at all, they will become equally important for our viewers and readers. John Hankey, in his recent article 'The interpretation of a railroad landscape', spoke to this very theme when he concluded that the best any of us can ever hope to do is to pass on to our audience 'a truth' rather than 'the truth'. This is because, Hankey says, we have only impressions of the past that have been passed on to us by 'middlemen' and we filter that second-hand

information through our own subjective cultural and social biases to form our own very idiosyncratic views. For each of us, those individual views become our truths.[7] Hankey is right, I think, as far as he goes. The fact is, however, that we here are pretty long in the tooth and that during our lives we have stored up literally millions of such truths. Yet we deem some more valuable than others and a very few we feel compelled to share with other people. We are here today to learn how to do that more effectively.

That makes all of us artists as we strive for the highest form of self-expression, an overt manifestation of how we view our world. Whereas Norman Rockwell used a brush and oils, and the Williamsburg restoration folks used Flemish brick patterns and 250-year-old recipes to illustrate their passions, we work with very large artefacts in our museums and very large notions and ideas in our books. It is all the same thing. Even my watch repair man, who dabbles in minute gears and mechanisms, saw a larger beauty to my watch. His artistry was to rehabilitate my timepiece, to make it perform as it once had when conductors relied upon similar timepieces to ensure that their trains ran on time and to avoid collisions between scheduled meets.

The most successful artists are those who draw from their own wellspring of truth in their presentations. For us, that presents some complex problems that a Rockwell, who could paint anything as long as the *Saturday Evening Post* would put it on its cover, never faced. Frankly, I do not know how to re-create my late-night journey across New York state. A museum could couple two passenger cars together, open their Dutch doors, douse the lights, turn up the air conditioning, throw snow in my face and spin telegraph poles on a Lazy Susan at 100 mph and the whole contrivance would still lose something. I am no longer 19 years old and headed to that home.

We cannot replicate our experiences; they were rooted in a specific time and mood in the first place. But we can trigger strong reactions in others and often do so in the smallest ways. For example, some years ago I ventured into Pennsylvania's wilds to ride the narrow gauge East Broad Top railroad. It was a great experience, but what stuck in my mind was totally unintended by the Broad Toppers. When I went into the lunch counter at the side of the station, I went through an old-fashioned wooden screen door, the kind that never had a pneumatic closing device. This door, covered with a dozen coats of paint, slammed defiantly behind me about a quarter of an inch from my posterior, just as doors 40 years ago always did. It had one of those looping black springs, half an inch in diameter, as a door closer; that was all. It instantly evoked an experience that the whole railroad represented: a trip back in years.

The smallest details can create larger and more important images, but it also works the other way. Years ago I stumbled across an abandoned stone quarry in northern Louisiana and standing in the middle of it was a steam engine and tender. The straight-stacked locomotive was probably built in the 1870s or a little later. It was all there, if a little down-at-heel and begrimed. But the context, the overgrown slag piles, the huge quarry pit and the short section of rail the loco and its tender occupied, caused me to look around to see if the engineer and his fireman were on their way to steam her up for a day's work. It was that real and quite unintentionally so. If we can abandon artefacts in such evocative poses, we must possess the intelligence and artistry consciously to arrange them in even more powerful landscapes or to write about them in more strikingly emotional ways.

And that brings me to the good news. Even though it is impossible for us to re-create for others our personal experiences and memories, it really does not make much difference. For anyone standing next to us at the moments that such events touched us, undoubtedly perceived them in a totally different manner; they too filtered reality through their own psychological and emotional granules to record it differently. The same holds true for our restorations and literature. No matter how closely they parallel our intentions, no matter how much time and money we spend on them, they will be viewed and read in myriad ways. If, however, we can at the conscious level present our enthusiasms in a logical and explanatory sequence, then any reaction we draw from our publics, no matter how far removed from our own expectations, is worth all our exertions. We touch them even if they do not like our work; even bad reviews show that we have made the reviewer think.

I do not pretend to know, for example, what a German tourist's reaction would be to the Smithsonian's rail transport gallery. I do know, however, that it would stem from the common roots of rail technology and probably from at least a modicum of interest, without which he or she

would have skipped the display. It would not be 'a truth' the visitor would depart with, but it would be 'his or her truth'; even if it is only the observation that most American steam locomotives lack the 'elephant ears' smoke deflectors which are familiar in Germany, that observation will be a highly powerful notion because it reflects the visitor's own ethnic and cultural tendencies. The impressions I have mentioned in this paper were, I must admit, just as serendipitous: the upper berth, the screen door, the Louisiana quarry. It is a mystery to me why all my other impressions recorded from years of waiting for and riding trains do not mean just as much to me. Why not the all-night gin games, the train wreck or the worst food I have ever ingested on the euphemistically named 'snack car' on the Texas & Pacific? My point is that nobody created the memories that have moved us – we did that ourselves.

Our only charge is to make sense of the railways' realities, to suggest how important they are to the world as a whole and to invite that world to come and see for itself. Ultimately, it does not matter through what prism we view the industry – visual, textual, artistic or mechanical – because all our approaches are equally legitimate. If this symposium is a rousing success, and we all develop a greater appreciation for other methodologies and approaches to separate railway cultures, it will add new dimensions to our own work. This is all to the good, especially when we are seeking to enthuse a younger generation that comes to us without benefit of any railroad experiences and armed only with potential interest. The more effectively we can present the realities of railroading across the continents, the more apt we are to touch young folks' spirits and engender in them a lasting interest in the subject. If we satisfy our own needs in the process, that is almost enough, but if we move others to see the railroads' beauty, variety, power, charm and importance, then we have ascended to the exalted ranks of the world's greatest teachers. Of course, like all teachers, we can never be sure of exactly what it is that we have taught.

But back to the theme of this conference. The symposium's organisers judged the common roots to be the basic railway technology as conceived in the UK and exported to the rest of the world, while they saw the branches as the observably different cultural, economic and social manifestations that developed. I have felt a little more free than that and have, I suspect, crawled out on a branch and have been diligently sawing it off behind me. I have tried to get above the tree and in so doing have implied that *we* are the tree's metaphorical roots and that therefore there are as many of them as there are branches. Each of our railroad experiences, no matter how indirect, has put down yet one more 'rootling' – I fear my biology here is a little suspect. And, to wear out my metaphor, we, in machine shops, artists' studios, archaeological digs, archives and offices in front of word processors, are the ones who give this whole business its nourishment. The branches are the artistic manifestations of our own experiences, our feeble attempts to re-create our emotional attachments and translate them into some physical truths that will create an awareness in others.

The more we understand why we dedicate our careers to this business, the more effective will be our efforts to represent it, and the healthier the tree's branches will become. Like the roots of a real tree, we splay out in all directions and take radically different approaches in our search for personal and professional nourishment. We provide different functions but, in the end, we have come together here, to enrich the tree's foliage, to identify ways to attract others to play in it, and to help us and them to find truth and meaning among the colourful leaves. There can be no higher calling.

Notes and references

1   This sentence is from a memorandum from Neil Cossons to Rob Shorland-Ball.

2   Leo Marx first broached this idea in his *The Machine in the Garden: Technology and the Pastoral Idea in America* (New York: Oxford University Press, 1964) and in his later work with Susan Danly, *The Railroad in American Art* (Cambridge, MA: MIT Press, 1988). See also Cupper, Dan, *Crossroads of Commerce: The Pennsylvania Railroad Calendar Art of Grif Teller* (Richmond, VT: Great Eastern Publishing, 1992); Simmons, Jack, *The Victorian Railway* (New York and London: Thames & Hudson, 1991).

3   See in particular the articles by Mark Smith and John Hankey in recent 1993 issues of *Locomotive & Railway Preservation*.

4   Stilgoe, John R, *Metropolitan Corridor: Railroads and the American Scene* (New Haven: Yale University Press, 1983)

5   The most famous of this genre are Fishlow, Albert, *American Railroads and the Transformation of the Ante-Bellum Economy* (Cambridge, MA: Harvard University Press, 1965), and Fogel, Robert, *Railroads and American Economic Growth* (Baltimore: Johns Hopkins Press, 1964). For the European version, see O'Brien, Patrick (ed), *Railways and the Economic Development of Western Europe, 1830-1914* (New York: St Martin's Press, 1983).

6   Sullivan, Louis H, *The Autobiography of an Idea* (New York: Dover Publications, 1956), 2nd edn, p258; Richards, Jeffrey, and MacKenzie, John M, *The Railway Station: A Social History* (New York: Oxford University Press, 1986); Grant, H Roger, *Living in the Depot: The Two-Story Railroad Station* (Iowa City: University of Iowa Press, 1993)

7   Hankey, John, 'Views of Chama: the interpretation of a railroad landscape', *Locomotive & Railway Preservation* (July/August 1993), pp50-52

The railway infrastructure

Railway buildings and structures in Britain

Gordon Biddle

The promoters of the first trunk railways in Britain had a strong sense of their pioneering role in providing a new and rapid transport system for the country's expanding industries. Although financed by private capital, railway building was regarded as a national undertaking from which the country at large would benefit. The profit motive was accompanied by enormous self-confidence in engineering works on an unprecedented scale which, it was believed, would last for ever. In this paper, time and space allow me to give only a taste of their extent and variety, in a blend of the outstanding, the typical and the unique.

Firstly, however, it is necessary to look briefly at what is left of the railway's forerunners: the horse tramroads and wagonways which, structurally, reflect the canal era during which most of them were built. The Causey Arch in County Durham (*c*1726) actually pre-dated the canals and was the widest single-span masonry arch in the world. The tunnel at Ticknall, Leicestershire, on the Ticknall Tramroad (1802) was built merely to pass beneath the drive to Calke Abbey out of sight of the house – as were some railway tunnels later - but even so it is typical and one of very few remaining.

There are equally few engine houses and winding engines remaining: these hauled tramroad wagons up or lowered them down inclined planes. A typical early railway example will serve to illustrate them, however. Middleton Top engine house (1831) on the Cromford & High Peak Railway in Derbyshire has been nicely restored, complete with its winding gear. Also related to winding engines are the remarkable, yet little-known, massive brick underground vaults beneath the head of Camden incline north of Euston station in London. The two boiler rooms still exist, each 30 ft x 24 ft, flanking a room 76 ft x 30 ft which contained the engine which from 1837 to 1844 wound the endless rope used for getting trains up and down the one-mile gradient from Euston. Today, main line trains still rumble overhead.

Railway civil engineering structures were the direct successors of those on canals and tramroads. What may be termed the earliest large bridge on a proper railway, the Skerne Bridge at Darlington (1825) on the Stockton & Darlington Railway, was in fact designed by an architect, Ignatius Bonomi, who may be justly called the first railway architect. From the thousands of brick and stone bridges on this country's railways, perhaps I can pick out Robert Stephenson's three dramatic stone flying arches on the London & Birmingham Railway (1837) near Coventry, one just east of the station and the others at either end of Beechwood Tunnel, five miles to the west. I K Brunel built a whole series of bridges on the South Wales Railway in Pembrokeshire and there are others elsewhere, all built later than Stephenson's, which seem to have gone largely unnoticed. Sometimes special decorative effects were applied to a bridge at the behest of a local landowner, in return for a reasonable price for his land or, indeed, any price at all. One of the most elaborate is on the Trent Valley Railway (1847) – now part of the west coast main line – where it crosses Shugborough Park, Staffordshire: the bridge bears the arms and insignia of the Earls of Lichfield. An architect, John Livock, almost certainly designed this one.[1]

When it came to tunnels, expense was often lavished on elaborate portals. The awesome thrill or sense of horror – according to taste and temperament – with which the early Victorians regarded the noisy and noisome passage of a railway tunnel seemed to make Gothic crenellations and turrets peculiarly appropriate, as at Clayton tunnel in Sussex (1841). Other designers thought classicism more appropriate, as Brunel demonstrated at Box in Wiltshire (1841), and as Robert Stephenson displayed in particularly massive form at Primrose Hill tunnel (1837) near Euston station in London. But appearances can be deceptive. Just as the need for the little tunnel at Ticknall was not dictated by the terrain, neither was the need for the Primrose Hill tunnel. The landowner here was Eton College and, like many others, when the College authorities got wind of the London & Birmingham Railway Committee's intentions they hastily laid out the line of a few streets, declared their land to be in course of development and gained both extra compensation and a clause in the Railway's Act of Incorporation requiring the line to tunnel beneath their estate. Furthermore, it had to be done in such a manner as to be able to support houses on top, with the southerly mouth sufficiently 'substantial and ornamental' to prevent the soil 'from giving way or slipping down'.[2] An open cutting would otherwise have sufficed. Similar difficulties were encountered when parallel tunnels were made in 1879 and 1921-22.

Viaducts are among the most impressive nineteenth-century railway structures as they stride across valleys. The engineers wisely let them speak for themselves with the minimum of ornament. There is a typically dramatic viaduct in stone at Cefn Coed near Merthyr Tydfil in South Wales (1868). One of the few that was deliberately ornamented is Balcombe in Sussex (1841), where 37 brick arches span the Ouse valley. There the architect David Mocatta added balustrades and end pavilions to J U Raistrick's viaduct. But, for me, the most impressive is Grainger and Miller's Ballochmyle viaduct in southwest Strathclyde (1848), where the central arch makes a dramatic leap of 181 ft, 163 ft high – at the time the widest

then attempted. (Plate 1) The structure has superb detailing.

Timber was used extensively by Joseph Locke on the Caledonian Railway and, most of all, by Brunel in South Wales and the West Country. It not only saved expense when capital was scarce but also enabled wooden viaducts and bridges to be erected quickly, allowing the line to start earning revenue at the earliest possible moment. Brunel built no fewer than 56 timber viaducts on what became the Great Western Railway through south Devon and Cornwall, employing characteristically ingenious techniques. Many were notable for their fan-type construction, as could be seen at Moorswater in Cornwall (1858). They were progressively rebuilt in stone or iron, sometimes using the original stone piers but often built alongside, leaving the old piers still standing, as they remain at Moorswater. The last of the Cornish viaducts survived until 1934.[3]

I believe that only three timber bridges now remain, the largest being the Barmouth viaduct across the Mawddach estuary in North Wales – still in use, although heavy trains now rarely cross it. The little wooden bridge at Wickam Bishops in Essex is now disused, but it is listed and being

Plate 1. Ballochmyle viaduct (1848), Ayrshire, in 1987. (Photograph by G Biddle)

restored. Lesser known is Aultnaslanash viaduct, a five-span trestle structure on the Highland Railway near Tomatin (1897), the only wooden bridge still in use on a British main line.

Iron was used almost from the beginning: first cast and later wrought. The Liverpool & Manchester Railway's bridge across Water Street, Manchester (1830) was replaced in about 1910 but its successor, although wider, is not unlike it and is representative of hundreds of other plate girder bridges up and down the country. At Conway in North Wales Robert Stephenson essayed a novel square-section tubular iron bridge (1849) as a prototype for his much larger Britannia Bridge across the Menai Strait. The castellated towers successfully blended with Telford's suspension bridge and Conway Castle alongside, as was intended, gaining the approval of the Commissioners of Woods and Forests and the Castle Governor, as required under the Chester & Holyhead Railway Act.[4] A few wrought-iron trestle viaducts were built in this country, of which two remain: one at Bennerley, Nottinghamshire, and the other at Meldon in north Devon, both disused. Meldon is by far the more interesting and spectacular – in reality it consists of two single-line trestles side by side, their legs entwined, the first built in 1874 and the second when the line was doubled in 1879. Lastly, in this brief survey of bridges, we must not omit the magnificent Forth Bridge (1890), a novel cantilever structure and the first large bridge to be built in steel.

However, we cannot leave viaducts without considering their place in the landscape, on which they made a greater impact than any other type of railway structure. John Ruskin fulminated against the effect of the railway and viaduct in his beloved Monsal Dale in Derbyshire.[5] Now we see them differently and, when they are disused, campaign for their retention. When it was proposed to demolish Monsal Dale viaduct there was an outcry; contrary to Ruskin's view, a century later it was considered to be an essential part of the landscape. Equally in towns viaducts had a particular impact which today is considered to form an important element in the local scene, to the extent of special floodlighting at, for example, Stockport and Accrington. At Durham the viaduct (1856) complements the cathedral and castle on their rock across the town; at Brighton the handsome London Road viaduct (1846) looks down on the town and for many years acted as a barrier to development up the valley.[6] Despite being constructed in blue engineering brick, Bordesley viaduct at Birmingham (1852) has a certain majesty in the way it dominates an area of mean streets, small factories and workshops with scenes that even today could come from Doré or Dickens. In Leamington Spa, Regency Bath Street is terminated, with what Pevsner called 'characteristically Victorian ruthlessness',[7] by the Great Western Railway's bowstring girder bridge of 1850. Until about 1960 it was hidden by the only slightly more acceptable plate girder bridge built a year earlier by the London & North Western Railway, running parallel and only a few feet away.

Let me now turn to stations. The first ones were very simple. The terminus of the Liverpool & Manchester Railway at Liverpool Crown Street (1830) comprised a sober Georgian-style office building with a canopy over the single platform supporting a wooden overall roof which looked like an afterthought. Out along the line many stations were not more than stopping places, perhaps at a level crossing, where a local inn might be used as a booking office, stage-coach fashion. On the Leicester & Swannington Railway the Ashby Road Hotel was used at what later became Bardon Hill station (1833), Leicestershire. It was eventually bought by the Midland Railway and used as part of the station until it was closed in 1952.

Proper lineside stations soon evolved, however, as the need quickly arose for basic accommodation such as a booking office, waiting room, conveniences (with or without elaborations and additions) and perhaps a house for the station master. Platform canopies appeared, complete with that very British appendage, the decorated valance, possibly first used by Brunel on the Great Western. Brunel designed a series of charming little Tudor-styled stations between London and Bristol, each with an integral canopy like that on the Oxford line at Culham, Oxfordshire (1845), which is now the only one left. It was the first of the 'company' styles, leading to standard features by which the ownership of a station could be recognised. During the next 60 years whole standard designs were developed, particularly comprehensively for wooden stations like Parbold, Lancashire, which is a typical example of late nineteenth-century practice on the Lancashire & Yorkshire Railway.

Before this strong element of standardisation emerged, however, country stations possessed a fascinating variety of styles. Fenny Stratford,

Buckinghamshire (1846), for example, like other stations between Bletchley and Bedford, was half-timbered to meet the wish of the Duke of Bedford for something in keeping with his estate at Woburn Abbey. Audley End, Cambridgeshire (1847), was built to a common design for the Eastern Counties Railway, to which a *porte cochere* was specially added for the convenience of Lord Braybrooke, whose mansion was nearby. Gobowen, Shropshire (1848), is a rare Florentine-style station, larger and, with one exception, quite different from the others on the Shrewsbury & Chester Railway, probably because it was used by the company's chairman who lived not far away.[8] Atherstone in Warwickshire (1847), lately restored, is the sole survivor of Livock's series of neo-Tudor and Jacobean stations between Rugby and Stafford which is still in use,[9] while Dunblane, Perthshire (1848), is typically Scottish, the work of the noted Victorian architect Sir William Tite, who designed many stations in England, Scotland and Northern France. It will be seen, therefore, that railway stations reflected all the stylistic variety of Victorian architectural eclecticism and that of the Edwardian years. Lynton & Lynmouth station (1889) on the narrow gauge Lynton & Barnstaple Railway is a good example of the late-Victorian Domestic Revival manifested in north Devon. By comparison, very little new building was done in the 1920s and 1930s, but what there was again embraced current fashions: Lea Hall, West Midlands (1938), in reinforced concrete, is a notable example.

Stylistic variety was equally apparent in large stations. In the first two or three decades of railways the concept of the great railway terminal was as a triumphal gateway. Architecture at the beginning of this time was still largely in the Classical Revival period so naturally the railway builders strove to express this idiom by imitating the monuments of ancient Greece and Rome. In London the first was also the greatest: the massive Doric Arch (or, more correctly, *propylaeum*) at Euston (1838), designed by Philip Hardwick to symbolise the London & Birmingham Railway as the gateway to the industrial wealth of the Midlands and the north. At the other end of the line he complemented it with Birmingham Curzon Street. One of our best smaller classical termini was surprisingly late: Bath Green Park (1870) fits most agreeably into the Georgian city, as it was designed to do. (Plate 2)

Another popular style was the Italian, adopted so prolifically as to be called 'the English railway style'.[10] Foremost is Chester (1848), by Francis Thompson, which had the longest station facade in the country: 1050 ft. But in the 1840s the so-called Gothic Revival was gaining ground. It was a successful attempt to revive medieval styles, provoking fierce arguments for and against. The term came to embrace almost anything from pseudo-Norman to Tudor and Jacobean, and some railway architects, anxious to be in the forefront of fashion, freely adopted it. Brunel designed Bristol Temple Meads (1840) in Tudor style; T M Penson chose an English collegiate style for Shrewsbury (1848); later in the century Middlesborough (1877) was an essay in rather coarse Victorian commercial Gothic by the North Eastern Railway's architect William Peachey. The Scottish equivalent – 'Scottish baronial' – appeared in notable form at Dundee West in 1889.

Stations had a much smaller influence on townscapes than viaducts, unlike the situation in Europe and North America where they were often deliberately chosen to form the focal point of a town. There are, however, one or two exceptions. Euston set an example by being fronted by Euston Square. The square was small but the concept was there, only to be quickly destroyed when the railway built an hotel in front of the Doric Arch.

One city, Liverpool, seized the opportunity presented by the extension of the Liverpool & Manchester Railway to Lime Street in 1836 and contributed £2000 to ensure that a suitable station facade faced the new square which the corporation was creating. But only the setting of Stoke-on-Trent can be called a truly railway creation: Winton Square was formed by Henry Hunt's richly Jacobean station facade together with his matching houses and North Staffordshire Hotel for the railway of that name. It was a deliberate essay in town planning by a small but proud and socially conscious local company.

At Carlisle (1850) two railways and the city council agreed on a central station opposite Robert Smirke's Citadel law courts. Tite produced a complementary Gothic design and the council laid out a small square. Fifty years later Leeds fared somewhat better. City Square was laid out in the 1890s to mark Leeds' incorporation as a city, on one side of which stood the Midland Railway's Queens Hotel; although no masterpiece, it did at least hide the disgraceful wooden shed that was Wellington station. Then in 1937 a good railway building came to dominate the square when the London Midland & Scottish Railway rebuilt the Queens Hotel: it is

Plate 2. Bath Green Park station (1870), in 1962, before cleaning. (Photograph by G Biddle)

arguably now the best building in the square.

Stations occasionally acted as a satisfying visual termination to the prospect along a street. The Great Western's Act of Incorporation[11] required it to build a street at Bath to satisfy Lord Manvers, not less than 30 ft wide where it crossed his land. The result was Manvers Street, to which, from a distance, Brunel's unusually asymmetrical facade does, in fact, present a symmetrical termination. The supremely classical Huddersfield Station (1847) occupies a square that is not really large enough for it, but it closes the vista up Northumberland Street in a satisfying manner and has a good sidelong aspect along the appropriately named Railway Street. The town plan and the station's place in it were principally due to the Ramsden family who owned most of Huddersfield at the time.[12] Tite's Southampton Terminus has the same effect in that town.

Newcastle, unfortunately, was a near miss.

Richard Grainger and John Dobson intended that the latter's great station should form part of their town-planning scheme, but the plan failed to reach completion. Neville Street, along the front of the station, was widened, but it needed a square to set the station off. As it is, because the foot of Grainger Street ends on a slight curve instead of opening out, the station's centrepiece is not fully revealed until the last moment.

The long facades of stations such as Chester, Carlisle and Newcastle were used to mask the train sheds that covered the platforms and tracks. Within a few years some railway companies started to build hotels across the head of train sheds. One of the first hotels to form part of a station, by G T Andrews, was at the original York station (1853) while the first in this manner in London was the hotel at Paddington of 1854 (the earlier one at Euston was detached), more elaborate than it is today after alterations made in 1936-38. At the time it was built it was the largest hotel in Britain, the first of the great luxury hotels. Others followed in London and elsewhere: the Grosvenor Hotel at Victoria (1861), built by a separate company in which the railway had an interest; the North Western at Liverpool Lime Street (1869-71) by Alfred Waterhouse, with over 200 bedrooms but only 8 bathrooms; and, most sumptuous of them all, Sir George Gilbert Scott's Midland Grand at St Pancras (1868-73). (Plate 3) From any viewpoint, inside or out, it had an incredible fantasy quality. Furthermore, it was 'a symbol ... of the whole Victorian epoch. It combines in one building the romantic aspirations, the stylistic display and the solid philistinism of the [eighteen] sixties.'[13]

But what of the train sheds behind these great buildings? The first ones were an anticlimax; low wooden or iron sheds that were cheap and easy to erect, open along the sides and roofed with slates and glass. Euston (1837) had a two-bay iron shed

Plate 3. The ultimate in Victorian railway hotels: St Pancras, London, in 1968, before cleaning. (Photograph by G Biddle)

designed by Robert Stephenson and Charles Fox. (Fox went on to become a partner in the well-known firm of Fox Henderson & Co which built the Crystal Palace.) It was not inelegant but it was dwarfed by the Doric Arch. The Euston roof was developed, and came to be perpetuated for a long time on many railways, particularly the London & North Western where it survives in that company's final form at Preston (1879-80).

In his design for a wooden roof at Bristol, however, Brunel included some elaborate Tudor detail to match his exterior, including imitation hammer-beams which disguised what is really a cantilever form of construction, 74 ft wide. Some small stations, too, had overall roofs. Brunel's belief in timber showed itself in his wooden stations as well as his viaducts. Not for nothing have they been called Brunel's barns; a number survived into this century, although only one now remains, at Frome, Somerset (1850). An example of a different kind of small train shed is still in use at Beverley, Humberside, where the roof was rebuilt in 1908 but to a design of G T Andrews' dating from 1845, hipped with wrought-iron trusses supporting timber and slating cladding. It was one of a number built in northeast England.

Pitched roofs like these were relatively narrow, particularly when compared with earlier timber roofs over shipbuilding slips at British naval dockyards, which from the 1840s were superseded by iron.[14] Some had spans nearly twice as wide as the largest contemporary railway roofs, until the iron arched roof was developed to satisfy demands for unobstructed space at large stations, combined with greater height to disperse smoke and steam. Newcastle Central (1850) was among the first, doubly notable for being sited on a sharp curve which produces some dramatic geometrical perspectives. The three spans were each 60 ft wide, on an outer ground radius of 800 ft. King's Cross station in London (1852) followed closely. It was the last of the large wooden station roofs and, for its size, was unique in having two sets of laminated timber ribs. They were replaced with iron in 1870 and 1887, but with the same profile, so that the station today appears much the same as when it was built.

A year later there was a big advance when Birmingham New Street station (1854) was completed on an irregular-shaped site with a single-span iron arched roof of 212 ft at the widest point. For 14 years it was unequalled, until the train shed at Liverpool Lime Street (1867) was enlarged for the third time since it was opened in 1836, giving us some indication of the rapid growth of passenger traffic. Twelve years later a second span was necessary, doubling the station's size.

The greatest train shed was finished in London at St Pancras (1868). It is 243 ft wide and 110 ft high above the tracks, and has been exceeded in width by only three other stations, all in the US, while no other is as high. It has many interesting features, not least the placing of the train shed deck at first-floor level in order to reduce the downhill gradient into the station and simultaneously to act as a tie for the arches and to form cellars underneath, for use as a goods warehouse into which wagons were lowered by an hydraulic lift.

It is not inappropriate to mention here that, nearly 90 years after the last major arched roof was built at Hull Paragon station in 1904, a spectacular roof of novel design in steel and glass was completed in 1993 at Waterloo International in readiness for the Channel Tunnel trains. Each span comprises two banana-span bow-string trusses of unequal length, pinned at a central joint, forming a striking perspective of asymmetrical arches decreasing in width along the gentle curve of the platforms. It is well within the nineteenth-century tradition of dramatic railway station engineering.

From the late 1850s flat ridge-and-furrow roofs, both transverse and longitudinal, were developed from Paxton's principles for the Crystal Palace. The transverse types were usually low with a narrow profile, like Stoke-on-Trent (1893), although some, like Perth (1887), were deeper and therefore more airy, an effect seen at its best in the later part of Glasgow Central (1906).

But there is more to railway structures than spectacular tunnels and viaducts, picturesque country stations and impressive train sheds. The humble goods shed, for instance, must not be ignored; after all, until recent years goods traffic was the mainstay of the railway. The country goods shed at Wooler, Northumberland, with its projecting canopy over the loading door, is typical, as is the interior of Wellingborough, Northamptonshire (c1857), with its wooden platform and hand-operated cranes. Large warehouses were built for special traffic, from the grain warehouse at Burton-on-Trent, now restored for use by small businesses, to the huge Deansgate goods station in Manchester (1898), with its massive warehouse mainly for

cotton goods and, facing the street, a quarter-mile row of shops and offices, all built by the Great Northern Railway.

Signal boxes deserve a place, too. Here again, there was enormous variety of shapes and sizes, mostly bearing recognisable characteristics of the railways or signalling manufacturers who built them. They range from the tiny Lambrigg Crossing box in Cumbria, a type built by Saxby and Farmer for the London & North Western Railway in 1867-72, to that railway's own huge Rhyl No 2 in North Wales, built much later to the company's standard design. (Plate 4) In between is the curious North Eastern Railway signal box tacked on to a house at Knaresborough, North Yorkshire, and the all-wooden box cantilevered out over the rails at Canterbury East in Kent. The variety is – or was – endless.

The railway companies also built houses for their employees. In 1921 there were over 27,000, excluding those forming part of a station. Among the earliest were the Great Western's at Swindon (1841) and the Grand Junction Railway's at Crewe (1843), where they formed new towns serving locomotive works. (Plate 5) Others were located out in the country, singly, or in small groups at stations, like those at Clynderwen on the South Wales Railway in Pembrokeshire, and the keeper's cottage at Hilton Crossing at Egginton Junction on the North Staffordshire Railway.[15]

To end this brief survey, we have what I might call a few odds and ends: important pieces of equipment, none the less, and of interesting design. No station was complete without its clock. Some were quite elaborate, like the one at Troon, Ayrshire. Platform seats were equally necessary, often bearing the station name like that at Mouldsworth, Cheshire. These days drinking fountains are no longer required, but a few still exist, usually carefully preserved, as is the example at Inverurie, Aberdeenshire, which was chosen from an ironfounder's pattern book. Some items were, of course, indispensable, such as the decorated cast-iron urinal at Garston, Liverpool.

In another paper Leslie Soane will be discussing some of the problems of maintaining historic railway structures in Britain. Meanwhile, I hope that I have given a taste of what there is; it may be a very small taste, but it is sufficient, I hope, to convey something of the flavour.

Plate 4 (above). One of the two largest remaining signal boxes in Britain, Rhyl No 2, in 1986. (Photograph by G Biddle) Plate 5 (below). Early London & North Western Railway houses in Victoria St, Crewe, in 1989. (Photograph by G Biddle)

Notes and references

A source of general reference to the sites referred to in this paper is Gordon Biddle and O S Nock, *Railway Heritage of Britain: 150 Years of Railway Architecture and Engineering* (London: Michael Joseph, 1983).

1 Biddle, G, 'The Railway Stations of John Livock and T M Penson', *Journal of the Railway and Canal Historical Society*, 31, 154 (May 1993), p61

2 London & Birmingham Railway Act, 3 & 4 Wm 4, cXXXVI, 1833

3 For a comprehensive recent account see Binding, J, *Brunel's Cornish Viaducts* (Penrhyn: Atlantic Publishers, 1993).

4 7&8 Vic, cLXV, 1844

5 Ruskin, J, *Works*, ed by E T Cook and A Wedderburn (1903-12), XXVII

6 For a wider examination of this topic see Simmons, J, *The Railways of Britain* (London: Guild Books, 1986), 3rd edn; Simmons, J, *Victorian Railways* (London: Thames & Hudson, 1992); Biddle, G, 'Railways in Towns', *Journal of the Railway and Canal Historical Society*, 31, 156 (November 1993).

7 Pevsner, N, and Wedgwood, A, *The Buildings of England: Warwickshire* (London: Penguin Books, 1966)

8 Biddle, G, 'The Railway Stations of John Livock and T M Penson'

9 Biddle, G, 'The Railway Stations of John Livock and T M Penson'

10 See the description of the Bricklayers' Arms Station in the *Illustrated London News*, 4 May 1844.

11 5&6 Wm 4, cCVII, 1835

12 Whomsley, D, 'A Landed Estate and the Railway: Huddersfield 1844-54', *Journal of Transport History*, NS, 2, 4 (September 1974), p189

13 Jordan, R Furneaux, *Victorian Architecture* (London: Penguin Books, 1966), p94

14 Sutherland, R J M, 'Shipbuilding and the Long Span Roof', *Transactions of the Newcomen Society*, 60 (1988-89), p107

15 For a detailed exposition see Biddle, G, *The Railway Surveyors* (London: Ian Allan & BR Property Board, 1990).

An American perspective on the built railway heritage

John P Hankey

First of all, why should we even bother to speak of a 'perspective?'. Is there for us Americans a distinctly 'American perspective' on railway preservation which somehow differs from a 'European', global or, perhaps, a cosmic perspective? How many American perspectives are there likely to be, and which ones are valid for our purposes? Is not the business of identifying, collecting or otherwise conserving tangible history essentially the same, whether it takes place in Great Britain, continental Europe or the US?

Common sense suggests that practitioners of a certain kind of history in a certain place will bring a unique perspective to their work. We in railway preservation (in all its forms) are no different. Knowledge of our perspectives helps us to understand the general shape of the field. It provides insights helpful for understanding the history itself and for presenting it to out audiences in effective, sympathetic, useful ways.

I hope that increasingly we will begin to think more explicitly of the historiography of railroading, and to tackle the questions which extend beyond boiler specifications and route miles. We have nibbled at the edges of some very bold assertions regarding the scope and influence of railroading in the US but we lack the rigour and intellectual framework as yet to defend them. The issues that I will raise in this commentary are examples.

I will begin with the assumption that 'railroading' – the entire system, the trains, buildings and tangible remains of all sorts – is a cultural artefact in exactly the same fashion as fine art, literature or the architecture of great cities. It is less self-conscious than other forms of cultural expression, but for that very reason it may be more honest and open to understanding. Defining the built railway environment in this way is an important first step in apprehending what the railroad means in America, rather than simply what form it happened to take there.

Considering the railroad in this way also permits us to ask broad questions:

- To what degree did emerging American values shape the evolution and application of the technology?
- Who built, used and paid for the railroads?
- How did the railroad – both the reality of its existence and the potential it offered – affect the course of American history?
- What were the original intentions of the railroad builders? What were the actual results? What were the unintended consequences?
- How did America 'know' its railroads?

There are more – many more – questions that we could ask. My point is simply to locate the discussion and ultimately to suggest that our particular perspectives bear directly on the kinds of questions we ask. Many of the answers are to be found in our own preservation efforts, a fact we may not fully realise.

Such questions, and the perspectives that accompany them, also provide an interesting framework for examining, or re-examining, the tangible legacy of railroading. Traditionally, that category includes whatever we consider to be in some way noteworthy or 'historic', according to whatever definition we are using.

The 'built railway heritage' – leaving aside for the time being all the intangible, ephemeral and non-object-based railroad history – includes equipment, things, places, works of civil engineering, systems and landscapes. For the purposes of my points, I would broaden the category to include all of railroading, including that which is not yet historic and that which will never be historic. The commonplace and disposable are often where the most interesting conclusions manifest themselves.

It matters not whether this built railway heritage is preserved in a museum, worked as a preservation activity, part of the present operating system or privately owned. It may even be of little consequence whether or not it survives, for these perspectives apply equally well to lost history. In fact, I would like to blur or perhaps obliterate as many boundaries as I can, for they have little meaning for the ideas to follow.

I have suggested that we regard the railroad as a cultural artefact, outlined general types of questions and characterised the legacy we may use to answer those questions. What are we to do with it? For practical people such as ourselves, the test of an intellectual exercise is whether it is useful in understanding, explaining or conducting our preservation activities.

All of these thoughts are tentative: use them like templates or gauges, or see if any of the conclusions agree or conflict with your own work. If nothing else, perhaps they will assist in understanding the large, vital and diverse panorama of American railroad history. I propose four broad clusters of ideas to help make sense of railroading in America.

The first cluster of ideas may be summarised by a reckless statement: the railroad was the single most important agent in the creation of the US as a functional, continental, unitary entity. Put another way, the railroad was responsible for the creation of modern America. Were it not for the timely introduction of this technology, the political, economic and physical development of the entire North American continent would have proceeded on a different basis, almost certainly with different results.

We are probably familiar with the interpretation that railroads in Europe connected established population centres and supplemented existing commercial routes, while railroads in the US usually opened wilderness areas to development. Put another way, railroading came to Britain (and to most of Europe) long after it was settled, domesticated and industrialised. It was an evolutionary and supplemental technology. In America, the railroad was revolutionary.

Transportation had always been vital to the survival of the colonies and of the early federal US, to the extent that the lack or limitations of traditional road and water transport hampered the growth of the republic in very real ways. The railroad represented a relatively inexpensive, all-weather, effective, flexible and rapid solution to the problem. Railroads (or something very much like them) were necessary, although not sufficient, for America to move beyond proto-industrialisation and a coastal existence.

For example, railroads facilitated, and in many cases initiated, the rapid and sustained westward migrations which filled the continent. Immigration was a powerful factor in the creation of the US, and the railroad made possible both relatively easy internal migrations and the wide dispersal of

millions of Europeans entering through a few east coast ports. It is difficult to imagine how we could have successfully occupied the remote corners and filled the empty places without the railroad to tie us all together.

By effectively removing barriers to internal trade and transport, the railroad itself became a tangible embodiment of American ideals. As the conduit for the nation's business, it gave form to political beliefs, provided a forum for the refinement of society and mirrored themes and trends at work throughout the nation.

The railroad was an incremental, expanding and highly visible demonstration of technological progress. Railroads operated across state boundaries, demanded a high degree of co-operation to become an integrated system and by their very nature brought a degree of uniformity and order to their communities (with the use of standard time, schedules and predictable mail delivery). As built in the US, they were democratic, accessible, widely dispersed and highly adaptable – as most Americans fancied themselves to be.

From this perspective, the railroad became the enabling device which allowed the US to attain its full potential. I believe that some vestige of this widely held nineteenth-century conclusion is today responsible for the railroad's place in our popular culture, and that this is why so many Americans respond emotionally to the traditional iconography of railroading.

Railroad history may thus be understood, preserved and interpreted in terms of the American secular religion. It has far more legitimacy than its traditional place in the history of technology. The built railway heritage thus takes its place alongside Civil War battlefields, Kitty Hawk, Yellowstone, Ellis Island and Graceland. It moves from the fringes of industrial archaeology to the very centre of the American experience.

The second cluster of ideas aspiring to become a perspective concerns a defining characteristic of the American psyche, one which manifests itself to this day. I summarise it with another reckless statement: Americans used the railroad as they used the axe and plough: to attain mastery over nature and to wilfully, completely, irreversibly change the very face of the land itself. The railroad is an agent of and metaphor for power, and Americans like power. Not unfettered raw power; we are distrustful of that. We also believe that power ought to be turned to some good end; that is traditional

American naivety. Railroading was an incredibly powerful technology, and we believed that we could control it and that it worked for the greater good of all.

For this concept of mastery over nature we may thank England's Francis Bacon, Elizabethan politician and philosopher, a man known in the sixteenth century as a 'projector'. Today he would be known as an entrepreneur or a businessman who also engaged in politics and philosophy. A central tenet of his influential philosophy was that man had both the right and the power to subdue nature and to turn it towards his own ends. The Earth and everything it provided was to be taken and used, with little regard for the consequences. Four centuries ago such a view must have seemed not unreasonable.

John Smith and Walter Raleigh and thousands of the earliest British colonists to the New World firmly planted that Baconian ethic on American shores, and we pay dearly today. The overarching theme of the first 400 years of European habitation in North America was that the Earth's abundance was there for the taking: the 'virgin land', the 'wild west', the mythology of the American destiny. The entire myth of America as a source of endless bounty derives from Elizabethan enthusiasm and modern notions of progress.

The railroad provided Americans with the most powerful tool of the nineteenth century. With it, they could expand agriculture almost at will. They could transcend what had been insurmountable barriers of time and distance. Deserts became inconveniences, mountains crumbled against the onslaught of steam drills and dynamite. Railroads called into being entire industries, while transform-ing us into a nation of commodities, mass con-sumption and industrialisation.

This expansive, almost savage, ethic may be read across the land in bridges, cuttings, locomotives and preserved landscapes. The National Park Service's site at Promontory is a fine example, celebrating the first transcontinental railroad. Big Bend Tunnel and the legend of John Henry are evocative symbols. The huge steam locomotives operated by Norfolk Southern and Union Pacific epitomise the quest for more power, larger size and higher productivity, and capture our fascination with machines.

Yet what we railroad enthusiasts might see as a dramatic railroad landscape or an impressive freight train may be regarded with equal validity as a scar upon the face of the Earth, a form of defilement. At the very least, railroads represented a fundamental shift in the relationship between man and nature. Roads and canals largely conformed to the contours of the land. Railroads did also, but to a much greater degree they required modification of the very Earth itself. For the first time, man engaged with nature using a large-scale technology and began to visibly, and symbolically, change the shape of the Earth in ways different from, for example, traditional agriculture.

In the same fashion, railroads made possible strip mines and other types of large-scale extractive industries, industrial and agricultural concentration (as in Pittsburgh for steel or in the plains states for cereal culture), and the rise of large cities. Railroading brought about an intensification of all sorts of other processes, each of which had lasting physical and perceptual results. These are not technically part of the railroad built environment, but they surely are part of our railway heritage. We might look on them as the real products of the railroad in history.

No matter what form it takes, our built railway heritage is an expression of aggressive conduct towards nature. Whether or not we accept that conduct as integral to modern western culture, the railroad and its heritage constitute a record of nineteenth-century American civilisation in the same fashion as the Mayan temples, irrigation systems and public spaces record the civilisation of 1000 years previously.

For my third cluster of ideas, I suggest that ambiguity is a defining American characteristic, and arguably one which has helped us to survive and prosper. Ambiguity of purpose, need and style characterised the creation of much of the American railroad network and ambiguity likewise character-ises our present efforts to preserve important aspects of it. That is not necessarily a bad thing, but it makes life complicated for us.

Different types of ambiguity lie at the heart of the American experience. People from around the world came to this 'new' place and created a 'new' political, social, economic and cultural entity unlike anything else on the face of the planet. Implicit in that process was self-consciousness, doubt and often guilt. Americans worked hard at creating a new, synthetic entity. Was this place better than the one left behind? What have we done to the environment?

We are a nation built around choices – options – and many of our social and technological structures reflect that preoccupation with personal freedom and access. The millions of willing immigrants who came to the US made conscious choices. Their place of settlement was usually a matter of choice, or at least more so than the places they had left.

In the process of creating a new country, if not a new nation, we were determined to shape the landscape to suit our purposes. We saw beauty in steel mills, progress in railroad yards, prosperity as a consequence of environmental degradation. The literature and fine arts of the nineteenth century reflect the debate, the soul-searching, the distress and the ambiguity associated with our hell-bent rush to industrialise.

In so doing, we translated much older forms and symbols into a sort of secular religion. As part of the ambiguity we felt about nature, we created national parks and preserved wilderness areas as examples of what we had lost. Perhaps as a response to such a brief national history, we came to regard a journey to the nation's capital as a sort of *hajj* – a holy pilgrimage. An amusing example is that, for decades, the Baltimore & Ohio Railroad printed brochures admonishing citizens that it was their duty to visit 'Washington, shrine of American patriotism'. A country so new and raw as the nineteenth-century US could not help but have an ambiguous relationship to its own history and feel compelled to invest in a variety of myths, symbols and substitutions.

The origins, conduct and results of railway preservation in the US over the past 100 years mirror that ambiguity. In general, it has been loyal, idiosyncratic, unsystematic and often for utilitarian or ulterior purposes. It has also been sincere, heartfelt, largely unburdened by informing ideals or larger purposes and quite effective.

Comparisons may be inappropriate, but consider for example the British National Railway Museum. It exists as part of Great Britain's national museum system and had (at least until the 1993 Railways Act) a formal arrangement with British Rail for the selection and preservation of equipment retired from service. The exhibition and interpretation of railroad history takes place in a larger context as part of a social policy.

In the US we have nothing of the sort. Perhaps the Smithsonian Institution's Air and Space Museum represents a transportation analogue, and the National Park Service and many state governments are active in large-scale railroad preservation. Yet transportation policy itself is in its infancy

across the Atlantic; federal articulation of a preservation policy is decades away, or perhaps simply inappropriate. The idea of some Washington bureaucrat telling our very private railroads to select equipment for preservation seems to us absurd.

That ambiguity, working along with some trace of guilt or responsibility, is apparent in so many of our preservation activities, just as it is in our entire built environment. Towns placed locomotives in public parks to be enjoyed as one does stuffed animals, but many (if not most) towns soon lost interest and permitted the locomotives to deteriorate. The metaphor of putting the horse out to pasture quickly lost its power.

We use these machines – the primary agent of the destruction of the natural landscape – to gain access to and view remnants of that lost landscape. The friction growing between advocates of railroad preservation and the rails-to-trails community, resulting from different goals for the same historic assets, is a simple fact of American life. Even our inability to agree on the need for some sort of national railway trust similar to the Railway Heritage Trust in Great Britain is an example of ambiguity, masquerading as individuality.

Like so much of American life, railway preservation operates in the general hurly-burly of free markets and individual choice. We celebrate the technology without much thought to its social or cultural contexts, its causes or consequences. What is accomplished results as much from a combination of traditional American voluntary association and social Darwinism as from an articulated vision for the place of railroad history in society.

Finally, we Americans were, perhaps more than at present, great proponents of setting things in motion and waiting to see how they turned out. The whole country was a grand experiment; people came to the New World to escape restrictions, tradition and the slowly grinding machinery of established culture. This resulted in the American fondness for change, novelty and a deeply ingrained tolerance for unintended consequences.

Railroads changed the America that existed prior to their introduction. They subsequently and dramatically altered both the course of national destiny and the texture of daily life. Noone could predict how. Noone seemed to want to try.

Perhaps only now are we beginning to appreciate how these massive systems work, and how they can shape and affect and drive society. They did not 'just happen', market forces notwithstanding. Nor can we really ever grasp the true causal relationships, the magnitude of influence or the net good – or harm – to have resulted.

This could be a universal perspective applicable to all human endeavour. Yet in America we have commonly avoided considerations of what railroads actually did, caused or made possible. We might make a list: railroads made it possible to settle and farm the entire temperate interior, which led directly and quickly to the destruction of virtually all native prairie; railroads were the proximate cause for the location and development of great cities such as Chicago; and the location of railroads determined the sites, orientations functions and characteristics of thousands of towns and communities across the continent.

Railroading acted with telegraphy and science to alter fundamentally the American perception of time, space, distance, measurement and speed. The railroad in the US was analogous to the church in medieval Europe: in the absence of a higher authority or civil system, both imposed some degree of order on emerging civilisations. The railroad was indeed America's universal religion.

We brush up against these conclusions; cautiously we approach new interpretations. American railroad preservationists and historians are on the verge of professionalisation and recognition as a field, perhaps in material culture, or American civilisation, or history or historic preservation. At present we are unaware of the boundaries of that field and unsure of our claim on it. That will change directly, especially with the involvement of the enthusiastic, university-trained young people who have declared their intention to make railroad history in one form or another their life's work.

Transportation is such a fundamental human activity, and its effects so profound and unpredictable, that a technology like railroading in a place like North America at a time like the nineteenth century will have profound consequences. So profound, in fact, that we have difficulty in grasping the ramifications. The next generation should have an easier time of it.

My last perspective, then, is one of ignorance, curiosity and optimism. We have realised, perhaps for the first time, what an immense and rewarding field we labour in; how little we really understand;

how great are the opportunities. Questions that no one thought to consider a mere 20 years ago are debated today, with substantial, positive consequences for the future of railway preservation. We see on the horizon a decided change in how we know and interpret both our built environment and the cultural history of railroading.

At the dawn of the Railway Age in the US, Americans were different from Europeans. They had made themselves different from the English, Germans, Dutch, French, Spanish and whoever else had once laid claim to a piece of the New World. Americans had not yet (and some might argue still have not) coalesced into one people, and certainly the millions of immigrants lent a shifting, evolving character to the nation. But we may define Americans by what they were not: they had ceased to be Europeans and were beginning to look to themselves for culture, technology and identity.

From their beginnings our railroads reflected all that was good, bad and ambiguous about Americans and America. Now railroading may serve as a lens: turned one way, it may be used to focus intense scrutiny on specific issues, themes and events. One can hardly find a better teaching tool for early twentieth-century race relations than a Jim Crow car; the steam locomotive is an almost perfect embodiment of the first Industrial Revolution. Turned the other way, that same lens – the railroad – reveals a broad landscape: physical, but also cultural, political and psychological. What compelled Americans to lace an immense continent together with iron rails in the space of a few decades? What does that feat reveal about the American character – about the perceived or real need to 'conquer the west' or seize what nature had to offer? The railroad is an effective vehicle for grasping in their broadest terms applied American ideals.

Perhaps that is what I find so exciting about railroad history and its tangible heritage. It has the potential to transcend its own reality and to speak to larger themes. The unique standing of railroading in America's development means that we can have it both ways: good railroad history is also good American history, and so much of the modern American experience played itself out on the railroad.

The railway buildings of Berlin and the Museum für Verkehr und Technik

Alfred Gottwaldt

The first German railway was opened in Bavaria in 1835. It connected Nürnberg to Fürth, only a few miles away. The first railway in Berlin, which was the capital of the kingdom of Prussia, was opened three years later in 1838; it connected the city to Potsdam.

At that time there was no united country of Germany. The various territories, such as Bavaria and Prussia, were separated by borders, by legislation, currencies, measurements and so on. These divisions were only partly done away with after the Franco-Prussian War of 1870.

When the Prussian Hohenzollerns established a united German Empire in 1871 the Prussian plans to form one national railway for strategic reasons did not succeed. The railways remained under the authority of the various semi-independent kingdoms and grand duchies. Only in southern Germany (Bavaria, Baden, Saxony, Württemberg) were there state-owned railway systems; in the north the railways were built and operated by private capital. Only a few lines which did not seem to offer profit were set up by the state but these were still in the established form of commercial companies.

As in London and in Paris, the first railways in Prussia were built as direct lines to connect Berlin with other major cities. Between 1838 and 1846 the five railway companies which built lines to Magdeburg, to Dresden, to Hamburg, to Stettin and to Breslau erected their first station buildings just outside the ancient Berlin town wall. (Plate 1)

These station buildings of the 'first generation' soon proved to be too small so most of them were replaced by typical 'cathedrals of the railway' between about 1870 and 1880. These larger buildings are described as the 'second generation', and in this

Plate 1. Exterior of Berlin's Hamburg Station. The station was in operation from 1846 to 1884 and was used as a museum from 1906 to 1943.

more elaborate style, three more termini were built by further railway companies between 1866 and 1872 for lines to Küstrin, Görlitz and Hannover. These eight different railways lines (seven of them built with private capital) projected like radials into the country around Berlin and a linking network developed only slowly. The different lines were connected between 1871 and 1877 by a Circle Line (the 'Ringbahn') close to their Berlin termini, which allowed freight trains to go round Berlin and also carried a few passenger trains to serve what were then the suburbs. A few years later one of the first viaduct or elevated railways of the world was built across Berlin: the City Railway ('Stadtbahn') was opened in 1882. Its route is from west to east through the capital, and runs mainly on the land of a disused canal. It carries one pair of tracks for local traffic and one for long-distance traffic, and all for passengers only. Its station buildings are integrated into the viaduct by large halls over the tracks thus forming a unique urban railway architecture.

Both the Circle and the City Railways were paid for by the state of Prussia; this state involvement reflected a growing trend. In 1875 the railways no longer made the profits which they had in the past. The Prussian Chancellor Otto von Bismarck took his chance and launched an extensive programme to buy up all Prussian railways; he saw their importance for the national economy and for military purposes. All railways serving Berlin had been nationalised by 1882. The state set up a Royal Prussian Railway Board which lasted until the end of monarchy in Germany in 1918-20.

The Royal Prussian Railway Board reorganised the functions of all Berlin stations. Of the 'first generation', only the station for the Hamburg line of 1846 was still in operation, and this was closed in 1884 but not replaced since another station was available to take over its trains.

In 1906 the old Hamburg Station in Berlin was made one of the first railway museums of the world under the name of the Museum for Transport and Construction ('Verkehrs- und Baumuseum'). Though it was given a new main hall of contemporary design, it still had the atmosphere of an early railway station. It was mainly paid for

Plate 2. Railway network of Berlin in 1900

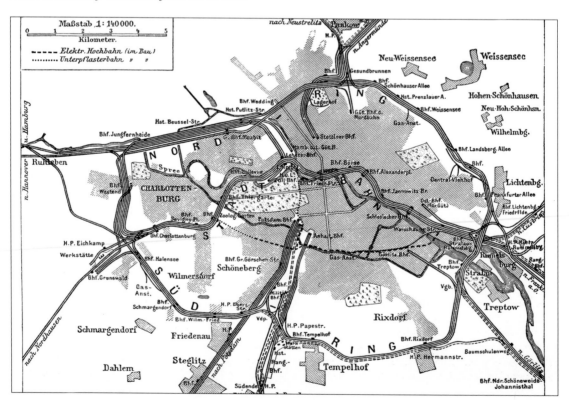

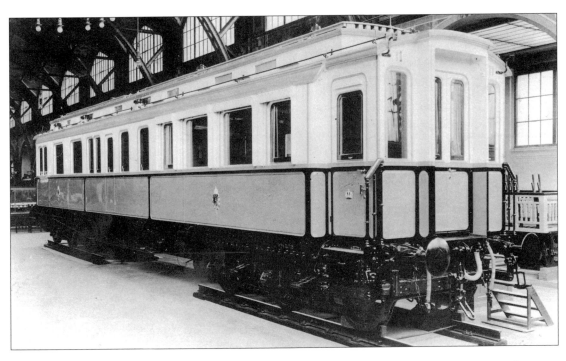

Plate 3. The German Emperor's saloon carriage from 1889. This was held at the Museum for Transport and Construction from 1921-43.

by Prussian State Railways, which at that time were a large and profit-making enterprise. It is said that about half the state revenues of the time were derived from railway operations, thus making the Railway Minister a most important man in the kingdom of Prussia.

The Museum for Transport and Construction was intended mainly for the education of railway-men. Its collections were very technical. There were many objects designed to teach the operation of signal boxes, signals and points. In 1935, on the 100th anniversary of the Germany railways, this museum was reorganised, and it then became a little more a place of history and tradition, thus underlining the idea of progress under the Third Reich.

All the German railways had been unified under the name of the German State Railways ('Deutsche Reichsbahn') in 1920. In Nürnberg there was another railway museum which had been founded by the Bavarian State Railways in 1899. The State Railways decided to continue operating both muse-ums; the coverage of the museums was divided along geographical lines into north (Prussia) in

Berlin and south (Bavaria) in Nürnberg. The celebrations of 1935 (and for the 150th anniversary in 1985) were of course held in the historic city of Nürnberg.

Before World War Two the railways of Berlin were modernised by the electrification of all subur-ban lines at 800 V DC, although the long-distance traffic remained steam operated. Before and after the Olympic Games of 1936 a modern under-ground railway from north to south was built for commuter trains, and its stations are remarkable for their contemporary architecture. There were also gigantic plans by the Nazi Party to do away with all the old termini and give Berlin two (or four) new central stations but these plans were cancelled during the War.

The Berlin Museum for Transport and Construction in the old Hamburg Station was closed because of air raids in 1943. Many of its objects were sent to small stations in the country-side to secure them from damage. Though the old Hamburg Station building was hit by bombs, more objects were lost from the various places to which they were sent outside Berlin than from the

Hamburg Station due to bomb damage. Some seem to have gone forever; others have made their way back from the transport museums in Prague and Dresden in recent years. We are very grateful to our colleagues there for their help in returning these 'lost' objects to Berlin.

After World War Two, when Berlin was partitioned, the former Museum of Transport and Construction ended up in the British sector. All railway operations in Berlin, however, were made the responsibility of the German State Railways which also ran all railways in the Soviet zone and then the German Democratic Republic (GDR). For political reasons it was decided that an East German authority could not operate a railway museum in West Berlin, and therefore the building remained closed until 1984.

The post-War sub-division of Germany and of Berlin itself also led to the closure of most of the old termini. They were damaged during the War but, more importantly, the new GDR wanted to run its internal trains into a station in East Berlin. Furthermore, the West Berliners were reluctant to use the East German trains which served West Berlin. Therefore many stations were closed and

knocked down, leaving great areas in the city without proper rail transport connections.

After the erection of the Berlin wall in 1961 any hopes of reopening the old Museum of Transport and Construction vanished and, as early as 1966, a group of enthusiasts began to develop plans for a modern transport museum of their own. Finally, in 1980, the government of West Berlin decided to establish a new technical museum which was to cover the history of both transportation and technology. The coverage of the new museum was much wider than that of the old; many other collections which had existed as separate institutions before the war (such as the Postal Museum, the Maritime Museum, the Aeronautical Museum and the Labour Protection Museum) were taken over by the new museum.

The initial proposal had been to convert the impressive hall of the Anhalter Station of 1880 into a transport museum, but this magnificent building was demolished in 1961. (Plate 4) There were, however, remnants of its locomotive depot and its freight yard together with a wide space covered by rusty tracks overgrown by trees known as the track triangle ('Gleisdreieck') close to the centre of what

Plate 4. Demolition of Anhalter Station in 1960

was then West Berlin. It was in this area that the 1980 scheme began to take shape. (Plate 5)

The first Director, Professor Günter Gottmann, came from the Deutsches Museum in Munich. He laid out plans for a museum integrating not only means of transport such as road, water, rail and air, but also communications such as printing, telephones, radio, film and computers, and technical hardware such as heavy industry, electricity, crafts, scientific instruments and household technology. A department for hands-on experiments was also planned as this was thought to be popular with visitors. All the exhibits were intended to form a conceptual network which would make clear the interdependencies between the various fields, although this has proved to be very difficult to realise in the historic buildings. But some simple things work: railway timetables are printed in the graphic arts department, thus inviting visitors particularly interested in railways to visit that department.

The first exhibition in the Berlin Museum of Transportation and Technology was opened on 14 December 1983. The first building stood by the side of the Anhalter Station; it had been a stable for

horses and carts which distributed artificial ice to restaurants and butchers in Berlin. One gallery was created for each future department of the museum. An adjacent hall of modern design was opened for the display of motor vehicles in 1985. Two historic locomotive roundhouses with turntables were repaired and rebuilt for the museum in 1987 and 1988, and they now contain the railway exhibition on 33 tracks. This is a permanent exhibition, and there are plans to erect a new building for water and air transport as well as to refurbish the old freight buildings for all the other fields the museum has chosen to represent.

After the War, for the political reasons mentioned above, many stations of the Circle and City Railways were closed. In 1984 the government of West Berlin took responsibility for those stations in its part of the city, and with them came the old Transport Museum. The historic collections that remained in the building formed an important addition to the new museum. It was decided to transfer the collections to the new museum and to give the historic old Hamburg Station another function as a museum of modern art. In the new museum, an exhibition called *Trains, Locos,*

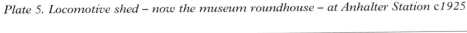

Plate 5. Locomotive shed – now the museum roundhouse – at Anhalter Station c1925

and People ('*Züge, Loks und Leute*') now incorporates the well-known collections from Hamburg Station.

Following the fall of the Berlin wall in 1989 and German reunification, many things have changed. Nowadays, a museum would not be able to get hold of a site as valuable as that of the new transport museum, which lies two miles from the heart of the German capital. The unified German railways, soon to be grouped together under the name Deutsche Bahn, are working very hard to improve the railway services in Berlin after 45 years of neglect. Many old railway buildings which have survived as ruins will have to go, and this process will greatly change the face of Berlin. New lines for high-speed trains from Hannover and Hamburg are under construction. There are also plans to dig a new tunnel for high-speed services from north to south under the city of Berlin and to build a new central interchange station. The proposed tunnel will begin only 100 yards from the museum and will be an important means of enabling visitors to see both the history and the future of German railways in one spot.

Editor's note

Alfred Gottwaldt describes the display philosophy adopted in the new railway galleries of the new Berlin Transport Museum on pages 210 to 214.

Horseshoe Curve and the Altoona Railroaders Memorial Museum, Altoona, Pennsylvania

Peter D Barton

Preface

The Altoona Railroaders Memorial Museum has long conveyed its mission in its name. From its inception the Board of Directors of the museum chose to break from the tradition of railroad museums which celebrate technology alone or focus their energies on the 'glamour' jobs of the train crews or the foresight of corporate magnates. The museum has taken on the task of telling the story of American workers engaged in work of mythical stature, in conceiving, building and running the transportation system that transformed a nation and made manifest the possibilities of the Industrial Revolution in the US. It is a story filled with creativity, bravery and hardship.

Historical overview

It was in Altoona that the early managers of the Pennsylvania Railroad (PRR) elected to develop the principal workshop and test facilities for the design, production and maintenance of the railroad's fleet of locomotives and rolling stock. During the peak of production, from 1920 to 1930, the Altoona Works employed over 17,000 people in four workshop complexes which stretched for six miles and totalled nearly 100 acres under cover. But what really triggered the development of the settlement of Altoona as 'Railroad City' was the topography of the area rather than corporate foresight. Altoona sits in the eastern foothills of the Allegheny Mountains which cross the states of Pennsylvania, West Virginia and Virginia, from northeast to southwest. The mountains rise 2000 to 4000 ft above the surrounding land, creating a formidable obstacle to transportation and commerce. Altoona developed as a locomotive staging point as railroads were built through the mountains.

The PRR was established in 1846 to construct and operate a railroad between Harrisburg and Pittsburgh, a distance of 249 miles. The early surveyors for the railroad found it best to follow the course of the Juniata River, west from Harrisburg to a point near Altoona, gaining 800 ft elevation in

about 100 miles. From Altoona westward to Allegheny Summit the railroad had to gain 1000 ft in elevation in little more than 12 miles. To accomplish this at a gradient that could be achieved by mid-nineteenth century 'steel wheel on steel rail' technology, the railroad was built on a steadily rising gradient on a ledge cut into the mountains. At Kittanning Point a system of 'cut-and-fill' was employed to enable the crossing of Logan Valley with a gradient not exceeding 1.8 per cent. The Kittanning Point cut-and-fill, about six miles west of Altoona, resulted in the formation of a large semicircular arc of 220 degrees which became known as the Horseshoe Curve.

The change of gradient at Altoona meant that Altoona became a strategic point on the railroad. Additional motive power was required to push trains over the summit, and because the rugged terrain put more stress on locomotives and equipment, the additional maintenance required became the driving force behind the decision to establish major workshop facilities at Altoona.

Horseshoe Curve National Historic Landmark

Opened in early 1854, the Horseshoe Curve, which was a striking railway feature in an area of great natural beauty, quickly took a predominant role in the promotion of passenger travel on the PRR. Early photographs of the Curve, taken around 1865, were widely circulated by the railroad as a means to promote travel. William Henry Rau, an early Philadelphia photographer hired by the PRR to photograph the landscape of the railroad and western Pennsylvania, took numerous images of trains on the Curve in the late nineteenth century. By 1879 the railroad had established a station and a park at the Curve site.

The railroad continued to expand, and by 1900 the main line of the PRR around Horseshoe Curve had grown to four tracks. In 1925 the railroad built a stone horseshoe decoration 34 ft long, painted white, in the side of the hill below the right-of-way. The PRR gave the nearby City of Altoona a permit to operate a park at the apex of the Curve in 1940, and the Civilian Conservation Corps built a rest house of stone to accommodate visitors. During World War Two the Curve and nearby summit tunnels were closed to the public and put under guard but the Curve was promptly reopened for public viewing after the War. A PRR class K-4 steam locomotive was placed on a short section of track beside the Curve in 1957. In 1966 the Horseshoe Curve was designated a National Historic Landmark by the National Park Service.

Lack of financial resources on the part of the City of Altoona led to a gradual decline in the upkeep of the park at Horseshoe Curve. By the mid-1980s what had been the pride of Altoona was becoming an embarrassment.

The number of visitors to the Horseshoe Curve site has remained high throughout the twentieth century. It has been estimated that an average of 50,000 visitors per year have come to witness the struggle of machines against nature and the forces of gravity over the last half century. Horseshoe Curve is instantly recognised as a site where a unique civil-engineering solution to a transportation problem has remained effective for over 130 years. The Horseshoe Curve serves today as the main line for Conrail – with over 95 million gross tons of freight passing annually in nearly 50 freight trains per day.

In 1988 the Altoona Railroaders Memorial Museum became a co-operating partner in America's Industrial Heritage Project (AIHP) – a nine-county organisation in western Pennsylvania formed to commemorate and celebrate the industries of coal mining, iron and steel fabrication and railroad transportation. AIHP was initiated by a federally appointed commission, which was authorised to identify and develop 15 sites of 'national significance' within the region; the commission chose Horseshoe Curve as its first project.

AIHP is a unique approach to heritage preservation, with the commission providing both the technical expertise to plan and design sites and the capital necessary to develop them. The commission seeks out private non-profit agencies or institutions which agree to operate the developed sites without long-term public subsidy. Thus a new public/private partnership for regional heritage preservation of significant sites was born. In the case of the Horseshoe Curve, the Altoona Railroaders Memorial Museum was chosen to operate and manage the planned development.

While Horseshoe Curve itself is a historic resource, the structures that existed at the park site were not historically significant. Thus, as planning for the revitalisation of the park at Horseshoe Curve got under way, it was determined that maintaining existing structures was not critical. What was important was to maintain the experience of the Curve and particularly the sensory experience of frequent train movements over a steep mountain gradient. The planners quickly decided that it was vital that any new facilities should be constructed at road elevation, some 100 ft below the trackside, thus maintaining the historic landscape of the Curve.

The planning team comprised representatives of the commission, the Altoona museum and local government. Community goals were addressed through a series of public planning sessions. What resulted was the clear indication that the Curve did indeed warrant new facilities and visitor amenities. The facilities which have been provided include a 4600 sq ft interpretative centre, architecturally designed to resemble a 'turn of the century' railway station with a number of large arched windows. Within this new centre the significance of the Horseshoe Curve is told through photographs, exhibits and film. A covered portico connects the interpretative centre to modern rest rooms and a gift shop in a second building of 2200 sq ft. A new set of stairs enables visitors to climb the hill to the trackside more easily. To improve access to the Curve itself further, a funicular, or inclined plane, was constructed. Two 12-passenger cabins take visitors from the interpretative centre to an upper observation area. The cabins were constructed and painted to reflect the heritage of the PRR. Improved highway access and a new parking lot complement the development. The total cost was some $5.8 million.

As the Horseshoe Curve park had always been 'free access', the challenge to the Altoona Railroaders Memorial Museum, which runs the site, is the agreement to operate and maintain it without charging an admission fee. Income for personnel and maintenance is earned through sales in the gift shop and the sale of funicular tokens. (Visitors can of course, walk the stairs at no charge.) During the 16 full months of operation since the new facilities opened on 25 April 1992 the site has seen in excess of 267,000 visitors, from across the US and around the world, who have come to learn of the significance of this nineteenth-century civil-engineering triumph that enabled the first all-rail crossing of the

Allegheny Mountains and the consequent changes to American society.

A key component of AIHP is its ability to spawn economic development through the enhancement of heritage tourism opportunities. To monitor the project's success, independent research is conducted annually by Pennsylvania State University, for example through exit surveys of visitors at selected sites. During 1992 the Horseshoe Curve was a survey site. The statistical research of visitors to the Curve reveals that the site was responsible for $8.3 million of economic activity across the region in only eight months of operation. Of that amount, the Altoona Railroaders Memorial Museum, as site operator, captured only a small percentage (less than half a million). The real benefactors of this heritage development are the businesses in the area. The public investment at Horseshoe Curve was returned to the private sector in excess of 100 per cent in less than one year!

Altoona Railroaders Memorial Museum

The Altoona Railroaders Memorial Museum has a somewhat atypical mission statement for a railroad museum. Its purpose is to honour railroad workers and their significant contribution to the culture and development of the railroad industry, and to preserve this rich heritage for the education, enjoyment and enrichment of present and future generations. It was to fulfil this mission that the museum was established in 1972. From 1972 to 1979 planning, site-locating and fund-raising efforts were undertaken. It was determined that the museum should be constructed on the site of the first (1850) railroad workshops built at Altoona. A five-acre parcel of land was acquired and construction of a 10,000 sq ft facility was completed and opened in late 1980. In the ensuing 13 years in excess of 350,000 people have visited the museum.

As the PRR's Altoona Works were arguably the largest and most sophisticated railroad workshops in the US, the museum quickly outgrew available space for interpretation of this complex history. Once again the museum formed an alliance with AIHP – this time to develop a 10-year management plan for the museum. Nearly three years in development, the management plan looked at a variety of alternatives for the museum's expansion over a period of several years. Suggested alternatives were the construction of additional new facilities at the site of the existing museum, or new construction elsewhere in Altoona.

The preferred alternative was for expansion of the museum into a historic ex-PRR structure adjacent to the present museum. This former PRR Master Mechanics' building was abandoned by Conrail in 1984 after serving three successive railroad companies for over 100 years. The Master Mechanics' building was part of a complex of railroad workshops known as the '12th Street Car Shops'. This 40 ft by 200 ft, 5 floor, 40,000 sq ft building was constructed by the PRR in three phases from 1882 to 1914. The building served a variety of functions for the railroad including stores department, master mechanics' drawing offices and library, medical department, police department, divisional dispatchers' and clerks' offices, and, most importantly, was the site of the first physical and chemical test department for the PRR. The chemical and physical test departments of the PRR at Altoona generated more patents than any other railroad in the US. The railroad tested materials and products extensively – contributing to the PRR's title of 'Standard Railroad of the World'.

The Master Mechanics' building is therefore a historic structure and one of the last extant structures from the 12th Street complex. The museum undertook extensive historical architectural and environmental surveys of the Master Mechanics' building and surrounding property. A 'historic structure' report was prepared as was a 'determination of eligibility' for National Register listing, thus enabling the grant of federal monies for building rehabilitation.

Fortunately, hazardous material investigations did not turn up extensive building or ground contamination. (Rail yard sites in the US have often been found to suffer from ground contamination by hazardous materials, thus making public use of such sites prohibitively expensive.) The most significant removal of hazardous material needed in the Master Mechanics' building is the removal or encapsulation of some 14 layers of lead-based paint applied to surfaces within the building over several decades.

Concurrent with site planning and design an interpretative planning effort was undertaken. An extensive research project was mounted to determine the 'key' interpretative themes relating to Altoona's railroad history. Answers to questions such as 'Why in the world Altoona?' were fundamental to relevant interpretation of the PRR and its impact on Altoona. An interpretative concepts planning process employing primary resources, the men and women who lived the Altoona experience, was utilised extensively in the development of storylines.

Armed with an interpretative plan and excellent historical research on the building itself, the planning team set out to determine a practical and realistic timeline and budget for development. As the cost for implementation was estimated to be about $20 million, the museum management had to develop a plan for the project which could be phased over several years. The federal commission simply does not have the resources to allocate funding for a project of this magnitude. The development was therefore broken into three phases. A key consideration for the phasing was that phase one should be complete in itself. If funding for future phases is delayed, the integration of each successive phase will become an addition to the existing museum and will not disrupt visitor circulation or experience to any large degree.

The first phase, the rehabilitation of, and fabrication of exhibits for, the Master Mechanics' building will cost around $10 million. This is now available and construction activity is scheduled for the first quarter of 1994. Opening of this part of the new museum complex is anticipated by late 1995.

The second phase of the project involves improvements to the site adjacent to the Master Mechanics' building and the existing museum facility. The museum complex is located on land used for the original PRR workshop construction of 1850. Foundations from the large erecting and machine shops are extant, and structures no longer standing will be interpreted through the use of new imaging techniques such as holography and 'ghosting'. Large industrial artefacts from the railroad workshops, donated by Conrail, will be set out on the various foundations as a visual indication that both the buildings and the machines used to construct railroad equipment created large vertical elements in the urban landscape.

Also planned for second phase implementation is the locating of at least a dozen wayside exhibits throughout Altoona. These will be placed at strategic locations relevant to presesnt or past railroad activity. Conrail (the successor to the PRR) continues to use Altoona for the maintenance and repair of its fleet of locomotives and equipment, so a large number of railroad enthusiasts are drawn to the area. The wayside exhibits will serve as a means to encourage this audience to visit key sites where

Conrail operations and workshop activity can be viewed.

The PRR was responsible for the development of many cultural and service amenities for its workers and families. Additional wayside exhibits will be placed at suitable locations commemorating the railroad's role in the development of the Altoona water distribution system, the hospital, the library and the sports field.

The third phase of the project addresses the development of the present museum building and its reconfiguration as a covered rolling stock building. The present collection of some 20-plus pieces of rolling stock is displayed outside, making proper curatorial care and preservation very difficult. Some $5 million have been budgeted for this final phase of construction to house and interpret the rolling stock.

The three extant buildings from the 12th Street Car Shops (other than the Master Mechanics' building) are currently in private ownership, operating as a freight car repair shop and an office for a steel fabricator. Since these buildings, too, contribute to the historic railroad landscape, regular meetings are held with the owners and their co-operation has been secured for appropriate facade treatments for their buildings. It is possible that these buildings might become available to the museum before the start of the final design process for the rolling stock structure. These historic workshops would then become the location for rolling stock protection and interpretation.

The entire development project is planned for completion by 1999 – the sesquicentennial celebration of the founding of Altoona.

Summary

This paper has presented two very different projects in terms of scope and goals for preservation and interpretation, and each has a different approach and solution. The first is Horseshoe Curve, an important civil engineering landmark which had little interpretation but which was a pleasant and serene setting to view trains struggling against the forces of nature and gravity. Careful planning developed structures at the Curve that were sympathetic to the landscape and not in conflict with the historic setting. These new structures contribute to the visitor experience through interpretation of the significance of the site. The structures and interpretative displays at the Curve represent a deliberate and comprehensively planned development which was made possible only by the co-operation of the many partners involved.

The second approach, the expansion of the Altoona Railroaders Memorial Museum, preserves, adapts and reuses an historic railroad building which itself served a variety of functions during its service for the railroad. The same principles of careful planning, extensive public involvement and key partnership development will ensure the success of this project as it did at Horseshoe Curve. Through this development the museum will become a catalyst for the revitalisation of Altoona's city centre, spawning additional economic development and creating an awareness that historic preservation and heritage tourism development are beneficial to the community.

The early Baltimore & Ohio Railroad and its physical remains

Herbert H Harwood, Jr

The Stockton & Darlington Railway had been open less than a year when an American from Baltimore came calling. Evan Thomas had been touring England and visited the railway mostly out of curiosity. His brother, a Baltimore banker, was worrying about a commercial crisis his city was facing and had heard about this new iron road on which cumbersome locomotives hauled trains of coal. Thomas sailed home and gave a non-committal but enthusiastic report – and suddenly one of the seeds of the railroad revolution in America was planted and instantly began growing.

Within six months the Baltimore & Ohio (B&O) Railroad had been created, on paper at least. Admittedly it was less a case of vision than desperation, but the Baltimoreans were off on the early nineteenth-century equivalent of a moon shot.

The B&O was not America's first railroad, nor even America's first steam-powered railroad. It was the first operating common carrier, or public railway, in the US when it started a short, horse-powered service on 24 May 1830 – even though this distinction lasted only about seven months. Nonetheless, the B&O can legitimately be called America's pioneering railway. It was the country's most ambitious early transportation project and its most influential; it was truly the B&O which set the standards for American railroading. (Unfortunately its fame also inevitably spawned some mythology which still haunts and confuses historians. A few myths will be mentioned, but beware of more when studying the railroad.)

This paper looks at the B&O's early history from the slightly different viewpoint of railroad archaeology: a study of the relics of the past which still exist to tell the story. Not only is the B&O one of America's oldest railroads but it is also probably the best preserved. The physical remains of over 160 years of life are still visible; to the perceptive historian they can sometimes tell a much more graphic and immediate story than can abstractions from books and documents. These structures speak about the struggles, the missteps, the successes and the everyday business of the railroad; they say things about how the company perceived itself and

how it wanted others to think of it. Some of the structures are obvious and maybe even over-familiar; other relics are hidden and barely known – adding the joy of discovery to the railroad archaeologist's adventures. And perhaps some are not what they seem to be at first.

Background: Baltimore marches into the unknown (1827-31)

By the early 1820s three young, aggressive, and ambitious seaport cities – New York, Philadelphia and Baltimore – were competing hotly with one another. While each had its own regional hinterland, their common battleground was what was then the far west – the Ohio River–Mississippi River–Great Lakes region. Already the country was expanding rapidly westward, and these areas promised major markets and raw material sources. The distances were great, however – anything from 350 to 500 miles depending on the specific port and the route inland.

New York was edging ahead in the contest, but Baltimore had some basic advantages of its own. In that era, of course, any inland travel was either by road or unimproved waterway. In this territory it was almost entirely by road: slow, difficult and very expensive. With freight shippers lucky to cover 30 miles a day overland, Baltimore was well placed in relation to its rivals; it lay some 200 miles closer to the western waterways. Furthermore, it had a superior system of roads and turnpikes, not the least of which was its connection to the government-built National Road, a modern (for the time) hard-surfaced highway which had been completed to the Ohio River at Wheeling in 1818.

In 1825, however, New York completed its Erie Canal, giving it a direct water-level route to the Great Lakes at Buffalo, New York. The canal made possible a spectacular cut in shipping costs; in some cases the freight rate between Buffalo and New York dropped from $100 per ton to $10-12. Suddenly Baltimore's fine road system was obsolete and its location less important. The city's merchants and bankers at first considered their own canal, but the terrain westward from Baltimore was nothing like the course of the Erie Canal. Not least, there were the Allegheny Mountains, reaching about 2600 ft, to cross. (A later canal plan contemplated no less than 246 locks and a 4-mile tunnel on the 150-mile mountain section; even so, water supply would have been uncertain at best.) Fortuitously, there was suddenly another alternative, albeit an enormously chancy one. The same year that the Erie Canal opened, so did the Stockton & Darlington Railway in England. The technology was clearly crude, the distance short and the environment quite different, but Baltimore's businessmen felt that they had little choice and decided to gamble on a railroad. In February 1827 they incorporated the B&O, to run from Baltimore to the Ohio river at Wheeling, Virginia (now West Virginia). (Wheeling was also the original terminal of the National Road.)

From the beginning it was clear that the B&O would be very different from the Stockton & Darlington, or even from the later and more advanced Liverpool & Manchester. When the B&O was incorporated in 1827, the longest railroad in the world – the Stockton & Darlington – was about 25 miles long, and was little more than a primitive mine tramway. Baltimore's merchants and bankers intended to build a railroad 380 miles long, through highly hostile terrain that no railroad had ever faced. They did not know how to locate the line, what tonnage would be hauled, how to design bridges and track for the traffic or what locomotive rolling stock designs would work. They did not know how much it would all cost or where the money would come from. In short, the B&O was one of the largest, riskiest and most daring projects of its day. Virtually everything had to be invented, adapted or learned the hard way. And there was much learning the hard way.

Undeterred, the Baltimoreans officially launched their railroad with a grand parade and ceremony on the 4th of July 1828. It was the biggest celebration Baltimore had ever seen and, taking relative population size into account, ever would. At the time the city's population was about 70,000 – and it was estimated that 70,000 people turned out. Charles Carroll of Carrollton, aged 90, the last living signatory to the Declaration of Independence, turned the first spadeful of earth to send the railroad on its way. Nobody noticed, perhaps, that on America's Independence Day Carroll was launching an English invention to save his city.

Construction proceeded feverishly, in some cases with construction crews working day and night. Two years of furious activity passed and by 1831 the finished line extended for just 13 miles to Ellicott's Mills (now called Ellicott City), Maryland. The company was running out of funds and close to bankruptcy. The development of the railroad was on the basis of trial and error, with many expensive errors. In a short time, in fact, the B&O became known as the university of American railroading; many other railroad engineers learned on the B&O, then went on to build other railways.

Many relics stand today which tell this story of experimentation, frustration and eventual success and some significant survivors are examined in the remainder of this paper.

Building bridges for eternity (1829-35)

An immediate and critical question to be resolved by those building the railroad was the design of the bridges. The B&O would need many, and some large ones; political pressures and the natural piedmont topography west of Baltimore combined to produce a rugged route. The line's first seven miles cut across hilly country at right angles to the drainage pattern; farther west it hugged the banks of streams which were barely more than creeks, crossing and re-crossing them and their little tributaries.

Railroad civil-engineering expertise was, of course, non-existent. The nearest source which the railroad could find was the US Army. Its military academy at West Point, New York, was the country's only formal engineering school at the time, and its exploration, road-building and other construction projects came closest to the skills needed for railroad location and construction. The B&O's directors managed to persuade the government to loan several experienced army engineers, most notably Lt Col Stephen H Long and Capt William Gibbs McNeill. (A later addition was Lt George Washington Whistler.) A second source of expertise was the civilian turnpike builders, particularly those who had helped build the National Road. Two in particular were appointed by the B&O: Jonathan Knight, as Senior Engineer, and Caspar Wever, as the new company's Construction Superintendent.

The engineers, builders and company directors quickly found themselves at odds over how to cross all the various valleys and streams. The pragmatic army engineers, experienced in wilderness road building, argued for a 'frontier' theory of construction. They wanted to build low-cost wooden bridges and trestles and get the line into operation as quickly and cheaply as possible; as traffic and finances built up, wood could then be replaced by more substantial structures. Construction Superintendent Wever, however, was a passionate advocate of the sort of heavy stone construction he had used in his turnpike building. An open fight developed. Wever – who was not an engineer and whose job was to build what the engineers told him to build – went directly to the B&O's President and directors, arguing for the 'permanence' of earth embankments, stone bridges and viaducts. It is highly possible that Wever implied to the company's directors that stone bridges would last forever and could be named in honour of particular directors.

In the event, that was the way it turned out. Stone was used and some magnificent and long-lived structures arose and were named after some of the B&O's early directors. The cost was enormous and construction progress was far slower than it should have been. But from the historian's viewpoint many fine relics survived to illustrate this crucial phase in the railroad's history.

Not the least of these was what is now America's oldest surviving railroad bridge, the justly well-known Carrollton viaduct, spanning Gwynns Falls within the present city of Baltimore. This spectacular structure is 297 ft long with a single 80 ft arch. Completed in 1829, it was named after the early B&O director and promoter, Charles Carroll of Carrollton, who had started the railroad on its way a year before. (Plate 1)

But the Carrollton viaduct is merely the most notable of these early B&O stone bridges. Scattered along 76 miles of the B&O's original main line west of Baltimore are at least 17 other stone bridges from the 1829-33 period. Some (such as the Patterson viaduct at Ilchester and the Oliver viaduct at Ellicott City) are only partial remnants of much larger structures; some still carry rail traffic; many others were bypassed during a massive turn-of-the-century line relocation project and now, hidden in deep woods, are known only to occasional hikers. (Plate 2)

By 1834 prudence had displaced pride; the B&O's infatuation with stone abruptly ended, and

Plate 1. The 1829 Carrollton viaduct in Baltimore is the earliest existing US railroad bridge; it remained in service in 1994, although no longer on a main line route. (Photograph by H H Harwood, Jr, 1974)

afterwards most bridges were built of wood and then iron. But its last stone monument was surely its grandest. Between 1833 and 1835 the B&O built a short but important 29½ mile branch from its main line at Relay, Maryland, to Washington, DC. At the point where the new Washington branch left the line at Relay it had to cross the wide valley of the Patapsco River and circle a hill on a horseshoe curve to continue south. To accomplish this, the engineer in charge, Benjamin Latrobe Jr, designed what was then the largest stone viaduct ever attempted in the US and which was also, necessarily, located on a curve. Named the Thomas viaduct in honour of the B&O's President, Philip E Thomas, it measures 612 ft long, 60 ft high, with eight arches each averaging 58 ft wide. Finally completed in July 1835, the Thomas viaduct remains in heavy main line service and is usually considered America's oldest surviving multiple-arch railroad bridge. (Plate 3)

The Thomas viaduct is such a timeless symbol of the B&O that it may be surprising to know that for much of its life the railroad wanted to get rid of the

Plate 2 (above). Typical of the many 'hidden treasures' along B&O's original main line is this 1831 stone bridge near Davis, MD. This section of line was abandoned during a major line relocation in 1902. (Photograph by H H Harwood, Jr, 1979). Plate 3 (below). The famous 1833-35 Thomas viaduct as seen from its southeast end at Elkridge, MD, in 1974. It continues in main line service carrying CXST and Conrail freight trains as well as commuter trains operated by the State of Maryland. (Photograph by H H Harwood, Jr, 1974)

bridge. As traffic volume and train speeds increased in the late nineteenth century, the viaduct's alignment became an operating nuisance. The sharp horseshoe curve of which it was a part was unnecessarily circuitous, required reduced speeds and created extra wear on wheels and rail. Ironically the original surveys had considered a much straighter, easier and more direct alignment – which also would have required a more modest bridge. Indeed, it was rumoured at the time that the viaduct's alignment was chosen so that the company could build a spectacular structure there. In any event, beginning in 1876, the B&O began buying property to bypass the viaduct, and construction of the cut-off route actually started in the mid-1890s. But financial problems intervened, and between one thing and another, the project was never completed. It remained alive but dormant until 1969, however, when some of the right-of-way was finally sold.

The B&O's stone bridge era ended early but gloriously. To many historians this impressive array of expansive masonry was a direct, if misguided, imitation of English railway 'permanent way' practice. That well may be so, but it is interesting to note that the most decisive force within the company was Caspar Wever, the Construction Superintendent, who had never been to Britain and whose experience and opinions came from his American turnpike work. Possibly in this case the 'common roots' went further back to the common root of them all: the Roman roads and aqueducts.

A permanent roadbed and how it vanished (1830-31)

The railway track bed might be thought to have indisputable 'common roots' but the B&O, as in so much else, chose to experiment. Initially, and electing for permanence over cost, the B&O adopted the Stockton & Darlington's technique of using granite blocks as its track base. The rail itself, however, was pure American expediency: a flat iron strip fastened to a wood stringer, which in turn was set on the stone blocks. Six miles of single track were laid using this combination of granite blocks, wood stringers and iron 'strap rail'. Another equally long section was 'temporarily' laid with very flimsy wooden sleepers until the stone blocks could be delivered and until some earth embankments had settled.

At that point the B&O's senior engineer, Jonathan Knight, had what he believed to be a better idea.

Rather than granite blocks and wood stringers, he decided to cut the granite into long, longitudinal sills. These would be placed end to end and the iron strap rail would be bolted directly to the stone, thereby eliminating the wood stringer and providing a continuous 'permanent' stone base for the rail. Knight's method became the B&O's standard, and about 25 miles of double track were laid in this way with each long granite stringer laboriously and expensively quarried, cut to form, finished to accommodate the rail, hauled to the site and set into the ground.

Mercifully for the company's finances, the process proved so slow that Knight had to revert to wooden sleepers as another 'temporary' expedient to keep construction moving ahead. In the meantime it became clear that the stone sill method was an irretrievable disaster. It was impossible to keep the track aligned or the strap rails secured; the rigid, unyielding track gave a rough ride and damaged equipment, particularly as horse power gave way to steam.

While the stone bridges were an expensive mistake, they were at least eminently usable. Nothing could be done with the stone roadbed, either the sills or the earlier blocks. Some stones were extracted for use in buildings and retaining walls but in most cases the railroad was forced, literally, to bury its mistake; time was now too short and capital too scarce to stop. The embarrassment almost completely disappeared under succeeding generations of new track and roadbed, gone from both sight and memory.

In June 1972 floods from Tropical Storm Agnes swept down the Patapsco River valley, washing out many sections of the original B&O main line. The stone roadbed reappeared, so well preserved in some cases that the iron strap rail could have been re-attached and the track put back into service. (Plate 4) Some was eventually reburied as the railroad was rebuilt but in many areas where the old line had been bypassed by relocations it can be found on or close to the ground surface. (Plate 5) Some of this original right-of-way is now a public park trail, and hikers who know what to look for can find numerous relics.

Locomotives like none before – or since (1830-37)

While track construction was proceeding, the B&O also had to work out how to pull its trains. By the

Plate 4 (above). Floods from Tropical Storm Agnes in 1972 exposed this section of 1830 stone stringer roadbed at Union Dam, MD, about 15 miles west of Baltimore. This section of original main line had been by-passed by a 1902 realignment. (Photograph by H H Harwood, Jr, 1972). Plate 5 (below). The same 1972 flood revealed both the original stone block roadbed construction (centre) and slightly later stone stringer technique used for the second track (right). The scene is at Ilchester, MD, east of Ellicott City. (Photograph by H H Harwood, Jr, 1972)

time construction started in 1828, steam power was reasonably well proven in England, and by late 1829 most of the principles of modern steam locomotive design had been worked out there. But the B&O had a particular problem. Its route up the winding Patapsco River valley had such sharp curves (14 to 18° in some cases) that the English locomotives of the time could not negotiate the line. Horses hauled the first service to Ellicott's Mills in 1830 and the company's directors almost concluded that they must be satisfied with a 380-mile horse-powered railroad.

Peter Cooper, a New York entrepreneur and inventor, had invested in some harbour-front land in Baltimore and was anxious to make the new railroad a success. In 1830 he put together the first steam locomotive built in the US. It was a tiny four-wheeled demonstrator which was able to work on the B&O's line: the engine everyone now calls the *Tom Thumb*. (Actually the name came much later, long after the engine was gone.) The *Tom Thumb* was not meant for everyday traffic; the idea was merely to show how steam could be applied to the B&O. It worked, and having served its purpose it was soon scrapped, but its odd, short wheelbase and its vertical-boilered, geared design formed the foundation for early B&O locomotives and started the B&O off on its own individualistic course of locomotive design.

The famous 1926 replica *Tom Thumb* at the B&O Museum in Baltimore has been pictured the world over and is still occasionally operated at railroad celebrations. Unhappily, it has minimal resemblance to the original. Cooper's engine was, at most, half the size of this surviving replica and probably had a different drive mechanism. Although no plans of the original engine have survived (and perhaps none ever existed), some good conjectural drawings have been made. If ever a good museum replica was needed, this is it.

Despite the success of the Cooper engine, steam came slowly to the B&O. After its own version of the Rainhill trials in 1831, the railroad settled on a more-or-less standardised design built around a vertical boiler with a short two-axle wheelbase and geared drive. Between 1832 and 1837 16 of these peculiar little creatures were built and hauled all of the B&O's traffic. Odd as they looked, they were practical, tough machines ideally suited to the B&O's corkscrew alignments. Although a dead-end design and soon replaced by more conventional horizontal-boilered locomotives, many worked on.

Some were still at work as shunters as late as 1892, 56 years after they were built, an amazing longevity record for a pioneer design. Three survive today, two at the B&O Museum in Baltimore and one at Dayton, Ohio.

Stations, real and not (1831-39)

The B&O needed to establish facilities for handling passengers and freight and, not surprisingly, the earliest surviving station in the US is on the B&O in Maryland. The question of the exact location of the oldest American *passenger* station is, however, not entirely straightforward.

In the past there has been debate over the competing claims of two early B&O stations, the Mt Clare station in Baltimore (Plate 6) (now a part of the B&O Museum complex) and Ellicott City, Maryland, 13 miles west of Baltimore. Both, it was thought, dated from the 1830-31 period when the railroad had just begun limited operations. Traditionally, most published histories gave the 'oldest' title to Mt Clare, which stands on or near the site

where the B&O sold its first passenger ticket.

But all railroad archaeologists – especially anyone working with the B&O – must beware of received wisdom. The firmest evidence indicates that Mt Clare's birth certificate was altered by over-zealous B&O publicists; the company's own annual reports clearly show that it was actually built in 1850 or 1851. By default that leaves Ellicott City, which was truly built about 1831 and probably deserves the title – but not for certain.

The stone Ellicott City depot is not the country's oldest *passenger* station. It was originally built as a multi-purpose operating building, a combination of freight depot, freight office, operations' construction office and, later, as an engine house. It did not begin handling passengers until 1856. So where, then, is the oldest passenger station?

We should recall an important aspect of early American railroad passenger operations that is now often overlooked. Many pioneering US railroads simply did not bother with passenger facilities, particularly at intermediate stations. Beset by high construction costs, meagre capital and long

Plate 6. The Mt Clare station in Baltimore has often been claimed as the oldest in the US, if not the world. It was actually built in 1851, more than 20 years later than legend states. Its site is significant, however, as the point where the first public railway operation in America began in May 1830. (Photograph by H H Harwood, Jr, 1970)

Plate 7. Probably the oldest surviving US 'railroad' passenger station is the former Patapsco Hotel in Ellicott City, MD, which was used by B&O passengers from 1830-56. Trains stopped alongside the hotel's second story (at right). (Photograph by H H Harwood, Jr, 1977)

distances to cover before adequate income could be generated, they had to get into business as quickly as possible and at minimum cost. Money was spent where it was most needed (or rather where the railroad thought it was most needed) on permanent way, bridges, equipment and freight facilities. Freight, unlike passengers, needed protection from weather and theft or damage; passengers could move and protect themselves. There had been no earlier tradition of providing shelter for passengers. Stagecoach passengers usually waited in roadside inns, taverns or stores, much like intercity bus riders a century later. Many early railroads simply continued this economical practice, including the B&O. At Ellicott City passengers used the stone Patapsco Hotel, located adjacent to the track directly across the street from the freight depot. (Plate 7) Built at about the same time as the railroad, the old hotel stands in reconstructed form today and is probably the oldest American railroad passenger station.

Apart from the B&O, at least three other examples of these early inn/railroad stations still exist in

the US, and perhaps there are more. One, about 10 miles north of Baltimore, and an almost exact contemporary of the Ellicott City hotel, is the present Valley Inn at Brooklandville, Maryland. It was built of stone in about 1830 on the Falls Turnpike Road and beginning in 1832 also served the infant Baltimore & Susquehanna Railroad which crossed the highway here. For those wanting to explore farther, there is also the present General Wayne Inn at Merion, Pennsylvania (west of Philadelphia), built in 1704 and used as a stop by the Philadelphia & Columbia Railroad between 1834 and 1850. And in West Newton, Massachusetts, the one-time Davis Tavern was also the Boston & Worcester's first western terminal in 1834.

Since these early inns were not railroad-owned structures the question remains: where then *is* the earliest true surviving American passenger station? Somewhat surprisingly, nobody really knows, so here is yet another challenge for railroad archaeologists. One contender, anecdotally dated at 1839, stands in West Brookfield, Massachusetts, on the one-time Boston & Albany Railroad main line. But another suddenly came to light in July 1993 on the B&O and teaches a superb lesson that all is not yet discovered.

Duffields, West Virginia, is a country hamlet 84 miles west of Baltimore on the B&O's main line to Cumberland, Maryland. Construction of this section of line started in 1839 and was completed in 1842. When it began work in 1839, the B&O built a little stone station at Duffields, which may have served as a construction office until the line opened three years later. Afterwards it handled all of Duffields' rather modest passenger and freight business until it was replaced by a newer and more fashionable building in 1884. To earn a few extra dollars for itself, the railroad then sold the old station into private hands and soon forgot it. After about 108 years the private owners apparently forgot it too; vacant and neglected, it was left to revert to nature, which quickly obscured it with trees, bushes and vines. Happily, a perceptive local rail historian has recently re-discovered and identified it. Enough vegetation was cleared away to reveal the bulk of the original station. (Plate 8) The

dark side of the story is that nature may return or worse may happen; the structure remains a friendless derelict.

Maturity but not normality (1842-57)

Thanks to political and financial misfortunes, it was not until 1842 that the B&O reached Cumberland, Maryland, at the base of the Allegheny Mountains. Fourteen years had now elapsed since it had begun building, the railroad was still only halfway to its goal at the Ohio River and the most difficult terrain still lay ahead. At Cumberland, however, the B&O hit the jackpot: bituminous coal. By the late 1840s coal began flowing eastward to the port of Baltimore in ever-growing quantities. Coal quickly became the B&O's staple, indeed its largest single commodity, and the major ingredient in whatever success the company had.

Coal also gave the B&O a new pioneering engineering challenge – how to design locomotives, cars and structures for hauling large quantities of a heavy, bulk commodity. (Until then the B&O's major business had been flour.) The B&O became

Plate 8. This unassuming 1839 stone station at Duffields, WV, was rediscovered in 1993. Disused by the railroad after 1884, it has since been privately owned. (Photograph by H H Harwood, Jr, 1993)

one of the earliest users of high-tractive effort locomotives, primarily ponderous 0-8-0s such as the 1848 *Memnon*, now preserved in more-or-less original form at the B&O Museum in Baltimore, and the only surviving American example of this early heavy freight locomotive design. Another innovation was the use of the first mass-produced metal freight cars, the curious iron pot-shaped hoppers introduced in 1845. By the 1850s the design had evolved into an eight-wheel, three-hopper car carrying 20 tons of coal. By 1870 the B&O had almost 2000 of them, and they were built into the 1880s. (Despite appearances, these eight-wheeled cars did not have bogies; the hoppers unloaded where the bolsters of the bogies would normally be.) The B&O Museum has two examples of these vehicles, survivors of a unique pioneering design and symbolic of the point in history where American railroads diverged up the branch of heavy-tonnage, high-capacity bulk freight haulage. This is the branch which now routinely sees 20,000-ton trains moved by 12,000 diesel horse-power locomotives.

As mentioned earlier, the B&O had abandoned stone construction in the mid-1830s and had been building wooden bridges and trestles as it worked its way west. These were quickly overwhelmed by heavier locomotives and trains and at an early date iron became the standard construction material. But, ever individualistic, the B&O used its own truss design, developed by its Master-of-Road Wendel Bollman. This complex, spiderwebby truss was first installed in 1850, patented in 1852, and for the next 20 years was built everywhere along the expanding B&O system. One of the first examples of standardised, prefabricated American railroad bridge construction, Bollman trusses came in varying lengths and numbers of spans, culminating in a spectacular (and long gone) example at Harpers Ferry, West Virginia, consisting of eight spans on an 'S' curve alignment which carried both a railroad track and roadway and included a set of points leading to a branch line part way across!

Like all early American iron railroad bridge designs, the Bollman truss was obsolete by the 1870s; as traffic and train weights increased, the

Plate 9. The sole surviving example of B&O's standardised Bollman truss design stands at Savage, MD, between Baltimore and Washington. The 1869 double-track main line bridge was moved to this location to carry a single-track freight spur to the Savage Mill (rear) in 1887. Now owned by Howard County, MD. (Photograph by H H Harwood, Jr, 1984)

railroad rapidly replaced its Bollmans, and by the early 1900s virtually all were gone. One, however, actually survived in working railroad service into the late 1940s and still stands on its original site at Savage, Maryland, roughly midway between Baltimore and Washington. Originally built in 1869 as a double-track main line bridge, the two-span structure was moved to Savage in 1887 to serve a single-track industrial spur. Not only is it the last of its peculiar type, but it is also one of the very few early iron railroad bridges surviving anywhere in the US. (Plate 9)

Finally, on 1 January 1853, the B&O began service to Wheeling on the Ohio River. It had taken 25 years, and by then the B&O was no longer unique in the railroad business. Railroads were being built everywhere and, thanks in large part to the B&O's painful pioneering, the technology was well-developed and even routine. But the B&O had at last come of age on its own. After that things moved quickly, for a while. By 1857 the B&O had established a through route between Baltimore, Cincinnati and St Louis. The journey was not particularly fast or easy, but the company now linked the east coast with the Mississippi valley and the expanding western frontier. Although initially it did not own or control the full route, the B&O could claim to be the country's longest trunk line – about 910 miles from terminal to terminal.

With its new status and with coal revenues swelling its depleted coffers, the company sought to show Baltimore and the world that the B&O was at last a major railroad. The company's main Baltimore passenger terminal was still a re-used downtown commercial building which pre-dated the railroad and which was reached over city streets behind plodding horses. Beginning in 1853, the railroad spent large sums of money on a new route into the city and a grandiose terminal, called Camden station. Designed by the architects Niernsee and Neilson, Camden was finally completed in two stages, the first in 1857 and the second, delayed by the Civil War, in 1865. Its ostentatious architecture is symbolic of the end of the early struggles and the beginning of power, prestige and (sometimes) prosperity. (Plate 10)

The completion of Camden station in 1865 is an appropriate point to end this paper, before the events of the late nineteenth century made a tangle of the B&O's life. Before ending, however, it is worthwhile to pause and ponder Camden station itself; its life is an example of how some structures survive against all odds as a result of pragmatic transformations which may ultimately result in preservation dilemmas.

Almost from the beginning, Camden station changed its form. By the late 1870s its high central tower was deemed structurally unstable and cut down. The mid-1890s saw a complete rebuilding and reorientation of the station's layout and facilities, with new trainsheds, baggage room, and a low-level platform to serve the new line to Philadelphia. More alterations came in the early twentieth century as the west wing was sacrificed for a warehouse office building and exterior canopies were added. In the interim, plans were made to abandon the station completely; by then it was operationally obsolete, architecturally unfashionable and in a backwater of the city. But the money never seemed to be available and Camden soldiered on into the 1980s, further stripped by a well-meaning but destructive 1951 renovation, but by then the oldest metropolitan passenger terminal still in active service. However, the B&O had given up all its passenger trains and Camden served only a state-operated commuter service.

Finally abandoned entirely, the tattered orphan at last found a rich guardian angel in the form of the Maryland Stadium Authority, which inherited Camden station as part of the site for the city's new baseball stadium. While unsure what to do with it, the authority decided at least to restore it to its 1865 glory; back came the tower, cupolas, west wing and all. Not brought back, however, were passenger trains, which now load in austere open quarters a block to the south. Is such a reconstruction history? Is it 'real', including, as it does, features from different dates? No matter, perhaps; once again the building, even if it is something of a facade, illustrates how far the Baltimore & Ohio came from the days when it was not sure it could get beyond Ellicott's Mills.

Plate 10. The restored Camden station in Baltimore. The central section was originally completed in 1857; the two flanking wings in 1865. Tower, cupolas, west wing (right) and other features were later removed or altered. (Photograph by H H Harwood, Jr, 1993)

Additional reading

Baltimore & Ohio Railroad Co, *Annual Reports*, 1828-51

Bell, J S, *The Early Motive Power Of The Baltimore & Ohio Railroad* (New York: Angus Sinclair Co, 1912; reprinted Felton, CA: Glenwood Publishers, 1975)

Harwood, H H Jr, *Impossible Challenge: The Baltimore & Ohio Railroad in Maryland* (Baltimore, MD: Barnard, Roberts & Co, 1979)

Harwood, H H Jr, 'History where you don't expect it: some surprising survivors', *Railroad History*, 166 (1992)

Harwood, H H Jr, 'Mt Clare: America's oldest station – or is it?', *Railroad History*, 139 (1978)

Hungerford, E, *The Story Of The Baltimore & Ohio Railroad* (New York: G P Putnam & Sons, 1928)

Long, S H, and McNeill, W G, *Narrative Of The Proceedings Of The Board Of Engineers Of The Baltimore & Ohio Railroad Co* (Baltimore, MD: privately printed, 1830)

Roberts, C S, *West End: Cumberland To Grafton 1848-1991* (Baltimore, MD: Barnard, Roberts & Co, 1991)

Sagle, L W, 'Baltimore & Ohio stations in Baltimore', *Railway & Locomotive Historical Society Bulletin*, 106 (1962)

Stover, J F, *History Of The Baltimore and Ohio Railroad* (West Lafayette, IN: Purdue University Press, 1987)

Vogel, R M (ed), *Some Industrial Archaeology of the Monumental City & Environs: A Guide for SIA Tourists* (Washington, DC: Society for Industrial Archaeology, 1975)

White, J H Jr, and Vogel R M, 'Stone rails along the Patapsco', *IA: The Journal Of The Society For Industrial Archaeology*, 4, 1 (1978)

Appendix: surviving nineteenth-century structures on the B&O Railroad within 100 miles of Baltimore

Miles from Camden station	Location*	Structure, date and comments
1 Main line and 'Old Main line' west; opened 1830-42		
1.5	Baltimore	Mt Royal station, 1896; grandiose Romanesque-Renaissance design, with iron trainshed; now Maryland Institute College of Art
0.0	Baltimore	Camden station 1856-65; second oldest surviving US city passenger terminal; restored to original appearance 1992; owned by MD Stadium Authority
		Camden warehouse, 1899-1903; huge eight-storey 430,000 cu ft brick warehouse; restored and owned by MD Stadium Authority
0.8	Baltimore	Mt Clare station, *c*1850; part of B&O Museum complex
		Mt Clare shop buildings 1870, 1884; site of first US railroad workshop; surviving buildings include spectacular 1884 roundhouse, originally a passenger car workshop; all now part of B&O Museum
1.9	Baltimore	Gwynns Run bridge, 1829, 1848; stone arch located on original main line
2.1	Baltimore	Carrollton viaduct, 1829; stone arch on original main line; oldest US railroad bridge
3.5	Baltimore	'Deep cut', 1828-30; at Patapsco Ave, west Baltimore; 3000 ft long, 60 ft deep rock cut; B&O's most serious original construction obstacle; took two years to finish; later widened for four tracks
5.9	Halethorpe	Herbert Run bridge and embankment, 1830, 1875; largest original embankment, with stone bridge
10.7	Ilchester	Patterson viaduct, 1829-30; originally four stone arches crossing Patapsco River; single arch remains on abandoned alignment
11.5	Lees	Stone bridge, 1830
12.8	Ellicott City	Station, 1831; stone; earliest US railroad station; now museum
12.8		Patapsco Hotel, *c*1830; Main St; used as passenger station 1830-56
		Freight station, 1884; brick; now part of museum

continued

		Oliver viaduct, 1830; originally three-arch stone viaduct over Main St and stream; now single arch; in present service
13.4	Oella	Sucker Run bridge, 1831; small stone bridge
14.9	Union Dam	Stone roadbed, 1831; longitudinal stringers on abandoned alignment; now reburied
17.9	Daniels	Bridge piers, 1838; built for wooden truss bridge on early line alignment; alignment now abandoned
		Stone roadbed, 1831; located at various places west of Daniels on abandoned original alignment; now state park trail
19.2 (approx)	Daniels (vicinity)	Three stone bridges, 1831, 1870; located on abandoned original alignment
20.3	Davis	Davis Creek bridge, 1831; in present service
21.8-24.6	Woodstock to Marriottsville	Three stone bridges, 1831, c1848; in present service
28.8	Syskesville	Station, 1883; brick; architect-designed; now restaurant
38.0 (approx)	Mt Airy (vicinity)	Inclined planes, 1831; various remains of planes 1 and 2 on east side of Parrs Ridge hill, including stone culvert
39.6	Mt Airy	Station, 1875-82; on abandoned alignment; now pharmacy
46.7	Monrovia	Stone bridge, 1831; on abandoned alignment
58.2	Frederick	Station, 1854; Italianate design; city-owned; restored
61.8	Doub	Tuscarora Creek bridge, 1832; stone; in service
65.2	Point of Rocks	Station, c1871, 1875; architect-designed brick structure with central tower; in present service
68.9	Catoctin	Catoctin Creek bridge, 1833, 1902; large two-arch stone bridge, extended on north side
72.1	Brunswick	Station, 1891; wood
75.8	Weverton	Israel Creek bridge, 1833; stone; in present service
78.2	Harpers Ferry, WV	Stone bridge piers, 1836; remains of original wooden truss bridge over Potomac River; later used for iron truss bridges
		Valley branch bridge, 1894; steel truss over Potomac River, originally built as main line crossing
		Station, 1894-95; wood; relocated to present site in 1931

continued

84.5	Duffields, WV	Station, *c*1839; small stone; second oldest surviving on B&O system
96.3	Martinsburg, WV	Shops, 1866-72; three large brick buildings remain, including roundhouse
		Station, 1849; originally built as commercial hotel; used as station after 1861 and bought by railroad 1866; later enlarged
		Freight station, 1881; brick; west of passenger station

2 Washington branch, south/west of Relay, MD; opened 1835

7.2	Relay	Thomas viaduct, 1833-35; large stone multiple-arch viaduct on curve over Patapsco River; in present service
10.4	Harwood	Bascom Creek bridge, 1834; stone; in present service
11.5	Dorsey	Deep Run bridge, 1870; stone; in present service
17.6	Savage	Bollman iron truss bridge, *c*1869; two-span over Little Patuxent River at Savage Mill; relocated here 1887; last Bollman truss in existence
19.4	Laurel	Station, 1884; brick; architect-designed Queen Anne style; restored; in present service

3 Philadelphia Subdivision (Baltimore to Philadelphia, PA); opened 1886

| 6.8-7.7 | Baltimore | Two truss bridges, 1885; located in east Baltimore at Bay View and Gough St, Highlandtown, on branch to Canton; Murphy-Whipple trusses; originally built for main line use; among oldest metal bridges still in present use in US |
| 32.5 | Aberdeen | Station, 1888; architect-designed; brick and wood; attributed to Frank Furness; last original station on this line; in present use |

4 Metropolitan branch (Washington, DC, to Point of Rocks); opened 1873 (Note: all mileages shown here are from Union Station, Washington)

10.4	Kensington	Station, 1891; wood; in railroad service
16.0	Rockville	Station, 1873; brick; gothic style, architect-designed; relocated and privately owned
21.1	Gaithersburg	Station and freight station 1884; both brick; architect-designed
34.8	Dickerson	Station, 1891; wood; restored and in present use

* All locations are in Maryland unless noted

Railway mechanical engineering

Old debts and new visions: the interchange of ideas in railway engineering

John H White, Jr

Be prepared for a considerable amount of movement during the course of this paper. We will be travelling from England to New England, then to the American south, then northward to Canada. Along the way we will touch down in Pennsylvania, Cuba and British Guyana. Be prepared, too, for a lengthy side trip to Russia during the reign of Tsar Nicholas. The distances are great and the itinerary jumpy (Monday, Liverpool; Tuesday, Lowell, Massachusetts; Wednesday, St Petersburg) but at least the schedule is rather leisurely. We have a century and a half to complete our journey. Our basic mission is not just a tour of past railway monuments but also to follow the trail of railway engineering ideas. How was the technology exchanged and how rapid and easy was the flow of information among nations?

My own view is that the international nature of technology leads to an unrelenting (indeed an unstoppable) transfer of ideas between nations and cultures. This exchange cannot be halted by border police, trade laws, internal security or language barriers. All efforts to stem the flow of technical information have failed from the beginning of the Industrial Revolution to the atomic age. Regressive measures may temporarily slow the exchange of ideas but they have never succeeded in throttling it. When the free exchange of information is not offered, industrial espionage extracts the desired data: in one way or another, the truth will out. Maintaining technical secrets is an increasingly difficult task. The ancient Chinese managed to keep the secret of silk manufacture for over 1000 years but the English were unable to hide the details of textile machinery design for much over 50 years. In more recent times the US government mounted an elaborate scheme to conceal the making of atomic bombs but a handful of amateur spies breached this mighty defence in just a few years.

I must make one more generalisation before moving on to the substance of this paper. Most of the individuals I will mention are unknown. I suspect few readers, even those who are railway specialists, will easily be able to identify Horatio Allen, Thomas Winans, Joseph Harrison Jr, George Washington Whistler or John Bloomfield Jervis. I ask for your patience, however, for these obscure figures are important to our story and all were prominent in their day, not just in the railway industry but also in financial and social circles.

Trade and invention

It is very important to begin at the beginning: the beginning of the age of steam railway travel was around 1830 in England. As news of steam railways reached North America, a parade of American engineers crossed the Atlantic to examine this new wonder.[1] Books were available and exhaustive studies by Wood, Gray and Treadgold were studied with care, but Americans tended to be hands-on mechanics and they wanted to see the steam railway for themselves.

William Strickland appears to be the first American to have visited Britain specifically to study railways. An architect, he was sent over in 1825 on a tour sponsored by well-to-do Philadelphia merchants who were eager to construct some form of overland communication to compete with the Erie Canal. Strickland published a report on his findings in 1826. Two years later construction began on the state public works, a 294-mile system comprising two railways and two canals. It was one of the largest transport projects of its time.

Other Americans followed in quick succession. Some came alone, such as Horatio Allen in 1828, while others, such as Whistler, McNeill and Knight, came in a group. Most came over with corporate sponsorship – the four men mentioned were all sent over by railways. Allen was sent not just to observe and file a report: though only 26 years old at the time, he was empowered to order rail and locomotives for the Delaware and Hudson (D&H) gravity railroad. Most American visitors stayed no more than a month but Allen remained for nearly eight months; we will come back to him.

It was not just a bunch of nosy Americans who were turning up at the trackside: Britain was becoming a Mecca for curious engineers from other lands as well. The Germanic states were amongst the first to send over observers. The King of Bavaria sent a minor noble, named Joseph von Baader, in 1815, just as the Napoleonic Wars were ending. Von Baader returned to Munich not just to report on what the British were doing but also to expand upon his own ideas for rail transport which included piggyback cars and compressed-air locomotives. But the inventor's difficult and cantankerous personality caused him to be expelled from the Court before anything of substance was accomplished.

Prussia, not to be outdone by a south German king, sent over two army engineers in 1826 and 1827.[2] They produced another lengthy report on the latest form of overland transit. The French came somewhat later, in 1830, but one of their number prepared what is perhaps the first book devoted exclusively to steam locomotive design. The author, G de Pambour, published his first work in 1836 covering the practical and theoretical operation of a steam locomotive. The engine under study was not French but a Stephenson *Planet* class.

It is a little difficult to say how British railwaymen reacted to this invasion of foreigners. For the most part the visitors seem to have been received hospitably and given help with their researches. Horatio Allen singled out George Stephenson as being especially gracious. Stephenson was a very senior and a very busy man yet he found time for this young and not very experienced technician. Allen said that the elder Stephenson was ' ... perfectly willing to converse on whatever topic I wished to introduce'.[3]

Not everyone was so receptive. Several American visitors from Lowell, Massachusetts, attempted to see the Vauxhall foundry (Liverpool), builders of marine and locomotive engines, in March 1839. They were met at the gate by the proprietor, George Forrester. Forrester looked at them 'rather hard but finally admitted us through his works in a hurried manner during dinner time'.[4] Perhaps Forrester felt these spies from the Lowell machine shops were simply out to steal his latest valve gear layout.

Why should Stephenson have been so open? Perhaps a generous and giving nature was natural to this simple man who, with so little education and no special advantages, had risen from very humble beginnings to become one of the most successful engineers of all time. Personally, I feel that Stephenson's genuine humility was the main reason

for his openness. There were other reasons, to be sure. The most obvious was the public nature of the railway. How could any part of it be kept a secret when it was laid out in the open for all to see? One need only have stood beside the track and watched a train go by or bought a ticket and ridden over the whole line or walked down a platform to see an engine being oiled and cleaned. A railway is not a thing easily hidden behind a factory gate. All else failing, information could have been secured from a co-operative employee such as one of the engine men in the local pub.

All of this would have been obvious to a bright and practical man such as George Stephenson. We must also remember that the Stephensons were not just engineers but were also consultants and vendors. They sold their services to whoever would hire them. Most of their work was done in Britain but Robert found at least one major commission in Canada on the Victoria tubular bridge in Montreal, and his father was reportedly in the pay of the Boston and Lowell (B&L) Railroad. During the 1830s drawings for rolling stock and two Stephenson-built locomotives were sent over to the B&L. It cannot be coincidental that the track for this line was a faithful reproduction of the track designed by Stephenson for the Liverpool & Manchester Railway.[5]

So it was not just good manners to be polite to Yanks – it was also good business. Robert Stephenson & Co, the locomotive plant in Newcastle, supplied about 60 locomotives to US customers. Before about 1880 the majority of American railways were built with rail produced in Great Britain because local mills could not match the British prices: America was therefore a major and valued export market.

American engineers who had visited Britain were home for no more than a few years before their role as visitors was reversed to that of playing the host; Europeans began to visit America to observe progress there. But why would anyone travel 3000 miles when he could go next door, as it were, and see the best railways in the world? The Americans were clearly building a very inferior style of railway, with flimsy, strap-rail track and shaky wooden trestles. Locomotives were loose-jointed, rambling machines that shot out appalling clouds of sparks and wood ash. Passengers sat in open saloon coaches offering no comfort or privacy. The reasons for the European interest lay in the costs of construction; the American system, for all its defects, was extremely cheap. Some lines cost only $20,000 per mile compared to the high-budget figure of $180,000 per mile in Britain, although much higher land costs helped to inflate British railway costs.

While low capital cost may have been the chief attraction drawing European transport experts to America, the size and scale of the system was probably an additional attraction. In 1837 David Stevenson, a Scottish engineer who spent three months in North America, recorded some 2700 miles of railways in the US, in service or under construction: more than double the mileage in the home of railways, Britain. Stevenson went on to publish a small book which seemed to stimulate the curiosity of European technicians for more information about American techniques that made such a large-scale and rapid railway building programme possible.[6]

No European visitors to America were more scientific or dogged than Franz Anton Ritter Von Gerstner. An engineer from Prague in Bohemia, Von Gerstner had already built the first railway in Russia (1836) after some earlier work in Europe. He landed in New York in November 1838 determined to discover how Americans had learned to build railways so cheaply and so quickly. It seemed to Von Gerstner that the British laboured forever in laying down their stone block track or erecting their giant brick viaducts and monumental stations. What took years in Britain, the Yanks did in months. The resulting railways were very different but they both accomplished the same end – they transported passengers and goods.

Von Gerstner began a tour of every major American canal and railway. He made detailed notes along each step of the way and was more and more impressed by what he saw. The technology and workmanship were often primitive but the fact that a system of cheap provisional railways was rapidly taking shape was most impressive. Traffic and population densities were low and a line might run for miles with scarcely a town or hamlet in sight. The trains moved slowly over the lightly built track and bridges but speed was not a priority in an underdeveloped nation.

In the pine forests of the Carolinas or the lonely valleys of Pennsylvania, Von Gerstner must have seen echoes of his native Bohemia, rural Austria or perhaps even the vast, open spaces of Russia. He must have realised that the transient style of railways that he was seeing on a daily basis was ideal

for most areas of the world. The undeveloped nations needed a minimal form of transport. Britain was an exception. It was a small, rich country, highly developed, densely settled and, unlike other countries, industrialised. It also had abundant capital. The elegant style of railway it was building was perfect for its needs – but less than perfect for the rest of the world.

Whatever grandiose plans Von Gerstner may have contemplated during this exhaustive tour of the US, they were cut short by his premature death in Philadelphia in April 1840. Fortunately, his monumental report, 725 pages in 2 volumes, was completed by his associate Ludwig Klein.[7]

Other European visitors to America were doing more than compiling thick reports. Karl Von Ghega, an engineer, spent nearly two years, from 1840 to 1842, studying the Baltimore and Ohio (B&O) Railroad as a model for the projected Semmering Pass railway. Von Ghega wanted to observe first-hand how a mountain railway was built and operated because he was Chief Engineer of the Alpine railway that cut across the Semmering Pass. The line opened in 1853 as Europe's first mountain railway: an Old World pioneering railway was patterned upon a New World prototype. What better example could be found to illustrate the exchange of ideas in the international engineering community?

There was at least one even more dramatic example of this exchange: the construction of the Moscow to St Petersburg Railway by American contractors. At this time the Tsar of all the Russias was the autocratic ruler Nicholas I (1796-1855) who believed in strict military control of his semi-feudal society. On most subjects Nicholas was a self-confessed reactionary, but he was remarkably progressive when it came to technical tools that might strengthen the military control of his rustic nation. A railway between the new capital and the old capital offered a fast way to move troops to quell insurrections.

In the summer of 1839 the Tsar sent two colonels, Melnikoff and Kraft, from the Corps of Engineers to the US. They were given a year to inspect the American system of railways. They were to seek out suitable surveyors, engineers and contractors to build the Moscow to St Petersburg railway and to supply it with suitable rolling stock, bridges, stations and repair depots. Britain, considered the workshop of the world and the ultimate source for technical data, was by-passed; Melnikoff and Kraft went directly to the US where the practice and experience of railway building was more closely related to what they believed was required. The colonels picked an American military engineer to head their railway project. He was Major George Washington Whistler, a reserved, formal man and every inch an army officer.[8] The three men got on well and the choice of Whistler was a good one, perhaps the best, for he had broad experience in railway surveys and building and had worked for several years at Lowell managing the Locks and Canals machine shop which made him familiar with locomotive construction. Whistler was one of the first to work as an engineer for the developing American railroad industry. He worked on preliminary surveys for the B&O Railroad in 1828. He made surveys for several other railways including the Paterson & Hudson River and the Stonington Line before going to Lowell in 1834. He was Chief Engineer for the Western Railroad in Massachusetts, a major east-west trunk line, at the time of the Russian colonels' visit. (Plate 1)

Melnikoff and Kraft returned to St Petersburg and in early 1842 the Tsar approved plans for the 420-mile railroad which, at the time, was the largest railway project undertaken anywhere in the world. Whistler arrived in St Petersburg in the summer of the same year. As work on the surveys and grading moved ahead slowly, thoughts turned to equipping the line. It was determined that all rolling stock would be made on Russian soil. The old Alexandrosky Arsenal, located near the gates of St Petersburg and occupying 160 acres, was prepared as a workshop. The colonels, being unable to find any ex-military engineers active in the locomotive business, recommended Eastwick and Harrison of Philadelphia and Ross Winans of Baltimore. Eastwick and Harrison were delighted by the offer because American locomotive business had been very poor since the economic panic of 1837. Ross Winans declined but sent his son, Thomas, instead.

The five-year contract was indeed a magnificent one with a cash value of $3 million, worth at least $300 million today. The contractors were to complete 162 locomotives, 5300 iron trucks, 2500 8-wheel freight cars, 70 passenger cars and 2 special 80 ft cars for the Tsar. The workshops were to employ over 1900 workers. Eastwick, Harrison and Winans were the envy of the railway rolling stock manufacturers' world. The contract was later increased to $5 million and other contracts followed which, in due course, allowed the

Plate 1. George Washington Whistler (1800-49) was an army engineer turned railway builder. He studied railways in England and constructed lines in the US and Russia. (National Encyclopaedia of American Biography *(New York, 1899), IX, p49)*

partners to retire as wealthy men. (Plate 2)

In fact, the contractors were hard-pressed to begin operations for none of them had start-up capital and the Russian government was not prepared to pay a kopek until the first engine rolled out of the workshop. Harrison went to Britain seeking a backer in 1843-44. At last he convinced the Welsh iron-maker William Crawshay to advance him the necessary credit to purchase materials needed to start work on their huge contract and thus it was that international co-operation lead to the successful completion of Russia's first trunk railway line.[9]

Plate 2. Locomotives and cars were manufactured in St Petersburg by the American contractors Joseph Harrison Jr (top left) and Thomas Winans (bottom right) for Russian service in the 1840s and 1850s. ((Top left) Bishop, James L, History of American Manufacturers *(Philadelphia, 1864), opposite p524; (bottom right)* Harpers Weekly, *28 June 1878; (top right and bottom left) Harrison, Joseph Jr,* The Locomotive and Philadelphia's Share in its Early Improvement *(Philadelphia, 1872))*

Despite Whistler's desire to finish the job, work on the railway went even more slowly as war diverted railway funds and cholera spread across Russia, killing many of the workers assigned to the project. Then Whistler himself was stricken and died after a long illness in April 1849. Another American army major, Thompson S Brown, took his place as project manager. Whistler's railway finally opened in the autumn of 1851. It continues in service today as one of the most heavily travelled lines within the former Soviet Union.

The Moscow to St Petersburg railway is perhaps the best example in this paper of technological cross-fertilisation: a basic plan was developed in Britain and then exported to the US where it was significantly modified and re-exported to a third nation, in this case Russia. Thus technology travels thousands of miles and undergoes modifications each step of the way to suit a new environment – a reminder of Darwinian theory.

Visitors who stayed on

Some people came to America not just to look and leave but rather to put down roots and make a new life. Most were young, untrained railway apprentices, although at least a few were experienced railway officials. The list is rather long and it is hardly necessary to chronicle each and every one, but a few examples might be instructive.[10] In the locomotive field William S Hudson, long-time Superintendent of the Rogers Locomotive Works (Paterson, New Jersey) easily comes to mind. Hudson was a native of Derby (itself a great railway centre) but learned the machinist's trade in Newcastle-upon-Tyne at the Stephenson works. He emigrated to the US in 1834 and worked for several eastern railways before becoming Rogers' works manager in 1852. Rogers was one of the largest and most progressive locomotive builders in the nation during Hudson's 29 years as Superintendent.

Despite his undoubted skills, Hudson's name is little known on either side of the Atlantic. William Buchanan's name is probably unfamiliar, too, though one of his locomotives – the 999 – is better known. This high-wheeled, American type set a world speed record – at least unofficially – in 1893 at 112 mph. Next to the *Rocket* it is probably one of the best-known locomotives in the world. Buchanan, its designer, was a poor Scot who came to Troy, New York. He started out as a punch-press operator, then went on to learn the blacksmith's trade from his father. In 1849, when just 19 years old, he took a job with the New York Central Railroad as a machinist. His boss was Walter McQueen, another recent immigrant from Scotland. McQueen went on to become Superintendent of the Schenectady Locomotive Works (predecessor of the American Locomotive Company). Buchanan rose more slowly through the ranks and finally became Superintendent of Motive Power for the New York Central in 1881. He retired in 1899, after half a century with the New York Central System. (Plate 3)

The master car builder's field was full of British immigrants as well. George Hackney worked for the London, Brighton & South Coast Railway until his middle years. He came to the US in 1861 and worked for the Northwestern and later the Burlington railroads before taking over the Santa Fe's car department. Hackney retired in 1889, only to be succeeded by another British immigrant, John Player, from Woolwich, who had learned the machinery trade whilst an apprentice in the Woolwich Arsenal.

The Scots, too, were well represented in the car departments of American railways. Robert McKenna, for example, came over in 1848 to work as a pattern maker. He eventually was appointed Master Car Builder for the Lackawanna Railroad and supervised their Scranton workshops for almost 30 years.

When it came to civil engineering, the railway industry showed more of a continental attitude. Albert Fink came from Germany in 1849 to find a job in the B&O Railroad drawing office. Later he became pre-eminent not only in managing the Louisville & Nashville Railroad but in establishing rates and traffic divisions for all southern railways. Octave Chanute, a native of Paris, did much to reform and rebuild the Erie Railroad, though today we tend to remember him as an aviation pioneer.

If street railways are included under the broad umbrella of rail transport, then several more British and European immigrants contributed to American developments. The cable railway system, which is still working in San Francisco, was invented by an Englishman, Andrew Halladie, from London. The largest builder of horse-cars in the US was John Stephenson, a native of Northern Ireland. Two pioneers of electric traction were foreign born; Leo Daft came from Birmingham and Charles Van Depeole from Belgium.

The spread of railways in the western hemisphere

How the railway came from Britain to the US has of course been told many times before. That Americans took up this technology with enthusiasm is also a familiar tale. Less talked about is the spread of railways elsewhere in the New World (see Table 1).[11] Latin America was in general far less enthusiastic about industrial development and steam railways than countries to the north. Such generalisations are dangerous and certain exceptions can always be noted but, in the main, the thesis is a sound one. The railway age was already a quarter of a century old before many South American nations opened their first line.

Cuba was the first of the Latin countries to open a railway, a short line out of Havana in 1837. The mainland saw no steam railway until 1848, when the British built a small line in Guyana; Mexico's first railway was not completed until 1850.

Plate 3. William Buchanan, an emigrant Scot, became Master Mechanic on the New York Central System in 1881. He designed the famous high-speed passenger locomotive 999 *in 1893.* (Scientific American, *3 September 1898)*

Table 1.1. *Selected railway mileages, 1885*

Continent	Miles (rounded to the nearest 100)
North America	137,400
Europe	114,200
Asia	15,200
South America	9400
Africa	3700

Source: Gaskell's Family Atlas of the World *(New York, 1886)*

Table 1.2. Selected railway mileages, 1850 to 1990

	1850	1900	1950	1990
Argentina	0	10,200	27,000	21,100
Britain	6600	21,900	19,400	9900
Brazil	0	9200	23,100	18,500
Canada	100	17,900	41,300	56,700
Russia	400	31,700	76,600	148,000
US	9000	193,000	223,000	136,000

Source: Rand McNally Atlas of World History *(1957),* The Economist Book: Vital World Statistics *(London, 1990)*

Note: No-one should be surprised that statistical sources do not always agree. For example, the Association of American Railroads' annual booklet, Railroad Facts 1991, *states that US Class One railways in 1990 operated 119,758 miles while non-Class One lines owned 42,712 miles making a total of 162,470 miles, which is rather different from that reported by the sources noted above. (*Railroad Facts 1991 *(Washington, DC, 1991), pp44-45.) Sadly, I cannot resolve these differences.*

In 1851 American contractors built a 50-mile line in northern Chile to service copper mines at Copiapo. British interests introduced railways in Brazil and Argentina in 1854 and 1857. Slow progress was made over the succeeding decades but Latin America never developed a dense or unified system of railways. Most lines were portages between sea ports, rivers or mines. Big trunk lines or transcontinental routes were almost non-existent. Basically, Latin America missed the railway age – at least in the intense way in which it gripped North Americans. It is hard to explain the reasons exactly but they are likely to have been a combination of cultural and economic factors and perhaps even a stubborn determination not to copy Yankee practice. It is also true that foreign investors were reluctant to risk capital in nations that tended to be controlled by unstable governments.

By 1890, after over 40 years of intermittent railway building, only about 22,000 miles had been constructed in the whole of South America, which was slow progress indeed, especially when compared to the 166,000 miles operating in the US. Many Latin American railways of this period listed their headquarters at New Broad Street or Bishopsgate or Finsbury Circus, all in London. The chairman invariably seemed to be someone named Sir George Russell, or Douglas Fox, while the secretary might have been William Leighton Jordan. There were certainly some Hispanic officials named and a few lines were locally owned but in the main

most railways south of the border appear to have been British owned and operated. In 1914, quite late in the colonial era, British investors controlled 60 per cent of railways in Cuba, about 40 per cent in Venezuela and about 66 per cent of those in Argentina. This may explain why so much British rolling stock flowed into South America and why machines like the Fairlie locomotive flourished in Mexico but never in the US.

Canada represents the compromise between the US, where too many railways were never enough, and the South American view that just a few were sufficient. Canada came into the railway age with some caution. The first line, the Montreal and Lake Champlain, opened in 1836 and was just 16 miles long.[12] The track was built on the American strap-rail plan, while the locomotive was a standard Stephenson Samson class 0-4-0. After the opening of the first line very little happened. In 1850 there were only 80 miles of railway in Canada but then a mild railway mania developed during the 1850s so that about 2000 miles of line were opened. British capital and management predominated but Canadian railways showed a strong preference for US motive power. In 1860, of the 449 locomotives in service, 247 were of US manufacture, 124 were imports from Britain and 78 were locally made.

The largest railway in Canada in pre-Dominion times was the Grand Trunk. It was built by the British contracting firm of Peto, Brassey, Betts & Jackson who were determined that the Grand

Trunk should be the very model of what was found in the home of railways. To ensure that very pure, British-style locomotives were used, Messrs Peto & Co opened the Canada works at Birkenhead near Liverpool in around 1853. The locomotives produced here were well-made machines, no doubt, but they proved unsuitable for service in Canada and all were eventually rebuilt with leading bogies. (Plate 4) Messrs Peto & Company's selection of U-rail and four-wheel cars also proved unsatisfactory and both rail and cars were replaced, at some cost, with T-rail and eight-wheel cars.

Many of the pioneer Canadian railway officials were British railwaymen who, like Peto, tended to defend and perpetuate what they had known at home. Some, however, were to prove more flexible and, ultimately, more successful. Richard Eaton emigrated to Hamilton, Ontario, in 1858 to take over the operation and maintenance of the locomotives of the Great Western Railway of Canada. Although imbued with the practices of the London & North Western Railway, the harsh climate, frozen tracks and frost heaves in the spring convinced Eaton that flexible locomotives were a necessity. The British style of engines with a rigid wheelbase and no leading or trailing bogies was simply not suited to North American service. Within six months Eaton was an outspoken advocate of the American style of locomotive. He refused to be influenced by British critics of the American locomotives who claimed that they were 'cheap and nasty', 'gingerbread peacocks' which 'wriggle themselves to pieces on a good road'.[13] Eaton went on to rebuild British locomotives with bogies and outside cylinders and continued this programme when he succeeded F H Trevithick (a nephew of Richard Trevithick) in 1862 as Superintendent of Motive Power on the Grand Trunk Railroad. Within a few years Eaton offered his own design for a 4-4-0. The general plan was a standard American eight-wheel engine but in its details – it is difficult to be complimentary or even neutral here – his engines

Plate 4. Canada's Grand Trunk Railway was built by the British contractor Samuel M Peto and his associates. No 70 was built at Birkenhead, England, by Peto in 1856. It is shown here as remodelled on American lines as a 4-4-0 from a 2-2-2. No 70 was finally retired in 1916. (Smithsonian Chaney Collection (negative 3445))

were just plain ugly. Readers may judge for them-selves in the picture of one of Eaton's creations built by Neilson & Co of Glasgow in 1868. (Plate 5)

Eaton's position was, of course, vindicated be-cause Canadian railways came to accept the Ameri-can method of railway engineering as did most other colonial railways. Yet there are certain stylistic nuances – the shape of the chimneys or cab roofs or other design elements – that made it plain which were Canadian locomotives and which were from an American trunk line.

Locomotive design – staying with a good thing

As a thermal engine, the steam locomotive is a pretty miserable thing, with an overall fuel effi-ciency rarely much over six per cent. On the other hand, it is a wonderfully practical and dependable unit of power. Even when poorly maintained, it will continue to move trains; no matter how poor the coal or water a steam locomotive will generally succeed in moving the train from one end of the line to the other. Steam locomotives are low in capital cost and can be repaired and operated by ordinary mechanics. For 125 years the steam locomotive was the principal type of locomotive used on railways all over the world, yet, in all that time, its basic arrangement remained unchanged. Locomotives grew in size and gained some new auxiliaries (such as feed water heaters and the like) but, in their fundamental plan, they remained faithful to a scheme worked out by the Stephensons in 1829-30. The combination of a horizontal boiler with fire tubes, a separate firebox and smokebox, a direct mechanical connection from the wheels to the cylinders, and the draught stimulated by ex-hausting the waste steam out of the chimney, was universal. Since most engineers tend to be con-servative, there was a general reluctance to break with the orthodoxy of the Stephensonian locomo-tive, especially in the early years of railway develop-ment.

When steam railways came to the US the Stephensonian locomotive was already established.

*Plate 5. Richard Eaton, a British railwayman, became an advocate of American railway practice after emigrating to Canada in 1858. While Locomotive Superintendent for the Grand Trunk, he designed some very durable, if not very beautiful, eight-wheelers. Twenty-five were built by Neilson & Co, Glasgow, Scotland, in 1868. (*Engineering*, 20 March 1868, p239)*

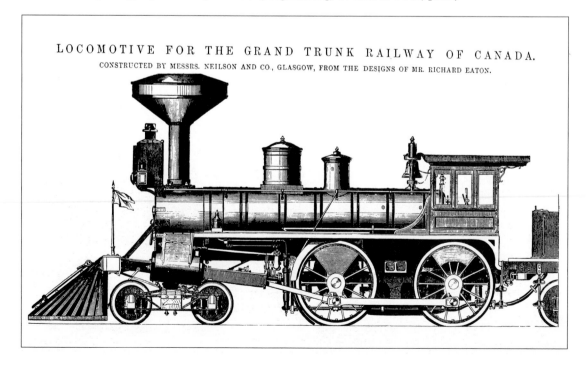

LOCOMOTIVE FOR THE GRAND TRUNK RAILWAY OF CANADA.

CONSTRUCTED BY MESSRS. NEILSON AND CO., GLASGOW, FROM THE DESIGNS OF MR. RICHARD EATON.

The more pragmatic railway builders accepted it as given; George Washington Whistler, for example, saw it as something to be exactly reproduced. In 1834, several years before his Russian expedition, Whistler was Superintendent of the Locks and Canals Machine Shop in Lowell, Massachusetts. He was charged with producing locomotives for the B&L Railroad, an enterprise financed by the owner of the Locks and Canals Company. Whistler was an experienced civil engineer and a fine draughtsman but he knew little about machinery design. Whistler employed a young English mechanic named James B Francis to help him in his task. The B&L had already imported two *Planet* type locomotives from Stephenson and Whistler, and Francis found the solution to their design problem by simply copying what Stephenson had wrought.[14]

The first engine produced at Lowell, named *Patrick*, was completed in June 1835. Even an expert would have sworn it was British built;

Whistler had taken the safe course and as a result produced no costly failures. The little *Patrick* (which weighed only eight tons) reflected well upon her builder. In January 1837 *Patrick* pulled a 401,496 lb, 35-car train (less the weight of the engine and tender) over the 26-mile B&L in 2 hours and 15 minutes. It is true the line was a relatively level one – the steepest gradient was a 10 ft rise in a mile – but the train was sizeable for so small a locomotive working in cold weather when the oil stiffened in the axle boxes and so retarded the train's motion.

Whistler went on to build more reproduction *Planets* not just for the B&L but also for railways elsewhere in the east. In all, he built about 60 lookalikes. We can still see a picture of the *Baltimore* produced in 1837 for the Baltimore and Susquehanna Railroad. (Plate 6) It shows the plagiarism and tinkering which has been going on and how the purism of the original has been

Plate 6. The Baltimore *built in 1837 by the Locks and Canals company is a copy of Stephenson's* Planet *class. Produced for service on the Baltimore and Susquehanna Railroad, it incorporated certain features, such as a bell and a cowcatcher, to adapt it for operation on a US railway of the period. (Smithsonian (negative 73-1352, detail))*

Table 2. British and American Planet *locomotives*

	4-4-0 Hinkley 1845	2-2-0 Stephenson 1830s	2-2-0 Locks and Canals 1830s
Cylinder diameter	13 inches	11 inches	11 inches
Cylinder stroke	20 inches	16 inches	16 inches
Driver diameter	60 inches (4)	60 inches (2)	60 inches (2)
Boiler diameter	37 inches	36 inches	34 inches
Tube length	9 ft 6 inches	6 ft 8 inches	6 ft 10 inches
Tubes (number)	88	129	66
Tubes OD	2 inches	1.625 inches	2.25 inches
Grate length	30 inches	N/A	22 inches
Grate width	39 inches	N/A	42 inches
Firebox depth	36 inches	N/A	37.5 inches
Tube surface	438 sq ft*	365.5 sq ft*	266 sq ft*
Firebox surface	39.3 sq ft	42.16 sq ft*	37 sq ft
Grate area	8.1 sq ft	6.5 sq ft	6.4 sq ft
Total heat surface	N/A	408 sq ft*	303 sq ft*
Weight (engine only)	15 tons	8 tons	11.5 tons
Steam pressure (estimated)	100 psi	50 psi	80 psi
Bogie wheel diameter	27 inches (4)	36 inches (2)	36 inches (2)
Tender	6 wheels	4 wheels	4 wheels
Tender tank (estimated)	1200 gallons	500 gallons	500 gallons
Tender weight (fuel and water) (estimated)	12 tons	5 tons	5 tons

* Calculated figures
Source: John H White, 1993

compromised in small ways. Notice the following additions: a pilot or cowcatcher, a bonnet chimney or stack with netting suitable for wood fuel, a bell and a whistle (the engineer's hand is on the valve handle of the whistle). These changes were necessary to make the engine safe for operation on American railways, where unfenced track and level crossings were the rule and not the exception, as was the case in Britain (see Table 2).

The products of Lowell were soon outclassed by larger engines but some of Whistler's *Planets* worked on for a generation or more. The *Baltimore*, for example, was rebuilt and enlarged in 1849 as a 4-4-0 and remained in service until 1865. Some New England railways seemed determined to squeeze the last mile out of their ancient Lowell-built engines. Plate 7 shows the Stonington Line's *Roger Williams*. This is one of Whistler's *Planets*, built in 1837 as a 2-2-0, as remodelled in 1846

with a four-wheel bogie and trailing wheels, a lengthened boiler and an added cab, headlight and hen coop cowcatcher. This cartoon of a locomotive steamed on until 1872.

Whistler was not alone in his readiness to imitate a successful design. M W Baldwin's first engine *Old Ironside* (1832) was yet another *Planet* duplicate. But, unlike Whistler, Baldwin abandoned the Stephenson design for his subsequent engines. Robert Stevens, however, Chief Engineer of the Camden and Amboy was determined, in 1831, to copy Stephenson's four-wheel Samson class. One engine was imported from Britain to serve as a prototype and Stevens assembled 15 Samsons. Some were built at local machine shops and some at the railway's Bordentown shops but vital parts for 10 of the machines, especially cylinders and valve boxes, were fabricated in Britain at Stephenson's plant in Newcastle-upon-Tyne.[15]

Plate 7. The Roger Williams *built in 1837 by the Locks and Canals for the Stonington Line was a near duplicate of the* Baltimore *shown in plate 6. The engine is shown here as rebuilt and enlarged in 1846. (Smithsonian Chaney Collection (negative 3581))*

Long after the *Planet* class was in production one New England engine builder found a way to perpetuate this old design. Holmes Hinkley of Boston started out as a carpenter at a time when if you built a barn, you built it like the one up at Jerry's crossroads, except perhaps a little longer or a little lower. Certainly it was never laid out on paper or started from scratch. Hinkley drifted into the machinery business and did so well that he decided to go into the locomotive trade in 1840.[16]

Hinkley's chief designer was an ex-ship's carpenter and pattern maker named John Souther. Souther too was not much given to drawing out on paper what could be observed under steam so he looked over what Major Whistler was doing for the B&L. Souther believed that the *Planets* were excellent locomotives (Plate 8) but thought it would make sense to make them a little bigger or, in fact, to double their size.

Thus was born the 'stretch' *Planet*. The wheel base was extended from 5 to 13 ft, the overall weight from 8 to 15 tons and the boiler length from 6½ to 9 ft. Increases in boiler diameter (from 30 to 37 inches) were more modest, and cylinders grew only from 11 by 16 to 13 by 20 inches. Apart from the increase in size, the only major alteration was in the running gear – a four-wheel bogie replaced the single pair of leading wheels and a second pair of drivers was added. But the firebox, smokebox, inside cylinders, crank axle and outside wooden frames were faithful copies of first-generation Stephenson locomotives. (Plate 9)

This was the real genius of American locomotive design – saving the best of the established Stephenson locomotive including the boiler and the cylinders and then modifying the running gear to meet the needs of a rough and ready track. A flexible style of undercarriage was required to offer the degree of movement necessary to stay on the rickety rails so common to pioneer America.

Hinkley became the largest locomotive builder in New England proving the soundness of the stretch *Planet* design. Between 300 and 400 engines were built on this plan before Hinkley modified his design in the 1850s.

The conservative, or mainstream, approach to

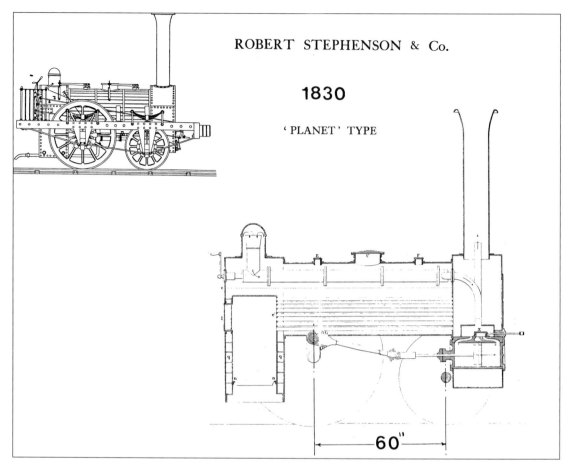

Plate 8. Robert Stephenson's **Planet** *of 1830 was at once elementary and sophisticated. It served as a basic design model for locomotive builders in all parts of the world. (De Pambours,* **A Practical Treatise on Locomotive Engines** *(London, 1836), p12)*

American locomotive design was little more than a process of modification. There was of course a more radical school. The failures of engineering can be instructive and some can, in time, lead to success. The drive to be different, to be independent, is very strong in some individuals. If the prevailing orthodoxy was for horizontal boilers, a certain faction called loudly for vertical boilers, and Americans seemed to exhibit a decided penchant for upright steam generators. The first such locomotive was Peter Cooper's *Tom Thumb*, a diminutive machine hardly bigger than a hand car. This 1830 creation was only a demonstrator and Cooper's plans to build more such engines on a larger scale never materialised. The cause of vertical boilers was

picked up in the 1830s by Phineas Davis and Ross Winans who built a dozen or so *Grasshopper* engines, mostly for the B&O; a few went to other lines and at least one was sent to Germany. (Plate 10) Winans built some eight-wheel engines with vertical boilers in 1844 but the limitations of the design were long recognised. The boiler could only be made so high and so large in diameter because of the clearance necessary for tunnels and bridges. The horizontal boiler, on the other hand, could grow – especially in length – unhampered, or at least less hampered than the vertical variety. And so this diversion from the standard Stephenson plan became a dead-end excursion.

There were many other dead ends that we will

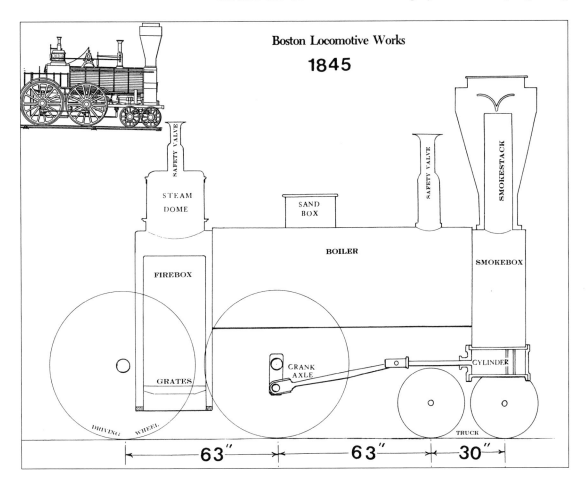

Boston Locomotive Works

1845

Labels: SAFETY VALVE, STEAM DOME, SAND BOX, SAFETY VALVE, SMOKESTACK, BOILER, SMOKEBOX, FIREBOX, CRANK AXLE, CYLINDER, GRATES, DRIVING WHEEL, TRUCK

63" — 63" — 30"

Plate 9. Holmes Hinkley of Boston enlarged Stephenson's Planet *design in about 1845. A four-wheel truck and a stack suitable for wood burning were added to adapt the engine for American service. (Drawing by John H White)*

not explore in this paper beyond mentioning the early fascination of various American inventors with rotary engines, oscillating cylinders, double fire-boxes and gear drives. It is easy to dismiss such schemes as impractical, ill-advised or even foolish but at least a few did point to the future.

A case in point is the bold scheme developed by Horatio Allen in the winter of 1830 and 1831.[17] (Plate 11) Allen has already been mentioned in connection with the D&H gravity railroad. In 1829, not long after returning from a visit to Britain as the D&H representative, Allen was appointed Chief Engineer of the South Carolina Railroad. The citizens of Charleston were planning a major trunk line to run 136 miles between the port of

Charleston and the town of Hamburg, opposite Augusta, Georgia. Several other long-distance lines were started around this time but most required decades to build – the South Carolina was completed in just three years after construction started in January 1830.

Allen adopted the pile system of construction so that the railway was built as a low trestle for most of its length, thus avoiding costly and time-consuming cuttings and embankments. Lumber was abundant from the dense forest of the region and the 5 ft gauge line was built for the phenomenally low figure of $14,000 per mile – very cheap even by American standards.

Allen's accomplishment was very impressive in

Plate 10. A number of American designers followed a perverse interest in locomotives with vertical boilers. The B&O made about a dozen little engines of this type, called Grasshoppers, *during the 1830s. Gear drives via jack shafts and fans rather than blast pipes set them apart from normal practice. (*Locomotive Engineering)

terms of cost and rapid completion but even its creator would admit it was a shaky, lightly built railway, likely to incur high maintenance costs after a few years of service. The structure was so fragile, in fact, that it could not even support the light locomotives of the time, few of which weighed much over 10 tons. The little *Best Friend* scampered over the wooden, roller-coaster line in a lively fashion but at 4½ tons it could hardly pull a paying load. Allen realised that a special style of engine with light axle loading was needed if his rickety South Carolina railway was to succeed.

What was needed was a new form of engine, with a long wheel base and many wheels to spread the weight out along a good length of track, but which was also capable of negotiating fairly sharp curves. During the winter of 1830 and 1831 Allen laboured over a design, helped in the planning stage by Christian E Detmold (1810-87), a German engineer who came to the US in 1826.

The result of these labours was a truly novel form of locomotive unlike any seen before or since. (Plate 12) It stood on eight wheels. The boiler had a common firebox at the centre of the engine, with four, not two barrels connected to smokeboxes fore and aft. There was no main frame; two independent wooden sub-frames carried the wheels which were secured to the underside of the smokebox so

Plate 11. Horatio Allen (1802-89) was a pioneer American engineer and was one of many to visit England at the dawn of the railway age. Allen designed the curious double-enders illustrated in plate 12. In later years he was prominent as a marine engine builder. (Smithsonian (negative 32, 257-A))

that they could swivel. A single cylinder was fastened to the bottom of each smokebox with the usual rod connection to a crank axle. Should both cylinders stop on dead centre it was necessary to 'pole' the locomotive to get started again. Side bearings fitted with rollers (there were no centre pins) carried the weight to the wheels. Ball joints at the crosshead and the ends of the main rods allowed freedom of movement when the sub-frames swivelled. (Plate 13)

The position of many important elements of the engine such as the steam dome, water pumps and cylinder lubricators are evident from the drawings. The position of the driver on top of the firebox is also clear – although it was not a safe or desirable place to stand. But how is this steam dragon fired? Where is the fire door? Where is the water kept? If the fuel is on a tender how is it delivered to the centre of the engine? There are many other

questions which cannot easily be answered.

Allen's engine was actually quite small, except for its overall length – 22 ft - and the height of the stack – 13 ft. The driving wheels were 60 inches in diameter and the leading wheels 36 inches. The estimated weight was between 8 and 10 tons.

As Chief Engineer, Allen was determined to see his plan transformed into a full-size, operating prototype. Allen wanted the engines, of which four were ordered, manufactured in England, but claimed that he was too busy building the railway to go abroad to place the orders. The contract was given instead to the West Point Foundry in New York City and the first of the double-enders went into service in February 1832.

As might be expected from such a novel design, the *South Carolina*, as the first engine was called, began to develop a long series of ailments ranging from clogged boiler tubes to broken crank axles. The locomotive blew up in December after about 10 months of very laboured service, but was rebuilt and returned to service in April 1833; final retirement and scrapping took place sometime before 1838.

The other double-enders, the *Charleston, Barnwell* and *Edisto* all arrived in 1833, but they proved no more durable than the *South Carolina*, and spent more time in the repair shop than at work. Months went by without a double-ender under steam, all of which was very embarrassing and very costly. A committee of investigations was organised to answer the complaints of certain stockholders who wondered why so much had been spent on new locomotives and yet so few trains were running.

The committee, perhaps inevitably, attempted to put the blame on outsiders: the problems were clearly not the fault of the railway's management. This was a predictable conclusion as the Chairman of the committee, Alexander Black, was a member of the railway's board. Horatio Allen, the Chief Engineer, was clearly not at fault because the design was perfectly sound and the engines proved very easy on the track – whenever they ran, that is. Hence, it had to be the fault of those rascals in New York who had built the locomotives. It was established that a cholera epidemic struck New York while the double-enders were being built and many of the workers at the West Point Foundry had fled the city to escape the plague; those who stayed were not necessarily the most skilful or experienced machinists. Why did West Point not delay the work until the best workers returned?

Plate 12. Allen's double-enders are among the most original, yet the least successful, American pioneer locomotives. Four were built by West Point Foundry in 1832 and 1833. (Brown's History of the First Locomotive in America *(New York, 1871), opposite p170).*

Because, presumably, the railway needed the engines and pressed for rapid delivery. As always, there was plenty of blame to go round. It is true that the workmanship of the West Point engines was not of the best but if the South Carolina's management truly believed in the double-enders, why did they decline to order any more? And why were all four cut up before 1838 and the salvageable parts incorporated in conventional engines? Indeed, if the Allen design was so sound why did no-one else copy it? It is difficult to form a conclusive judgement on Allen's interesting experiment, but despite the problems, his originality may have been the germ of subsequent developments elsewhere.

Many years later a series of successful articulated steam locomotives was introduced. Robert Francis Fairlie devised a double-ender in 1863 that was very similar to Allen's general design.[18] British railways showed scant interest in the patented Fairlie design, but other nations, especially Mexico, introduced Fairlies with enthusiasm. Other designers of articulated locomotives, such as Garrett and

Mallet, eliminated the central firebox scheme – the worst feature of both Allen's and Fairlie's plan – and went on to build world-class engines that were true titans of the rails. None of these latter inventors were influenced by Allen's experiments nor does there appear to be a very direct linkage. But direct or indirect, Allen's double-enders remain the ancestors of the principle of articulation which made possible the largest steam locomotives ever constructed. (Plate 14)

Before leaving the subject of invention and the locomotive, we should consider popular notions that engineering or scientific improvements are a series of sudden or dramatic advances: the 'big bang' theory. Personally, I feel that most technical advances come in tiny pops and splutters so muffled that few of us can hear them. The best and most innovative engineers are those who have the good judgement to select the good and discard the bad. Such a man was Horatio Allen's sometime boss and long-time associate, John B Jervis. At the very moment that Allen was developing plans for his ill-fated double-enders, Jervis was trying to reform the

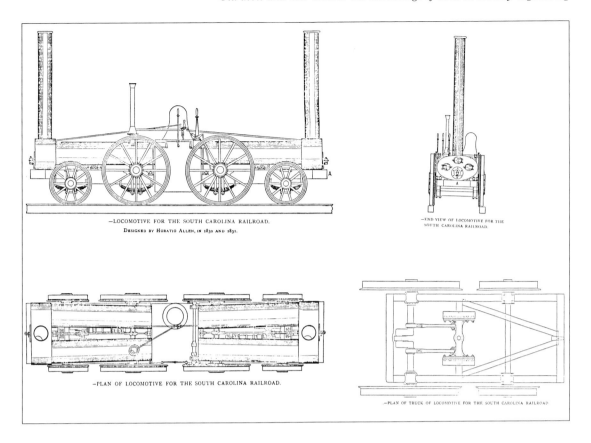

—LOCOMOTIVE FOR THE SOUTH CAROLINA RAILROAD.
DESIGNED BY HORATIO ALLEN, IN 1830 AND 1831.

—END VIEW OF LOCOMOTIVE FOR THE
SOUTH CAROLINA RAILROAD.

—PLAN OF LOCOMOTIVE FOR THE SOUTH CAROLINA RAILROAD.

—PLAN OF TRUCK OF LOCOMOTIVE FOR THE SOUTH CAROLINA RAILROAD

*Plate 13. The double-enders had many peculiarities including single cylinders, double-barrel boilers, a central firebox, twin smokestacks and an offset steam dome. There was no main frame. Wooden sub-frames were attached by pins to the underside of the smokeboxes at the fore and aft of the engine. (*American Railroad Journal *(February 1890), pp82-86; (March 1890), pp113-17; (April 1890), pp174-76)*

running gear of the rigid British locomotives brought over for some of America's pioneer lines. Unlike Allen, he did not believe in being radical. Jervis took more of a middle position and one that led to change without the trauma of revolution. Jervis found that a leading bogie, composed of an independent sub-frame with four wheels and a centre pin, could transform a rigid Stephenson locomotive into a flexible machine capable of taking most curves. This simple alteration was first tested by Jervis in 1832. Its merits were so obvious that it was adopted by every American locomotive builder within five years and eventually the leading wheels became a standard feature on most locomotives throughout the world. Jervis' idea was never patented and hence it was given over freely to the

engineering community. Indeed, Jervis was careful not to claim the principle of the bogie as his own, acknowledging its earlier British origins, but he rightly took credit for the successful development of leading wheels.

The exchange of ideas continues

The give and take of ideas was not limited to the first years of the railway era but continued for decade after decade down to the present time. Just who took or gave the most cannot be accurately calculated. The exchange was never equal or formal and the pattern of exchange was episodic, rising, falling and even disappearing for years at a time.

A complete list of the trade-offs would be tedious

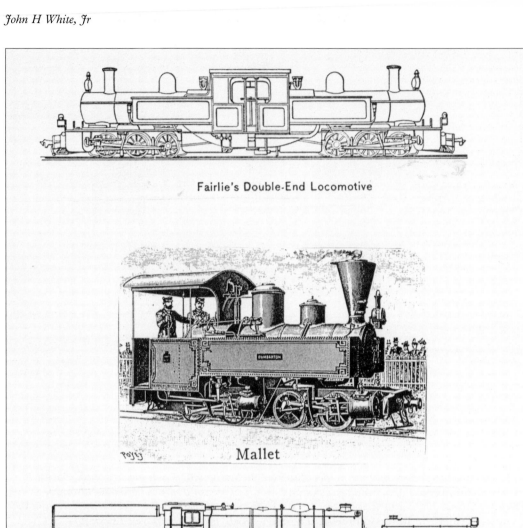

Fairlie's Double-End Locomotive

Mallet

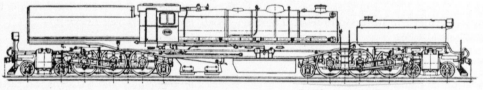

Union-Garratt   Built by J. A. Maffei

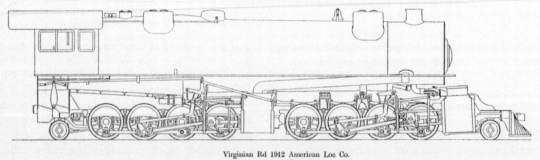

Virginian Rd 1912 American Loc Co.

Plate 14 (left). Successful articulated locomotives developed many years after Allen's 1831 design are related to the ill-fated engines shown in plates 12 and 13. ((Fairlie) Sinclair's Development of the Locomotive Engine *(New York, 1907), p193; (Mallet) Harter's* Transportation: A Pictorial Archive *(New York, 1984), p73; (Garrett) Wiener's* Articulated Locomotives *(New York, 1930), p228; (Mallet 1912) Jahn's* Die Damplokomotive *(Berlin, 1924), p335)*

to go through point by point but some idea may be gained of the common or collective debt. Major British contributions should include the steam railway itself as a common carrier of people and goods; it would be difficult to name a more fundamental contribution. The steam locomotive in its most basic and enduring form, as already explained earlier in this paper, was widely copied and subsequently developed. The British track gauge of 4 ft 8½ inches is now a world standard and the Block System of signalling which permitted a dense traffic to operate safely and at high speeds has also been almost universally adopted.

Bessemer steel, so necessary for stronger and safer rails, boilers and axles, was another British invention. Steel rails were credited as the single most important improvement to railway operations after about 1880. Cheap steel made strong rails affordable.

From continental Europe came the French injector, an ingenious device introduced around 1858 which eliminated the problem of the feed water pump. Another Frenchman, Bourdon, devised an accurate steam pressure gauge that became the standard form all over the world by about 1860 and which did more for boiler safety than any other single invention. The highly successful Mallet articulated locomotive has already been mentioned. Credit should also be given to the Walschaert's valve from Belgium and the Schmidt superheater from Germany.

All of these items were important to the American railways; some were obviously essential. The Americans took and took and took but they also developed techniques and principles which were taken up in Britain and elsewhere. Mention has already been made of the leading bogie and of locomotives built on a scale that noone else dared to copy.

The eight-wheel bogie vehicle, for freight and passengers, has become an international standard since its development in the 1830s. So, too, has the American plan of passenger carriage with its end entrance, centre aisle and seats on either side of the aisle. And what of brakes? Few modern railways could function without the (American) Westinghouse air brake introduced in 1869. In the design of track, American engineers provided some fundamental improvements including wooden sleepers, hook head spikes and the flat bottom rail which is now found in daily service on every major railway in the world, with the exception of the London Tube system.

Welded rail may or may not be an American invention but Americans were pioneers in this area of technology. Welded rail is now an essential element of the modern railways and one that represents a great advance in the strength and durability of the permanent way. The origins of welded rails are uncertain, but they were used by some American street railways from about 1890. Experimental main line installation began in 1933 on the D&H Railroad and the technique became standard practice within a generation.

In the area of communications, Americans developed working systems, if not inital prototypes, for both the telegraph (1844) and the telephone (1876). Both became essential to the control of trains and so did much to promote efficient and safe railway operations. Today radio is used widely in many aspects of train operation and, if Marconi is accepted as the inventor of the wireless, Italy can be included in the pantheon of notable contributors.

Signalling made at least a few leaps forward in North America. Automatic block signalling – signals controlled by an electric current and not by a human operator – were introduced in regular service in 1868 by Thomas S Hall of Stamford, Connecticut. Centralised traffic control, as it has evolved in America, is surely the most important twentieth-century advance in signalling, for it allows one person to control up to 300 miles of railway safely. Trains can be stopped, told to proceed or switched from one track to another with all the ease of the operation of a model railway layout.

An American case can also be made for the diesel-electric locomotive. It was not invented in America, and engineers from many nations laboured to make the diesel a practical unit for the everyday haulage of trains. Yet I feel this goal was first achieved in North America. A diesel shunter built for the Central Railroad of New Jersey in 1925 worked on, day after day, until its retirement 32 years later. It was not alone, for other diesel locomotives worked for other main line companies and commercial, rather than experimental, passenger and freight diesel units went into production in the 1930s. These machines proved so tough, so reliable and so economical that American railways were able rapidly to abandon the traditional steam locomotive. Dieselisation swept through the industry in only 15 years, and the last main line steamer chuffed off into history in 1960.

In summary, it seems clear that the fabric of railway development is truly a tangle of international 'common roots' that cross and recross one another. The pattern is surely complex, but the separate branches are just as surely a rich and vigorous growth which continues to this day. Although the US pioneered main line electrification in the late nineteenth century, a new electric locomotive design adopted in 1980 came from Sweden. And today new high-speed trains from Swedish and German manufacturers are being tested in America for service between Boston and Washington. In truth, there is nothing new.

Notes and references

1 Biographical data for people mentioned here and elsewhere in the text is drawn from a variety of sources. My principal sources include *A Biographical Dictionary of American Civil Engineers* (New York: ASCE, 1972); Marshall, John, *Biographical Dictionary of Railway Engineers* (Newton Abbot: David and Charles, 1978); and Stapleton, D H, 'Origins of American railroad technology 1825-1840', *Railroad History*, 139 (1978), pp65-77.

2 Oeynhausen, C, and Dechen, H, *Report on Railways in England ...* (Berlin, 1829)

3 *The Railroad Era, First Five Years of the Development* (New York, 1884)

4 Clark, Edwin R, 'Early locomotive building in Lowell, Mass', *Railway & Locomotive Historical Society*, 7 (1924), p33

5 Harlow, Alvin F, *Steelways of New England* (New York, 1946), p1131. The B&L reproduction of the British stone block track proved a costly failure. The hard frost of New England winters heaved up the tracks.

6 Stevenson, David, *Civil Engineering in North America* (London, 1838)

7 Von Gerstner's great study has been translated into English and will be reprinted in about 1996 or 1997 by Stanford University Press, Stanford, California.

8 Parry, Albert, *Whistler's Father* (Indianapolis, 1939)

9 *Philadelphia Public Ledger*, 28 March 1874

10 Most of the biographical data in this section is drawn from my volumes on early locomotive design written in 1968, and the most recent freight car book. See White, John H Jr, *American Locomotives: An Engineering History 1830-1880* (Baltimore: Johns Hopkins University Press, 1968); and White, John H Jr, *The American Railroad Freight Car* (Baltimore: Johns Hopkins University Press, 1993). For William Buchanan, see Becker, G P, 'William Buchanan', *Railway & Locomotive Historical Society Bulletin*, 37, pp33-40.

11 *Poor's Directory of Railway Officials*, published annually by H V Poor, offers limited data on South American railways. Pages 1244-60 of the 1890 volume are particularly useful. See also Lavis, F, 'The status of the railways of North and South America', *International Rail Congress 1905*, pp51-123.

12 Information on Canadian railways is largely drawn from Brown, Robert R, 'Early Canadian rolling stock', *Railway & Locomotive Historical Society Bulletin*, 56 (1941), pp30-54; Lavallée, Omer, 'Grand trunk railway of Canada', *Railroad History*, 147 (1982), pp12-33; and Lehmann, F, 'Richard Eaton', *Railroad History*, 165 (1991), pp63-82.

13 Dorsey, Edward, *English and American Railways* (New York, 1887), pp98-99

14 Gibb, George S, *The Saco-Lowell Shops* (Cambridge, MA: Harvard University Press, 1950). See also notes 1, 5 and 8.

15 White, John H, Jr, *The John Bull: 150 Years a Locomotive* (Washington, DC: Smithsonian Institution Press, 1981)

16 White, John H, Jr, 'Holmes Hinkley and the Boston Locomotive Works', *Railroad History*, 142 (1980), pp27-52

17 Data on Horatio Allen is drawn from S M

Derrick's *Centennial History of the South Caro-lina Railroad* (Columbia, 1930); and *American Railroad Journal.* A three-part biography of Allen by Matthias N Forney appeared in the February, March and April 1890 issues of this journal.

18 The story of articulated locomotives is well summarised in Lionel Weiner's pioneering book of that name published in 1930. Since then the subject has been filled in with books on the Mallet and Garrett by A E Durrant, and R A S Abbott's small volume on Fairlies (1970). Robert A La Massena's two-volume set, pub-lished in 1979, concentrated mainly on US Mallets, though other articulated locomotives are mentioned. See Weiner, L, *Articulated Locomotives* (New York, 1930); Durrant, A E, *Mallett* and *Garrett* (New York, 1974); and La Massena, R A, *Articulated Locomotives in North America* (Silverton, 1979)

The early British rolling stock inheritance

Philip Atkins

The world's first steam locomotive was built in 1803, and nearly two centuries later, in 1993, a handful were still being built in China. Between times, around 650,000 have been constructed, of which some 180,000 were built in the US, about 150,000 in Germany and 130,000 in the UK. (The next countries in the world league table, Russia and France, came very much further down the list at about 40,000 each).[1]

The early development of the steam locomotive in Britain can be traced through surviving examples and, increasingly through authentic replicas which fill gaps in the story. Nothing survives from the very early developments but, during the last few years, the Ironbridge Gorge and Welsh Industrial and Maritime Museums have produced working replicas of Richard Trevithick's pioneering locomotives of 1803-4, with their single cylinders, huge flywheels and cog transmission systems.[2] (Plate 1)

The oldest genuine surviving steam locomotives are William Hedley's *Wylam Dilly* of 1813, which is preserved in the Royal Scottish Museum in

Plate 1. An engraving of Richard Trevithick's pioneer locomotive of 1803. In recent years full-size working replicas of Trevithick locomotives operating on these principles have been built by and for the Welsh Industrial and Maritime Museum and by the Ironbridge Gorge Museum. (Science Museum collection)

Edinburgh, and *Puffing Billy* of 1814, which can be seen in the Science Museum in London. Both these locomotives were designed and built for work on primitive plateways at collieries on Tyneside and both had working lives of about 50 years. An even longer life of 90 years was claimed for a successor, George Stephenson's Hetton Colliery locomotive, officially dated 1822, which operated until 1912. It is now preserved as a part of the National Collection and displayed at Beamish Open-Air Museum.

During the 1820s steam locomotive construction was largely confined to the northeast of England, where the first public railway to be worked by steam, between Stockton and Darlington, opened in 1825. Although inaugurated by George Stephenson's 0-4-0 *Locomotion* (now preserved in Darlington) it tends to be forgotten that the Stockton & Darlington (S&D) initially depended heavily upon horses.[3] When the plans for the Liverpool & Manchester Railway (LMR) were started shortly afterwards, the use of steam locomotives was by no means a foregone conclusion; the Rainhill trials of October 1829, which were held to settle the matter, finally established the practical feasibility of steam locomotives for railway use.[4]

Several locomotives took part in the Rainhill trials, including Timothy Hackworth's 0-4-0 *Sans Pareil*, but pre-eminent was George and Robert Stephenson's *Rocket*. Both these locomotives are preserved in the Science Museum. *Rocket* has spawned a number of replicas, including a working one built for the National Railway Museum (NRM) in 1979, which, in its yellow and white paint, conforms more closely to the popular perception of this epoch-making locomotive than the blackened remains of the original. (Plate 2) *Rocket* was the first steam locomotive to function according to the fundamental principles upon which virtually all of its more than half a million successors would operate. These principles were:

- direct drive from the pistons on to the wheels through connecting rods, rather than through a system of levers, as employed on earlier locomotives
- a multi-tube boiler, providing a much greater and more efficient heating surface than possible with earlier single-flue arrangements
- utilisation of the exhaust steam to provide a draught on the fire, so that the harder the engine was worked, the stronger was the draught on the

fire, and the greater the amount of steam produced to supply the demand.[5]

Stephenson successfully combined other people's ideas in his locomotive work so it is not entirely surprising, as John White has pointed out in his paper, that nobody subsequently came up with any alternative system which was substantially better. Even the Union Pacific Railroad 'Big Boy' 4-8-8-4s, built over a century later and, at around 550 long tons, weighing well over 100 times more (but utilising precisely the same rail gauge), operated on entirely the same principle as *Rocket*.

John White's paper has shown that there was international interest in British railway developments well before the appearance of *Rocket*. Almost simultaneously with the construction of *Rocket*, John Urpeth Raistrick, in the West Midlands, made and exported to America the *Stourbridge Lion* which was one of the last of the 'primitive' steam locomotives to be built. *Stourbridge Lion* incorporated an indirect drive by a lever system and a single-flue boiler,

Plate 2. The remains of **Rocket** *(1829) as preserved in the Science Museum in London. This was the progenitor in function of over 600,000 steam locomotives built worldwide to the present day. (Science Museum collection)*

which relied upon natural draught, as is evident from the exceptionally tall chimney. A very similar locomotive, *Agenoria* (also of 1829), built by Raistrick, worked at the Shutt End Colliery in south Staffordshire and, remarkably, has survived to become part of the National Railway Collection displayed at York. It is apparent from a brief inspection of *Agenoria* that steam locomotives working on these principles could not work at speeds in excess of 100 mph, or single-handedly haul trains of several thousand tons weight: locomotives built on Stephensonian principles were capable of such development.

The *Stourbridge Lion* was supplied to America's first railroad, the Delaware & Hudson (D&H), by the latter's resident engineer, Horatio Allen. This was the first steam locomotive to run in America, in May 1829. A replica of the *Stourbridge Lion* was built by the D&H in 1933.[6]

A sizeable proportion of Robert Stephenson & Co's early output was exported to America, including their 50th engine, *John Bull*, built for the Camden & Amboy Railroad in 1831. Now over 160 years old and displayed at the Smithsonian Institution in Washington, it can claim to be the world's oldest operable steam locomotive,[7] and is a fine testimony to British engineering and American conservation expertise. It is interesting to recall that, as early as 1839, Britain was briefly importing locomotives *from* America; the Birmingham & Gloucester Railway obtained some 4-2-0s from Norris & Co of Philadelphia.[8]

A remarkably high number of early British examples of primitive locomotives survive in relation to the small numbers built during that period. These range from the *Wylam Dilly* of 1813, already mentioned, to the Canterbury & Whitstable Railway 0-4-0 *Invicta* of 1830, now preserved by Canterbury Museums and the earliest locomotive to work in southern England. Ironically, only the LMR 0-4-2 No 57 *Lion*, of 1837, survives from the post-primitive decade of 1831-40 although this decade witnessed the rapid development of the modern locomotive.[9] The most probable reasons are that the initial novelty factor no longer applied and that engines of this era were rapidly superseded by others. The seminal locomotive of the period was the Stephenson 2-2-0 *Planet*, built for the LMR in 1830, only one year after *Rocket*. In the *Planet* cylinders were placed where they would remain in most future designs, at the front of the locomotive, adjacent to the smokebox and exhaust

system, whether located inside or outside the main frames. Although no original *Planet*-type locomotives survive, the Museum of Science & Industry in Manchester completed a working replica *Planet* in 1993, thereby filling a notable void in the British Locomotive inheritance.

In his paper John White has made the interesting point that the first locomotive to be built in America, in 1831, by Mathias T Baldwin, *Old Ironsides*, was effectively a transatlantic version of *Planet*. After a shaky start Baldwin established, in Philadelphia, what would become the world's largest locomotive building company: it would eventually produce 59,000 steam locomotives up to 1955, or about 1 in 11 of the world's total.

In 1833 the *Planet* 2-2-0 was enlarged into the *Patentee* 2-2-2, still with iron plate and timber sandwich frames and inside cylinders. Examples of Patentees built by the Stephensons and others were the first locomotives to see service in a number of European countries. As early as 1835 an Englishman, John Cockerill, was building Patentees in Belgium, and his eponymous enterprise would remain prominent amongst the remarkably numerous Belgian locomotive builders for well over a century.

During the 1930s replica Patentees were built in Germany, Italy and the Netherlands, in order to commemorate the railway centenaries in these countries. The only remaining British Patentee is also a replica, the Great Western Railway (GWR) 7 ft gauge *North Star* at Swindon GWR Museum. The original locomotive was built by Robert Stephenson & Co in 1835 for the 5 ft 6 inch gauge New Orleans Railroad in America. The Railroad quickly foundered and the engine was returned and re-gauged to 7 ft ¼ inches for sale to the GWR. The engine, which ran until 1871, was initially preserved but regrettably was broken up in 1906. In 1925 a replica was re-created for the GWR participation in the S&D's centenary celebrations held in that year. This replica incorporated a number of components of the original which had been saved by various individuals.[10]

Equally regrettable was the destruction, in 1906, of the Gooch broad-gauge 4-2-2 *Lord of the Isles* of 1847. This outstanding design was effectively the ultimate development of the Patentee concept and nothing as big was built for the standard gauge for almost 50 years. A working replica of a sister engine, *Iron Duke*, was constructed for the NRM in 1985.

It was to contest the claims made by Brunel for the superiority of the 7 ft gauge that the newly constituted, standard-gauge London & North Western Railway (LNWR) at Crewe Works built the maverick 2-2-2 named *Cornwall* in 1847. As now preserved in the National Collection, this engine bears little resemblance to its short-lived original configuration, whereby the driving axle actually passed *through* the top of the deliberately low-slung boiler barrel to maintain a low centre of gravity.[11]

Entirely conventional from birth was the little Grand Junction Railway 2-2-2 of 1845, still referred to as *Columbine*, despite losing its name 120 years ago. The *Columbine* owes its survival to the mistaken belief that it was the first locomotive to be built at Crewe Works (it was actually the 20th). The so-called Crewe-type evolved with outside cylinders to avoid the need for an expensive and vulnerable crank axle. The oldest Crewe-type still extant is the Paris to Rouen Railway 2-2-2 No 33 *Saint Pierre* built at Sotteville in 1843 under the direction of the British engineer W B Buddicomb, former Locomotive Superintendent of the Grand Junction Railway. This engine ran until 1916 and is now preserved at the French National Railway Museum in Mulhouse.[12]

By the 1850s locomotive design had effectively settled down to a conventional format, although there are few surviving locomotives as examples. As late as the mid-1840s 'deviant' designs were still being built as evidenced by two locomotives in the National Collection: Edward Bury's Furness Railway 0-4-0 No 3 *Old Coppernob*, displayed at York, and S&D 0-6-0 No 25 *Derwent*, on loan to the North Road Railway Museum in Darlington. *Coppernob* is a late example of the 'Bury' type, with its attractive hemispherical firebox and bar frames. British practice remained faithful to plate frames; by the 1950s this was about the only *major* feature to distinguish British from latter-day American practice.

Timothy Hackworth's idiosyncratic *Derwent* is an unusual locomotive to have been built as late as 1845, with a tender at each end and a return-flue boiler which required firing from the front of the locomotive.[13] The outside cylinders are at the rear and drive *Rocket*-fashion on to wheels whose cast centres are remarkably similar to those of *Locomotion*, which is displayed beside *Derwent*.

John White has made extended reference in his paper to European and American visitors who came to Britain in the 1820s and 1830s to inspect, at first-hand, the exciting railway developments taking place and to report back. A visitor who came, stayed and made a significant contribution to British locomotive engineering was the German, Charles Beyer (1813-76). Born in Saxony, Beyer arrived in Manchester in the early 1830s and became a draughtsman to Sharp, Roberts & Co. He rose to become Chief Draughtsman, before leaving to set up his own enterprise elsewhere in Manchester in partnership with a Yorkshireman, Richard Peacock. Beyer, Peacock & Co was established in 1854. Beyer was a consummate designer, who subsequently employed other Germans on his senior design staff. Their influence was apparent in the elegant simplicity of Beyer, Peacock designs, especially in chimney profiles and driving wheel splashers. An early example is the 2-2-2 *Don Luiz* built in 1862 for the South Eastern Railway of Portugal, which ran until 1934 and is now preserved in Lisbon. Beyer's aesthetic influence can be detected in such diverse locomotives currently displayed in York as the LNWR 2-4-0 No 790 *Hardwicke* (1892), the Midland Railway (MR) 4-2-2 No 673 (1897) (Plate 3), the South Eastern & Chatham Railway 4-4-0 No 737 (1901) and even the Great Central Railway 4-4-0 No 506 *Butler Henderson* (1920).

It is easy to forget that the concept of railways substantially pre-dated the invention of the steam locomotive, being primarily devised as a means of transporting minerals, particularly coal. The oldest design of railway vehicle in the National Collection is the Peak Forest Canal Truck which dates from the close of the eighteenth century (1797). (Plate 4) This truck incorporates unflanged wheels running on plate rail. Its immediate successors are chauldron wagons from the northeast of England which have flanged wheels running on smooth rails. Few railway goods vehicles of the first half of the nineteenth century still survive, possibly because, unlike locomotives, they were substantially made of wood, were often worked to destruction and not at the time regarded as particularly worthy of preservation since they were so commonplace.

A greater number of early passenger vehicles survive, including some replicas. In 1930 three pairs of LMR replicas – second class and third class (literally open thirds) – were built for the LMR centenary celebrations of that year. The oldest genuine passenger vehicles to survive are three from the originally isolated Bodmin & Wadebridge

Plate 3 (above). The sole surviving ex-MR 4-2-2 'spinner', recorded at Bedford c1904 as MR No 118, now preserved with modified smokebox and chimney as MR No 673. This engine was built at Derby in 1897 as a late example of the single driving-axle express locomotive. (N Thompson collection, NRM). Plate 4 (below). The Peak Forest Truck, as preserved at the NRM. The design (c1797) pre-dates the steam locomotive. (NRM collection)

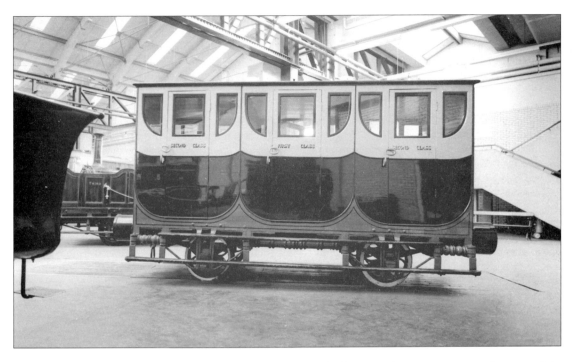

Plate 5 (above). Bodmin & Wadebridge Railway four-wheel composite passenger coach, reputed to date from 1834, the oldest passenger vehicle in the National Collection. (NRM collection). Plate 6 (below). LNWR Royal Diner No 76, which was exhibited new at the Paris Exhibition of 1900. This illustration dates from 1976 when the vehicle still wore all-over claret livery. It has since been fully restored to LNWR lake and flake white livery lined out in gold leaf. (NRM collection)

Railway. (Plate 5) These three are of slightly uncertain date, but were built between 1834 and 1840. A particular gem is Queen Adelaide's saloon built for the London & Birmingham Railway in 1842 which clearly reveals the 'stage coach' origin of early railway passenger stock. A similar construction is shown by the S&D Composite No 59, built around 1845. All the above mentioned vehicles are in the National Railway Collection at York.

Unlike locomotive design, carriage design progressed relatively slowly for many years until, during the 1890s, there was a rapid adoption of bogie stock and the first appearance of corridor and vestibule vehicles. The flowering of late nineteenth-century British railway carriage design is epitomised by the 12-wheel LNWR Royal Diner No 76, whose external appearance has a strong American influence. (Plate 6) The vehicle was awarded a gold medal at the Paris Exhibition of 1900. At this event several British locomotives, none of which now remain, were also awarded gold medals.

Only once more, perhaps, would British practice receive such acclaim abroad, when GWR 4-6-0 No 6000 *King George V* appeared at the Baltimore & Ohio Iron Horse centenary celebrations in the US in 1927. The design of the locomotive reflects the merging of British and American practice, post-1900, with a measure of French influence.[14] No 6000 is preserved in the National Collection, and displayed, appropriately, at its birthplace, Swindon.

From common roots at the dawn of the steam locomotive age British and American locomotive practice remained relatively separate for much of the nineteenth century but came together at the beginning of the twentieth century. Thereafter the two strands increasingly converged, with British practice following the American lead. The British Railways Standard 4-6-2s and 2-10-0s introduced in the early 1950s, smaller size and plate frames apart, were in overall concept remarkably similar to the Pennsylvania Railroad K4s 4-6-2s and I1s 2-10-0s designed nearly 40 years earlier.[15]

Notes and references

1 Atkins, C P, 'How many, where and when?', *Steam Railway*, 116 (December 1989), p71

2 Owen-Jones, S, *The Penydarren Locomotive* (Cardiff: National Museum of Wales, 1981), p32

3 Holmes, P J, *Stockton & Darlington Railway 1825-1975* (Ayr: First Avenue Publishing Company, 1975), p194

4 Thomas, R H G, *The Liverpool & Manchester Railway* (London: B T Batsford Ltd, 1980), p194

5 Reed, B, *The Rocket: Loco Profile No 7* (Windsor: Profile Publications, 1970), p24

6 Shaughnessy, J, *Delaware and Hudson* (Berkeley: Howell-North Books, 1967), p476

7 White, J H, *The John Bull – 150 Years a Locomotive* (Washington, DC: Smithsonian Institution Press, 1981), p138

8 Reed, B, *Norris Locomotives: Loco Profile No 11* (Windsor: Profile Publications, 1971), p24

9 Reed, B, *150 Years of Steam Locomotives* (Newton Abbot: David and Charles, 1975), p128

10 Unpublished correspondence concerning the reconstruction of the *North Star* in 1925 (Great Western Railway correspondence file NRM/CORR/GWR/1, National Railway Museum, York)

11 Anon, 'An historic locomotive: the *Cornwall*, London and North Western Railway', *The Railway Gazette* (5 July 1918), p13

12 Stuart, D H, and Reed, B, *The Crewe Type: Loco Profile No 15* (Windsor: Profile Publications, 1971), p24

13 Young, R, *Timothy Hackworth and the Locomotive* (London: Locomotive Publishing Company, 1923), p406

14 Rutherford, M, *Castles and Kings at Work* (Shepperton: Ian Allan, 1982), p144

15 Atkins, C P, *Britannia – Birth of a Locomotive* (Pinner: Irwell Press, 1991), p92; Atkins, C P, *The British Railway Standard 9F 2-10-0* (Oldham: Irwell Press, 1993), p92

Purchase or adaptive redevelopment: the British locomotive in Sweden

Lars Olov Karlsson

The first evidence of railways' common roots in Sweden and Britain was provided by the Rainhill trials in 1829. One of the competing locomotives, *Novelty*, was built by a Swede, John Ericsson, in co-operation with the British engineer, John Braithwaite. The Ericsson/Braithwaite team had no luck at Rainhill; George Stephenson won the competition quite justifiably: *Novelty* could never have been developed like *Rocket* into a more efficient locomotive. After the trials Ericsson returned to London, built several more locomotives but turned his attention to other inventions. He experienced financial trouble and later went to the US where he developed the propeller, the hot-air engine and the Monitor fighting ship. *Novelty* was soon scrapped but not forgotten and will be mentioned subsequently in this paper.

Railway plans in Sweden

John Ericsson never returned to Sweden but he kept in contact with several Swedes about railway development in Sweden. One of the Swedes was Adolf Eugene von Rosen, who, during the 1840s, visited Britain and studied the developing railways there; his visit was, essentially, industrial espionage.

In Sweden a few industrial railways had been built in the eighteenth century, all horse powered and none open to public traffic. Sweden was then a poor country with few industries. Communications were mainly by water, along the coast, on lakes, rivers or canals. Von Rosen saw the railways as a way to develop his country and when he returned to Sweden he started a campaign to build railways to connect all the main centres. There was no great enthusiasm for such proposals from the Swedish government. Von Rosen was given permission to build railways according to his plans but at his own expense. He was unable to find the financial help in Britain he had hoped for and most of his railways were never realised, or at least not by him.

In the meantime the Frykstad Railway, the very first railway for public traffic, opened in western Sweden connecting a lake system with a navigable river. The railway was opened in 1849; it was powered by horses and mainly conveyed goods.

In the early 1850s the Swedish government became seriously interested in railway development, but with the initial object of connecting different waterways. Plans were, however, drawn up for a state railway network of main lines connecting the bigger cities, as well as the waterways, with each other. Branch lines and lines of local interest were to be built by private companies. The government appointed Nils Ericson [*sic*], brother of John Ericsson of Rainhill fame, to plan and build the State Railways. He was a colonel at the military Waterway Building Corps and later admitted that, at the time, he did not believe in the idea of building railways in Sweden but since the King had asked him personally, he had obeyed orders as a good officer! Ericson had complete authority to plan, design, build and equip the railways but when he was appointed on 22 January 1855 he knew nothing about railways and needed help. Very few Swedes at that time did know anything about railways. Von Rosen was reluctant to help as he had himself hoped to be appointed to build the State Railways. Ericson did, however, find a Swedish engineer named Stieler who had worked on railways in France. Ericson gave Stieler the commission to buy locomotives, coaches, wagons, rails and other equipment for the Swedish State Railways.

The first Swedish locomotives

There had been a number of attempts in the early 1850s to develop locomotives in Sweden. In 1853 the company Munktells of Eskilstuna (still in business but now building tractors for Volvo) built a small narrow gauge 0-4-0T locomotive to be used by contractors building a local railway in Norberg. It was called *Förstlingen* ('Firstling') and was designed and built without any help from outside Sweden. However, it was a failure and had to be returned to Munktells having done very little work. It was rebuilt to standard gauge and put to work as a contractors' locomotive on the Nora to Ervalla line, which, when it opened in 1856, was to be Sweden's first standard gauge locomotive-powered railway. Here *Förstlingen* did some work until it was eventually scrapped in 1882. Some parts of the locomotive have been preserved in the Swedish Railway Museum.

In 1855 Munktells did build another locomotive, the second in Sweden. It was a narrow gauge 0-6-0T called *Fryckstad*, and it was used in 1856 to replace the horses on the Frykstad Railway. Perhaps the engineers at Munktells had studied some successful locomotives; *Fryckstad* had a superior design. It worked on the railway for 20 years and was then used for another 20 years in the construction of military forts. Later it was stored, forgotten, but it was eventually rescued for the Swedish Railway Museum.

The State Railways turn to Britain

Despite the success of *Fryckstad*, Ericsson and Stieler were not impressed with Swedish efforts to build railway equipment. Ericsson decided to follow German standards in building the railway infrastructure in Sweden; German railway civil-engineering practice was seen as somewhere between high British standards and contemporary simple American standards. Locomotives, rails, bridges and axles for the coaches and wagons were to be bought in Britain and the coaches themselves in Germany. The goods wagons were entrusted to Swedish factories but were to be equipped with British fittings.

Stieler went to London and, through friends, he contacted the then rather new Beyer, Peacock and Company in Manchester. They were known as designers and builders of reliable, simple locomotives. The first locomotives bought were 2-4-0s for mixed traffic; 45 were built between 1856 and 1872, some of them in Sweden. The first Swedish locomotive of this type was built in 1861 by Nyköpings Mekaniska Verkstad. The Swedish-built locomotives were not, however, up to British standards, and most locomotives continued to be bought from Britain. The 2-4-0 was built to contemporary British standards and had, for instance, no driver's cab. However, it proved impossible to work without protection, especially during the hard Swedish winter. All locomotives were soon provided with a roof and some side sheets as protection for the driver.

Locomotives of the 2-4-0 mixed traffic type, later called class B, were in use until 1909, most of them by then equipped with new Swedish boilers with Belpaire fireboxes. One of the first of the class, *Prins August*, built in 1856, was put aside for preservation in 1906. It was later taken into the Swedish Railway Museum and partly restored to its original condition. In 1956, when the Swedish State Railways celebrated their centenary, it was restored to working order using a 'new' boiler, from an 0-4-2 from a private railway. This boiler was a replacement built in Sweden in the 1920s but very close to the original in size and construction since the original design of the 0-4-2s was also from Beyer, Peacock and Company. *Prins August* has since been maintained in running order and can still be used; in 1992 it operated on some short trips outside the museum in Gävle.

Locomotives for different uses

The Swedish State Railways also bought some second-hand locomotives in Britain to use during the construction period. They were never taken into the operating fleet and little information about them has survived, though two of them, *Ajax* and *Titan*, are known to have been 0-4-2s from the London & South Western Railway. Six new saddle tank 0-4-2s were built between 1858 and 1879 for contractors' work. They were also a standard Beyer, Peacock design which was used in many countries. One, *Thor*, built in 1861, is preserved in the Swedish Railway Museum, and a broad gauge sister engine is preserved in Finland.

When the first part of the Swedish State Railway system opened in December 1856 the only need was for mixed traffic locomotives. As the lines became longer, and traffic increased, there was a need for other types of locomotives too; 0-6-0s were ordered for goods traffic, 2-2-2s for fast passenger trains and 0-4-2Ts for local passenger trains.

There were several types of 0-6-0s for goods trains. The first 14, later to be called class F, performed well and were used until 1911, although most of them were rebuilt with new boilers in the 1880s. The next class, later to be class G, was similar but a little heavier. Of this type, 51 were built between 1866 and 1874. They had long lives even though several of them ran in the very north of Sweden. The last class G 0-6-0 was taken off shunting duties in 1936. Two of them were preserved: *Jernsida* from 1867 and *Vik* from 1875. Parts from the two engines were used to make one, *Jernsida* ('Ironside'), and the remaining parts were scrapped. Research has subsequently found that it is probably mainly *Vik* that is preserved, with the name plate and possibly a few other parts from *Jernsida*!

A few 0-6-0s were bought from other builders, mainly to provide a comparison with the Beyer, Peacock designs. One locomotive, later class M, was bought from the London & North Western Railway works in Crewe. It was a standard Ramsbottom-designed locomotive of class DX but it was not considered successful in Sweden although it worked until 1883, when it was scrapped. The other deviation from Beyer, Peacock orthodoxy were 12 0-6-0s, later class H, which were bought in 1874 from Sharp Stewart in Manchester. They were very similar to the G class, and also had long lives. The last one was scrapped in 1951, having been used as an industrial shunter in its last years.

For express train duties, 32 single wheel 2-2-2s were built between 1863 and 1873, some of them in Sweden. They hauled the first fast trains between Stockholm and Göteborg, connecting the cities by a trip taking 14 hours, including stops for meals. Today the tilting X2000 train makes the same journey in less than three hours!

The single wheelers, later called class A, were soon replaced by heavier locomotives on main trains but continued to haul lighter trains until the turn of century. One of the class, *Göta*, was preserved in 1906 for the Swedish Railway Museum. It was displayed in the museum until 1980 when it was taken out and put back in running order. It still has its original boiler and very little work, other than cleaning, had to be done to it before it was able to steam again. *Göta* has since made several long trips and runs very smoothly. On the main line speeds of up to 70 or 80 km/h can be reached without any problems. The maximum official speed is 30 km/h, but the locomotive does not have a speedometer ...

For shunting and local train services, several small 0-4-2STs were bought from Beyer, Peacock; they were of more or less standard construction but none has been preserved. The complete frame of one, with wheels, was discovered in the mid-1980s in use testing weighbridges in the harbour of Narvik in northern Norway. It was offered to the Swedish Railway Museum, but unfortunately it was scrapped by mistake before the museum had the opportunity to confirm its interest.

The end of an era

The end of good relations between the Swedish State Railways and the firm of Beyer, Peacock came very suddenly. The last delivery comprised six long boilered 0-6-0s in 1872. They were not of standard type but had been designed for the Köln to Minden Railway in Germany. The long boiler construction made the rather heavy locomotives sway and oscillate. They were hard on the track, very quickly became unpopular and were confined to shunting duties.

The poor performance of these locomotives is sometimes said to be the reason for the change in locomotive purchasing policy in Sweden and the break in relations with Beyer, Peacock but the assumption is too simplistic. The British-built locomotives had been very successful and were to be the mainstay of the locomotive fleet for many years to come. There were other reasons. By 1872 the State Railways in Sweden had almost achieved their original objectives. Most main lines were built, at least in southern Sweden, and the organisation was changing from an emphasis on building to running railways. A special motive power department was created and Fredrik Almgren was appointed as director in 1873. Almgren's training had been principally with Borsig in Berlin so, quite naturally, a new German era started on Swedish State Railways. Almgren began to develop his own locomotives, but his first locomotives were ordered from Borsig in Berlin. Borsig built locomotives for the Swedish State Railways for some years, but it was soon found that the Swedish locomotive builders had acquired the experience to build reliable locomotives. With the exception of 20 locomotives bought from the US around the turn of the century, nearly all future steam locomotives for the Swedish State Railways were to be built in Sweden.

Private railway locomotives

The fact that only the main lines in Sweden were built by the state, leaving branch lines and local lines to private interests, has already been mentioned in this paper. Of the roughly 17,400 km of railway built in Sweden, 69 per cent or 12,000 km were built by more than 200 private companies. There were small companies with just a few kilometres of line and a few locomotives, and companies with lines very similar to the main lines and with over 100 locomotives. Most of these private lines were taken over by the State Railways, or closed down, during the 1930s and 1940s. They were built to many different gauges, but the most important ones were standard gauge. The most extensive narrow gauge lines were built to a gauge of 3 ft (Swedish) or 891mm, but some early lines were built to 4 ft (English) or 1219 mm, 3 ft 6 inches or 1067 mm or 600 mm.

The first private railways also turned to Beyer, Peacock or other British builders for locomotives. The largest of the Swedish private railways was the Bergslagernas Railway (BJ) which ran the principal route from Falun to Göteborg. The company was faithful to Beyer, Peacock, buying all its first locomotives from the firm. There were standard passenger 0-4-2s, goods train 0-6-0s and shunting 0-6-0STs, all of them very British in design. At a later date locomotives of these types were also built in Sweden, and some of them had very long working lives. The last 0-6-0 worked into the 1970s when it was bought for preservation. Another of these 0-6-0s, No 27, built in Manchester in 1880, was taken over by the Swedish Railway Museum in the 1950s. BJ bought their last two 0-6-2ST Beyer, Peacock engines in 1908; they were built for heavy shunting and were used until the 1940s. They were the last conventional steam locomotives built in Britain for any Swedish railway company and also the last bought from Beyer, Peacock. Two steam railcars and one narrow gauge locomotive were built by Sentinel for Swedish buyers in the 1920s, but neither design was very successful.

Another big private line buying British locomotives for a long period was the Stockholm–Västerås–Bergslagernas Railway which ran from Stockholm to Västerås and Ludvika. They bought their locomotives from several British companies starting with some 2-4-0s and 0-4-2STs, followed by 0-6-0Ts and 2-6-0s from Sharp Stewart. Later they bought 4-4-0s from Neilson, Reid and Company, and 2-8-0s from Nasmyth Wilson. The 2-8-0 locomotives were built for a Mexican line but were never sent there.

The Gefle to Dala Railway, from Gävle to Falun, bought all their early locomotives from Britain, mainly 0-6-0s from Beyer, Peacock. This line also operated what is thought to be the earliest-built locomotive to run in Sweden, an 0-4-2 bought second-hand from Sharp Stewart in 1856. The locomotive was built by Kirtley in 1841 for the Manchester, Sheffield & Lincolnshire Railway and was scrapped in 1874.

Smaller Swedish private railways bought locomotives from a variety of British builders. The very small 0-4-0T *Elfkarleö* was built in 1873 by Henry Hughes of Loughbough and brought to Sweden in 1876. The original appearance is unknown and was probably significantly changed when it was rebuilt with a new boiler in 1900; it was given to the Swedish Railway Museum in 1945. The very small dimensions suggest that it may have been built as a tramway engine. It is now restored to full working order, and is used occasionally every year on the museum site. It is so small that when it shunts modern wagons and coaches it looks as if it is built to a different scale from modern equipment.

The Oxelösund–Flen–Westmanlands Railway (OFWJ) later became a part of the Grängesberg to Oxelösund Railway (TGOJ). This is now one of the last private railways in Sweden but forms part of the State Railway system as an associated company. The railways in the TGOJ of today were all built by British capital. From the beginning they were all very British in style and appearance. OFWJ bought their locomotives from Sharp Stewart. From their first locomotive fleet from 1876, two have been preserved. No 8, an 0-4-2, is now in full working order at the Swedish Railway Museum, while 0-6-0ST No 1 is displayed, but not working, at the local technical museum in Eskilstuna.

Narrow gauge locomotives

On the narrow gauge most of the very first locomotives were from Britain. A few have been preserved, such as the 0-4-2ST *Helgenäs* from an industrial 600 mm line. It was built by Hudswell Clarke in 1889 and still has its original boiler. It is occasionally in use on the museum line in Mariefred but it is so small that it cannot be used for any regular traffic.

Of the early locomotives for 3 ft (Swedish), or 891 mm, and 3 ft 6 inches, or 1067mm gauge, few British-built engines have been preserved. One is the 0-6-2T *Lovisa Tranaea*, built by Avonside in 1875 for the Nordmark Klarälven Railway and now displayed at the local railway museum in Hagfors. In the same museum is a small 0-4-2ST built by Henry Hughes in 1874 for the same railway. There is also an 0-6-0T built by Fletcher Jennings in 1873 for Ulricehamns Railway preserved in the local museum in Skara. It has, however, been heavily rebuilt so that what used to be a saddle tank locomotive now has side tanks.

More unusual standard gauge locomotives

A variety of slightly unusual British-built standard gauge locomotives has been preserved in Sweden. An 0-6-0ST, *Karlskoga*, built by Fox Walker in 1873 is preserved in its old home town of Nora by a museum railway. It was built for the Nora to Karlskoga Railway, but was sold off for industrial use before the turn of the century. In the 1950s it was brought back for display on a plinth at Karlskoga station and after many years outdoors it was finally returned to running condition some years ago.

A line in Sweden built by British capital was the first iron ore line between Luleå and Gällivare in the very north of the country. To work the line, the Swedish and Norwegian Railway Company bought five 0-4-0STs from Black Hawthorn and 18 0-8-0s from Sharp Stewart. The company ran out of money and the 0-8-0s were never paid for; only a few of them had reached Sweden and they were returned to the builder. All of the class were resold to British and German railways. The tank engines were taken over by Swedish State Railways which bought the line very cheaply and finished the work. Instead of the heavy Sharp Stewart 0-8-0s, old Beyer, Peacock locomotives were put on the heavy iron ore trains; sometimes three class G 0-6-0s had to be used. Very un-British was the fact that the Swedish and Norwegian Railway company introduced air rather than vacuum brakes to Sweden on this line. Later Swedish locomotives for the ore trains were fitted with New York Air Brake Company equipment but the air-pumps were not built in the US. On the air-pump on the museum's compound Ma class 2-8-0 is the inscription: New York Air Brake Company, Moscow Factory, Russia.

British influence

Approximately 465 locomotives were supplied to Sweden by a number of British builders, a small proportion of the total of about 3450 steam locomotives used in Sweden. The British locomotives worked hard and reliably for many years but seem to have had very little influence on subsequent locomotive development in Sweden.

Several Swedish locomotive builders started by copying British designs. When the Nydqvist & Holm Company (later NOHAB) were building their first locomotive, *Trollhättan*, for the Uddevalla-Vänersborg–Herrljunga Railway (UWHJ) they built an almost exact copy of some locomotives built by the British firm of Slaughter, Grunning and Company for the 4 ft gauge Borås to Herrljunga Railway. When UWHJ was widened from 4 ft to standard gauge in 1899 NOHAB bought their first locomotive back and later gave it to the Swedish Railway Museum. After *Trollhättan* NOHAB designed a few locomotives themselves, but when they built locomotives for the Swedish State Railways they used Beyer, Peacock designs. The other big steam locomotive builder in Sweden, Motala Verkstad, followed the same course. Their first locomotive, a crude 0-6-0T named *Carlsund*, was built for a Belgian-owned mining company in Sweden probably using Belgian plans, or at least Belgian specifications. The next locomotives they built were to Beyer, Peacock plans.

Although newer locomotives constructed in Sweden show little British influence, it can be argued that inside cylinders and simple construction principles were carried over from the period of British influence. A few railway companies still ordered locomotives with the typically British crowned funnel. It seems, however, that British builders lost interest in Sweden at the end of the nineteenth century despite apparently good opportunities to continue to sell more locomotives there. British locomotives had a good reputation and prices must have been competitive, especially from the bigger builders. Was the Swedish market too small for Britain? Was it more interesting and easier to sell to countries within the Commonwealth? Answers to these questions remain the subject of research and enquiry by the Swedish Railway Museum.

Electrics and diesels

It is interesting to note that history repeated itself when electric and diesel locomotives were introduced. The very first electric line in Sweden, the Djursholmsbanan, opened for electric passenger service in 1895. Four electric rail cars were built in Sweden but the electric equipment was supplied by Mather & Platt in Britain. This equipment was not a success so it was soon replaced by Swedish equipment which was designed partly in Germany.

When the first diesel locomotives were required after World War Two by the Swedish State Railways, they turned to Britain. Two standard British Electric 0-6-0 (similar to British Rail Class 08) locomotives were bought in 1949. They were used for shunting, at first in Göteborg and later in the iron ore harbour of Luleå. They were very reliable; they worked and worked. In the early 1970s, still working well, they were sold for industrial use because they were not compatible with other Swedish diesel locomotives. They worked on until 1992; one of them was even rebuilt with radio control. They were then both donated to the Swedish Railway Museum. Only these two diesels of British manufacture came to Sweden. The next order for diesels went to Germany and later diesels were built in Sweden under licence from the US and Germany. As with steam locomotives, it seems that British manufacturers had a good product but failed to sell it.

The War Department 2-8-0s

There is a postscript to the history of the British-built steam locomotive in Sweden. During the 1950s two further British-built steam locomotives came to the Swedish State Railways; they were two 2-8-0s of the War Department (WD) type which were imported from Holland. At that time diesels and electrics had taken over most of the traffic in Sweden but it was a military requirement that steam should be kept as a strategic reserve. Several hundred steam locomotives were put in store all over the country. The military authorities appreciated, however, that the locomotives in store were old and wanted to investigate the possibility of exchanging the existing reserve stock for more modern types of steam locomotives then on sale in Europe very cheaply. Two old WD locomotives were bought from Holland and rebuilt to Swedish

standards. New drivers' cabs were made, the tender was reduced from four to three axles (to fit the shorter Swedish turntables) and some of the fittings were exchanged for Swedish designs. Needless to say, the rebuilding costs were very high and no more locomotives were purchased. The two WD locomotives were allocated to class G11, tested and then put in store. One was later sold to a British preservation society and the other was scrapped.

Novelty, *again*

With the two ex-WD locomotives, the history of the British-built steam locomotive would have ended, if it were not for the Swedish Railway Museum and the preservation movement. In 1981, as the Swedish railway system celebrated its 125th anniversary, the *Novelty* replica built in 1980 by Locomotion Enterprises was brought to Sweden. It seemed appropriate to display at the celebrations the first locomotive built by a Swede. *Novelty* had not worked very well in Britain at Rainhill in 1980, but when it arrived in Sweden it was fully workable and was demonstrated. Local people in Gävle became so fond of the little engine that they begged money from a local foundation and bought it. The replica was then donated to the Swedish Railway Museum where, for the moment, it remains inactive because the Swedish boiler inspector does not fully agree with Ericsson's construction principles! *Novelty* was a beginning and, for this paper, an appropriate end. It exemplifies the common roots which were important to the early development of Swedish locomotives but which led to the separate branches of the modern Swedish State Railways.

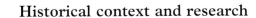

Historical context and research

Railways in their context

Jack Simmons

I hope, in this paper, to open up a large subject which reflects the diversity of experience of those who are interested in railways but look at them from different points of view: different aspects of their technology, for example, different departments of their daily work, the different uses made of the facilities that they have offered to their customers. I shall be looking here at the railways from the outside, from the standpoint of those who have used and observed them as instruments of daily life, in a way in which they have been considered too little or too narrowly in the past.

Let me begin by quoting some sentences written by Charles E Lee. They come from his short book *Passenger Class Distinctions*. He writes there of

the ever-increasing tendency to make the fundamental mistake of recording a fact as if it were an isolated phenomenon, without considering it in true perspective in relation to the social and economic conditions prevailing ... Railways came into general use in the first half of the last century because of the increasing need for the transport of heavy concentrated loads along fixed routes, often with gradients unsuited to canals; not because they had just been invented. The urge to develop the steam locomotive was provided by the high cost of horse feed during the Napoleonic wars ... When invention does not coincide with real need, it usually languishes.

Lee's purpose in writing in this way was 'to draw attention to the difference between an item of news and what has come to be called background material. News tends to be recorded, and indexed, while attendant conditions do not.'[1]

Lee had no academic pretensions, nor did he set himself up to preach sermons about the way in which the history of railways ought to be written. He just got on with the job, and he left behind him a body of more than 20 books, booklets and substantial papers, which are still used by serious students.

There was nothing strikingly original in the remarks just quoted. What *is* striking is to see how often they are disregarded, almost 50 years after they first came out in print. The economic historians, of course, have not disregarded them. From

Sir John Clapham onwards some have made it their business to attend carefully to the part the railways played in shaping the British economy. But I am writing here, as Lee was too, of those who have written specifically about railways, of the history of companies, their mechanical equipment and the services of trains they provided.

The chief explanation of the failure to look enough at the development of railways 'in relation to the social and economic conditions prevailing' at the time is that those who have set themselves to write about it have concentrated their minds too much on recording what happened, and when, and not enough on answering the question 'why?'. Very often the answer to the question 'why?' will be found by looking carefully at the condition of the country or the district in which the railways were growing up; not at its social and economic condition alone, but at its political, cultural and moral condition too. Those 'conditions' add up to what I am calling the 'context' within which railways were projected, built and made to work.

This paper discusses five examples of various kinds.

Railways and government

We may begin by looking at railways in the context of government. In Britain the national government played very little direct part in the development of railways, and the part it did play was almost wholly negative. In Belgium the national government itself laid down the main lines of the railway system in 1834, and the French government did the same for its own country, in a different way, in 1842. In Britain nothing of that kind occurred. Here the railways were built by companies, running on their own chosen routes, and they were financed by shares taken up by private investors. With the exception of a small number of short lines built to serve naval or military installations, the national government commissioned and paid for no railways of its own. The companies had to obtain parliamentary authority to build their lines, and that was frequently refused. On some matters the government legislated in the interests of safety; it imposed obligations on the companies, to carry the mail on the instructions of the Post Office and soldiers with their equipment. It did almost nothing positive towards determining the system beyond taking a decision that Holyhead should be the packet station for the conveyance of the mail to Ireland, rather than any of two or three rival ports – a decision which settled the route of the railway to reach it.

The government made two further efforts to shape the pattern of railway development. In 1844 it tried to control the submission to Parliament of Bills for the construction of new railways, but although the body charged with the task, presided over by Lord Dalhousie, performed it well by throwing out many schemes that were evidently unsound, the companies succeeded in persuading the government to bring its work to an end after a single year, leaving the forces of private competition stronger than they had been before. In 1846 a commission was appointed to consider proposals for running railways into the heart of London. It produced an intelligent report, which was accepted by the government, and the policy it recommended, of excluding the railways from a large area at the centre of the city, was adopted and maintained, but only for 14 years. It was overthrown in 1860, when a private company was given power by Parliament to build a line into and through London, close to St Paul's Cathedral. Thereafter, the British government would sometimes prevent railway companies from doing what it considered foolish or wrong; it would seldom do anything to require them to do what was right. The principal exception was provided by the Regulation of Railways Act of 1889, which obliged railway companies to fit adequate brakes to their passenger trains, but that measure was forced through by public horror at one appalling accident.

Why should the state have stood aside in this way in Britain? Because the power of commercial enterprise – its political power in votes – was far stronger there than it was in France, and, the country being protected (then) by its insular position behind strong sea defences, the government had much less need to seize and maintain tight control of the railways for reasons of national security. All this left railway companies free to provide what services they chose, for the conveyance of passengers and freight – much more free than the railways in Belgium or France or Germany. To their customers it was in some important respects a better service –

faster and more frequent than those elsewhere in Europe. In Britain, for example, by the 1880s almost all consignments of goods travelling up to 200 miles were delivered on the day following their despatch. In Belgium – a much smaller country – three days were required for all such deliveries.[2] The Belgian government was satisfied to set a lower standard than the one that was acceptable in Britain. The higher British standard was due largely to the strength of competition between the railway companies; a force that scarcely operated in Belgium at all. There was only one large town in England 200 miles from London that was not served by at least two competing railways, namely Hull; Liverpool, Manchester, and Leeds were served by three. These British goods trains battled along by night, often at 30 mph and more (without continuous brakes), taking goods put on to the railway in the late afternoon or evening, to be ready for distribution early next day.[3] By this means, though there were others, the whole machinery of industry and trade was able to turn orders round more quickly in Britain than anywhere on the European mainland.

It was the same with passenger trains. At least until the 1890s the service was substantially faster and more frequent in Britain than it was on the mainland of Europe, and the facilities it provided for third-class passengers using the best trains were much more liberal as well. That is – please note – a *European* comparison only.

In the US, where the railways were also competitive enterprises, and (at least until 1887) not much subject to the authority of the federal government, the passenger services were in this respect more like those in Britain. But even there they were still not framed as favourably to the passenger. A candid and very well-informed American writer observed in 1882 that 'for number of trains and for speed England leads the world, surpassing entirely Continental Europe and the United States'.[4] On the European mainland, governments had the will and the power to keep down the cost of providing railway services, and in this matter they were slow to relax their grip.

Until the 1880s the British government took a rather detached view of railways, interfering with them as little as possible, and this was largely due to the presence in Parliament of a substantial body of directors of railway companies, collectively called 'the Railway Interest'.[5] That interest reached its peak numerically in 1873, when nearly one-fifth of the members of the House of Commons sat on railway boards. The companies had therefore a good chance of making their opinions known in Parliament and, on occasion, of acting for the advantage of railways in general.

Here and there the railways came to form some of the very stuff of parliamentary politics. In the 1860s railway matters, of various kinds, played an important part in one or more elections in at least seven English towns: Harwich,[6] Southampton,[7] Salisbury,[8] Launceston,[9] Shrewsbury,[10] Stockport[11] and Carlisle.[12] Under the terms of the Reform Act of 1867 many railway employees became qualified to secure the franchise. At the general election of 1880 their votes were held to have determined a result at Sheffield.[13] The steps taken by F W Webb to control the voting of the men employed in the London & North Western Company's works at Crewe, and their ultimate, ignominious failure, are well known.[14]

Here we approach the history of railwaymen as a community: an important subject that has been treated so far mainly in connection with the development of trade unions, though it is really much wider than that. It does not, however, form part of the substance of this paper.

Railways and leisure

Let us now turn to look at the railways' part in the enlargement and diversification of leisure. For most people in Britain, before the railways arrived, a 'holiday' meant one day off work: Sunday perhaps (though a good many people worked on seven days a week), Christmas and Boxing Days, Easter Monday, Whit Monday. Those townsmen who wished could take a stroll into the country or into one of the large open spaces around London. Even that might be a rare event. The prosperous John Gilpin's wife remarked to him in 1782 that after they had been married 20 years '... yet we/no holiday have seen.'[15]

The well-to-do moved about the country in coaches or on horseback or travelled for holidays to watering-places like Scarborough and Bath; some went on extended 'tours' and so became 'tourists'. But the total number of all those people was very small, and it remained so until steam power enabled them to be conveyed in large groups all together. Steamships carried large numbers of passengers along the estuaries of the Clyde and Thames from 1815 onwards, and then up the east coast from London

to Leith, where by 1824 a regular service was maintained, one of the ships being named *The Tourist*. The railways soon took up this practice. In 1836 one of the Stockton & Darlington Company's carriages was also called *The Tourist*.[16]

A steamboat or a railway train had the capacity and the power to take passengers by hundreds, whereas most road vehicles had to reckon theirs by tens. They offered, decisively and clearly, a new kind of popular holiday making. And the railway enjoyed one great advantage over the steamboat in that the effect of bad weather was much less disastrous than it was on the sea. As long as the cheapest trains, the excursions, were made up of carriages open to the sky, the passengers might get drenched by rain, just as they might on the ship, but the motion of the trains rarely induced any kind of sickness, as all steamers did, and they generally ran in any kind of weather. Many steamboat services were provided only in the summer months.

Accordingly, the number of people able to take the cheaper kinds of holiday that railways offered grew steadily. And they were free to grow in Britain as the companies thought fit to provide them, the decisions being a response to popular demand. Elsewhere in Europe the running of every additional train had to be sanctioned by civil servants; we know, from special enquiries made into the management and operation of railways there on behalf of the British government in 1909-10, that the number of such trains in France, Belgium, Germany, Austria and Italy was very small compared with that in Britain.[17]

But one thing in Britain acted in the opposite direction: in some parts of the island this kind of travel – every kind of travel indeed – was restricted or forbidden on Sundays, or altogether forbidden. The old sincerities and formalities of church and chapel going were still strong, and the railways always had to take account of them. In 1914 nearly two-thirds of the whole railway system of Scotland was shut down on Sundays, except for a few mail services; in England and Wales more than one-fifth was closed. On those lines that were open, the number of trains run was much restricted. There was, for example, only one day-time train on Sundays from London to Newcastle, arriving there just before midnight.

True, this arrangement was not due solely to religious scruple. It was often a convenience to the railways themselves, in allowing the engineers much fuller possession of the lines on one day in the week, where they needed repair or reconstruction; some concession of that kind was more often necessary in Britain than on the Continental railways because the traffic they carried was much heavier. On the whole of the European mainland there was, I believe, one railway line that was closed to Sunday traffic, the Yverdon & Ste Croix in Switzerland, and that was less than 16 miles long.[18]

The reduction or prohibition of Sunday traffic represented a limit placed by the railways on the expansion of popular travel. But it was accompanied by a concession of a kind that had not been seen very much before. Some railway companies, the South Western and the North Western being among the first, offered tickets at reduced fares to passengers making their outward journeys on Saturdays and returning on Mondays, so cutting out the demand for Sunday trains. By the 1870s this type of holiday was coming to be called a 'weekend'. The French adopted the phrase *le weekend* early in the new century, and with it they coined another, *la semaine anglaise*, or the English week, to indicate a working week of 5 or 5½ days.[19] Both expressions were slightly derisive, suggesting that the British people were lazy. Whatever the truth of the matter, the practice came to stay, and it was actively fostered by the railways as a profitable branch of their own business. 'I'm going away for the weekend': that is an agreeable incident of life today that we owe to the Victorian railways. As for the contempt that our European neighbours may have felt for this indulgence, it was perhaps tinged a little with envy: for the number of working hours in the British week had been reduced below those customary in most industries on the Continent, the wage rates were generally higher, and, on top of all that, the practice of granting holidays with pay was becoming more common in Britain before 1914.

Railways and coal

So there are the railways opening out the prospect of pleasure, and being bound more and more closely into the texture of middle- and working-class life. Let us turn now to their part in providing the country with the ordinary necessities of living, and here I choose particularly the distribution of coal. This was the single most important kind of freight they handled, indispensable then both in manufacturing industry and in domestic life, and moreover one on which the railways themselves were almost completely dependent.

The conveyance of coal had been a prime purpose of railways from their beginning, and it continued to be that down to our own time, even after the railways had been nationalised. Other fuels were much more freely used elsewhere in the nineteenth century, particularly wood for cooking and heating, but Britain had no huge forests comparable, for instance, with those in Germany and America.

Railways never enjoyed a monopoly in this branch of transport. A very large quantity of coal was conveyed away from northeastern England by coastal shipping. It was not until late in the 1860s that the amount of rail-borne coal brought into London exceeded that brought in by sea. Then, with the improvement of ships engaged in the coasting trade in the later nineteenth century, the railways' lead was gradually reduced, until by 1900, so it seems, ships once again carried more than half the coal that London demanded.[20] But when the coal had been taken there, whether it was by rail or sea, it had to be distributed throughout Greater London. Some of that work was done wholly by road, but a great deal of it was managed by the railways, the coal being handed over to the merchants in suburban station yards.

It was the same at small country stations, and some very substantial coal-merchants' businesses were founded, wholly or partly, on their work at these rural depots. Richard Coller, for example, resigned his post as stationmaster at Narborough to become a goods agent at the nearby town of King's Lynn. In 1849 he went entirely into the coal trade, supplying the depots of small merchants at stations. There were eventually 18 of these, stretching right across Norfolk to Norwich. He became a wealthy man, and in due course Mayor of Norwich. His firm was eventually absorbed into Charrington's.[21] The same sort of activity, extending also into building materials, was an important ingredient in the making of two businesses that became well known nationally, Ellis & Everard and Joseph Ellis Ltd. They were both founded in Leicester and quickly extended their operations, based on station yards, into Northamptonshire and southwards as far as Hitchin.[22]

As a general rule, the arrival of railways brought the price of coal down directly the lines were opened, and that was often noted gratefully: at Chester, for instance,[23] at York[24] and Carlisle.[25] However, the benefit did not always prove lasting.

By 1856 the price at Darlington was observed to be higher than it had been before the Stockton & Darlington Railway was opened 30 years previously.[26]

Railways and public health

The railways' movement of coal came to underpin the domestic life of a large majority of people in Britain. They also offered some important contributions to the improvement of public health.

They greatly assisted the development of some large and important hospitals; not only by the conveyance of materials required for the erection of their buildings, but also, here and there, by making special provision for the transport of staff, patients and visitors to and from them. One example is the gradual improvement in treating people who were mentally disordered. Private railway lines were carried into at least four big, newly built mental hospitals – Cheddleton, Hellingly and Whittingham in England, and Bangour in Scotland. Each had a railway of its own, a branch taken off one of the companies' lines and built in collaboration with it.[27]

An example of current research into the use of railways, that lies altogether outside railway history as it has been conventionally written, is an investigation into the treatment of hospital out-patients. One of the team, an NHS consultant, thought that the enormous increase in mobility brought about by railways from the 1840s onwards might have its bearing on the earlier history of this subject. Together we decided that an investigation of the hospitals' registers of out-patients (where they survived and showed the places from which the patients came) might afford some interesting clues. I suggested he seek the assistance of the National Register of Archives (that admirable source of knowledge), and enquiries by that route are now in progress.

Such services rendered by railways to the community, and there were many more of the same kind, which careful research could uncover, were valuable, and positive. But the Victorians seldom looked at the matter in this way. When they discussed the effects of railways on health, it was usually in the opposite sense, to draw attention to the evils they produced, not the good.

The best-known treatment of the subject is the short book published by the *Lancet* in 1862, called *The Influence of Railway Travelling on Public Health*. Most of the 'influence' it treats is bad. It concentrates the reader's attention on the dangers the railways brought with them to the health of the passengers they carried. These included, for instance, the posture that the carriage seats forced upon those who occupied them, helping to give currency to the idea that a new disease, had emerged, 'railway spine', and warning commuters of the risks they ran from the fatigue produced by their daily journeys. There was truth, of course, in that last contention, but the statement of it here was unbalanced, making no attempt to weigh against it the benefits to health that these people enjoyed from using railways, allowing them, for example, to live at greater distances from their work near the centres of crowded cities. Six years later another medical paper published a different presentation of the same topic under a more eye-catching title: A Haviland's *Hurried to Death; Or, A Few Words of Advice on the Danger of Hurry and Excitement, Especially Addressed to Railway Travellers.*

The dangers presented by railway accidents certainly began to grow more alarming in the 1860s, and were constantly laid before a popular audience by *Punch* through the cartoons of John Tenniel, who never let up on the railways' misdeeds nor had a good word to say for them. These accidents were matters of fact, dangers to health and life that no one could deny, and shown by the inspectors' reports again and again to be due wholly or in part to the companies' mismanagement. There is no sign, however, that they had any effect on the determination of the British public to travel by train. Looking at the figures for the 10 years 1867-76 – which covered the dreadful accidents at Brockley Whins, Wigan, Norwich, Shipton, Abbots Ripton and Radstock – we find that, while the system grew in length by 19 per cent, the number of passenger journeys over it grew by 93 per cent.

The truth is that once the railways had established their system over the whole of Great Britain except the far northwest of Scotland, they had come to be taken as part of the normal equipment of daily life, like the postal service and the rapidly expanding sewerage system. Few people thought it worthwhile to remind the country of the benefits it owed to the railways. What made news, lively reading, was the exposure of misconduct. As the media demonstrate today, bad news is the best-selling news.

Here and there something was done to right the balance. Only four years after the publication of the *Lancet*'s little book, a surgeon of unquestionable authority was able to show that there was no such thing as 'railway spine'.[28]

Railways and social class

One theme from general social history which has, however, attracted very little attention from social historians is whether the railways, as they developed, served to raise or to lower the barriers between classes in Britain.

The only extended account of the distinctions made by railways between their passengers is Lee's, which I have already mentioned. But his aim was a restricted one: to set down distinctions that were imposed by the railways in response to the decrees of government. He performed this task excellently, and his little book must be the starting point of any enquiry made into this matter. But its business is not with broad intentions or with the consequences to the whole community.

The railways inherited their decision to provide accommodation for more than one sort of traveller from the stage-coaches, which had offered their passengers two. The more expensive provision was that enjoyed by those who travelled inside the vehicles, totally enclosed, the doors having glass windows. The cheaper provision was offered to the much more numerous passengers who rode in the open air, beside the coachman, on the roof or (occasionally) in a boot at the back of the vehicle. If the weather was fine and the driver drove well the cheaper accommodation might be thought preferable; and it was sometimes sought after not simply for reasons of economy. But, as a rule, those who could afford the higher fares levied for travelling inside the coaches paid them.

The railways took over this practice, charging more for totally enclosed accommodation and less for that in open vehicles furnished either with a simple canopy over the passengers' heads or with no covering at all. But they soon introduced a very small change of language, which helped to produce far-reaching results. The stage-coaches called their two categories of passengers 'insides' and 'outsides': a sensible use of words, based on matters of fact. Similarly, the early steamboats, which started just before the railways, called the two kinds of accommodation they offered 'cabin' and 'deck': a distinction that related merely to the part of the ship in which the passengers travelled. But the railways came to take scarcely any 'outside' passengers, seated on the roofs of the carriages (that was soon seen to be

dangerous because of the numerous bridges that crossed over their lines), and they had no decks. So they adopted a different mode of distinguishing between their passengers. At least as early as 1834 they had begun to speak of their trains as being of two 'classes', first and second, and by 1837 the Grand Junction, the first trunk railway in Europe, started out in business by speaking of 'first- and second-class passengers'.[29] The only earlier use of the terms 'first-' and 'second-class', to designate persons individually, referred to candidates examined at universities.[30] The railways adopted these expressions, with the differences they implied in importance between the two classes, extensively and soon: at Manchester (Liverpool Road) from 1830 onwards.[31] Whishaw tells us that at Ayr station, 'along the platform is an iron railing, which separates the first-class from the second-class passengers in their progress to the carriages'. In his account of the grand station at Derby he speaks of the 'different booking-offices and waiting and refreshment rooms, for first and second-class passengers, which are quite apart from each other'.[32]

There had been many class distinctions made in the treatment of stage-coach passengers, particularly at the inns where they stopped *en route*. The differential behaviour of innkeepers and their servants to travellers according to their social class and wealth was notorious, and often satirised, but it was no more than a reflection of established social custom. The railways now systematised it, applying it rigidly in a numerical formula to every one of their passengers and proclaiming it by the arrangements at their stations and in their trains. The rigidity began to seize on the passenger from the moment he or she purchased a ticket.

The British railways set out then with two classes, but they very soon added a third to them, cheaper than the other two, and made some experiments with a fourth, not always successfully: the Chester & Birkenhead company, having taken it up, discontinued it in 1842.[33] In 1844 there came to be a fifth class, called 'Parliamentary' because the accommodation and running of the trains carrying passengers at a standard fare of a penny a mile were regulated by Act of Parliament. In the course of the next 20 years two more classes appeared, or at least fares at two new rates came to be charged: 'express', for travelling by the fastest trains, and 'workmen's', for travelling in trains put on to carry men (and presently women) into and out of large towns at the lowest prices of all. By 1864 the

British railways might therefore be held to exemplify a seven-class system.

Railway companies had developed the concept of class to a high degree, but they soon started to retreat from this position. Fourth class disappeared in Britain in the 1870s, and the practice of charging express fares declined, until by 1882 it was not to be found anywhere except in the extreme southeastern corner of the country.

From the late 1860s onwards a new tendency was appearing, much more important than the withdrawal of certain categories of travelling. The number of journeys being made every year in the third class was greater than in either the first or the second – soon indeed in both of these put together – and the margin of difference was growing wider. One of the English companies made two startling decisions in quick succession. The Midland, which had ceased to levy express fares as early as 1859, decided in 1872 to put third-class carriages into every one of its trains, including the fastest. Then, in 1875, it went on to abolish second class altogether throughout its system, lowering its first-class fares a little at the same time, and upholstering the wooden seats in its third-class carriages to the standard of that in the old seconds. Most of the other companies were greatly incensed by these decisions. But as far as the first decision was concerned, they were obliged, however little they liked it, to follow suit wherever their services and the Midland's competed, for example between London and Manchester, Leeds and Sheffield. With regard to the withdrawal of second class, they were under no such compulsion, and the Midland's policy was not widely adopted until 1891-93, when second class disappeared throughout Scotland and from several large companies' systems in England (except in certain kinds of services, mainly suburban). The rest had all followed suit by 1912, except for the London & South Western and the South Eastern & Chatham, which fell into line in 1918 and 1923, respectively.

On the mainland of Europe things went differently. In the late 1880s third-class passengers were admitted to only 7 per cent of the express trains in Switzerland, to just over a quarter of those in France, to less than half those in Austria-Hungary, to 59 per cent in Belgium, to 72 per cent in North Germany and to 81 per cent in Holland. In Great Britain the percentage by that time was 93.[34] By 1914 third-class passengers, though they were still excluded from a good many international expresses, were admitted to all but quite a small number running wholly within the national boundaries of states in mainland Europe. However, express supplements were payable in almost every country (some of them very substantial, and falling most heavily on third-class passengers); and the seating in third-class carriages nearly always comprised bare wooden boards with bare wooden backs. In comfort, there could be no comparison between a long third-class journey made in Germany and in Britain. Moreover, no other European country went over to an entirely two-class system, as Britain had done, before 1945.

Today, passengers travelling at the cheapest rates are admitted to almost every European train, and the seating has come to be not much different from that in first-class vehicles. But it has taken a long time to reach this result.

Our judgement on these matters might perhaps run something like this. The British railways experimented, and at some points they fumbled in their efforts to achieve a sensible relationship between the facilities they provided for passengers in different classes. However, they quickly came to adopt arrangements that were a great deal more favourable to third-class passengers than those anywhere else in Europe, and the changes reviewed above had resulted, before the end of the nineteenth century, in a perfectly clear democratisation of travel in Britain, corresponding quite closely to the advance towards democracy to be seen in its politics.

This does not, of course, mean that the British railways' arrangements were necessarily right. In economic terms they were certainly questionable. I hope that in the future a careful effort will be made to analyse them: statistically as figures, and then in terms of their profits, drawbacks, disadvantages, and side-effects.

That is the last of the topics that I want to discuss in order to illustrate the intimacy of the connection between the railways and the whole community of Great Britain. I should like to direct your attention to a great source of information on some of these matters which has scarcely been exploited: the railways' working timetables and the special notices that were issued to supplement them. These were all printed, but they were never published. They were compiled for the use of the companies' servants only, to guide those who were responsible for the trains' progress – drivers and firemen, guards, signalmen, station staff – through their task of getting the trains to their destinations. How much time was allowed on each journey for the shunting work that goods trains had to be ready to perform in the yards of the stations they stopped at? What was to happen if a train was likely to run out of its course or for some reason had to be re-timed?

Only the passenger trains appear in the public timetables. In the working timetables they can be seen side by side – in competition, I sometimes feel – with other trains of all kinds: fast and slow freight trains, those carrying mail and newspapers, milk and other perishable goods. Here, too, we can see the movements of light engines and empty rolling stock, all of which had to be slotted into their places in and out of the paths of revenue-earning trains.

The special notices indicate the very wide range of exceptional services that railways might be called on to render: to take a theatrical company or a circus on tour, for instance, or to take any kind of summer excursion, whether as a treat for a Sunday-school or as a works outing. There will never again be such a picture of the movement of passengers and freight over large tracts of the country at single moments of time.

But a caution must be given here. The numbers of working timetables and special notices that have survived are small in relation to the numbers that were actually produced. These books and pamphlets were all throw-aways. On many railways each of them bore the distinct instruction that the previous one was to be destroyed. The Highland company spelt this out even more precisely: as soon as one of its working timetables ceased to be current, it was to be 'torn up for lavatory use'.[35]

There is no complete set of working timetables and notices for any British company. The largest collection is in the Public Record Office at Kew; but it contains, for example, no working timetables for such important companies as the Lancashire & Yorkshire or the Great Central. There is a good collection at York in the library of the National Railway Museum; it is much smaller than that at Kew, but is still being extended. A higher proportion of these timetables and notices is preserved in the Scottish Record Office in Edinburgh than at Kew for the English companies. But, although this literature is fragmentary and incomplete, it can be immensely valuable to anyone interested in the history of railways. The railway holdings of the Scottish Record Office are witness to the better evidence for the history of railways in Scotland than remains for other parts of the UK. I should like to add that, in some of the matters I have been dis-

cussing today, recent work bearing on the history of Scottish railways has been more widely informative than that dealing with those in England or Wales. C J A Robertson's *Origins of the Scottish Railway System* is the fullest, the best-informed and most richly documented study that we have of the history of railways in any part of Great Britain. It covers the years 1722-1844, and, when it was published 10 years ago, we looked forward to seeing the work continued to become a complete history of railways in that country of a quality that few other countries anywhere could equal. But alas, the author was overtaken by grave illness, and he died in December 1992. His book will be an enduring monument to his memory.

It is in Scotland, too, that an extended study of the development of tourism is being carried forward, by Alastair Durie in the University of Glasgow. We all know that we have a tourist industry today that is very important to the British economy. No one has ever investigated its emergence carefully and comprehensively before. Durie's work on Scottish tourism will, I know, demonstrate the very large part that the railways played in tourism, first in conjunction with travel agents and then on their own account. When it is published – in three or four years' time, I hope – it will be a large-scale illustration of one part of my theme: the close, the intimate involvement that the railways came to develop with the whole life of the country they served.

I will return for a moment, in conclusion, to the government. We have observed, so far, only the distance that was maintained between it and the railways in Britain. But there were occasions when the government turned directly to the railways for help. Sometimes it was for the purpose of meeting civil disorder: riots at Manchester in 1842 or (improbably) at Strome Ferry in 1883, for instance. The government asked for troops or police to be transported to the seat of trouble at once. There may be differing views about the rightness of the government's action in repressing these disturbances as it did. But it *was* the government, this was its conception of good order, and it called on the railways for aid in enforcing it. They did what they were asked to do, promptly and exactly. When it came to the national emergencies of war, they did the same, on a far greater scale: in conveying soldiers to South Africa in 1899-1901 through Southampton, and the British Expeditionary Force through the same port in 1914; in taking evacuated children and their families away from London and the great cities in 1939; in bringing back troops making their way from Dunkirk to any part of the southeast coast that they could reach in 1940; in carrying out the greatest task of all, Operation Overlord, in 1944.

The British railways were not devised with any such purposes in mind. They were instruments of private profit. But their work completely tran-

scended that original purpose. They quickly became, and then they remained for the best part of a century, the huge instrument on which the greater part of the inland transport system turned. The full extent of the debt that the country owed to its railways has never been computed; some parts of it will always remain hidden from us now. I hope this paper has done a little to stimulate and encourage further exploration.

Notes and references

1   Lee, C E, 'Passenger Class Distinctions', *Railway Gazette* (1946), p4

2   Grierson, J, *Railway Rates: English and Foreign* (London, 1886), pp120-21

3   Foxwell, E, and Farrer, T C, *Express Trains English and Foreign* (London: Smith Elder, 1889), pp30-31

4   Minot, R J, *Railway Travel in England and America* (Boston, 1880), p14

5   See Alderman, G, *The Railway Interest* (Leicester: Leicester University Press, 1973).

6   Hanham, H J, *Elections and Party Management* (London: Longman, 1959), pp59-62

7   Patterson, A T, *History of Southampton* (Southampton: Southampton Record Society, 1966-75), II, pp167-69

8   Mack, E C, and Armytage, W, *Thomas Hughes* (London: Benn, 1952), pp221-22

9   Robbins, M, *Points and Signals* (London: Allen & Unwin, 1967), pp76-77

10 *Victoria History of Shropshire* (Oxford: Oxford University Press, 1979), III, pp229-30

11 Sheffield Public Library, Wh M 418 (1868)

12 Hanham, H J, *Elections and Party Management*, pp85-90

13 Lloyd, T, *The General Election of 1880* (Oxford: Oxford University Press, 1968), p118

14 See Chaloner, W H, *The Social and Economic Development of Crewe* (Manchester: Manchester University Press, 1950), chp 6.

15 Cowper, W, *Poetical Works*, ed by H S Milford (Oxford: Oxford University Press, 1954), 4th edn, p346

16 Tomlinson, W W, *The North Eastern Railway* (Newcastle: Andrew Reid, 1915), p400

17 *Parliamentary Papers* (1909), LXVII, p394; *Parliamentary Papers* (1910), LVII, pp65, 168, 416

18 See Simmons, J, *The Victorian Railway* (London: Thames & Hudson, 1991), p395, note 77.

19 *Le Petit Robert*, under *week-end* and *semaine*

20 Simmons, J, *The Railway in Town and Country* (Newton Abbot: David & Charles, 1986), p44

21 Fraser-Stephen, E, *Two Centuries in the London Coal Trade* (London: Charringtons, 1952), pp85-7

22 Ellis, C D B, *Centenary Book of Joseph Ellis Ltd* (Leicester, 1939), pp31-32, and *Centenary Book of Ellis & Everard Ltd* (Leicester, 1946), pp5-12

23 Parry, E, *Railway Companion from Chester to Shrewsbury* (Chester, 1849), p11

24 Armstrong, A, *Stability and Change in an English Country Town* (Cambridge: Cambridge University Press, 1974), pp41-42

25 Mannix and Whellan, *History, Gazetteer and Directory of Cumberland* (Beverley, 1847), p40

26 Mewburn, F, *The Larchfield Diary* (1876), p141

27 Some details of these lines are given in Croughton, G, Kidner, R W, and Young, A, *Private and Untimetabled Railway Stations* (Oxford: Oakwood Press, 1982), and in Turner, J H, *The London Brighton & South Coast Railway* (London, Batsford, 1977-79), III, p169. The Bangour hospital is fully and well described by C McWilliam, with a reference to its railway, in *The Buildings of Scotland: Lothian* (London: Penguin Books, 1978), pp90-92.

28 Erichsen, J E, *On Railway and Other Injuries of the Nervous System* (London, 1866), p46

29 Webster, N W, *Britain's First Trunk Line* (London: Adams & Dart, 1972), p105

30 *Oxford English Dictionary*, under 'class' and 'first-class'

31 Fitzgerald, R S, *Liverpool Road Station,*

Manchester (Manchester: Manchester University Press, 1980)

32 Whishaw, F, *The Railways of Great Britain* (London: Weale, 1842), 2nd edn, pp116, 374

33 *Journal of the Royal Statistical Society*, 8 (1849), p222

34 Foxwell, E, and Farrer, T C, *Express Trains English and Foreign*, p95

35 Scottish Record Office, BR/TT(S)/60/17, p42

American railroads and urban promotion

H Roger Grant

During its first century the American railroad enterprise spawned literally thousands of villages, towns and cities throughout the country. Atlanta, Georgia; Creston, Iowa; De Smet, South Dakota; Hooker, Oklahoma; Hornell, New York; Hope, Arkansas; Las Vegas, Nevada; Miami, Florida; West Chicago, Illinois; Willard, Ohio; Port Arthur, Texas; and Tacoma, Washington, for example, were all railroad-sponsored births. While sometimes considered to be largely a regional or western phenomenon, urban promotion by railroads occurred nationwide. Carriers needed centres of population to generate freight, express and passenger business, and used towns for operational, equipment-repair and locomotive-refuelling purposes.[1]

Hundreds of communities existed prior to the coming of the iron horse, yet this triumph of technology directly affected even established places. Those localities that attracted railroads prospered; occasionally some grew in a spectacular fashion; Chicago, Kansas City and Los Angeles illustrate great railway-created metropolises. Settlements which developed as a result of the railway reflected the fact that trains reduced the cost, time and stress of travel much more than either improved roadways or waterways.

Communities which failed to attract a railroad usually faced a bleak future. Take the case of two villages, Morris and Washington, in rural Connecticut whose founders had located them on hilltops in characteristic Puritan fashion. When the Shepaug Railroad, a later component of the New York, New Haven & Hartford, built its 32-mile-long line between Hawleyville and Litchfield in the early 1870s, promoters decided not to serve directly either Morris or Washington because of their lofty elevations. Wishing to minimise construction costs, the railway company exploited the gentle gradients of nearby valleys. How did residents of Morris and Washington respond to the Shepaug's strategy? These townsfolk made adjustments in a typical manner. While Morris remained on the steep hill east of the Shepaug depot, some of its commercial interests acquired trackside locations for their businesses. Washington, too, continued where it had always been, but a new settlement, appropriately called Washington Depot, developed along the track several miles north of the original townsite. Predictably, Morris and Washington remained somnolent villages; neighbouring communities, like Danbury and Waterbury, with excellent railroad services into the heart of the town, prospered.[2]

While the Shepaug caused only minor adjustments to patterns of urban settlement when it crossed an established part of southern New England, other railroads in the east produced wholly new communities. While the 13 original states had long passed through their frontier stage by the second quarter of the nineteenth century, there remained lightly populated areas that the railroads could develop. The presence of an 'iron highway' gave rise to settlements, some of which grew into more than a depot, a general store and a few houses. These larger places were commonly the site of a railroad junction, an administrative centre or a workshop facility.

A good illustration of the 'railroad town' is Hornell, New York. Located in one of the state's rugged 'Southern Tier' counties, this community emerged with the arrival of the New York & Erie (Erie) Rail Road in the middle of the century, won incorporation as a village in 1852, and became a city in 1888. Like similar places, Hornell hoped to become an important transportation centre, and it did. The town began to thrive after the Erie built a branch line to Buffalo which connected at Hornell with its original 447-mile route between the Hudson River and Lake Erie. Hornell could soon claim more than a strategic location; it subsequently served as headquarters of an operating division ('three divisions of the Erie end and begin here') and as a centre for repairing equipment. It also sported an assortment of water, coal and sand facilities. By the 1890s the community had 13,000 residents who worked not only for the railroad but also in glass, shoe, silk and other industries. This 'creation of the Erie' had in addition '11 churches; 4 newspapers; 5 schools; 2 banks; 6 hotels; [and a] sanatorium'.[3]

As railroads pushed beyond the trans-

Appalachian west, a zone of transition developed. This meant that while serving many existing communities, some of which owed their vitality to locations on lakes, rivers, canals and improved roadways, railroads also created numerous urban places. The latter, in fact, surpassed the former in substantial numbers.

The state of Illinois nicely depicts the presence of this zone of transition. Town promotion before 1850 had benefitted from access to Lake Michigan, the Illinois, Mississippi and Ohio rivers and the Illinois & Michigan Canal, and, to a lesser degree, the National Road. Settlements with these geographical advantages took root much more deeply than those laid out by promoters without much thought to felicitous locations. Admittedly, except for Chicago, 'Nature's Metropolis', the state's communities did not seem destined for greatness. The federal census of 1850 enumerated only four urban places with populations in excess of 5000: Chicago (29,963), Quincy (6902), Galena (6004) and Peoria (5095).[4]

But the railroads radically transformed Illinois. They brought in tens of thousands of settlers, energised commerce and industry, and produced an enormously altered urban landscape of 'Beautiful Suburban Towns' and 'Picturesque Communities'. The Chicago & North Western Railway, for one, aggressively promoted communities along its evolving system. The company focused on the suburbs along Chicago's 'North Shore' area, most of which owed their existence to a predecessor company, the Milwaukee & Chicago Railroad, which opened in the 1850s. Evanston, Wilmette, Kenilworth, Glencoe, Highland Park, Lake Forest, Lake Bluff and Waukegan evolved into true 'steamcar' suburbs.[5]

Once the process of railroad and town development began, the impact took various forms. Growing communities along these Prairie State rail lines usually drained commerce and population from 'inland' or 'interior' settlements without access to railroads, causing some of them to disappear. By the late nineteenth century Chicago, with more than a million residents, could rightfully claim to be America's rail Mecca, for nearly all of its 24 railroads were major trunk lines. Moreover, scores of Illinois communities had populations exceeding 5000 and several railroads. Many of these towns traced their origins directly to the iron horse. This was particularly evident when railroads established their division or terminal points, usually spaced at regular intervals. Places like Centralia, Decatur,

Effingham, Galesburg, Savanna, Stockton and West Chicago were either wholly launched by carriers or grew enormously because of their presence.[6]

The technique of creating communities began with the first railroads and evolved into a *direct* promotional role by the railway companies or by related firms. While the activities of the pioneer Illinois Central Railroad have been chronicled in Paul Wallace Gates's classic study, *The Illinois Central Railroad and its Colonization Work* (1934), the story was repeated many times in the zones of transition and throughout the trans-Mississippi west. Indeed, the actions of the Illinois Central and an allied land company served as a prototype for many carriers. Railroads large and small, from the Northern Pacific to the Quanah, Acme & Pacific, employed variations of the Illinois Central's approach to town promotion.[7]

The Illinois Central possessed several unusual characteristics, including its degree of federal support, vast length and a north-south ('wrong-way') main line, but its relationship to on-line communities differed drastically from other railroads. The construction of tracks from Galena, the thriving lead-mining centre in the northwestern corner of Illinois, to Cairo, near the confluence of the Ohio and Mississippi rivers, followed soon after the company received its charter in 1851. The railroad decided to build a 'Chicago Branch' between Lake Michigan and the main line at Centralia (named for the railroad). The 252-mile appendage soon eclipsed the Galena segment, and by the late 1850s became the primary focus of the company's town promotion efforts.[8]

The Illinois Central could not establish towns on or near its routes because of a charter provision. This legal impediment, however, failed to prevent well-positioned officials from exploiting the financial opportunities offered by urban development. Several directors of the railroad and the engineer who supervised construction of the line organised the Associates Land Company to acquire public lands along the proposed railroad for town promotion purposes. When the Chicago Branch was projected, there were only three settlements along the route. Twenty years later there were 28 communities, 13 of which had been laid out and promoted by the land company.[9]

The methods employed by the Associates were wholly practical. The group gave the Illinois Central land for depots, yards and other facilities. When prospective buyers of town lots inspected the land company's offerings, either in person or on paper, they discovered towns laid out to a standard plan. Streets ran at right angles: east-to-west avenues were named for trees and north-to-south streets were numbered sequentially. The parcels nearest the depot and the railroad corridor commanded the highest prices, while 'out-lots', furthest from the tracks, were the least expensive.[10]

Obviously, the labours of the Associates would have aided the Illinois Central. Companies like this Chicago-based railroad encountered enormous expenses. For one thing, the army of employees hired during the Age of Steam meant a massive payroll commitment. Carriers had to fill their freight cars and passenger coaches if they were to be economically viable. Ideally, increased traffic from burgeoning communities would have covered fixed costs and generated interest for bondholders and dividends for stockholders.

However, the ownership of lands for towns along the right-of-way could also benefit those intimately involved with such ventures. The economics were straightforward: creation of communities permitted acquisitive individuals to obtain a greater share of the profits from heightened real-estate values. More money could be made by selling town lots than by peddling larger tracts outside urban areas. Although the advent of the railroad might have boosted the price of an acre of farm land from several dollars to 10 or 20 dollars per acre, a small acreage sold as commercial and residential parcels frequently yielded thousands of dollars. No wonder then that railroad leaders pushed hard for the success of fledgling settlements in which they shared the profits. As Arthur E Stilwell, founder of the Kansas City Southern and the Kansas City, Mexico & Orient railroads, recalled in an autobiographical sketch,

The buying of townsites, laying them out, naming the principal streets after the directors of the road or my friends, and booming these newly found communities as desirable places for people to locate, constituted no small part of my work.

Stilwell's most notable venture, Port Arthur, Texas, the southern terminus of his Kansas City Southern, originally the Kansas City, Pittsburg & Gulf, stemmed from the formation in 1895 of the Port Arthur Townsite and Land Company and the Port Arthur Townsite Company, in which he, of course, held a sizeable interest.[11]

The model for converting empty lands at trackside into townsites in a rational and profitable fashion, developed by the Associates shortly after mid-century, continued for decades. The efforts of Arthur Stilwell attest to the persistence of this railroad official/land developer arrangement. When railroads pushed beyond the zone of transition into the largely unsettled west or even into parts of the Florida peninsula, mostly between the 1860s and the 1910s, their townsite opportunities soared.

The saga of the Minneapolis, St Paul & Sault Ste Marie Railroad ('Soo Line') extending through a sparsely settled section of North Dakota demonstrates the grandness of the town-building phenomenon. By the turn of the century this company was well established in both the upper Mississippi River valley and the northern plains. The Soo Line served North Dakota, a state since 1889, but an area with large, undeveloped parts. Its tallgrass prairies resembled the central plains at the time when the Union Pacific and Kansas Pacific pushed toward the Rocky Mountains in the decade following the American Civil War.

Rapid development occurred in North Dakota early in the twentieth century, however, and publicly and privately financed myth-makers boomed the state as an 'empire in the making'. Country newspaper editors claimed that their hometowns 'were taking on metropolitan airs'. Settlers often ignored earlier negative comments about the state, and particularly its western part; the 'hell with the fires out' description was hardly apt during this expansive time.[12]

Following the example of its competitors, the Great Northern and the Northern Pacific, the Soo Line commonly constructed lines ahead of major settlement. When the company completed its 212-mile 'Wheat Line' between Thief River Falls, Minnesota, and Kenmare, North Dakota, in 1905, it energetically broadcast a plethora of urban opportunities. A typical advertisement proclaimed:

27 New Towns, Hustling, Hurrying, Enterprising Commercial Centers now open to the Merchant and Investor in Minnesota and North Dakota. Read the Names: Viking, Radium, Alvarado, Oslo, Medford, Lankin, Adams, Fairdale, Nekoma, Loma, Alsen, Calio, Egeland, Brumbaugh, Armourdale, Mylo, Rolette, Overly, Gardenia, Kramer, Russell, Eckman, Hurd, Grano, Tolley, Coleharbor, Garrison. These towns will all be important commercial points, and offer exceptional opportunities to those desiring business locations.[13]

Rather than form a subsidiary for town promotion,

the Soo Line preferred to work with private town development firms. In the case of the Wheat Line, it continued an affiliation with the Minnesota Loan & Trust Company. This Minneapolis-based organisation apparently had no direct financial relationship with the railroad's officials and directors. The Soo Line employed its own townsite agent, however, who co-ordinated activities within the firm. Along the new western extension towns were laid out *before* the trackage was installed; earlier, the opposite approach had been used. The *Minneapolis Times* explained that the altered policy 'enabl[ed] business men to get located and have their buildings up and stocks in readiness for the heavy fall business, when the construction crews arrive'.[14]

While the financial relationship between the Soo Line and the Minnesota Loan & Trust Company is sketchy, it is obvious that the railroad wished to maximise traffic along the Thief River Falls to Kenmare extension. Through its town promotion efforts, the railroad believed that it could create trading patterns resulting in increased business. This was critical, as the Great Northern, a powerful and aggressive rival, was also building in the vicinity.[15]

The way in which the Soo Line handled town promotion suggests that railroads varied their methods depending upon the territory and the competition; there was no single blueprint that the carriers slavishly followed and examples of differing approaches abound.

One railroad that exemplifies the flexible nature of town promotion was the Chicago Great Western Railway (CGW), the 'Maple Leaf Route'. Built largely during the 1880s, this railroad fashioned its Midwestern network of lines relatively late; several other trunk roads were already entrenched in the nation's mid-section. The CGW faced more than stiff competition between its principal terminals of St Paul, Chicago and Kansas City. Because it crossed a heavily settled territory, there were limited opportunities for community building. Nevertheless, the railroad's arrival sparked more than a score of new settlements in northwestern Illinois, southern Iowa and northwestern Missouri.[16] (Plate 1)

The first strategy of town building used by the CGW differed noticeably from that later employed when it built from Fort Dodge, Iowa, to Omaha, Nebraska. As soon as trains rolled between St Paul and Chicago, and later into St Joseph and Kansas City, Missouri, the company watched property owners and speculators subdivide agricultural land

on their own along the line into town lots. Although the CGW did not bother to select specific sites, it encouraged promoters to develop communities no farther than 10 miles apart.[17]

Construction of the Des Moines, Iowa, to St Joseph, Missouri, segment in 1887 and 1888 illustrates the CGW's initial forays into urban development. When the trackage opened, no important towns, except Savannah, seat of Andrew County, Missouri, were served. This seemingly foolish strategy resulted from several factors. Rough terrain explains why several county-seat communities were missed. The railroad also wished to avoid direct confrontation with competitors. The company penetrated what the Chicago, Burlington & Quincy Railroad (CB&Q) considered to be its rightful sphere of influence. The CB&Q wanted to protect its local monopolies; in fact, this vindictive rival temporarily blocked the CGW's entry into St Joseph. Another explanation is cost. Management understood that if a community failed to grant adequate concessions or subsidies, the cost of real-estate acquisitions might reach ruinous levels. Apparently financial inducements were not forthcoming from the larger communities. A final consideration, perhaps foremost in the builders' minds, was the notion that their line might ultimately benefit by *avoiding* established places. Since horse-drawn conveyances and poor-quality roads limited the range of travellers, alert merchants and their rural clientele would certainly have gravitated toward a new rail artery. Once established, these places would have depended upon the railroad company for most of their transportation needs. And this happened; more than a dozen villages appeared along the 158-mile stretch of track.[18] (Plate 2)

The financial relationship, if any, between CGW management and railroad-spawned communities prior to the turn of the century is unknown. A few officials may have acquired rural lands that eventually became town lots; perhaps, too, they tipped off friends about investment prospects. Since no company townsite affiliate emerged, the gestation process of town promotion rested with outside interests. While the rail leaders possibly missed chances for personal gain, the steady, even rapid expansion of a majority of these 'up-and-coming'

Plate 1 (right). Chicago Great Western Railway map, c1940. (H Roger Grant collection)

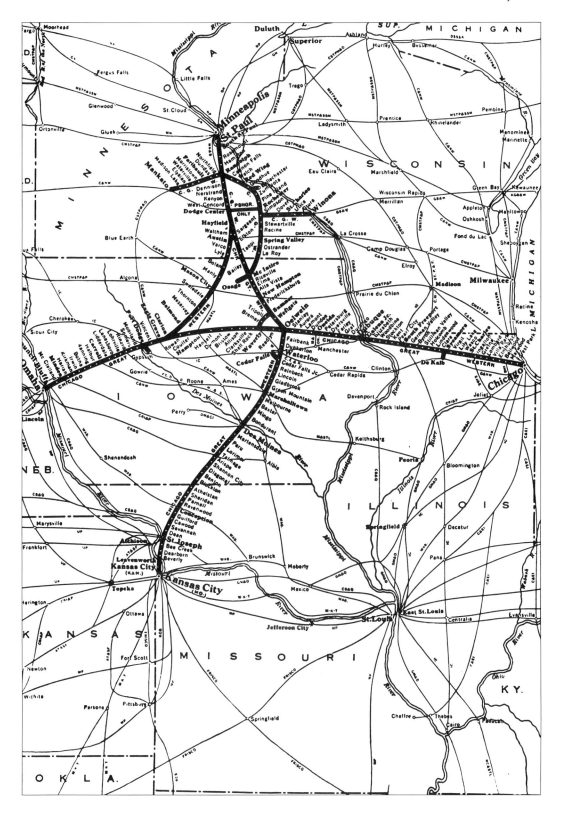

towns must have pleased them; after all, urban growth meant increased traffic and presumably greater corporate earnings.

Not all backers of the Maple Leaf Route ignored the potential for personal and corporate profits from land development. Shortly after the road opened, its founder, A B Stickney, and several of his business associates, purchased a large tract of virgin land five miles south of St Paul, Minnesota, and speedily erected a sprawling stockyard. Soon a meat-packing plant appeared nearby, and both facilities flourished. The complex, in fact, might be considered a forerunner of the latter-day industrial park.[19]

Severe economic dislocations caused by the financial panic of 1893 delayed expansion of the CGW. But, as prosperity gradually returned, rumours spread that the company planned to absorb several short lines and enter new rail centres. Such tales had validity. The company acquired additional properties, including the 88-mile Mason City & Fort Dodge Railroad. With the latter under CGW control after 1901, plans emerged to extend

it into both Sioux City, Iowa, and Omaha, Nebraska. In the early months of the new century, survey crews located possible routes. Although cost considerations mostly explain why Sioux City was never reached, construction of an 'airline' or direct route between Fort Dodge, Iowa, and Omaha, a distance of 133 miles, began in August 1901. The line opened 27 months later.[20]

The decision to make the CGW an airline between Fort Dodge and Omaha meant that a number of well-established communities would be missed. Only three county-seat towns would be served. One survey had followed a path that would have passed through a host of bustling places and theoretically offered greater opportunities for freight and especially passenger traffic.[21] The rejection of the 'established town' route occurred for reasons other than its somewhat longer length. As the backers knew, choosing existing communities often increased construction costs dramatically, a factor that partially explains the avoidance of most existing settlements when the St Joseph line was selected. Admittedly, local subsidies might have

Plate 2. A Chicago Great Western freight train pauses at the station in Peru, Iowa, about 1920. The town, called Peru by the railroad and East Peru by the residents, was a few miles from the pre-railroad settlement of Peru. When the company built its Des Moines, Iowa, to St Joseph, Missouri, extension in the late 1880s, residents relocated to trackside. (H Roger Grant collection)

developed, but the expense of acquiring houses and businesses escalated construction costs.[22]

Areas devoid of settlements existed along the Omaha extension, and the CGW launched the Iowa Townsite Company (ITC) to create the required on-line communities. Constituted on 10 July 1901, under the laws of Minnesota, with a modest $10,000 of capital stock, this venture consisted of five organisers, all Stickney lieutenants. The railroad itself later acquired the securities. According to the ITC's charter,

Its business shall be the buying, owning, improving, selling, and dealing in lands ..., and laying out townsites, subdividing lands into town lots, streets and alleys, and improving the same, and selling such lots ....[23]

These functions were hardly unusual. (Plate 3)

As soon as the CGW fixed the route to Omaha, townsite personnel scoured the countryside for choice locations. Nothing was to be left to chance. A newspaper account noted, 'The old system of letting settlements spring up here and there wherever [there] happened to be an oasis on the desert has been sidetracked, forever, for a more scientific method.' The ITC considered several specific matters in its allegedly 'scientific' approach to community making. An acceptable site had to abut a prosperous farming area; it had to be not too close to established places; and it had to be at the right 'frequency' along the route, for stations were to be at least five miles apart. Whenever the firm picked a location, it acquired from 40 to 400 acres and then laid out streets and made necessary improvements. These usually included concrete pavements and possibly a water and sewerage system. The major thoroughfare, the one extending from the depot through the heart of the commercial district, might have been surfaced with crushed stone or paved with brick.[24] (Plate 4)

The first and most successful of the Maple Leaf Route's new communities along the Omaha extension was Lanesboro, in northeastern Carroll County. This site seemed especially promising

Plate 3. Wightman, Iowa, was one of several towns established by the Iowa Townsite Company when the Chicago Great Western built its Omaha extension. Located in Calhoun County, this community never became much more than a sleepy hamlet. Since housing was limited, the company included apartment space in the depot. The laundry of the agent's family flaps in the breeze in this c1912 photograph. (H Roger Grant collection)

Plate 4. This c1910 view of Rinard, Iowa (Calhoun County), reveals the commercial district of one of the new communities established in a 'scientific' fashion by the Iowa Townsite Company early in the century. (H Roger Grant collection)

since it was the only point in Iowa that lacked urban competition within a 12-mile radius. In fact, the merchants who served the territory realised the potential threat and vigorously objected to the proposal. In March 1902 the ITC purchased 280 acres from farmer George Lane. For the next several months employees prepared the property, mostly conducting surveying and grading work. Since the railroad was to pass on a diagonal, the town was to have its principal business district and an adjoining park parallel to the tracks. The remaining sections were to follow the traditional rectangular grid pattern.[25]

Lanesboro began to take shape by the end of 1904. The ITC filed the town plan with the county recorder on 4 October, and three days later the sale was held. Hundreds flocked to the event. Many believed that 'it will be one of the best new townsites ever offered to the public as a business or residence location', but others came solely out of curiosity. Unlike subsequent townsite auctions, buyers arrived by horse and buggy and farm wagon. The CGW was unable to provide

excursions because crews were still installing track and a mammoth bridge over the Des Moines River near Fort Dodge. The sale followed a set format, for by then the art of town lot disposal was fully developed. After a hearty free lunch served in the undeveloped park, the participants crowded around a large chalkboard that showed lot numbers and locations. (Plate 5) Bidding was brisk for the best commercial properties and active for choice residential lots. The day's events encouraged the organisers: about 90 lots sold at prices ranging from $155 to $340 for businesses and about half that for homes. The ITC also peddled additional parcels, mostly residential, during the following months. Soon this 'beautiful new town site [that] sits like a queen on the magnificent prairie' saw a platoon of carpenters, masons and painters start their assignments. By March 1903 an Oelwein, Iowa, newspaper reported that:

We are in receipt of volume 1, number 1 of the *Lanesboro Journal* ... showing the development of Lanesboro from last October when the site was a prairie without a house

Plate 5. By the early years of the twentieth century town lot sales had become ubiquitous. This photograph, converted into a 'real-photo' postcard, shows a crowd gathered to bid on lots at Polk, Nebraska, on 11 September 1906. Polk developed along the Union Pacific's 112-mile branch from Valley City, Nebraska, to Central City, Nebraska. (H Roger Grant collection)

till the present when it has a newspaper, bank, grain elevators, lumber yards, stores, saloons, school house, and about 500 population.

The paper concluded: 'Another town made by the Chicago Great Western Railway.'[26] (Plate 6)

While Lanesboro emerged as 'one of the prides of the Great Western', the ITC continued its town organising efforts. At the time of the initial lot auction, the firm announced through the regional press and a folder, 'New Town Sites', that it expected to develop nine more places. These 'scientifically selected' localities included Roelyn (Webster County), Rinard and Wightman (Calhoun County), Lidderdale (Carroll County), Magill and Tennant (Shelby County) and Bentley, McClelland and Gilliat (Pottawattamie County). Several town names honoured the CGW's leading English stockholders, for at this time the company relied heavily on foreign investors.[27]

The process of townsite auctions continued. The sales of lots were good and new communities,

which surrounded the railroad corridor, sprang up, promising traffic which was controlled solely by the CGW. Yet, the ITC witnessed one still-birth: Magill. This community appeared in Shelby County, six miles southwest of Tennant and four miles northeast of Minden. While planned as the tenth town, Magill's *raison d'être* seems to have been as much for a place to service helper locomotives which assisted heavy freight trains over Tennant Hill. The least successful of the new towns, Magill never sported much more than a depot, water tank, grain elevator and stock pens. Probably the place was too close to Minden, and conceivably, too, it failed to attract the energetic people so necessary for urban growth.[28]

The work of the ITC is an example of the ubiquitous town promotion ventures in which railroads had engaged for decades. Rail transport made community development deliberate, rather than random, in thousands of instances. Urban builders sought orderly, ideally permanent development along their lines, especially when tracks preceded

Plate 6. Lanesboro, Iowa, the most successful of the new towns launched by the Iowa Townsite Company, received a brick rather than wooden depot, an indication of the faith held by the railroad in this Carroll County location. (H Roger Grant collection)

settlers. While communities started along the CGW's Omaha extension failed to become 'New Chicagos', they had been situated in what their founders considered was a logical, even scientific fashion. The fact that railroads permanently altered the map of the US (and for that matter the world) is obvious. Contemporaries often charged that this town-making process was designed for promoters. What happened in the west, especially after the Civil War, they said, was merely another example of greed and corruption. Admittedly, a cosy relationship existed between some railroad officials and townsite schemes. The activities of the Associates and Arthur Stilwell reveal that tie and it is very likely that some nefarious dealings occurred. But railroad companies regularly encountered enormous costs, and traffic that frequently failed to pay expenses. Bonds, commonly sold at a deep discount, and stock prices therefore remained low. If additional income were generated through sales of town lots, the company financial picture improved.

What should be remembered is that railroads demanded conveniently located stations. Companies, for one thing, required appropriately spaced terminals and repair facilities. While some trains during the era of town creation moved at what contemporaries considered to be breath-taking speeds – 'ballast-scorching' was the popular phrase – in reality, they travelled slowly by present-day standards. The Milwaukee, Lake Shore & Western annual report of June 1876 informed stockholders that: 'The highest speed allowed Express Trains [is] 35 miles per hour; Schedule speed of Express Trains [is] 15 miles per hour; [and] Schedule speed of Freight Trains [is] 12 miles per hour.' If train crews worked 10 or 12 hours in a day, they experienced difficulty journeying more than 100 miles. That distance became a standard length between crew-change points. No wonder these railroad towns developed in a predictable manner. Take the main stem of the Union Pacific across Wyoming: the average distance between each of the terminals, Cheyenne, Laramie, Rawlings, Green River and

Evanston, was 102 miles. Repair and major refuelling and servicing facilities were typically part of these regularly spaced installations.[29]

Much more closely placed stations also provided railroads with the necessary operational facilities. In the era of train orders by telegraph, a company needed agents located every few miles in order to handle 'meets' safely and efficiently. Moreover, water tanks were commonly installed at short intervals to satisfy thirsty steam locomotives. While some of these 'tank towns' resembled Magill, Iowa, more substantial communities sometimes developed around these vital railroad structures.

Residents, too, benefitted from the plethora of communities born of rail transport. With handy access to the rails, they paid lower shipping rates; settlers in places that lacked rail access encountered more expense since they had to rely on overland drayage. Obviously, too, trackside patrons profited from the speed and accessibility of the railroad. The historian John L Stover argues:

When the ... rail network was built to completion in the half-century before World War I, the nation needed every railroad that was constructed ... In a day when the farm wagon was the main mode of transport, closely spaced lines with depots located every few miles made real sense.[30]

Convenience was only part of the story of town creation. Carriers, particularly in the trans-Mississippi west where towns were laid out before settlers arrived, wished to control the trade patterns of the hinterland. They wanted 'their' communities to prosper, and they disliked incursions by competitors. The CGW suffered retaliation when it sliced through the CB&Q's territory, and the Soo Line and Great Northern crossed swords in North Dakota early in the century.

The Great Depression of the 1930s finally ended the process of railroads building towns. Yet the final phase also involved the electric interurban railways. During their heyday these commuter lines spawned communities, mostly in suburban areas.

What occurred in Southern California in the early twentieth century is the premier illustration of the interurban contributing to urban development. The construction of the Atchison, Topeka & Santa Fe and the Southern Pacific railroads had already led to the creation of numerous communities by 1890.

Most were agricultural towns. Such places as Pasadena, Riverside and San Bernardio were founded in anticipation of trans-continental rail connections. Knowing, of course, that the steam railroad had fostered urbanisation in the Los Angeles basin, Henry E Huntington, an experienced railroader and a major beneficiary of the estate of his uncle, Collis P Huntington, a founder of the Southern Pacific, launched the Pacific Electric Railway in 1901. Huntington's interurban and his principal real-estate arm, the Huntington Land and Improvement Company, permanently shaped the greater Los Angeles area. Thousands of individuals flocked to this sun-drenched El Dorado to buy Huntington suburban lots and to build homes. They then travelled to and from work, shopping and recreational sites on the 'Big Red Cars' that sped along the approximately 600 route miles of the Huntington interurban. Alhambra, San Marino and South Pasadena for example, owed their being to the masterful efforts of the creator of the 'Greatest Electric Railway System in the World'.[31]

Communities which had not particularly gained from their steam or electric railroad connections might, nevertheless, develop by default as a result of motorway building. Restricted access, multilane highways, created mostly by the National Defence Highway Act of 1956, significantly affected where people lived and worked. If an interstate was accessible from a community, there might be explosive expansion. But these super highways, unlike waterways and most of all railways, rarely gave rise to new places; Breezewood, Pennsylvania, 'the city of motels', is exceptional. Rather, these thoroughfares caused adjustments and relocations, not all that different from the experiences of Morris and Washington, Connecticut, when the Shepaug Railroad arrived.

Unquestionably, interstate highways altered the face of the country. 'The two-mile strips bordering these huge arteries should incorporate [to form] their own state called Interstate,' comments Linda Nieman in her autobiography, *Boomer: Railroad Memoirs*. 'East of the Rockies they would belong to New York; west would be LA.' While Nieman exaggerates, she correctly perceives that transportation routes continue to affect the geography of the US. Nevertheless, it was the railroad that left the most indelible mark upon the national map.[32]

Notes and references

1 Brown, A T, and Glaab, C N, *A History of Urban America* (New York: Macmillan, 1967), pp107-32

2 Goodwin, L W (interview, 16 May 1992, Northfield, Connecticut); *Poor's Manual of Railroads* (New York: H V Poor, 1887), p106

3 Mott, E H, *Between the Ocean and the Lakes: The Story of Erie* (New York: J S Collins, 1899), p506. The community was called Hornellsville before the turn of the century.

4 Cronon, W, *Nature's Metropolis: Chicago and the Great West* (New York: W W Norton, 1991); *Seventh Census of the United States: 1850* (Washington, DC: Robert Armstrong, 1853), pp703-17

5 *Beautiful Suburban Towns* (Chicago: Chicago & North Western Line, 1904); Ebner, M H, *Creating Chicago's North Shore: A Suburban History* (Chicago: University of Chicago Press, 1988), pp21-42

6 *Report on the Population of the United States at the Eleventh Census: 1890* (Washington, DC: Government Printing Office, 1895), I, pp101-17; *Official Railway Guide for the United States and Canada* (New York: National Railway Publication Company, June 1892), p757

7 Gates, P W, *The Illinois Central Railroad and its Colonization Work* (Cambridge, MA: Harvard University Press, 1934), pp122-32; See Oster, D B, 'The Hannibal and St Joseph Railroad, government and town founding, 1846-1861', *Missouri Historical Review*, 87 (1993), pp403-21; and Hofsommer, D L, *The Quanah Route: A History of the Quanah, Acme & Pacific Railway* (College Station: Texas A&M University Press, 1991), pp27-35

8 Stover, J F, *History of the Illinois Central Railroad* (New York: Macmillan, 1975), pp31-57

9 Gates, P W, *The Illinois Central Railroad and its Colonization Work*, pp122-25

10 Gates, P W, *The Illinois Central Railroad and its Colonization Work*, pp122-25

11 Overton, R C, *Burlington West: A Colonization History of the Burlington Railroad* (Cambridge, MA: Harvard University Press, 1941), pp269-89; Stilwell, A, and Crowell, M R, 'I had a hunch', *Saturday Evening Post*, 200 (1927), p26; Bryant, K L, *Arthur E Stilwell: Promoter with a Hunch* (Nashville: Vanderbilt University Press, 1977), pp98-100

12 Henke, W A, 'Imagery, immigration and the myth of North Dakota', *North Dakota History*, 38 (1971), pp414-500

13 *The Official Guide of the Railways* (New York: National Railway Publication Company, June 1906), p598

14 Hudson, J C, *Plains County Towns* (Minneapolis: University of Minnesota Press, 1985), pp61, 66, 83-84

15 Hudson, J C, 'North Dakota's railway war of 1905', *North Dakota History*, 48 (1981), pp4-19

16 See Grant, H R, *The Corn Belt Route: A History of the Chicago Great Western Railway Company* (DeKalb: Northern Illinois University Press, 1984). The Great Western gave rise to the Illinois communities of Elizabeth, German Valley, Kent, Stockton and Woodbine; Iowa towns of Arispee, Athelstan, Blockton, Diagonal, East Peru, Knowlton, Lorimor and Shannon City; and the Missouri settlements of Parnell, Ravenwood and Sheridan.

17 Grant, H R, 'Seeking the Maple Leaf Route roundhouse', *Missouri Historical Review*, 76 (1982), pp405-20

18 Grant, H R, *The Corn Belt Route*, pp26-27

19 *South St Paul Daily Register* (South St Paul, Minnesota), 6 October 1937, 31 December 1937

20 *Corporate History of the Chicago Great Western Railway Company* (Chicago: Chicago Great Western Railroad, 1920), p23; *Daily Nonpareil* (Council Bluffs, Iowa), 7 November 1903

21 *Messenger* (Fort Dodge, Iowa), 16 May 1901

22 *Herald* (Carroll, Iowa), 7 May 1902; *Daily Nonpareil*, 8 April 1902, 25 June 1902; *Oelwein Register* (Oelwein, Iowa), 1 May 1901

23 'Articles of incorporation of Iowa Townsite Company', State of Minnesota, Office of the Secretary of State, 1901, pp218-19

24 *Messenger*, 2 September 1904

25 *Herald*, 12 February 1902; *Messenger*, 18 July 1901, 4 March 1902

26 'Plat of town of Lanesboro, Carroll County, Iowa', Office of the Carroll County Recorder, Carroll, Iowa, 4 October 1902; *Herald*, 3 September 1902, 8 October 1902; *Dearborn Democrat* (Dearborn, Missouri), 26 September 1902; *Messenger*, 21 January 1903; *Oelwein Register*, 18 March 1903

27 *Messenger*, 1 October 1902, 16 November 1903; *Daily Nonpareil*, 24 December 1902. Three members of the Great Western's London Finance Committee received a town named in their honour: The Rt Hon William Lidderdale, Howard Gilliat and Sir Charles Tennant, Bart.

28 *Ravenwood Gazette* (Ravenwood, Missouri), 28 August, 1903; *Messenger*, 9 September 1903, 11 November 1903, 21 October 1903. The Great Western also became involved in Moorland, Iowa, along the Omaha Extension. This Webster County hamlet near Fort Dodge owed its creation to the arrival of the Des Moines & Fort Dodge Railroad (later the Rock Island and the Minneapolis & St Louis) in 1882, but in August 1902 the Iowa Townsite Company laid out the 'Iowa Townsite Company's Addition' to the north end of the community and adjacent to the soon-to-be-completed line to Omaha. Incorporated officially in 1902, Moorland's population reached 137 by 1910.

29 *First Annual Statement of the Milwaukee, Lake Shore and Western Railway Company* (Milwaukee: J H Yewdale & Sons, 1876), p3; Union Pacific System Timetables, 7 September 1919, pp15-18

30 Stover, J F, *The Life and Decline of the American Railroads* (New York: Oxford University Press, 1970), pp102-12

31 Hofsommer, D L, *The Southern Pacific, 1901-1985* (College Station: Texas A&M University Press, 1986), pp59-60; Fredericks, W B, *Henry E Huntington and the Creation of Southern California* (Columbus: Ohio State University Press, 1992), pp125-26

32 Nieman, L, *Boomer: Railroad Memoirs* (Berkeley: University of California Press, 1990), p214

The archaeology of the world's oldest railway station building

J Patrick Greene

This paper describes the current state of research into a remarkable industrial building, the 1830 warehouse which forms part of the Liverpool & Manchester Railway's terminus in Manchester. It also describes the methodology that has been adopted to restore and adapt the warehouse to perform a new function as part of the Museum of Science and Industry in Manchester. It must be emphasised that this endeavour is one to which many organisations and individuals have contributed. The first is Ron Fitzgerald, whose study of the site was published by the Royal Commission on Historical Monuments in 1980. His book helped to draw attention to the importance of the site, which was saved by Greater Manchester Council from dereliction and the threat of demolition.

The Liverpool & Manchester Railway, which opened on 15 September 1830, had as its chief engineer George Stephenson. Whilst he was involved in the design of civil-engineering structures, others were responsible for buildings. There *was* a grand design for the railway, as embodied in the Liverpool & Manchester Railway Act of 1826. In reality, however, detailed design work occurred whilst construction was under way. Nowhere was this more marked than at the Manchester end of line, where the entire complex was subject to relocation, a series of last-minute decisions, and a building programme of breathtaking speed. The principal elements of the scheme were a bridge across the Irwell, a viaduct on the Manchester bank, a departure station for passengers and a warehouse for merchandise. The following chronology explains the evolution of the scheme and particularly the building of the warehouse, and the break-neck pace of its realisation.

Chronology

1826

5 May	Liverpool & Manchester Railway Bill passed. Terminus to be built in Salford.
June	Construction of line started.

1828

8 December	Land acquired for Manchester terminus.

1829

14 May	Extension of Parliamentary powers to Manchester terminus.
May	Tenders for Irwell bridge invited.
June	Discussions with carrying contractors opened.

1830

January	Contract with New Quay Company to carry goods and provide warehousing not ratified at last minute. Decision of Railway Company to act as carrier instead.
March	Bridge piers and abutments on banks complete.
3 April	Tenders invited for construction of five brick warehouses.
26 April	Contract let to David Bellhouse. Two warehouses to be completed by 31 July; remainder by 15 August.
1 July	First bridge arch centre erected.
19 July	First bridge arch keyed; second centre in place.
24 July	Warehouse nearing completion; whole range roofed.
28 August	First locomotive passed over bridge.
15 September	Railway opened; meal for 1000 in warehouse.

Plate 1. Survey in progress before restoration, 1991.

The speed of construction of the warehouse is astonishing. From the acceptance of the Bellhouse tender on 26 April 1830 it took just 90 days to get the roof on. As we shall see, construction of the roof required the completion of the entire timber frame within the warehouse. The laying of the floorboards could have followed, but these too must have been in place by 15 September 1830 when the opening took place in the completd warehouse. The occasion must have been a subdued affair, for William Huskisson (President of the Board of Trade) had been fatally injured during the ceremonies which opened the railway. The Prime Minister, the Duke of Wellington, had been so discouraged by Huskisson's death and by hostile demonstrations, recalling the Peterloo massacre 11 years earlier, that he remained in his carriage and was taken back to Liverpool. Despite the trauma of what must rate as a contender for the title 'The World's Worst Opening Ceremony' the railway proved an astonishing success.

Notwithstanding the speed of erection of the warehouse, no concessions were made in terms of either appearance or structural quality. Now, 164 years later, it remains virtually as it was built, with its timber frame intact for 80 per cent of its volume. Four of the five bays remain; the fifth was converted into the museum's *National Electricity Gallery* in 1986, with the timber retained for repair to the frame elsewhere in the building. Externally it is a very attractive building, brick-built with major openings framed in gritstone, which was also used for window sills and lintels, door lintels, the cornice, lunettes and copings. The roof covering was slate-torched (ie, plastered) on the underside.

The form and operation of the building has been described by Fitzgerald, who has made a convincing case for identifying Manchester canal warehouses, such as the Grocers', Middle and Merchants' Warehouses on the Bridgewater canal, as the model. In all of these, boats were taken into the building for unloading; at Liverpool Road Station railway wagons were turned through 90 degrees on small turntables and were rolled into the building to be unloaded at wharves. Remains of a turntable base were found when the upper surface of the viaduct was waterproofed in 1984. In addition to unloading at the wharves, goods were moved vertically, either within the building through hatches, or externally between floors using loop holes and hoists. At the rear of the building goods could be lowered from each floor using counter-balanced hand-operated hoists to yard level, from where horse-drawn wagons would take imported materials to mills and factories, and bring finished goods for export. The warehouse can be seen, essentially, as an inland extension of the Liverpool docks, serving the rapidly expanding manufacturing region around Manchester. The crane lofts and many of the hoists survive, as, in places, does one further means of moving goods between floors: wooden chutes lined with sheet iron. Horizontal movement was achieved using trolleys. These caused abrasion on the storey posts that formed part of the timber frame, and where this seriously weakened the structure, individual posts were eventually replaced with cast-iron columns.

The specification for the building was that it should provide storage capacity for 10,000 bales of cotton. It is doubtful, though, whether the basement was ever intended to be used for the storage of cotton, for it would have been too damp. Whilst not actually wet or suffering from floods, moisture would have entered through below-ground walls

and the floor. This explains the use of cast-iron columns here, not, as Fitzgerald suggested, as a precaution against occasional flooding, but to avoid the insidious effect of damp at the point at which the foot of a timber post would have sat on a stone base. The basement could have been used for storing more robust merchandise than cotton, and indeed it appears to have been adapted for the storage of high value material (possibly bonded goods) by attaching iron strips to the underside of the floor above. This would have prevented floor boards being prised up by anyone intent on pilferage.

The iron strips are the sort of detail that has been revealed during the current programme of research into the building. In the early days of the creation of the museum it was assumed that the timber frames would have to be removed and replaced by a concrete floor. We have taken a contrary view, making our priority the retention of the greatest possible extent of the building, and making subservient to this the use to which it is put. The first step was to clear the building, a task carried out by museum staff over a number of weekends in 1991. The next stage was a thorough survey of the

Plate 2. Interior view of ground floor during restoration, 1993. The large timber trestles supported rail tracks for trucks unloading inside the building.

building by the Greater Manchester Archaeology Unit. In parallel with this, a design brief for the restoration was developed by the museum in conjunction with its architects, structural engineers and quantity surveyors. Fund-raising resulted in the accumulation of grants totalling £2.1 million, provided by the European Union, Central Manchester Development Corporation, English Heritage, the Department of National Heritage and the museum itself from visitor income. Restoration started in March 1992 and was completed in June 1993. I will describe some of the results of the research, and how the restoration was tackled.

Building materials and methods of construction are two of the topics that have been examined, and considerable information has been obtained, particularly about the timber. The major structural timbers such as beams, joists and the components of the double queen-post roof trusses, purlins, wall plates and tie beams are European pine (*Pinus silvestris*). Small section timbers such as floor boards and rafters are also pine. The storey posts are of oak. Pads above the storey posts, incorporated to resist the punching shear on the main beams when the building was loaded, are greenheart. The sills of loading bays and other doorways are African oak (*Oldfieldia Africana*), which was first used by the English and French navies two centuries ago, and was traditionally used in buildings for applications which required high levels of strength and resistance to both fungal decay and abrasion.

A remarkable feature is the presence of marks on many of the main pine timbers. More than 650 sets have been recorded. They are not assembly marks (although these do occur on the roof trusses using the usual roman numerals). These marks often consist of a string of characters cut up to 3 mm into the timber, sometimes extending for a length of about 1 m. The longest that we have detected comprises 21 characters. The average length is eight characters incorporating curved as well as straight lines. Some characters can easily be recognised as Arabic numerals. Others appear to be letters and yet others to be Roman numerals.

What is the significance of the timber marks? They are definitely not carpenters' marks; one proof of this is that many have been halved during sawing prior to the assembly of the frame. It is therefore safe to say that they were not inscribed at saw yards in Britain. They must therefore relate to an earlier stage of the trade in timber. In 1830 *Pinus silvestris*

was being imported in large quantities from the Baltic (a term generally used to cover the Scandinavian peninsula as well as the mainland as far as timber is concerned). Oak from Baltic ports was already being imported into east coast English ports in the medieval period. By the late seventeenth century the Royal Navy had begun to use Baltic oak, because of the inadequacy of English forests, with large quantities of plank imported in 1677 for the construction of 30 ships of the line. In the eighteenth century Baltic pine too was being imported. One hundred and fifty thousand loads were rushed from Dantzig for repairs to ships prior to the Battle of Trafalgar. Merchant ships had been using Baltic wood for much longer. The use of Baltic wood as a building material on land followed a similar progression.

The mechanics of the trade were these. Trees were felled during the winter in forests that might be as much as 950 miles away from the coast. The forests of members of the Russian aristocracy were a particular source: merchants (usually Jewish) bought stands of timber, but the estate was responsible for felling. The trees were dragged across snow-covered ground to the rivers, and then floated down in huge rafts to the ports: the Oder to Stettin, the Vistula to Dantzig, the Niemen to Memel, the Duna to Riga and the Neva to St Petersburg. In Scandinavia the principal timber ports were Drammen, Kristiansand, Frederikstad and Göteborg (Gothenburg).

In the port the timber was collected in 'ponds' formed by booms in the river, where it was sorted into types. The best timbers were used for masts. Others were sent to saw mills for conversion into baulks (greater than 200 mm square), planks (between 50 and 200 mm thick), deals (boards) and battens (narrow boards). It could be sawn more cheaply in the Baltic than in England, using wind power (sometimes it was taken to Holland for processing). However, baulks might simply be axe-dressed, which is the form in which our timber seems to have been exported from the Baltic.

English merchants resident in the Baltic ports were responsible for most of the trade in timber to England. They would buy timber from the Jewish merchants, who had brought it from the interior, and would organise the sawing or dressing, expecting a commission of at least three per cent on its value.

To ensure quality, the major ports had 'brackers' who inspected the timber and divided it into three qualities, marking each piece. In Dantzig, K was marked on Crown timber (the best), B (later W) on second quality, and BB (later WW) on third rate. The bracking system was an assurance of quality control; brackers were chosen by the municipality, worked under oath and their word was final. It is highly likely that this is one of the components of the marks visible on the Manchester timbers. Others might indicate the merchant. But what about the numerals? A clue to their significance is provided by practices operating in the London docks earlier this century. There, wood stored in the form of rafts in ponds was measured, and its size marked on each individual timber to facilitate its sale (pricing was per volume of timber). The number of each raft was also inscribed. A special instrument, a scribing iron, was used to leave a shallow groove in the surface. As straight lines were easier to mark with a downward stroke of the scribing iron than curved ones, Roman numerals were used (is this the reason W was eventually adopted in Dantzig instead of B?). In the case of the London marks, they are described in the *Port of London Authority Monthly* in March 1934 as 'a strange variety of Roman lettering incomprehensible to the layman'.[1] The Manchester timber has curved as well as straight lines for the characters. Circular marks could be produced with a more complex scribing iron such as one in the Museum of London collection which has a point and curve-ended blade. It seems highly likely that the marks incorporate measurements. One recurring set of characters is BWh.

If the timber marks were applied in the Baltic ports, rather than at English ports or timber yards, then they should be found outside England. When I was in Copenhagen in early 1992 I sought out a comparable building to put the theory to the test. Gammel Dok, recently restored as an exhibition space by the Danish Architectural Association, was a promising candidate. There, on many of the principal timbers, were marks of a similar kind. Their Baltic origin cannot be doubted. Further confirmation is provided by work carried out by Gavin Simpson of Nottingham University at Lincoln and Ely Cathedrals. Timber marks have been found in timbers used for roof repairs at both cathedrals, including timbers used at Lincoln in about 1840. The cathedral accounts show that deal boards from the Baltic were being used from 1682, and pine baulks from 1762. There is now considerable progress being made with the development of

dendrochronological series for pine from the Baltic, particularly by Gavin Simpson, and by Neils Bonde in Copenhagen. By identifying the different patterns of tree ring development resulting from the different sub-climates of the region from which the timber was extracted, it will not only be possible to use pine timbers for dating, but also to identify the source. Our timbers will be made available for that purpose.

The timbers used on the 1830 warehouse would have been imported into Liverpool and then brought up the Mersey and Irwell Navigation to Manchester. David Bellhouse and Son, the successful tenderers for the warehouse contract, had become by the 1820s the leading timber importers in Manchester, with steam-powered sawmills at Eagle Quay on the Rochdale Canal. There were large timber yards alongside the Irwell, including some established by the Old Quay Company about 200 m from the warehouse site.

Timber was brought by Bellhouse in barges up the river system using, from 1824, a steam tug. The Bellhouse company had, by 1830, become a vertically integrated business. Thus not only did it construct buildings, but it also supplied and manufactured many of the components. As well as timber yards, David Bellhouse acquired brick land in Oxford Road, Manchester, and by the early 1820s, having acquired the Eagle Foundry in 1815, the company was casting its own iron beams for building projects. From 1816 David Bellhouse and his son David became heavily involved in the speculative building of warehouses. They were therefore well placed to tender to build the 1830 warehouse: not only were they experienced in warehouse construction, but they had a very large labour force that could be mobilised for the rapid campaign of building. By 1830 it was the son, David (1792-1866), who managed the company. The father continued to operate as a timber merchant until his death in 1840. In 1821 he had given evidence to the House of Commons Select Committee on Foreign Trade opposing the view that Canadian timber was prone to dry rot. He had a vested interest as he had started importing timber from Canada during the Napoleonic closure of the Baltic ports. He estimated that 85-90 per cent of the timber he used was North American pine for the construction of houses and 'middling' buildings, the remainder being Baltic pine for 'heavy' buildings.

The 1830 warehouse fell into this second category. The Bellhouses may have had an incentive to use timber for the interior structure rather than brick, but this should not necessarily be seen as a vested interest operating. Timber was a perfectly acceptable material for this purpose, and it had the advantage of speed of assembly which must have proved a great advantage under the circumstances in which the warehouse was built. It is unlikely, however, that David Bellhouse was the designer of the warehouse. Ron Fitzgerald suggested that this was Thomas Haigh, a Liverpool builder who undoubtedly designed the two 1831 warehouses. A further piece of evidence, brought to my attention by Keith Falconer, has emerged to support that theory. Haigh was commissioned to design a set of warehouses for the Gloucester docks in 1825 but these were never built. Their appearance is, however, strikingly similar to the 1830 warehouse and quite unlike the three warehouses on the Bridgewater Canal with their round-headed windows. Under the circumstances in which the Railway Company found itself in January 1830 with its decision to act as carrier, what better than to find a local architect with warehouse plans already on the shelf which could be used as the basis for inviting tenders?

The sequence of construction that our study has ascertained was as follows. Firstly, the viaduct was built carrying the railway line 150 m from the Irwell bridge, incorporating a beam bridge over Water Street. The viaduct had to follow a shallow curve to accommodate both the alignments of the Irwell bridge and Liverpool Road. The warehouse was started after the viaduct had been completed. Its structure butts up against the viaduct, and had to be built to a curving plan as a result of the viaduct. The width of each gabled bay of the warehouse corresponded to the width of the viaduct arches, which coincided with the warehouse. The first operation in building the warehouse was to excavate the alluvial silts and clays of the river bank site to a depth of about 7 m. The brick walls, with stepped foundations, were built on to the firm, stable clay, and the foundations for the basement cast-iron columns were constructed in the form of four courses of stepped brick. Set on each brick foundation was a sandstone block 0.6 m deep and 0.9 m square in plan. The top of this sandstone was neatly hollowed to receive the base of the cast-iron column. The major beams of the lowermost timber floor were supported on the cast-iron columns and were set into the walls. They in turn supported joists, on which floorboards were laid. A brick floor

incorporating a shallow drain completed the basement, which was given some light and ventilation by perimeter light wells.

The building, despite the original specification of 'five warehouses' and the split completion date for two and three warehouses, was built as one unit. As the brick outer walls and cross walls rose, so the timber frame had to be completed floor by floor until eventually the roofs were placed on the building. The carpenters' marks on the elements of each truss suggest that they were manufactured and assembled, and then hoisted into position. Finally the roof was slated and torched, incorporating lead gutters in the valleys, and cast-iron downpipes were attached to the north and south faces of the building. With the structure complete, floors could be laid and doors and shutters could be fixed to openings (doubtless starting on the lower floors as their frames were completed, whilst work progressed on the upper floors).

The archaeological survey revealed many details of the operation of the warehouse. One feature was gas lighting. The building seems to have been supplied with gas lighting from the outset: not surprising as there was a gas works only 700 m from the station on Water Street. The network of gas pipes and fittings was recorded. Another feature was stencilled numbers on many of the storey posts, which show that each compartment of each bay was numbered to facilitate the location of stored goods. Some numbers had been repainted several times. There were traces of signs, with legends such as 'Carters and others are warned not to stand under the jiggers' and 'Cotton waste and mineral oil are not to be stored in this warehouse', which also provide some clues as to its operation.

A warehouse in operation for nearly a century and a half would be expected to undergo changes, but many of those that can be seen occurred quite soon after its completion. The erection of offices is one example. An office at the western end of the building at track level is clearly placed where goods entering and leaving the building by rail could be checked. Its construction is timber stud partitioning infilled with brick. The blocking of a doorway in the dividing wall alongside was accompanied by the installation of a glazed window in the loading bay door facing onto the track. The desks used by the clerks, complete with holes for gas lighting, remain in the office. Likewise, an inserted office at yard level was used for supervising goods entering and leaving the site by road.

Changes to the lifting apparatus in the building were introduced soon after its completion. A steam engine was installed in 1831 immediately to the west, alongside Water Street. Blocks of gritstone set into the west wall provide information on how the power was transferred into the building. Sets of four large blocks originally held cast-iron bearing boxes. A scratch mark which describes an arc of 4.3 m diameter on the inner face of the west wall, on the top floor, suggests that a flywheel was part of the original arrangement. The system was subsequently remodelled with a vertical shaft supported on a plinth which survives in the basement alongside the west wall. The power was transmitted within the upper floor of the building by belts (and eventually perhaps by rope drives) to the hoists that had been designed purely for manual operation. The apertures which formerly contained wall boxes for mounting line shafting can be seen in the dividing walls.

Another change which occurred soon after the completion of the building was the construction of a mezzanine floor in bays one, two and three to increase the capacity of the warehouse, probably also in 1831. In that year the order was also given to construct two further warehouses.

1831 also saw the construction of major new facilities on the passenger side of the operation. A passenger station had been built in 1830 to the south of the viaduct, fronting Liverpool Road. A drawing shows work nearing completion, with the warehouses beyond and the viaduct visible to the right. It was against this part of the viaduct that the extension was built in 1831. It comprised a parcels office and shops at street level, and a carriage shed at rail level (disguised on its street side by a 'domestic' facade). This building was poorly constructed and suffered greatly when the site was allowed to slip into disrepair. Its restoration necessitated complete dismantling and re-erection, which revealed further information about the constructional history of the site. It was found that each of the viaduct arches, where they faced the street, had been given a brick facing incorporating iron-barred window openings and doors. Most of these were blocked when the 1831 range was erected, but it is clear that in 1830 they were intended to have a function. The most likely use to which they might have been put was as additional storage units for the brief time before the shops and carriage shed were built.

What are we to make of such sudden changes to both the warehousing and passenger facilities of the Liverpool & Manchester Railway? I believe they demonstrate that the promoters, although optimistic about the success of their venture, with a station designed to meet those expectations, were caught unawares by just how successful it turned out to be. Every change initiated within a year of the railway opening – the mechanisation of lifting apparatus, the construction of offices, the building of the mezzanine floor in the warehouse, the construction of two new warehouses and the expansion of passenger facilities – can be explained as a response by the railway company to a higher volume of goods and passenger traffic than that foreseen. The need to rethink the arrangements at the Manchester terminus of the line is perfectly understandable, for this was the first railway to link two major centres of commerce and population. There were simply no precedents upon which the railway company could base accurate projections of volume of business. The company therefore had to respond quickly to problems of success. The figures bear this out. The railway carried 72,000 passengers in its first 15 weeks of operation in 1830, and in 1831, 445,000 people. In 1831 43,000 tons of merchandise were carried and the following year, 159,000. By 1835 the total had reached 230,000 tons. It is a classic case of new technology being used to respond to an existing market demand, but in turn stimulating new and largely unpredictable demand.

I have described in detail a number of aspects of the archaeology of the 1830 warehouse. Much of the information that has survived is subtle, or easily lost or damaged. An appreciation of that fact has had a profound effect on our approach to the scheme of restoration and adaptation. On the one hand we require a building that is suitable for a variety of museum functions. On the other it is essential that we retain the maximum possible of the original structure, to be treated in such a way that the maximum amount of information about its construction and use is preserved. Having established that philosophy, the design team (museum staff, architects, engineers and quantity surveyors) developed a strategy that also recognised the necessity of phasing the work according to the availability of finance.

The first part of the programme was the internal cleaning of the building. A gentle abrasive and careful application of the air jets was essential, as well as good induction training for the operatives and liaison between the contractors and my museum colleagues. In consequence it proved possible to clean the timber work without raising the grain, whilst preserving the stencilled numbers and timber marks. Indeed, the process enabled additional information to be obtained.

The design work for the scheme needed to take account of future use of the building, particularly access and services. Two service cores in bays one and three have been created for this purpose, with timber removed for reuse elsewhere. It was originally estimated that it would be possible to retain some 70 per cent of the main structural timber framework, but that new floorboards, rafters, doors and shutters would be needed. Having adopted a 'minimum intervention/maximum retention' policy, however, it became clear as the design work progressed that a much higher proportion of original material could be repaired and preserved. This proved very demanding in terms of time, with a drawing required for every opening and an assessment of every structural timber. In consequence, a preservation rate of about 90 per cent of the timber framework has been achieved and about 80 per cent for rafters, floorboards and doors.

Inevitably, the worst-affected timbers were those in the valleys of the roofs where the gutters had long since failed, and on floors below, where water had trickled down through the building. The other main source of failure was, inevitably, where structural timbers were built into the perimeter walls. Wall plates, and the ends of beams and joists had frequently suffered wet or dry rot. Their collapse sometimes resulted in brickwork movement.

The technique of repair that we decided upon in a preliminary exercise in a 'test bay' was the piecing of new or reused timbers to replace rotten ends. In some cases a simple bolted half lap joint is used. Elsewhere a metal flitch plate, bolted through the timber, provides the strength to the joint. The bolts could then be hidden using circular wooden pellets. In the case of those storey posts that had suffered particularly severe abrasion during the operation of the warehouse, the weakened section was removed and replaced with a length of oak of identical scantling to the remaining post. As with the beam repairs, the use of hidden metal plates to strengthen the joint permits the maximum amount of original timber to be retained.

The floorboards were lifted as each zone of the building was treated. Once joists had been repaired, the boards were replaced in their original position. One modification was introduced, however. A

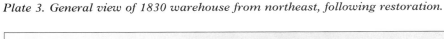

Plate 3. General view of 1830 warehouse from northeast, following restoration.

steel strip was inserted into the edges of adjacent boards to create a sealed joint to prevent dust falling through and to improve noise insulation. The pattern of floorboarding, like so many other elements of the building, shows evidence of the way in which it was used or modified. For example, the position of the original rail entrance for trucks is easily seen in the form of transverse boardings. The system of bringing trucks into the building for unloading ceased in the 1860s and a flush floor was created to maximise storage space.

To make the building usable it was necessary to improve its environmental and energy performance. Window openings have been glazed; originally only those alongside offices had glazing. The roof has also been modified by inserting insulation around the original rafters and below the slates. One bay, however, has neither of these modifications. Bay four is to be used to show how the warehouse operated, so it has wooden shutters to the windows and a torched underside to the slates.

To enable our presentation of the warehouse to be as accurate as possible, a programme of research into its operation is now under way by my colleagues. It includes a range of sources, from the minute books of the Liverpool & Manchester Railway in the 1830s to the memories of railway employees in the twentieth century in the form of an oral history project. In archaeological and historical research, good fortune is always a useful ally. In the case of our warehouse, one of the questions we wish to answer is: 'What was stored in it?'. Although storage of 10,000 bales of cotton was specified in the contract documents, it is probable that it was thought of as a performance specification rather than an intention of use. Manchester's voracious appetite for cotton must have resulted in considerable quantities passing through the 1830 warehouse and the two 1831 warehouses, but it is clear that from the outset the range of goods was much wider. For example, the railway company ordered posters to be displayed in the warehouse warning employees that stealing oranges, and oysters from barrels, would lead to instant dismissal. The 1850 OS map marks butter rooms,

grocery rooms and corn stores. An insurance survey on 1889 marks 'Flour, Paper and Sugar and Cereal Goods'. Undoubtedly the range of stored foods varied enormously over time, but the good fortune that I mentioned has come to our aid in two instances. When I and my colleagues were engaged in the arduous and filthy task of clearing the warehouse in 1991, a ledger was found in one of the crane lofts. It details the stored goods in 1905. Subsequently, the contractors working on the structure found a second ledger, dating from 1895. The careful briefing of the contractors' employees had paid off.

This briefing paid off again when fragments of a painted glass panel were found. Its subject could not be more appropriate, for it shows a warehouse with all the activities taking place in the yard outside. It provides an inspiration for our intended display inside, and especially outside, the restored warehouse. The first phase opened at the end of 1993.

In this paper I have described the position that we have reached to date in our research into the 1830 warehouse, and our approach to its restoration and future use. Research is continuing, and much will be discovered to add to and modify the information in this paper. There is a general point to be made about the nature of industrial archaeology. Since the term was coined there has been a search for a distinctive methodology for a separate subject. I believe that it is more helpful to regard industrial archaeology as an integral element of historical archaeology. A range of sources have contributed to this study: structural analysis, scientific analysis of building components, recording of fittings and loose artefacts, comparison with structures elsewhere in Britain and abroad and documentary evidence (written, cartographic and pictorial). They are entirely equivalent to the sources that one would use for earlier buildings or sites: in my case I would draw a direct comparison with the approach taken in studying a medieval monastic site. I very much hope the 1990s will be the decade in which industrial archaeology takes its place in the mainstream of archaeological enquiry.

Notes and references

1   *Port of London Authority Monthly* (March 1934), pp112-16

Railways and landscapes

J Allan Patmore

Enthusiasm for railways takes a wide variety of forms. Many are concerned with minutiae: more rarely is a broader view taken and the railway set in the life and landscape of its times. There are some honourable exceptions,[1] and it is in the shadow of these that this paper was conceived. The view is that of a geographer rather than an historian or a museum curator, and the concern is for the railway in its landscape setting, an extremely difficult theme to encapsulate in museum display. For practical reasons, the illustrations are taken entirely from the British scene, but it is hoped that the underlying themes may stimulate and serve a wider application.

At the end of the twentieth century it is hard to imagine the visual impact created by the railway in the middle years of the nineteenth. Motorway construction may give some idea of the physical upheaval, but the sheer scale of direct landscape change is hard to envisage, let alone the economic and social revolutions which accompanied it. But, as with motorways, innovation and intrusion were soon replaced in public perception by passive and unthinking acceptance, as the new transport form became the universal carrier for all except the most local of needs. In the years since 1914 that universality has rapidly declined with the application of the internal combustion engine and the pneumatic tyre to the road vehicle. Almost half the British rail network has closed, much of it reabsorbed into the landscape, leaving little trace except to the most discerning eye.[2]

The pattern of railway expansion and contraction has chroniclers in plenty and is not the concern here. The focus is rather, in a more static sense, on landscape impact, whether that impact in the longer term is of a permanent or more transient nature. Three themes are sketched: the direct relationship of the railway to the physical landscape; the distinctive landscape of the railway itself; and the impact of the railway on the landscape of settlements.

The railway and the physical landscape

In fitting the railway to the contours of the existing landscape, the railway engineer sought a variety of often conflicting aims: the most direct route with the minimum of curvature and gradient, and the least remodelling of the landscape with expensive earthworks, viaducts and tunnels. In practice, of course, numerous compromises were reached in the trade-off between initial cost and subsequent operating restrictions.

In the vertical plane, the limit was the absolute restriction on the ability of steel wheels to surmount a gradient on steel rails without total loss of adhesion. That ability may be artificially boosted by rope-worked inclines, as on the Cromford & High Peak Railway, or by rack-assisted traction, as, uniquely in Britain, on the Snowdon railway, but in either case there are severe penalties on load and speed. Gradients as steep as 1 in 14 have been worked by steam traction by adhesion alone, as on the Hopton incline of the Cromford & High Peak. For main lines the limit has been nearer 1 in 35 but with a penalty on speed accepted, as well as the frequent need to provide banking assistance, as on the Great Western Railway's South Devon banks (1 in 36 to 1 in 46) or the Lickey incline on the Birmingham & Gloucester (1 in 37). With the growing power of the steam locomotive, and of later diesel and electric traction, these limits became of lesser importance. In the nineteenth century, for example, the climb from Queen Street, Glasgow, to Cowlairs at a gradient of 1 in 41 was deemed sufficiently severe to need the assistance of ropes and a fixed engine, but in the twentieth century such assistance was abandoned, though a rear-end banker was long retained. In more recent years, electric traction has almost negated the formidable physical obstacle of the 1 in 75 ascent of Shap Fell on the West Coast main line.

The subtleties of the relationship between gradient, cost and traction ability are well illustrated in

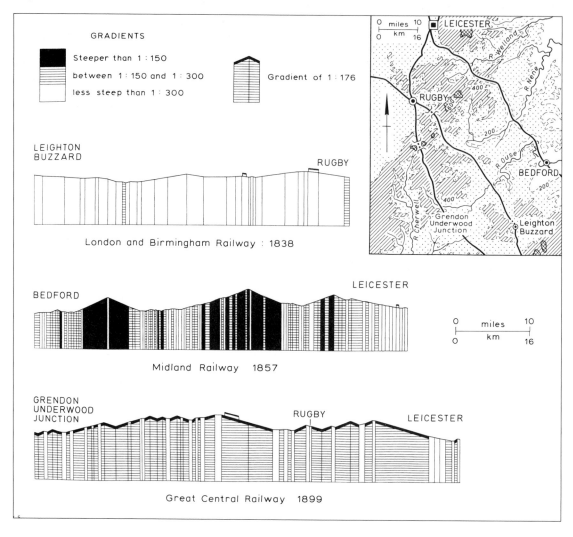

Plate 1. Contrasts in the gradient profiles of three main lines in the South Midlands

Plate 1. Here three erstwhile main lines crossed the Jurassic uplands of the South Midlands, roughly at right angles to the grain of the country. In terms of relief, there is little to differentiate the routes chosen by each line, but the gradients used differ considerably. The oldest route, from Leighton Buzzard to Rugby, is that of the pioneer London & Birmingham Railway of 1838. Its engineer, Robert Stephenson, had a very conservative view of the capabilities of contemporary steam traction and sought to limit gradients to a maximum of 1 in 330, following his father's dictum of no more than a vertical rise of 16 ft per mile. The result was a magnificent but expensive alignment with monumental cuttings and embankments. Some 20 years later the Midland Railway built its route from Bedford to Leicester at a time of financial stringency for the company. Earthworks were minimised – and costs reduced – by accepting gradients as steep as 1 in 120. The third route, part of England's last main line before the new Channel Tunnel link, was built by the Great Central Railway to maximise speed rather than reduce cost. With the developed steam locomotive at the end of the nineteenth century, a ruling gradient of 1 in 176 was chosen to this end, and much of the section illustrated here was laid out to that precise gradient, up hill and down dale. These three routes show three very different responses to similar terrain, dictated by the financial and technical circumstances of design and construction.

It is not, of course, only in the vertical plane that such restrictions are felt. Tight curves can equally limit speed. A narrower gauge than standard may permit very tight curves indeed, but at the expense of both load and speed. At the other extreme, lines suitable for speeds of 100 mph will need a minimum curve radius of at least 1¼ miles. Nevertheless, the railway is generally more flexible in the horizontal than in the vertical plane. This is aptly illustrated in Plate 2 which shows the north-south

Plate 2. Road and rail crossings of the North York Moors

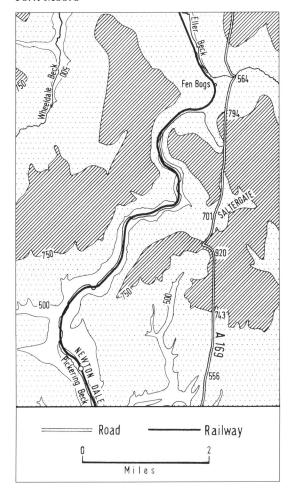

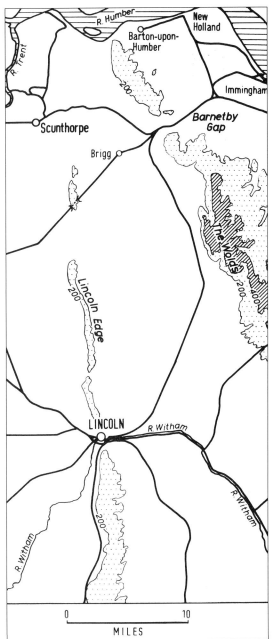

Plate 3. Railways and relief in Lincolnshire

crossing of the North York Moors. The early road (now the Whitby to Pickering A169) keeps to the relatively dry uplands, where it has a direct route, but at the expense of frequent oscillations in height. The later railway (originally the horse-drawn Whitby & Pickering Railway of 1836) utilises the glacial overflow gorge of Newtondale, where much lesser gradients obtain, but at the expense of a very wet route and relative sinuosity. To this day no road follows this section of the now preserved North Yorkshire Moors Railway.

The sensitivity of the railway in the vertical plane means that even quite modest landscape features may exercise a profound effect. In the relatively subdued terrain of Lincolnshire (Plate 3) the presence of the Witham gap through the Lincoln Edge or the Barnetby gap through the Lincolnshire Wolds has led to a marked focusing of railway routes – nine converging on the former and six on the latter.

Plate 4. The railway in the valley of the lower Wye

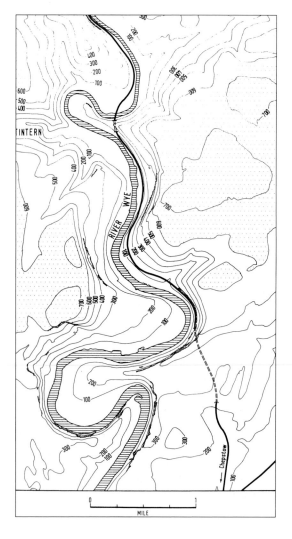

The impact of relief has many subtle variations. It is an obvious truism that railway engineers seek valleys to align their routes at lower levels, but much must depend on the nature of the route offered by the valley. In the incised meanders of the lower Wye, on the Welsh border (Plate 4), the railway tries to follow the banks of the river from the north. At Tintern the tight meander radius defeats it; the line crosses the Wye and of necessity tunnels through the meander neck rather than trying to follow the river course. Further south the steepening valley sides and the prospect of further tight curves force the engineer to tunnel to the east, out of the valley altogether. Indeed, at times, a valley may not be the most suitable route at all. Much of the route of the former London & South Western Railway branch to Bude from the northern flanks of Dartmoor (Plate 5) follows not the valley but the watershed between the Tamar and Torridge basins, where as far as Holsworthy the smoothest, least obstructed path is found.

In open country between towns the railway has relative freedom to choose a route and can thus be more sensitive to relief. Within towns that freedom is more restricted, and more expensive solutions, in an engineering sense, may have to be adopted. The pioneer London & Greenwich Railway, London's oldest railway, had no hills or valleys to cross, but the terrain was already intensively utilised. To avoid excessively frequent level crossings, the railway was built on a viaduct 3¾ miles long with 878 arches.[3] The viaduct, though costly to construct, avoided the purchase of the wider strip of expensive urban land which an embankment would have necessitated.

Elsewhere in London is a classic instance of the detailed relationships between relief and railway location (Plate 6). In the approach of main line railways from the north were three critical features: Euston Road, with the termini to be sited on its northern side; the descent from the relatively high ground immediately to the north; and the pre-existing Regent's Canal. These features left little room for manoeuvre, but the three main lines adopted different solutions. The London & Birmingham (1837) came through the high ground in Primrose Hill tunnel, over the canal, and then down a relatively steep gradient at 1 in 70 to a ground-level terminus at Euston. From 1837 to 1844, indeed, trains leaving Euston were rope-hauled to Camden: the bank was the steepest gradient on the whole route to Birmingham. At King's Cross (1852)

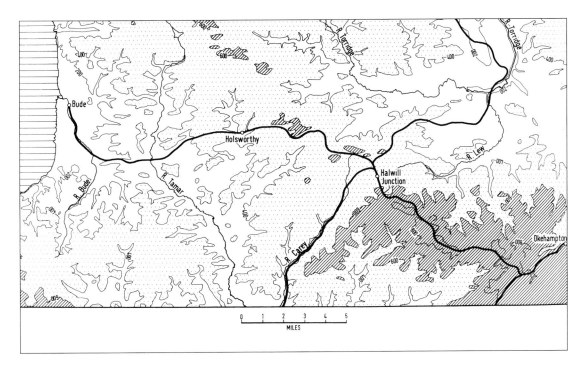

Plate 5. Railways and a watershed: the Bude branch of the London & South Western Railway

the canal was much nearer Euston Road. The Great Northern line has a ground-level terminus, and in consequence tunnels under the canal in dropping down from the higher ground beyond. At St Pancras (1868) the Midland also had little distance between the canal and its intended destination. It crossed over the canal, but then avoided an excessively steep drop to ground level by raising the terminus on arches some 12 to 17 ft above road level. The space at ground level below the platforms was used for the storage of beer from Burton-on-Trent, the supporting arches of the 'first floor' station being spaced in multiples of beer-barrel diameters.[4]

The landscape of the railway

The railway not only fitted in to the existing landscape, but created a very distinctive landscape of its own. The sheer scale of railway building necessitated the creation of a multitude of earthworks and structures, often long outlasting the railway itself.

Along the right of way, bridges were the most frequent and prominent structures. Something of

this proliferation had been foreshadowed in the canal-building era of half a century before with the profusion of canal overbridges, often in the distinctive style of an individual company. Techniques had been developed and refined, culminating on the Ellesmere Canal in the delicate Pontcysyllte aqueduct of 1803, over 1000 ft long and 120 ft above the River Dee. The canal builders' achievements were rapidly eclipsed by the railway engineers. Great viaducts in brick or stone proliferated, with countless numbers of smaller structures. Growing mastery of the use of iron, and subsequently steel, brought larger and even more striking structures. The first iron railway bridge, that on the Stockton & Darlington Railway over the River Gaunless, is preserved in the grounds of the National Railway Museum. Its successors were far too large for such treatment. Perhaps the best known are Robert Stephenson's 1849 Britannia tubular bridge across the Menai Straits, with its two main spans 460 ft long and 90 ft above the water, and Baker and Fowler's Forth Bridge of 1890 whose giant cantilever spans are each 1700 ft long and whose total length is 1.4 miles.

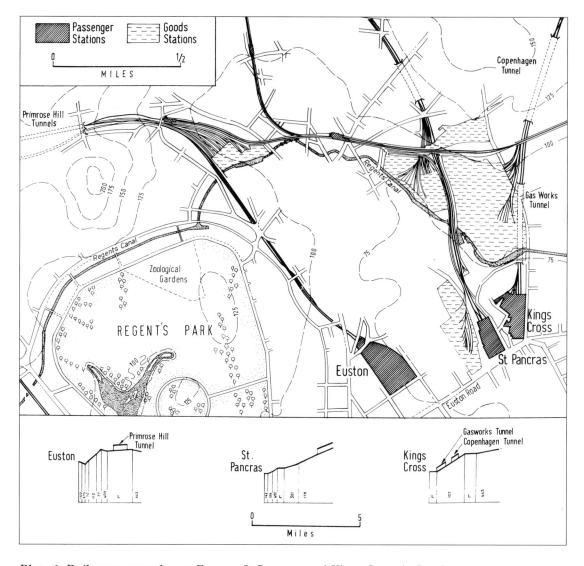

Plate 6. Railway approaches to Euston, St Pancras and Kings Cross in London

Like bridges, stations varied from the humble to the grandiloquent.[5] For 16 years, from 1833 to 1849, the Leicester & Swannington Railway used a modest public house as its Coalville station. Such modesty did not last long: the London & Birmingham heralded its approach to London at Euston with Hardwick's magnificent Doric arch and flanking pavilions, the true gateway to the north. Its destruction in the rebuilding of the 1960s was an act of great vandalism. Grandeur was often magnified by the linking of station to prestigious hotel, of which Gilbert Scott's St Pancras is the archetypal

example. Station buildings ran the whole gamut of architectural style and fashion. Companies had their own distinctive styles, often repeated at many of the smaller stations along a particular line. To the discerning eye, the station building is as much a key to date and location as locomotive and rolling stock.

Station buildings owed much to wider architectural trends, but in one respect at least the railway made its own distinctive contribution. The need, from the earliest days, to shelter passengers from the elements led to the evolution of the great train sheds: light, airy structures covering the maximum

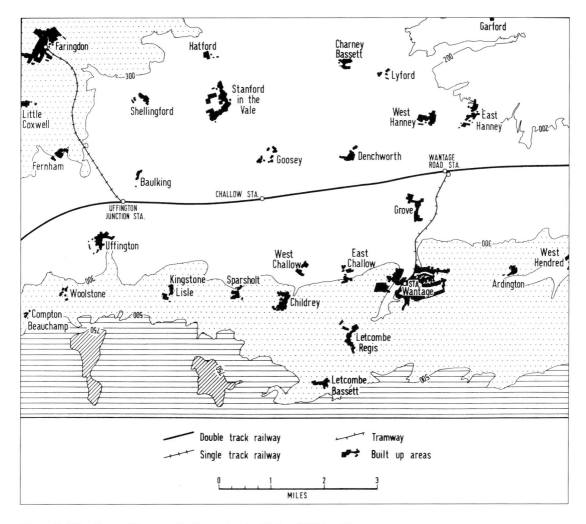

Plate 7. The Great Western Railway in the Vale of White Horse

of space with the minimum of support. Many remain virtually unchanged from the heyday of their Victorian development. Barlow's St Pancras shed has a single span 240 ft wide and 100 ft high. Its counterpart at Manchester Central is now the hall of the GMEX exhibition centre. More complex, and equally striking, is the great curved shed of York's 1877 station, with spans 81 ft, 55 ft and 43 ft in width.

Station complexes are a distinctive element in the landscape. High platforms in the British tradition are usually arranged in pairs, but oddities exist. At one time the Great Western Railway had twin facilities for up and down trains on the same side

of the tracks for some of its stations. Elsewhere, as at Chester and Cambridge, a single long platform with central crossovers served traffic in both directions. Inverness still has a distinctive Y-shaped layout, but without the working complexities of earlier years.

The railway landscape, of course, was far more than bridges and stations. Formerly, hundreds of acres were devoted to such ancillary facilities as marshalling yards, carriage sidings and motive power depots. But the stamp of railway character was not only in such major landscape features but also in the minor details. Prior to 1923 each railway company had its own distinctive house style, as evident in the characteristic design of signals as in stations or train sheds. Even through the years of grouping and of nationalisation, much of that intricate character remains: British Rail may have had a unified management, but happily the British railway is still far from a unified landscape.

The railway and settlement landscapes

The impact of the railway did not, of course, cease at the boundary of railway property. Its wider economic and social impact is beyond the purpose of this paper, but it had a direct influence on the landscapes of many of the settlements it served.

That impact was often least, in a direct sense, on rural areas. Most early railways were conceived as trunk routes, their essential purpose being interurban travel. Brunel's Great Western Railway of the 1830s was designed primarily for the London to Bristol traffic. Nowhere is this more evident than as it sweeps through the Vale of White Horse

(Plate 7), ignoring the lines of small villages and market towns on the northern and southern flanks of the vale. Only later in the century, as the railway became more nearly a universal carrier, did branches steal out to the larger settlements. Such branches were frequently lines of character, but, equally, were often the first to succumb to the competition of road traffic.

The wider fortunes of urban centres frequently reflected their position in relation to the railway network. Stamford in Lincolnshire was an important town on the Great North Road (A1) in the heyday of coaching traffic, and is still, despite its bypass, a considerable road focus (Plate 8). Its first railway was the 1846 Syston & Peterborough, running east from Leicester. It was, however, bypassed by the main east coast line (the Great Northern Railway), opened in 1852 and passing through Peterborough. Despite a branch from Essendine, opened in 1856, the town stagnated as Peterborough flourished.

Plate 8. The railways of Stamford, Lincolnshire

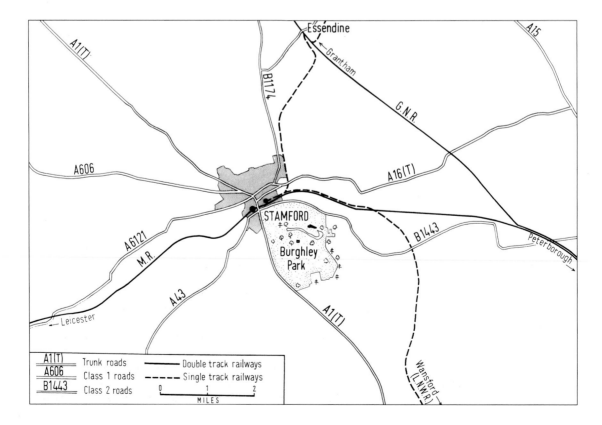

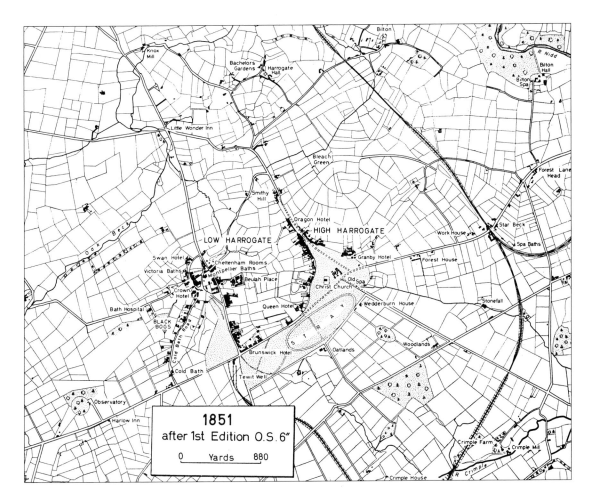

Plate 9. Harrogate in 1851

The railway created its own towns. Some, like Swindon, were the centres of railway workshops; others like Middlesbrough or Barry formed round ports built by the railway as traffic outlets. With growing excursion traffic, seaside resorts often reflected direct railway investment. Whitby's rise as a resort beyond its earlier port function owed much to George Hudson's investment in the West Cliff development to foster traffic for his York & North Midland Railway. Around the major cities, and London in particular, the pattern and progress of suburban development closely reflects the development of the railway – both surface and underground lines.[6]

Most towns of consequence owe something in economy and in landscape to the presence of the

railway. As illustration, one final example must suffice. In the early nineteenth century Harrogate[7] was a minor Regency spa some 22 miles west of York. The original hamlet, High Harrogate, was the residential and shopping focus: almost 1½ miles away, Low Harrogate, with its numerous springs, was the new treatment centre of the resort. By the middle of the century they were still small settlements with a combined population of 3500 and visitors limited in numbers by the difficulties of access.

The nascent spa did not attract the early railway promoters, but in the feverish speculation of the mid-1840s conditions rapidly changed: in 1848 the tiny settlement gained two separate railway lines. (Plate 9) Harrogate, unusually, lies astride a ridge between two valleys, and this posed problems for the railway promoters.

The first line, a branch from the route between Leeds and York of George Hudson's York & North Midland Railway, tackled the problem directly in approaching from the southeast. Cutting across the grain of the country, considerable engineering works were needed. A ¾ mile tunnel was followed by a 31 arch viaduct 110 ft high over the Crimple Valley before the line tunnelled again to the Brunswick terminus which was sited half way between the twin Harrogate settlements. This was an expensive way to serve a village of 3500 souls.

The second line, that of the Leeds & Thirsk Railway, approached from the south. Following the Crimple valley, it minimised costs by skirting Harrogate to the east before swinging round through the low ground of Starbeck to the north. At Starbeck was the station for Harrogate, over a mile

from High Harrogate and two from Low Harrogate.

In 1854 both routes became part of the North Eastern Railway, and the new company soon sought to rationalise the situation. The Leeds & Thirsk route best served Leeds; that of the York & North Midland Railway approached closest to the centre of the settlement. A new station site was chosen in the open ground between the twin villages, and a new line was built linking the Leeds & Thirsk route at Pannal to the York & North Midland approach across the Crimple viaduct, then, on another new alignment, to a new central station and on to Starbeck. This alignment had gradients as steep as 1 in 66, but the convenience for passengers of the location of the new station far outweighed operating difficulties. When the new lines were opened in 1862 the old Brunswick station was closed and its site incorporated into the open

Plate 10. Harrogate in 1878

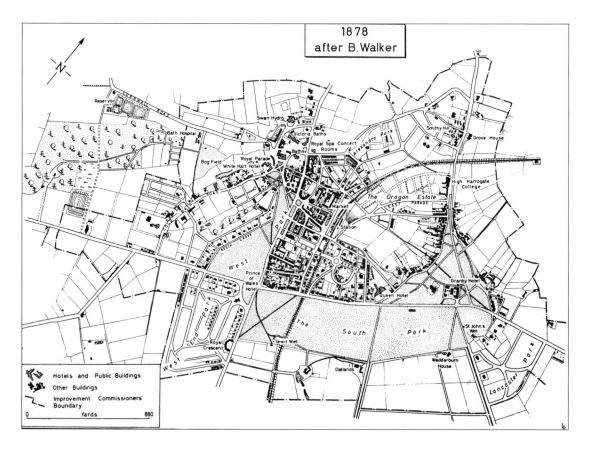

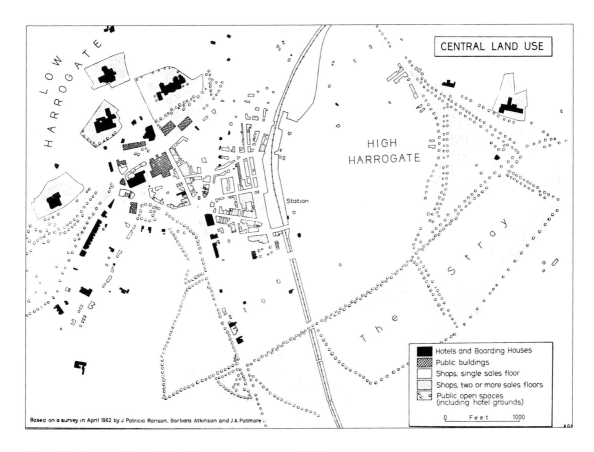

CENTRAL LAND USE

L O W
H A R R O G A T E

HIGH
HARROGATE

Station

T h e   S t r a y

Hotels and Boarding Houses
Public buildings
Shops, single sales floor
Shops, two or more sales floors
Public open spaces
(including hotel grounds)

0   Feet   1000

Based on a survey in April 1962 by J. Patricia Ronson, Barbara Atkinson and J.A. Patmore

Plate 11. Non-residential land use in Harrogate, 1962

ground of the Stray to compensate for land taken from the Stray for the new route. (Plate 10) The direct Crimple Valley route to Starbeck lasted for freight traffic until 1957 when it too was closed, whilst the circuitous York & North Midland line east of the Crimple viaduct was closed in 1964.

If seeming contradictions in the town's railway alignment can only be explained by this historical excursion, the impact of the railway went far beyond its direct presence. Linked to Leeds and the West Riding in particular, Harrogate flourished in turn as a spa, a resort, a dormitory town and an administrative centre in its own right. Even more interesting were the internal morphological changes. The 1862 station, built originally on open land, rapidly became a focus for new development. The prime shopping area grew along the streets linking

Low Harrogate and the station (Plate 11): High Harrogate atrophied and became no more than a fossil remnant of the Regency spa. The pull of the railway remains today. New offices were built astride the station building in the 1960s, and the station site is now (1993) straddled by a new indoor shopping development and its attendant car park. Yet even now the commercial tide ceases abruptly on the line of the railway: the landscape to the east remains purely residential. (Plate 11)

Harrogate is far from unique in having so much of its evolution and present-day landscape linked to the railway, but it serves to emphasise again that the railway has implications far beyond its role as a means of transport. In this, as in countless other instances, the landscape impact of the railway is far from the least of its fascinations.

J Allan Patmore

Editor's note

This paper was given as an illustrated public lecture during the symposium. The majority of illustrations were not suitable for reproduction, and the text in consequence is a shortened version of the original.

Notes and references

1 The seminal text on the railway and the landscape is Appleton, J H, *The Geography of Communications in Great Britain* (London: Oxford University Press, 1962). Other major references are Simmons, J, *The Railway in Town and Country 1830-1914* (Newton Abbot: David & Charles, 1986) and Turnock, D, *Railways in the British Isles: Landscape, Land Use and Society* (London: Adam & Charles Black, 1982).

2 See in particular White, H P, *Forgotten Railways* (Newton Abbot: David St John Thomas, 1986), pt 3.

3 Course, E, *London Railways* (London: Batsford, 1962), p21

4 White, H P, *A Regional History of the Railways of Great Britain* (London: Phoenix House 1963), III: *Greater London*, p148

5 For an introduction to this theme, see Biddle, G, *Victorian Stations* (Newton Abbot: David & Charles, 1973); Biddle, G, *Great Railway Stations of Britain* (Newton Abbot: David & Charles, 1986); and Hoole, K, *Railway Stations of the Northeast* (Newton Abbot: David & Charles, 1985).

6 See in particular Course, E, *London Railways*, chp 10.

7 Patmore, J A, *An Atlas of Harrogate* (Harrogate: Harrogate Corporation, 1963)

Preservation and interpretation

The British experience: railway preservation in the UK

Rob Shorland-Ball

The *Concise Oxford Dictionary* offers an explanation of 'preservation' as '... being kept safe from injury or destruction ...' and '... the keeping safe of a name or a memory ...'. In this brief paper I would like to keep in mind that relatively wide definition in the context of railway preservation.

In the UK, at least, the term 'the railway preservation movement' has gained currency in the last few years. In many minds it tends to be applied in a quite narrow sense to preserved railways and their rolling stock and particularly to those which are operated or cared for in whole or in part by volunteers. Professional museums, and especially the National Railway Museum (NRM), are perceived as concerned with but not necessarily part of 'the movement'. Beyond or alongside both are the private collectors, primarily of small objects which they term 'railwayana', several of whom are acknowledged experts in their own field.

What is lacking is an intellectual discipline binding these and other disparate parts of the subject of railways together and giving it coherence. Several papers in this symposium touch on the issue; I come back to it in my 'summing-up' paper. Here I am proposing a holistic view of that sum of the parts of the railway context which have been or are being preserved.

The hardware of railways, large and small, is an important element of the subject but it is sometimes forgotten that the preservation of such hardware extends to the infrastructure of the working railway itself. Leslie Soane's paper tells us of the Railway Heritage Trust which (in the words of the Trust's 1991-92 annual report) '... assists British Rail's business in their stewardship of over 1,000 listed buildings and structures'.

There are more than 90 operating preserved railways in the UK. David Morgan's paper on the Association of Railway Preservation Societies enlarges on that aspect of preservation.

There are large library and archive collections, particularly at the Public Record Office in Kew and here at the NRM. Together these collections include company records, both financial, personal and technical; photographs; posters; printed ephem-era; engineering drawings and printed books. In studying the latter we are greatly helped by the two volumes of George Ottley's incomparable *Bibliography of British Railway History* which provide a classified, annotated and fully indexed guide to over 12,000 items on the development of rail transport in the British Isles.

Railway preservation in the UK, then, has a number of roots and many branches.

Jack Simmons, who has probably done more than any other historian to set the railways in context, writes: 'The railway cannot properly be thought of as a work of engineering, an economic and administrative device, alone. It was forged and maintained by human beings for the service of other human beings.'[1] As soon as railway construction started in earnest artists and writers recorded their impressions of a phenomenon which was to have far-reaching consequences; Charles Francis Adams, writing in 1886, noted:

The great peculiarity of the locomotive engine and its sequence, the railroad ... was that it burst rather than stole or crept on the world. Its advent was in the highest degrees dramatic. It was even more so than the discovery of America ....[2]

At first, of course, there was little thought of railway *preservation* – the railways were a new symbol of progress and change. One hundred years later, however, in 1925, the centenary of the opening of the Stockton & Darlington Railway was celebrated, turning 'the spotlight of nationwide publicity on the railway past' and '... many relics of the pioneering days were displayed to the public for the first time'.[3]

Another event in the 1920s that facilitated railway preservation and changed official thinking was the formation of the Big Four railway companies in 1923. Some 120 companies were amalgamated in four groups to create the Great Western Railway (GWR), the London, Midland & Scottish Railway (LMS), the London & North Eastern Railway (LNER) and the Southern Railway (SR). As the new companies sought to establish their identities, an appreciation of railway history was seen as useful. A company-centric view was advanced that suggested that, after 1923, railway history could be expressed very simply as the sum of events and achievements leading to the formation of the four new companies.[4]

The Stockton & Darlington celebrations in 1925 were seminal in awakening public interest in the history of railways. More than 100 locomotives and other rolling stock – including some of the finest examples of contemporary practice – were displayed in Darlington and took part in a procession on part of the Stockton & Darlington line. One result of the celebrations and the desire of some officers of the Big Four companies to perpetuate their historical origins was the creation, by the LNER in York, of Britain's first major railway museum. It opened to the public in 1927 and became the genesis of what is now the NRM (although the genesis was slow and often tortuous). European railway museums in Hamar, Norway (1897), and Nuremburg, Germany (1899), were started much earlier but there the railways were state enterprises so the concept of a national museum was easier to realise. The NRM in York was opened by HRH The Duke of Edinburgh on 27 September 1975. In 1992 HRH The Duke of Kent opened the 'new' NRM which, after a £6.5 million rebuilding and redisplay programme, has doubled in size; it now has four acres of covered display space in two huge halls as well as yards for display and operation.

This, in brief, is the 'official' arm of railway preservation but, as I mentioned earlier, the movement has several roots and many branches.

Amateur students of railway history have flourished for many years but, initially, their interest was expressed in writing about railways, in photographing them and recording locomotive performance. Many were educated men – clergymen, university lecturers, school teachers – who had the time and the means to pursue what, for some, became an all-absorbing hobby. They formed societies – The Stephenson Locomotive Society (SLS), the Railway Correspondence and Travel Society – and clubs – The Oxford Railway Club – and they published journals to communicate the results of their work and research.

Essentially their interest was intellectual, although the SLS did acquire the London, Brighton & South Coast Railway 0-4-2 *Gladstone* for preservation in 1927 on the basis that the locomotive represented 'the unique achievement of a unique locomotive engineer'.[5] From the beginning it was intended to house the locomotive in a museum and it duly went to York (with the approval of the LNER) and is now displayed in the NRM's South Hall.

Alongside the intellectuals have grown the army of railway enthusiasts who, at best, make a contribution to the sum of railway knowledge. At worst, they constitute the platform-end number-gatherers, the 'foamers', 'glazers' and 'fans-living-with-Mom' whom we all know too well. Unfortunately, there is no satisfactory definition of a railway enthusiast that distinguishes the obsessive from the expertly well-informed collector, photographer or railway author. Sadly, it is the former – the obsessive – who has coloured the public perception of those concerned with recording and preserving the railway heritage.

The period of practical preservation of railway hardware (other than in museums or by the railway companies themselves) had early beginnings with the preservation – and restoration to working order – of the Liverpool & Manchester 0-4-2 *Lion* in 1927-30. But the more significant step of preserving a complete railway came in 1951 when the Welsh narrow-gauge Tal-y-llyn was taken over as a (just) working concern by a preservation society. The 1 ft 11½ inch gauge Festiniog Railway followed in 1954 and the first standard-gauge preservation, the 'Bluebell Railway' from Sheffield Park to Horsted Keynes in Sussex, came about in 1959.

The way has never been easy. The establishment attitude to railway preservation was well illustrated by a legal battle in the 1950s between the Festiniog Railway and the Central Electricity Authority (CEA). In brief, the CEA was developing a hydro-electric power scheme which would flood part of the northern end of the Festiniog track bed. At that time the preservation society was slowly reopening the abandoned railway and the northern end was still derelict. In the course of a legal hearing, Counsel for the CEA said: 'My personal view is that your railway is just a hobby for elderly gentlemen and young men. It is playing trains.'[6] This uncalled-for legal *bon mot* was widely reported in the newspapers at the time and still colours perceptions of the work on which we are engaged.

It is indeed true that young men, and particularly children, have always had a soft spot for railways. In 1946 Thomas the Tank Engine was born – and a whole generation (of which I am part) grew up with Thomas stories. Despite their simplistic nature they serve as an entertaining introduction to railway operation. But they do nothing, it must be admitted, to enhance the gravitas of the study of railways as an academic discipline.

In many eyes the accusation of 'playing trains' became even more apt in the 1960s when preservation of British Rail lines and locomotives began as a reaction to the closure of many lines and the demise of steam traction on BR. The first steam locomotive to be privately preserved and operated was GN 0-6-0T No 1247 in 1959. The last BR steam locomotive was withdrawn in 1968. The end of steam saw a great wave of sentiment for the steam railway which has been nurtured by videos and magazines and underpinned by the preservation of several hundred steam locomotives. Some are famous (like *Flying Scotsman*); some are epics of restoration (like *Duke of Gloucester* or *Blue Peter*); many are humble industrial 0-6-0 tank engines; and many more are still scrapyard wrecks.

The significance of our UK railway heritage was officially celebrated in 1975 by the 'Rail 150' exhibition and cavalcade recalling the 150th anniversary of the Stockton & Darlington Railway. In 1980 an even more splendid occasion was 'Rocket 150' when a great cavalcade at Rainhill on the Liverpool & Manchester Railway marked the 150th anniversary of the Rainhill Trials where, in 1829, *Rocket* triumphed against all comers. Working replicas of *Rocket* (owned by the NRM), of *Sans Pareil* and of *Novelty* took part in the celebrations.

So the 'preservation tree' is almost complete: museums – and particularly the NRM; armchair students of railway history; specialist photographers; specialist collectors; those preserving, restoring and operating whole railways or items of rolling stock – including, now, diesel as well as steam locomotives; publishers of books, videos and magazines.

I have omitted modellers, not because I do not admire their work and believe their contribution important. I suspect, however, that is not mainstream in the context of this paper. Modellers are not preserving reality, rather mimicking it in miniature, but they have an important part to play, especially in research and interpretation, and should not be forgotten.

When detail obscures the overall pattern we say that we 'cannot see the wood for the trees'. In the case of the railway preservation tree I believe that we cannot distinguish the trunk – the core – because of the vigour and profusion of the branches. The railway preservation movement has enormous vitality but its various parts do not always communicate well (if at all). In museum terms, a great number of objects, 'things', have been collected and some have been restored and operated. The central significance of the railway as a force that literally 'changed the world' has often been lost – in swirls of smoke and sentimental attempts to re-create what is called the Era of the Steam Railway (always written with a capital E, S and R), referred to as 'the Glory Years', but actually comprising relatively few years within recent living memory.

The historian John Kellett, writing in 1969, noted that:

> ... the imbalance and inadequacy of existing published treatment [of railway history] will be rectified only as the extra-ordinary spell which has been cast over the subject is broken, and contributions are made to railway history by writers whose main interests extend beyond the railways themselves and to whom the sights and sounds of the steam locomotive are not so overwhelmingly personal a memory[7]

The best historians have always been aware of the significance of railways and their work illuminates the *raison d'être* for railway preservation – the trunk of the tree. Eric Hobsbawn describes the impact of the railway on social and economic development:

> ... the 100,000 railway locomotives pulling their almost three-quarters of a million carriages and wagons in long trains under banners of smoke ... were part of the most dramatic innovation of the century, undreamt-of – unlike air travel – a century earlier .... The railways collectively constituted the most massive effort of public building as yet undertaken by man. They employed more men than any other industrial undertakings. They reached into the centres of the great cities, where their triumphal achievements were celebrated in equally triumphal and gigantic railway stations, and into the remotest countryside where no other trace of 19th century civilisation penetrated.[8]

If any one body – in the UK – is to illuminate, however inadequately, the trunk of the railway tree, I believe it should be the NRM. We must nurture and help the branches, where it is appropriate for us to do so, and we should set standards in those areas where we have particular expertise. We should complement the work of preservation which is being carried out elsewhere. And we should lead, as I hope we are doing in this symposium, in the opening up of avenues of scholarly enquiry and academic research.

Notes and references

1   Simmons, J, *Railways: An Anthology* (London: Collins, 1991)

2   Addams, C F, *Railroads: Their Origins and Problems* (New York and London, 1886), revised edn

3   Hopkin, D W, 'Railway preservation: railways, museums and enthusiasts' (unpublished master's thesis, University of Leicester, 1987)

4   Hopkin, D W, 'Railway preservation'

5   Maskelyne, J N, President of the Stephenson Locomotive Society, to members, quoted in Hopkin, D W, 'Railway preservation'

6   Quoted in Boyd, J I C, *The Festiniog Railway* (Lingfield: Oakwood Press, 1975), 2nd edn, II, p553

7   Kellet, J, *Victorian Studies*, 13, 1 (1969)

8   Hobsbawm, E, *The Age of Empire* (London, 1987)

The National Railway Museum, York

Christine J Heap

To begin this paper I want to look again at the mission statement and first core objective of the National Railway Museum (NRM). The mission statement of the museum is to enhance the public understanding of railways and to be the principal public trustee of the nation's railway collection; its first core objective is to develop the collections and apply to them the highest standards of management and care. These taken together imply both the breadth of subject coverage and the high standards of curatorial care which the museum aims to achieve. Hidden behind these worthy aims is a hint of the delicate balancing act which the museum has to perform in order to collect in a way that accurately represents the history of the railway, without overstretching its resources and compromising its standards of care.

The NRM's stated aim in collecting is to preserve, record and illustrate the history and development of railways, railway engineering and associated railway manufacturing industries in the British Isles from the beginning of the Industrial Revolution to the present day. The brief is a wide one. No aspect of railway manufacture or operation is specifically excluded. The museum collects examples of structural engineering, architecture, locomotives and rolling stock, signalling, personalia, railway office pencils, posters, photographs, art, ceramics, uniforms, tickets ... the list goes on.

The collection groups which are used at present to administer the collections illustrate the breadth of collecting within the museum. Falling within three main groups these are:

- *railway engineering and technical development*: locomotives and rolling stock; railway infrastructure; signalling and telecommunications; tools of the trade and personal accessories
- *railways in society – 3D collections*: road vehicles; stationary engines; railway shipping; fixtures and fittings from railway buildings; railway models; tickets, passes and labels; passenger comforts; railway furniture; railway uniform and costume; tools of the trade and personal accessories; railway timepieces; railway textiles; railway heraldry; toys and games; miscellaneous and curiosities; railway numismatics
- *railways in society – 2D collections*: NRM archive (history of museum); archive collections (railways); written and printed ephemera; maps and plans; photographic collections from official sources; pictorial (fine art) collections; posters, notices and handbills; photographic collections from other than official sources; postcards; film

The aim of the museum in collecting so widely is to cover all aspects of railway history. In its collecting and in its displays it is attempting to tell the complete story of railways. It is not simply the technical development of locomotives and rolling stock which is of concern, nor only issues of railway safety, in terms of railway signalling and safety equipment, nor even just the nostalgia of railway travel which the museum is trying to represent, but the full economic and social impact of the railway on society. Deciding what to collect in this context is extremely difficult. Deciding what *not* to collect is even more difficult for arguments can be put forward on several fronts to justify any particular acquisition.

What criteria then should the NRM use to guide its acquisitions? In some areas, the decision has already been made for us. The division of archive material between the Public Record Office in Kew, the NRM in York and the Scottish Record Office in Edinburgh is very clear. The PRO takes the administrative, economic, civil-engineering and personnel records of the railway in England and Wales; the NRM takes the mechanical engineering records of the railway in England; and the Scottish Record Office takes all material which relates to Scotland. There is also an understanding between museums that whenever possible they will not compete for material. The NRM therefore leaves most collecting relating to Scotland's railways to museums in Scotland, Welsh railways to museums in Wales and Irish railways to museums in Ireland.

When it comes to the remaining material, there is no easy answer. One solution would be to collect everything and therefore not have to make any decisions at all, but in reality the volume of material concerned makes this an impossible option. Each item collected, whether it is a locomotive, a uniform, a pencil or a drawing, has to be stored, conserved, catalogued and made available to the public. Already the museum has more than 250 items of rolling stock, around one million negatives, 500,000 drawings, 3600 items of railway uniform and 5500 tools of the trade. A second option would be to collect nothing further: to draw a line beneath the present collections, say on the coming into law on 1 April 1994 of the Railways Bill which privatises the railways, and let the existing artefacts form the national railway collection. This is a feasible option, but it would be a denial of our present collecting policy of continuing to represent the modern railway, and is, therefore, not acceptable. A third option, and the one which has been adopted by the NRM, is to give very serious consideration to each item offered before a decision on its acceptance or rejection is made. An acquisitions committee sits regularly to discuss and sometimes agonise over the pros and cons of each potential new acquisition. The committee asks such questions as:

- is the item particularly significant in the history and development of railways?
- is it typical?
- does it fill a gap in the existing collection?
- is it a good example of its type and in good condition?

Arguments can be put forward in favour of almost anything which comes before the committee, and it is fair to say that we have, on occasion, some robust discussions on the meaning of 'particularly significant' when trying to decide if an item is of particular significance in the history and development of the railways. Nevertheless, about 50 per cent of the material offered to us is finally rejected by the committee. It is important to get the decision right, both from the point of view of future generations who will want to see the national collection, and from the point of view of the impact of collecting on the museum's resources.

As we have seen, the first core objective of the museum is to develop the collections and apply the highest standards of management and care. The task is to ensure the long-term preservation of the items collected whilst also making them available for research, education and enjoyment. In order to do this, both physical and human resources are required. Adequate storage accommodation is required for all the different materials represented in the collection, ranging from paper to textiles, from metal to ceramics. A wide range of conservation skills is needed, and a substantial amount of cataloguing effort is demanded. The NRM has a good track record in a number of these areas. The opening of the new Foundry Lane stores in 1990 has led the way in the storage of small railway objects in the 3D collections. The store is secure, well equipped and well organised. The recent upgrading of one of the drawing stores to meet the Public Record Office requirements for appointment as a place of deposit for public records is a further step in the right direction for the 2D collection.

Considerable skills are available in the workshops for restoration and conservation work on the locomotives, rolling stock and other items of railway engineering. The London & South Western Railway tri-composite coach on display in the South Hall demonstrates the standards achieved. Specialist outside conservators are used for paper conservation, picture restoration, uniform repair and for particular tasks such as the Euston gates now on display in the Great Hall. Cleaning and microfilming of drawings is carried out to a high standard by outside contractors.

Great effort is being put into getting all the objects in the inventory on to the computer database. The negative collection is being copied to optical disc and each image described for the text database. A handlist of periodicals has recently been produced and plans are being formulated for the transfer of the book records to computer.

However, there are still many problems to be faced. There are already great pressures on storage space. A number of items of rolling stock are not stored under cover because the museum does not have the space to accommodate them. Negatives acquired from the Western Region of British Railways are stored in London and are not accessible to the public because the museum does not have any suitable storage space in York. Drawings from railway company works are stored at York in basement accommodation which does not meet the criteria for archive storage laid down in the British Standard BS5454 and which risks damage through flooding. Many of the existing stores are already full. There is still much conservation work needed on drawings, textiles and rolling stock. There is a large backlog of cataloguing of drawings, signalling equipment, tools and photographs.

The museum is looking seriously at both its acquisition and its disposal policies and asking hard questions about its role. Disposal or de-acquisition policies are being defined and applied across the board. Talk of disposal causes great alarm in many circles but, if properly regulated, disposal is a valid option for a national museum. De-acquisition is only applied to items which are in bad condition, which are duplicated or which no longer accord with the museum's collecting policy. Most items in fair-to-good condition which are de-accessioned from the national collection are offered to and accepted by other public institutions and therefore continue to be available to the public. The notion of a core national collection is being developed, but not everything of significance is nor can be located at the NRM. The concept of a broader national railway collection is thus evolving, whereby particularly important items preserved elsewhere can be formally recognised as 'of national significance'. Loans out from the NRM already ease some of the pressure on storage for large items but, of course, have an administrative and staff cost in servicing them. Preservation *in situ* is another option for certain types of material, although security for such items is always a problem, as the unhappy fate of the Huskisson memorial, recently vandalised on the trackside site where it was erected to commemorate Huskisson's death in 1830, has shown.

There are no easy answers to the questions posed in this paper. There are no effective conclusions, at least as yet. Perhaps the best we can say is that we are working towards a better and wider understanding of what the national railway collection is, should be, and can be given the level of funding available to it. But the aim nonetheless is clear, as set out in our mission statement. We aim for excellence.

Additional reading

British Standard Recommendations for the Storage and Exhibition of Archival Documents: BS5454 (London: British Standard Institution, 1989)

Caring for Collections – Strategies for Conservation, Maintenance and Documentation (American Association of Museums, 1984)

Lord, B, *et al*, *The Cost of Collecting: Collections Management in UK Museums* (London: HMSO, 1989)

Lowenthal, D, *The Past is a Foreign Country* (Cambridge: Cambridge University Press, 1985)

Lubar, S, *et al* (eds), *History from Things: Essays on Material Culture* (Smithsonian Institution Press, 1993)

Royal Commission on Historical Monuments, *A Standard for Record Repositories* (London: HMSO, 1990)

Standing Conference on Museums and Archives, *Code of Practice on Archives for Museums in the United Kingdom* (London: HMSO, 1990)

The Association of Railway Preservation Societies

David Morgan

The Association of Railway Preservation Societies (ARPS) is the umbrella body of private preservation in the UK. As the Chairman of the ARPS, I appreciate the opportunity to outline how it started in the UK, how it developed, how it operates today but, most importantly, how it is organised.

As a nation Britain claims to have invented the railway; even our £5 note depicts our most famous engineer, George Stephenson, and the locomotive, *Rocket*. It is only natural, therefore, that we should also claim to have been the first to recognise the need to preserve railways.

The first foray into railway preservation was the Tal-y-llyn narrow gauge line in Wales. Tom Rolt, an author and engineer, visited the railway, realised that this picturesque line was about to be lost to posterity and, in 1950, wrote a letter to *The Times* seeking support. As a result of the replies Rolt received, a meeting was convened in Birmingham and the Tal-y-llyn Railway Society was born. This was probably the country's first railway preservation society, as opposed to a society dedicated to research into the history of railway development. The acquisition of the railway from the family which owned it was negotiated and teams of volunteers slaved away restoring the line to working order. Now the railway is operated as a tourist attraction, run principally by unpaid volunteers, but also relying on a small nucleus of paid staff. The Tal-y-llyn was soon followed by other narrow and miniature gauge railway schemes, but it was another decade before the emergence of the standard gauge preservation movement.

In 1960 both the Bluebell Railway in Sussex and the Middleton Railway on the outskirts of Leeds in Yorkshire were taken over by preservation societies. The Middleton had the distinction of being the country's first Parliamentary railway, having been authorised under an Act of 1758; it is a reminder that there were railways before the advent of the steam locomotive. However, it was the Bluebell Railway which captured the public imagination. British Rail, in closing the line, had failed to appreciate that the Act empowering the opening of the line many years earlier required that a minimum of four trains run each day. The courts compelled British Rail to reinstate the service until another Bill was rushed through Parliament. Apart from generating useful publicity, the delay allowed the Bluebell Railway Preservation Society time to generate sufficient support to preserve the line. Both the Middleton and the Bluebell projects were undertaken by volunteers, aided and abetted by professional railwaymen, with very little money. One of the founders of the revived Bluebell line was a retired naval officer, Captain Peter Manisty, who was one of the first to recognise the need for the new preservation bodies to get together. Manisty convened the meeting in 1959 of seven of the pioneer preserved railways to discuss the setting up of the umbrella organisation which later became the Association of Railway Preservation Societies.

It is useful to know the historical background to the evolution of the railway preservation movement in order to understand the culture behind it as well as the motives of some of those participating. Indeed, railway preservation is building a history of its own, particularly now that some preservation companies have operated their railway for longer than their forebears. I hope that in due course this museum will recognise that preservation history.

I suspect that many of us in the early days thought that we would run railways better than British Rail. Alas, we did not achieve that ambition but we discovered a new market: the leisure industry. It may seem laughable now, but many of us honestly thought that we would provide a public transport service. One person who recognised that we would not was John Snell, the Managing Director of the Romney, Hythe and Dymchurch Railway, a 15 in miniature railway in Kent, who dismissed anyone who thought he was in the public transport service as 'a menace to society'! The irony is, however, that it is now John Snell's railway which is under contract to Kent County Council to provide school transport to several hundred children every day during term time. Contract work, however, is very different from operating a full public timetable and depending only on local business.

Today there are 65 standard gauge railways and 63 miniature steam centres and museums covering 385 route miles, crossing over 600 bridges and calling at over 220 stations to pick up and set down over 8 million passengers each year. Nearly 1000 steam locomotives have been preserved and a growing number of diesel locomotives and railcars.

The backbone of all this achievement has been the work of unpaid volunteers and armchair supporters who have delved into their pockets to invest, lend, give or raise funds, all for no return other than the pleasure of seeing complete railways, rolling stock and railway infrastructure and equipment brought back to life. The usual development of preservation projects has been for regional railway societies to promote a company limited by shares, which allows them to raise capital, or a company limited by guarantee, which allows them to charge an annual subscription and, possibly, claim charitable status. While such companies seek to be profitable, any profits are invariably ploughed back into the enterprise. Today there are over 160 societies and companies, including, interestingly, about half a dozen railway ship societies. The ARPS is helping those engaged in restoring and operating locomotives, both steam and diesel, rolling stock and other railway equipment, to achieve and maintain what we consider to be high standards. The ARPS furthers the work of preserving the railway heritage by publicising the activities of the various societies and presenting their case to both government and industry. Indeed, the ARPS has proved so successful in the pursuit of its aims that a growing number of overseas preserved railway organisations, from the US, Canada and most countries of Europe, have become affiliated members.

In a wider role, the ARPS promotes steam railways and museums to the general public, organises awards and competitions to ensure high standards and, in particular, promotes the development of rigorous museological standards within the railway preservation movement: where appropriate, ARPS members have been encouraged to apply for registration under the national Museums and Galleries Commission guidelines. The ARPS provides advisory services and information to members, organises meetings and seminars and provides a forum for the exchange of information and experience within the preservation movement. As the preservation movement has grown, the ARPS has been joined by another trade association – the Association

of Independent Railways – whose members are the general managers of about 50 railways. Both organisations have combined to create the Railway Clearing House to lobby government.

I believe that we in the UK can no longer ignore the European dimension of railway preservation. The directives issued by the European Commission have an increasing impact on legislation affecting our member railways; the recent batch of safety regulations being a good example. Following the first ARPS international conference in Utrecht in 1989, we held a second conference in Hamelin where it was agreed by colleagues from France, Germany, Belgium, Holland, Sweden and elsewhere that there was a need for a European umbrella organisation. Following negotiations by a working party, that organisation is being registered as the European Federation of Museum and Tourist Railways or La Fédération Européene des Chemins de Fer Historique et Touristique. This is an international association registered under Belgian law as FEDECRAIL and launched in April 1994 at a seminar and general meeting at Louvain University, near Brussels.

Finally, and particularly since ARPS was mentioned, I must respond to Dr Cossons' comments during the symposium about an absence of scholarship in the railway preservation movement. I would confess that my own personal knowledge of railways is limited: I have never claimed otherwise. But that is not true of all railway preservationists and the scope of the papers at this symposium, many written by self-confessed enthusiasts, testifies to the depth and breadth of knowledge within the movement. While a train spotter with his array of badges and cameras may be the laughing stock of cartoonists, those active in the field of independent railway operation are a very different breed. I share Dr Cossons' belief that too much focus is given to locomotive restoration, but I do think that he fails to give adequate recognition to initiatives such as the Ian Allan Railway Heritage Award and the ARPS Carriage and Wagon competition which encourage attention to other branches of railway preservation. I support Dr Cossons' proposals for enhanced scholarship in the preservation movement and the idea of widening public interest in railway history. I am not sure, however, that one necessarily leads to the other, but I know, for example, of one enthusiast, a man of little formal education, once a soldier, then subsequently a railway signal man, who is researching the impact of railway development on the economics and corporate law of this country. I am sure that there are many similar examples.

I believe that railway preservation answers a need. The fact that we enjoy the active support and participation of over 100,000 members and 8 million passengers seems to me to provide one significant justification for our activities.

Technology assessment and 'edutainment'

Kilian T Elsasser

Introduction

Museums today have, according to Stephen E Weil, three basic responsibilities: to preserve, to study and to communicate.[1] 'To preserve' subsumes the two basic duties of collection and conserving and thus satisfies the more comprehensive view of the purpose of a museum defined by the International Council of Museums (ICOM). More important in the case of creating a new exhibition is 'interpretation' and 'exhibition' which are covered by the overall term 'communication'. Communication as a goal for present-day museums is much more appropriate than either exhibition or interpretation alone because the word reflects a more encompassing task. Communication includes not only displaying artefacts and describing them with labels but also educating the visiting public by conveying ideas and values to them. Communication implies a two-way exchange of ideas and needs, involving the audience in the making and the evaluation of displays. Many museum people see audience involvement as controversial because it can be argued that to make an intelligent choice about content requires the audience to have previous knowledge about the subject. It is often the case, therefore, that museum communication is, in practice, only one-way.

This paper will concentrate mainly on the communication of messages from the creator of the exhibition to the public. An exhibition in a museum does not of itself provide a learning situation as does the classroom. There is no two-way communication between the creator of the exhibition and the visitor; indeed, there is very little communication between the visitors themselves. The motivation of the average museum audience is to do with leisure and does not involve specific learning objectives. Even if a museum visit is orientated towards education, successful learning situations require preparation and consolidation time which is not normally available during museum visits.

Museum displays which are made for a broad public and intended to impart a substantive message are much more characteristic of mass-media communication than of the educational situation.[2] 'The public' consists of a heterogeneous body of people whose behaviour and responses, in the museum context, are likely to be individualistic, inconsistent and unpredictable. The content of museum displays is created and the display media chosen without consideration of the wishes of the public because those wishes are not known. Visitors cannot be gathered together in the kind of social network that will help them to give each other some direction in the interpretation of the exhibition. It can be argued, therefore, that it is worth adapting mass-media tools for museum interpretation, without forgetting the ultimate goal of educating the visitor, which is to achieve a two-way communication between teacher and taught.

Visitors passively consume the content of the exhibitions without necessarily understanding or learning from what they see. The content of an exhibition will be compared with knowledge acquired previously; linking new with old is essential for acquiring new knowledge. Such linking is achieved and reinforced by discussion of the content with those who have, in the eyes of the visitor, a certain authority. The credibility of the institution where the exhibition is displayed helps that reinforcement. The museum visitor has no choice in the topics within an exhibition nor in the way that they are structured. The only way a visitor can make a choice, other than by choosing not to visit at all, is to concentrate on particular parts of the exhibition and to ignore others. The selection of aspects of the exhibition is based on how interesting and how visually appealing they are, on what the visitor already knows and even on how the visitor feels. It follows, therefore, that by choosing topics within an exhibition, by presenting them in an eye-catching way and by drawing on academic credibility, the museum can both attract the attention of an audience and also stimulate a learning effect.

The layout and content of exhibitions and displays have to catch the attention of the visitor. Instead of interpreting a topic in a careful analytic structure, an exhibition should tell a thrilling story. It should, as Jeshajahu Weinberg, the Director of

159

the US Holocaust Memorial Museum in Washington DC, says, 'drive up the blood pressure';[3] it should provoke an emotional response and perhaps discussion with other visitors. Ideally, the main message of an exhibition should build on something about which the general public is knowledgeable and to which it is attracted.

In the sort of museums with which we are all concerned, it is not enough to tell a dramatic story; the content has to include an evaluation and a contextual explanation of the technology concerned: a 'technology assessment'. Not only has the functioning of past technology to be explained but also the social, economic and cultural importance of that technology. The context also has to be presented. The more recent a particular technology, the more important it is to talk about consequences rather than function. Our concern today is more about the consequences of applied technology, and less about the possibilities. A technology assessment in an exhibition should include the positive and negative aspects of a development and show how contemporaries dealt with the situation. The presentation of several subjective perspectives will allow visitors to identify with the issues raised in an exhibition. A more or less open-ended story, which includes different perspectives, will allow the visitors to draw their own conclusions.

Having discussed the theory, I now want to compare the theory about exhibitions as mass-media communication with the contents of exhibitions as technology assessment at the Swiss Transport Museum. In particular, I want to look at the question of credibility, content and the relationship between sponsors (in this case Swiss Federal Railways) and museums.

Content

From the foundation of the Swiss Transport Museum in 1959 to the early 1980s, the vehicles, as the core of the museum collection, stood for progress and a national identity which was shaped in the pre-World War Two period. The railways in Switzerland as a national organisation were, apart from being almost the only means of transportation, a symbolic network tying together the nation and enabling it to withstand the destruction of World War Two. Main line electrification of Swiss Federal Railways, completed in 1936, could be seen as a symbol of independence from foreign energy sources. The museum, and especially the railway

displays, were reminders of the strength of the country and the successful prevention of direct involvement in World War Two. In addition, the vehicles and the whole museum celebrated the successful industrialisation of Switzerland.[4] Economic growth meant progress, which was reflected in the aim of the museum which was, until 1992, according to its statute, the promotion of increased traffic by land, water and air.[5]

The symbolic content of the artefacts and of the displays slowly became obsolete as a result of criticisms of the concept of continuous progress and questioning of the constitution of the Swiss national identity in the 1970s. Nevertheless, having been such a success in earlier periods the artefacts were left on display in what had become the traditional layout, but their symbolic meaning had been eroded and the audience of the museum had changed. Today's average visitors are not necessarily reminded by the artefacts of specific periods and events in Swiss history; they have not seen the core locomotives of the museum collection such as the *Crocodile*, the *Landi-Lok* or the *Red Arrow* in service. The railway no longer has the importance it had in Swiss life before the predominance of the motor car. Visitors are generally less familiar with the railway and have less interest in the subject. Present-day exhibitions of railway material must, therefore, be restructured to help visitors understand the significance of the tons of iron and steel which constitute a major part of the museum's railway galleries.

The first significant change at the museum came with the expansion of the exhibition space in the railway department in 1982. A new hall of about 1700 sq m was built, and the old and new halls were connected with a roof covering about 2100 sq m, thus tripling the covered display space. Because of financial constraints, the main emphasis of this expansion was on the protection of as many historic vehicles as possible. Thus the display could almost have been compared to a storehouse and the displayed items were not well interpreted. The committee which created the exhibition included representatives from groups interested in all aspects of railways and their history. As a result, many labels ended up enumerating facts such as speed, power and provenance, or in describing the machine in technical terms such as:

You will notice the two close-coupled motor bogies with their large front parts, the short central body with the driver's cab and the driving mechanism with jackshafts and coupling rods.[6]

The interpretative tools failed to connect the artefacts with one another and they did not relate the artefacts to a context familiar or accessible to the lay public. The labels gave the impression that they were written for a privileged audience of very knowledgeable railway enthusiasts, or *Pufferküssers* (buffer kissers), as they are called in Switzerland.

I believe that it is not enough, however, merely to make connections between the artefacts and to relate them to particular periods; interpretation has to be part of a story. This new interpretative approach has begun its first trial with the exhibition *Safety on the Railways*, sponsored by Swiss Federal Railways, which opened in late 1993. The thread of the story is the development of signalling and safety devices from the beginning of railways to the present day. The highlight of the exhibition is a link to the working railway showing signalling on the St Gotthard line which lies just outside the museum. Other themes are the principles of rail-guided transport, explained by interactive games; historical developments, illustrated by objects; and the changing nature of human responsibility in railway safety. Both the content and the complex synthesis of different communication media, such as interactive games, videos and labels, represent a development to be emulated in future railway displays.

My predecessor, who created the exhibition, had a hard task ensuring that it would not become a public relations exercise for the financial backer, Swiss Federal Railways, and the suppliers of signalling and safety equipment. The influence of Swiss Federal Railways can still be seen in the omission of accidents as an exhibition topic, despite the fact that they were often the impetus for the introduction of new safety measures, and in the public relations photographs that introduce and close the exhibition. Despite these shortcomings, it is probably the best of the displays in the museum for content, or storytelling, and for the use of inter-relating display media.

Credibility

The credibility of the displays depends on the credibility of the institution as a whole; high-quality displays will enhance the credibility of the museum in the long term. Quality of exhibition content, and objectivity and independence of viewpoint in dealing with contentious topics, are the factors that define credibility. This is especially so where pressure from sponsors has to be set aside in the interest of objectivity.

Visitors who pay an entrance fee have the right to see something of more integrity than can be seen for free in every railway station and trade fair. In the short term, it may be very enticing to allow a sponsor to use the museum as a public relations vehicle, but the end result may be to damage the museum's reputation for independence. The sponsor may gain in the short term but sponsors who can be persuaded to take a longer-term view will benefit from an association with a high-quality exhibition which is perceived to be both authoritative and objective. Finally, the museum can fulfil its duty of education based on as independent a view as possible which is a core prerequisite if the museum is to be a credible opinion-maker.

The quality of the content of an exhibition depends on the quality and state of the collection. The emphasis of the Swiss Transport Museum collection is on historical vehicles, especially from the beginnings of electrification, and on model locomotives in 1 in 10 scale. The remainder of the collection consists mostly of disparate objects with little background information on inventory. There is rudimentary documentation of the archive collections but the makeshift ordering of the archive for reference use has meant that much of the background information about the documents has been lost.

The museum's original collection management plan was based on many fewer objects, and documentation was largely replaced by the personal knowledge of the founder generation of curators about the artefacts and the notion that the history of a particular object would not be of interest although the fact that the artefact was an example of its type would. The state of the collection and the archive makes efficient use of both difficult when working on the creation of new exhibitions and displays. Although the collection management shortfalls of the last 30 years cannot be made good because of lack of time and financial resources before the anniversary of Swiss railways in 1997, work on a new exhibition for the anniversary will allow some improvements. An inventory can be made of some parts of the collections, and making these parts better known will also enhance the 1997 displays. The work will act as 'capital' for future exhibitions, as well as adding to the knowledge of

Swiss railway history which is the foundation of the very existence of the museum. The partners and sponsors of the 1997 displays want to have as striking and attractive an exhibition as possible. The museum, which depends heavily on entrance and membership fees (in 1992 about 77 per cent of the proceeds), needs an exhibition that will attract as many visitors as possible.

Superficially, the most efficient investment might seem to be in attractive display techniques and in making as many economies as possible in curatorial, conservation and interpretation work on the objects displayed. The case is being put to the sponsors, however, that funding collection management work, research and interpretation is essential to the work of the museum in general and to the anniversary exhibitions in particular.[7] The issue of funding priorities for sponsors is one which goes to the heart of the question of credibility. In addition, investing in collection management, despite financial constraints, makes good sense for the museum. Knowing one's own collection is a prerequisite of preservation and interpretation which are both part of the goal of a museum. Efforts in preservation will enhance the chances of new applications for public funding which is necessary if the Swiss Transport Museum is to survive in the long term. If sponsors can be shown to have supported such investment, it helps the museum in its applications for regular public funding.

Instead of presenting an analysis, a new exhibition has to tell a thrilling story. Exhibition planning must be holistic, must concentrate on content and must ensure that the presentation and interpretation of each artefact is subordinated to the main messages of the exhibition as a whole. Particular artefacts may have to serve as examples which stand for the general message and there must be a formal structure within the exhibition which encompasses the topics chosen. This seems obvious, but the museum committee which provides the connection between the railway companies in Switzerland and the museum itself consists mainly of *Pufferküssers* who are fascinated by interesting details that are not necessarily important to the general public. Nevertheless, the railway enthusiast committee members do represent a core audience. For them, the best exhibitions possible are the most comprehensive, especially if their favourite artefacts are on display. Railway enthusiasts need little interpretation because they have the background knowledge to see the single artefact in a contextual perspective. For them the artefacts evoke images that provoke an immediate emotional and intellectual reaction.

Unlike the *Safety on the Railways* exhibition, the 1997 display space of about 8000 sq m cannot be densely furnished with display material without creating too much of the same, even if the resources to do so were available. Various points, such as the fact that railway enthusiasts form a core audience, the fact that a large number of visitors have no specialist knowledge, the financial situation and the need to equate sponsors' wishes with museum requirements, suggested a division of the new exhibition into three parts. In the first part, the sponsors (the railway companies) have space to present the current railway and its future. The second part will deal with a topic of critical importance for Swiss railways and Switzerland – the conquering of the physical barrier of the Alps. It will be presented with the most up-to-date display techniques possible in order to attract a broad audience and to change public perceptions of the museum and its exhibitions. In the third part, the museum will create a structured study collection with the vehicles as the central feature to satisfy the wishes of the core audience of enthusiasts. The study collection, arranged under headings such as steam locomotives, the beginning of electrification, tramways, rack railways and promotion of tourism, may also satisfy members of the general public who have been interested by the exciting experience of the second part of the exhibition – the heart of the whole display.

The section of the exhibition presenting the railways of today and of the future will promote railway transport, and such relatively overt promotion reflects the close relationship between the museum and Swiss Federal Railways and the private railway companies. The museum is seen, especially by Swiss Federal Railways, as its shop window, presenting the past, present and future of railways in Switzerland. The historic vehicles are mainly owned by Swiss Federal Railways and are on loan to the museum. The railway companies support the museum with a substantial annual contribution and are responsible for considerable investments such as the 1997 exhibition (they are providing three million out of a total of eight million francs). In addition, through their direct involvement in the subject matter, the railway companies have a particular interest in presenting their own story.

The study collection section of the exhibition

needs to have a clear layout and intellectual framework which is readily comprehensible if it is to serve both a general and an enthusiast public. The presentation should not go into technical details but should include a technology assessment to explain how the development of railways shaped the structures of society, and *vice versa*. The displays will put the vehicles in their historical context by adding artefacts and documents to complement the large objects, and highlights of the collection will be indicated as such. Such a method of presenting a study collection offers new possibilities to the railway enthusiast and gives to the general public an introduction to the history of Swiss railways with the option of more detailed study if required. The financial and space savings resulting from this type of presentation allow for further development, especially in the year 2002, on the 100th anniversary of Swiss Federal Railways. If by then the company has not been re-privatised, there will be an opportunity to update parts of the study collection.

The central and most dramatic part of the 1997 exhibition will be the presentation of the role the railways played and still play in conquering the physical barrier of the Alps, with special emphasis on the St Gotthard railway line with its 14.6 km long tunnel. A particular highlight for the visitor will be the interpretation of the construction of the tunnel from 1872 to 1882. Visitors will travel in small time cars through a reconstruction of the tunnel as it was being built and they will experience (as far as is practicable) the conditions endured by the workers drilling the tunnel. At the beginning and end of the story there will be animated reconstructions of the process of deciding the route of the tunnel; the negotiations between the director of the St Gotthard Railway Company, Alfred Escher, and the building contractor, Louis Favre; life in the construction camps; and discussions by engineers about the development of drilling machines. At the end of the visitors' journey, the museum will create, to substantiate the validity of the reconstruction, a display of significant artefacts relating to the building of the tunnel. The overall theme of this section of the exhibition will be 'routes through the Alps yesterday, today and tomorrow', and will embrace topics such as 'locomotives of the St Gotthard railway', 'the consequences of building the St Gotthard tunnel' and 'the new railway Alpine base tunnels for the year 2000'.

On an emotional level, the story will allow the audience to identify with the people who built the tunnel. On an intellectual and political level, the topic will touch on several aspects of relevance to modern life in Switzerland, such as the difference between languages. Louis Favre, the French-Swiss building contractor, and Alfred Escher, the German-Swiss Director of the St Gotthard Railway Company, had to deal with each other and stood for both cultures. More complex is the question of foreign immigrants, especially Italians, who were mainly responsible for building the tunnel, and who have settled in large numbers ever since.

The relevance of an historical exhibition to the current situation is illustrated by the consent of Swiss voters in 1992 to the building of two new railways through the Alps in two main tunnels (Lötschberg and St Gotthard) up to 50 km long. On the level of national identity, the St Gotthard story means dealing with one of the core themes of Swiss national identity since the thirteenth century. There is no opportunity to deal with this subject in depth in this paper but of direct importance for the new exhibition is the fact that during World War Two the St Gotthard was seen as part of a physical and symbolic fortification against negative foreign influences: keeping open the railway line provided a talisman and a bargaining counter in negotiations to prevent Germany from attacking Switzerland.

The growth in international and political interrelations since World War Two has called into question the 'splendid isolation' of Switzerland and thus the mythical significance of the St Gotthard. These changes make it possible to review and re-present the history of the St Gotthard as a transit line servicing the continent: a door to Europe instead of a fortification. The notion of the St Gotthard railway as a transit line through the Alps is a theme which appeals to foreign visitors who make up a significant part of the museum's visitor profile.[8] A final and important theme of the new exhibition is that of historical progress in a nineteenth-century context. The history of the St Gotthard project covers an important period in the shaping of Swiss society in political, economic and social terms.

Conclusion

Effective communication through the medium of an exhibition should reinforce the visitors' existing knowledge and, by introducing new concepts and knowledge, offer new meanings which are appropriate to present perspectives. Besides an attractive presentation, the exhibition has to convey a sense of authenticity and, especially for a museum, the choice of subject has to take into account the historical memory which the site itself or the collection can convey.[9] The uniqueness of the objects in the collection distinguishes the museum from an attraction, a theme park or a fun fair. By communicating the wealth of its unique collections the museum can successfully compete with other attractions in the leisure market.[10]

The main theme of the 1997 exhibition, *Railways Through The Alps*, is believed to have a wide appeal because it contains a dramatic story. Display techniques will allow visitors to identify with the tunnel builders in ways proven to be popular in other exhibitions. Swiss visitors can relate to references to the development of their national identity and to future development of trans-Alpine railways. The fact that today's Swiss visitors will not identify in particular with the former symbolic meaning of the St Gotthard means that the new exhibition can take a different approach to its role in Swiss history. The collapse of eastern bloc communist ideologies has allowed for a new perspective on the history of the tunnel workers and has made it easier to include a more balanced and objective social history in the exhibition.

This special feature within the overall exhibition theme, of the epic story of the St Gotthard tunnel, will be seen by visitors to the museum as a new approach to railway displays. It will catch the attention of the visitors and will be something to talk about, which, on the one hand will help to further discussion, and on the other hand may promote a second visit to the museum.

Swiss Federal Railways have agreed, in principle, to invest two million francs in the 1997 anniversary exhibition at the Swiss Museum of Transport. The association of public transport (consisting mainly of private railways) will support the exhibition with one million francs. Three million francs will be provided by minting a special edition of a five franc coin celebrating the anniversary in 1997. The remaining two million francs will need to come from sponsors who must be convinced of the worth of the museum's proposals and of the approach to the exhibition outlined in this paper. The changing meaning of technology in general and the role of the transport museum, in particular, today give the opportunity to plan and to build an exhibition which will help in the redefinition of the transport museum's place within society and may help educate the public. The museum's task is a formidable one but we look forward to achieving our aims and to presenting an innovative and exciting exhibition in 1997.

Notes and references

1   Weil, Stephen E, *Rethinking the Museum* (Washington and London: Smithsonian Institution Press, 1990), p57

2   Graf, Bernhard, and Treinen, Heiner, *Besucher im Technischen Museum* (Berlin: Gebr Mann Verlag, 1983), p126

3   Strand, John, 'The storyteller: Jeshajahu Weinberg of the US Holocaust Memorial Museum', *Museum News* (March/April 1993), p40

4   Graf, Ruedi, 'Schweiz-Hilde', in Marchal, Guy (ed), *Arfundene Schweiz, Konstruktionen nationaler Identität* (Zurich, 1992), p241

5   At the general meeting of 1992 the second article of the statutes of the Museum of Transport Association was changed from the promotion of traffic to the promotion of an understanding of the questions raised by the development of traffic and the consequences of such development.

6   Label for electric freight locomotive (1'C)(C1') *Crocodile* of the St Gotthard line

7   Addyman, Peter, and Gaynor, Anthony, 'The Jorvik Viking Centre – an experiment in archaeological site interpretation', *International Journal of Museum Management and Curatorship*, 2 (1994), p7

8   Visitors from abroad make up 15 to 33 per cent of the total, according to a study undertaken during three weeks spread over the year 1989. Konso, *Besucher im Verkehrshaus der Schweiz 1989* (Basel: Konso, 1990)

9   Meyer, Marcel, 'Historical show design at tourist sites', *Technology in Leisure and Entertainment: Maastricht Conference Proceedings*

(London: Andrich International, 1993), p35

10 Winter, Ursula, 'Industriekultur: Fragen der Aesthetik im Technik- und Industriemuseum', in Zacharias, W (ed), *Zeitphänomen Musealisierung* (Essen: Verlag Klartext, 1990), p259

The Dutch Railway Museum

Paul van Vlijmen

On 20 September 1839 the first public railway was opened in the Netherlands. The celebratory first train, composed of nine carriages filled with dignitaries and other guests, was pulled by two steam rail cars, *De Arend* and *De Snelheid*. The locomotives were built by Michael Longbridge in Bedlington, England. The first engine drivers, John Middlemiss and Thomas Mann, were also English. The former later became head of the vehicle maintenance shop in Haarlem, and worked on the locomotives behind closed doors to ensure that none of his technical secrets would be divulged. However, all the maintenance work carried out on *De Arend* did not prevent it from eventually being discarded and dismantled in 1857; at the time the concept of a museum to preserve railway artefacts did not exist.

The Amsterdam to Utrecht line, built by the state, was extended to Arnhem, beyond which the former Prussian border came into view, and with it a technical problem. The Dutch government had determined that the railway track gauge should be 2 m, only to realise later that a conversion was necessary for the connection with Germany, which had adopted the Stephensonian 'standard' gauge of 4 ft 8½ inches. After much political bickering, a critical railway act 'regulating the laying of tracks by the state' was finally produced on 18 August 1860. The Company for State Railway Operations, which had been established in 1863, was charged with the management of the state-built railways. Thereafter the railway network expanded rapidly and large railway bridges were constructed.

Of the more than 10 companies operating lines around 1880, the Company for State Railway Operations, the HSM and the NRS were the most important. Co-operation among the companies was out of the question. In fact, the companies refused to have their trains connected up to those of other companies; they denied each other access to their respective lines; and they had their own opinions on how to run operations. For example, the HSM wanted a second eastern connection to Amsterdam but the NRS, which operated the Amsterdam to Utrecht line, prohibited joint access. The new eastern line, which was built in 1874, never became a success and, as early as 1939 the Maliebaan Station on this line was closed for passenger transport, something that was subsequently to be of great significance to the Railway Museum.

During World War One economic and social conditions deteriorated and materially affected the railways. The provisioning of neutral Holland became increasingly more difficult. Food had to be rationed on the basis of food stamps, and coal became scarce and therefore expensive. As a result of this, the executive boards of the various larger railway companies decided to bury the hatchet. On 1 January 1917 a new regulation co-ordinated their so-called 'common interests' and the name Dutch Railways was born, even though it was not until 1 January 1938 that the old companies ceased to exist and NV Nederlandse Spoorwegen ('Dutch Railways') became a fact.

After World War Two, from which the railway company emerged ravaged and plundered, the task of rebuilding and modernising the railways was taken vigorously in hand. In the 1960s and 1970s Dutch Railways experienced serious competition from automobile traffic and, at the same time, the cost of public transportation rose. In 1968 the government signalled the beginning of the rail modifications and innovations that are still evolving today, making Dutch Railways a modern and vital part of everyday life.

With the building of the line from Amsterdam in 1843, Utrecht became the railway city of the Netherlands. During the expansion of the railway network Utrecht acquired, as it were, an increasingly central position, especially after 1917, when the railways' headquarters were located there. It is, therefore, logical that the Dutch Railway Museum should also be established in Utrecht. The basis of the museum's collection consists of the collection of G W Van Vloten. A civil servant employed by Dutch Railways, Van Vloten began collecting unusual and historic objects in his youth. Among these was a collection of railway artefacts and archives. The latter collection, in particular, continued to grow until finally his home was bursting at the seams. In 1917 the board of directors of the railways offered him the use of a room in one of its main administrative buildings for storage but the building was sold in 1921 and Van Vloten was forced to move his collection again to a room in another administrative building.

Although the idea of founding a national railway museum was already a subject of discussion in 1910, the plan was only realised in 1927. In that year the executive board of Dutch Railways, together with Van Vloten, decided to create a museum with the aim of 'bringing together objects of historic or other interest to gain an understanding of rail- and tram-ways in general and those of the Netherlands in particular'. Van Vloten sold his collection of railway-related objects to the museum, while Dutch Railways donated larger items such as models and objects of a technical nature. Thus, on 7 January 1927, the Dutch Railway Museum Foundation was inaugurated as an independent institute.

The first museum was housed on the top floor of a building next to the exit from Utrecht Central Station. In nine small rooms the collection, or at least a part of it, was displayed in a technically, historically and aesthetically responsible fashion. The then director, Asselberghs, was successful in creating a modern and appealing museum on the basis of the existing collection. Meanwhile, the collection continued to grow. Preserving and displaying the smaller acquisitions presented few problems but this was not the case with the large steam locomotives. With the exception of a few horse-drawn streetcars, the entire collection of rolling stock was stored in several sheds and could not be displayed with the smaller artefacts.

World War Two and the German occupation foreshadowed great changes for the Dutch Railway Museum. The German demand for more office space forced the museum to seek new accommodation quickly. Thanks to Asselberghs' close contacts with the Ministry of Education, Arts and Sciences, it was possible to obtain temporary housing in the Rijksmuseum in Amsterdam. Before the War the eight rooms allotted to the Railway Museum had housed the Dutch maritime history department. The Germans considered this subject too patriotic and had the area cleared. In 1942 the small object collection of the Railway Museum was once again opened to the public.

In September 1944, however, the Rijksmuseum had to close its doors as the fighting front advanced and the collection was once again lost to the public. The small objects were stored and, fortunately, were spared the destruction of the War. Less fortunate was the rolling stock which was damaged in bombing by the allied forces; two horse-drawn streetcars were destroyed. What remained was subject to further destruction because the retreating Germans, in vengeance, blew up several of the museum's locomotives. After the War these locomotives were lovingly and skilfully restored to their former state.

At the end of the War the Rijksmuseum required all its space to display its art treasures, which had been stored in the basement. The Railway Museum was unsuccessful in finding new quarters and, between 1946 and 1952, like Sleeping Beauty, the museum's small object collections slumbered on the upper floor of a building with something of the feel of a fairy-tale castle: Amsterdam Central Station. And here too a prince came to the rescue: the President of Dutch Railways, Dr ir F Q den Hollander, brought new life to the dormant museum. In the summer of 1951 he designated the long-disused Maliebaan Station in Utrecht as the permanent home of the Dutch Railway Museum.

The history of Maliebaan Station began with its opening on 10 June 1874. However, the flow of passengers proved less than expected and on 15 October 1939 it was closed to passengers and thereafter used only as a marshalling and freight station. Once the designation of Maliebaan Station as a museum was confirmed, work was immediately begun on preparing the building for its new use. The ticket counters and wainscoting in the main hall were removed and new parquet floors and lighting installed. Once this was completed, it was time to move the collection – for the last time. On 28 November 1953 the main hall and the historical department were opened to the public. The modern department, which focuses on current railway developments, was completed less than a year later. On 5 November 1954 the entire Maliebaan Station was in full use as the Dutch Railway Museum.

The years that followed were devoted to restoring the rolling stock that had been damaged during the war. One by one the restored steam engines rolled into the museum. The old station canopy which, in contrast to the museum building itself, had not been renovated, was replaced by a smaller canopy, offering better protection to the collection displayed on the tracks outside. Great efforts were also devoted to refurbishing the carriages. Although the

collection certainly had gaps, the quality of the
carriages was some compensation. The end of the
steam era in the Netherlands (1958) saw the arrival
in the museum of the NS steam locomotive No
3737. Built by the Werkspoor Amsterdam in 1911
and kept in operational order, this locomotive is
one of the showpieces in a collection which steadily
continued to expand. The new Director, Miss
Asselberghs, the former Director's daughter, continued the development of the museum, modernised it
and produced publications on the collection. For
many, in fact, she became the voice of railway
history. She retired in 1984.

1989 marked the 150th anniversary of the railways in the Netherlands, an event that Dutch
Railways and the Dutch Railway Museum seized
upon as a means of drawing national and international attention both to the railway system and to
the museum. The museum, thanks to the financial
support of Dutch Railways and numerous other
sponsors, was given the opportunity to renovate the
interior of the museum totally. By then the original
installation was 35 years old and in great need of
refurbishment. Work was begun in 1987 on a
design which was finalised during the course of
1988. In August of that year Maliebaan Station was
cleared so that the new plan could be implemented.

The vision of the renovation plan was to create a
design which would be as surprising, clear, unusual
and 'timeless' as possible, and one which would
endure for decades both visually and technically.
The presentation of the collection was guided by
three 'A's: amazement, awe and admiration.

The design of the display cases and other museum furnishings was kept fairly sober in order to
allow the objects to be shown to their best advantage. The materials used, steel and glass, and the
scale of the furnishings, were intended to exude a
railway atmosphere, with its intrinsic solidity and
stability. The application of glass supports for the
model tracks is technically ingenious, as is the
silkscreen treatment of the concave and convex
walls and the use of magnetic foil as a frameless
support for posters and prints. All the subjects
presented in the new displays have been individually designed as a constant delight to the eye.

In 1985 the site behind the museum where
the rail yard of the station was formerly located
had been annexed to the museum, thus allowing
more room for expansion. Simultaneously with
the renovation and rearrangement of the museum's
interior the square in front of the station buildings

was drastically altered with the support of munici-
pal funds. The rolling stock standing on the square
was moved to other locations in the museum
grounds and two car-parking areas were built.
Dutch Railways made every effort to make the area
suitable for the anticipated number of visitors.

In 1988 a signal box was re-erected and a so-
called 'classic' signalling system with semaphore
signals and signal wires installed near the newly
constructed visitors' track. As the Dutch Railway
Museum is the only such museum through which
modern trains pass, it also became necessary to
build a level crossing with automatic half-barriers.

In June 1989 the rejuvenated Railway Museum
was opened. In July the railways gave the starting
signal for their major anniversary exhibition entitled
Tracks Through Time in and around the enormous
fairgrounds of the Jaarbeurs in Utrecht. The exhibition attracted an overwhelming number of visitors
from which the museum also profited: more than
210,000 visitors were counted, a record that will
not easily be broken for quite some time.

One has always to look toward the future. Currently the museum's main focus is on the expansion
of its existing facilities, both as an interesting museum and for commercial reasons. For the most
part the indoor section of the museum requires only
maintenance and small alterations and improvements. The same, however, cannot be said for a
part of the rolling stock collection. Although the
museum is the proud owner of a large number of
exquisitely restored objects, others are in dire need
of restoration. Among them are the famous diesel-
electric triple-carriage train of 1934, the first
stream-lined model, which once was a sensational
sight on the railway network. Another is the beautiful motor coach of the South Holland Electric
Railway Company of 1908, the first electric train in
the Netherlands. Yet another is the early wooden
compartment coach with 110 seats which, as far as
seating capacity is concerned, is the largest coach
the railways ever had in their fleet. All of these are
extremely valuable collectors' items that are in
urgent need of repair and the Railway Museum
considers itself fortunate to have found sympathy
and willingness to help fund this work on the part
of Dutch Railways.

In other more commercial areas the museum has
not stood still. In the summer of 1992 a large
restaurant seating 140 people was built in the
grounds behind the main museum building. This
restaurant is vintage railway as it is constructed in

the style of the former State Railways and using fragments of a Van Gend & Loos warehouse. As is more or less common in many museums, receptions, dinners and parties are organised here. The catering is provided by a franchised service which also runs the restaurant during regular visiting hours. Fifty per cent of the restaurant's profits and losses are assumed by the museum.

The museum regularly conducts surveys among its visitors. Information is collected on geographical origin, spending pattern, age, family make-up, length of visit, etc. On the basis of this information, we know, for instance, that there is a demand for a large model railway track. A start has been made on the preparatory work for this track, which will have a surface area of at least 200 sq m and will be built on a scale of 1 to 43.5. Such a large layout requires a large building to house it as there must be enough room for the many additional visitors the museum hopes to draw with this unique attraction. The track will illustrate the planned future of Dutch Railways and will give visitors an insight into the second railway revolution which is related to high-speed travel. A large part of the railway network will be converted from two to four tracks, thus making it possible for high-speed EuroCity and InterCity trains to operate unhindered by slow local trains.

Another of the museum's recent activities is the construction and operation of a 7¼ inch gauge model track approximately 1000 yards long in the museum grounds. A five-carriage TGV and a Dutch four-carriage InterCity train currently operate on the track. While the museum itself owns a 7¼ inch steam locomotive, it regularly allows steam engines owned by others to take a spin.

Visitors frequently enquire about special activities and we know that many of our visitors would prefer to see all of our steam engines operating all day, every day! However, because of technical limitations and environmental legislature this is not possible and, perhaps, not even desirable but, in order to satisfy the demand, the museum organised the first grand Steam Festival in May 1994. In addition to a number of the museum's locomotives, steam locomotives from 'museum lines' in the Netherlands were on display, as well as a selection of steam cars, a steam carrousel from England, farming machinery, steamrollers and much more.

As far as personnel is concerned, the Railway Museum now has 38 full-time equivalents. In 1985 there were only 12. The number of employees has substantially increased from 2 in 1984 to 70 at present, including part-timers. For a facility of its size, the museum has a modest budget: total expenditure for 1993 has been estimated at approximately £800,000 or about $1,250,000. A third of the income is covered by a subsidy from Dutch Railways; one-third comes from profits on net assets; and one-third is drawn from the sale of admission tickets and other trading activities.

The Dutch Railway Museum, for all its 66 years of existence, remains a dynamic institution. The museum enjoys a fruitful relationship with Dutch Railways and seeks to celebrate the continuing story of railway development in the Netherlands.

The Steamtown solution

John A Latschar

Steamtown National Historic Site in Scranton, Pennsylvania, has been surrounded by a certain amount of controversy ever since it was created in 1986. Over the past several years the park has endured an extraordinary amount of media coverage, and has been labelled by some as a 'pork barrel' project. The most common questions which we hear from the media and others can be summarised as: 'Why was this park created?'; 'What about that second-rate collection?'; and 'How can you justify spending $66 million on a railroad museum?'.

My response to these questions and others is in two parts: I will briefly summarise 'what we are doing', and then discuss in some detail 'why we are doing it'.

What are we doing?

Steamtown National Historic Site was created in October 1986 by US Public Law 99-951. The purpose of the park, according to the US Congress, is 'to further public understanding and appreciation of the development of steam locomotives in the region'. That is an exceedingly broad mandate, and it took the National Park Service several years of thought and study to arrive at a comprehensive plan for the development and operation of the park.

In developing that plan, we first had to assess the condition of the resources which were donated to the National Park Service to create the park. Then we had to determine how those resources could best be preserved and interpreted for the benefit of the public.

The City of Scranton donated to the National Park Service a 67-acre railroad yard which was the former home of the Delaware, Lackawanna & Western Railroad (DL&W). It is a rich historical site, which had been in continuous railroad operation since 1851, and was first recorded by the famous George Inness painting 'The Lackawanna Valley' in 1855. The site included 4½ miles of yard track and sidings and 13 historic structures built by the DL&W between 1865 and 1939. Some of the structures, such as the office/storage building (1909), the locomotive shop (1865-1949) and the

sand tower (1917), were in very good condition. Some of the structures, such as the roundhouse (1902-1937), were not.

The National Park Service also received a donation of 29 steam locomotives and 88 steam-era railroad cars from the Steamtown Foundation. Again, some of this collection was in reasonably good shape and some was not. We may debate whether or not the collection we received was of second-rate significance. We will not debate the fact that most of it was in second-rate condition when we received it.

We are now, in 1993, in the fourth year of our five-year development programme. To date, we have completed the rehabilitation of the historic 13-stall portion of the original roundhouse; we have placed a new turntable in the repaired turntable pit; we have completed the construction of two museum buildings; and we will soon complete the construction of the visitor centre and theatre. In addition, we have accomplished a considerable amount of less visible construction work, including the repair of 9 railroad bridges, the rehabilitation of 13 miles of railroad track, and the installation of new utility systems – water, sewerage, electrical, heating and cooling – through most of the park.

We have also begun the slow and painstaking process of restoration of the historic collection of locomotives and railroad cars. To date, 3 steam locomotives and 11 passenger cars have been returned to operating condition, and 3 railroad cars have been restored to museum display condition. In addition, 17 locomotives and cars have been 'cosmetically' restored, for interim display to the public.

By the time we have completed all this development, we will have spent $66 million. Approximately $2 million of that sum will be spent on planning, $11 million on design and $53 million on construction. Again, these sums represent a lot of 'unseen' but required work, such as the removal of hazardous wastes and the completion of air-quality studies, historical studies and archaeological investigations.

The major projects left to be completed are the construction of entry roads and parking, the completion of utility systems, the construction of our passenger excursion depot and the production and installation of the displays for the museum buildings. If all goes well, everything will be finished by the spring of 1995.

Why are we doing it?

I have summarised what we are doing. The larger question is: 'Why are we doing it?'. As I mentioned, the National Park Service took several years of study and planning before the development concept plan for the park was approved and published in 1989. Contained in that plan are Steamtown's four 'management objectives', which have driven all our construction, exhibition, interpretation and operational plans ever since. Our four management objectives are to:

- provide a setting evocative of steam railroading which retains the historic industrial working character of the yard, incorporating the preservation of historic structures to the greatest extent possible
- provide sufficient year-round facilities and programmes so that visitors can understand the role of steam railroads in the growth of the US, while allowing opportunities for hands-on, active experiences, including riding on a steam-era train and showing how a steam-era railroad operated
- preserve and restore the locomotives and cars in the collection for the purposes of exhibition, interpretation and excursion
- use the site and collection of rail-related artefacts as tools to interpret the cultural and industrial heritage of the northeastern US.

About half of these management objectives can be accomplished through standard museum exhibits and interpretative programmes. This is relatively easy to do, and relatively inexpensive. Through the interpretative exhibits in our museum buildings, we should be able to provide our visitors with an appreciation of the evolution and operation of steam railroads. We should also be able to provide them with an understanding and appreciation of the enormous economic, political, social, environmental and industrial impacts of the railroad industry on the northeastern US during the steam era. And, of course, we will try to give our visitors an understanding of the lives of people who worked on the railroads and whose lives were influenced by the railroads.

The other half of our management objectives will be accomplished through the operating part of the park, through what we call the 'operating railroad museum'. Developing and running an operating railroad museum is much more difficult and much more expensive than building and running a static railroad museum. In order to explain why we came to this decision, I must explain a little past history.

Treatment of resources

The National Park Service had two significant choices when it arrived at Steamtown and began to assess the resources which had been inherited. Firstly, we could choose to treat our buildings either as static historical structures or as functioning buildings. Secondly, we could choose to treat our collection of locomotives and railroad cars either as static historical objects or as functioning pieces of equipment. In both cases, we chose 'functioning'. This was an expensive decision, and one which has led to a lot of questions. I would like, therefore, to take some time to explain our justification for the operating philosophy.

The historic structures at Steamtown National Historic Site are typical of the steam era. None of them has any great architectural merit as an individual building, unlike, for instance, the Mt Clare roundhouse at the Baltimore & Ohio Railroad Museum. However, none of our structures was designed with an architectural purpose in mind. Rather, they were all designed and operated as part of a working rail yard system. In that sense, they are all very real and very authentic. Therefore, we made the decision to treat them as part of a designed rail yard system, and not as individual buildings.

In other words, we think that the value of our historic structures is in how they functioned within a designed rail yard system, and not in what they looked like. It follows that the best use of those structures is to bring them back to life as functioning buildings, in order to use them to interpret to the public how that rail yard system was designed and operated. We realise that this is not a popular decision with those who rate the historic significance of buildings solely upon their architectural merit.

In the same way, our railroad equipment is also typical. We have 29 steam locomotives built between 1887 and 1944, and 88 steam-era railroad cars. None of these locomotives or cars has any great individual significance. We do not have the *C P Huntington* or the *Governor Stanford*, which are proudly displayed at the California State Railroad Museum. All we have are typical working locomotives and cars that hauled the freight, delivered the mail, provided a passenger service and connected America.

In other words, we may not have any locomotives or cars which are significant individual symbols in American history, but they all have significant value as working pieces of equipment. We think that the value of our collection is in what it did, and not what it looked like.

And what did it do? The locomotives and cars in our collection worked, operated and produced as part of an engineering system designed to transport goods and people. Therefore we consider our collection, like our historic structures, to be part of an 'operating engineering system'.

Railway preservation

The National Park Service came to this decision, in part, because we brought a slightly different viewpoint of railway preservation to Steamtown. To us, railway preservation is a relatively recent offshoot of the overall field of historic preservation. We do not consider railway preservation to be a field unto itself. Over the past few years there has been a lot of worthy debate taking place within the railway preservation community concerning the need to adopt standard preservation criteria. We would like to suggest that many of the criteria and standards which have been accepted in the general field of historic preservation are directly applicable to railway preservation, and should be considered during this debate.

For example, there is now a general consensus regarding the preservation of historic structures. In the US this consensus has been published as the *Secretary of the Interior's Standards for Rehabilitation*.[1] A principle preservation tenet codified in the *Standards* is the notion that the long-term preservation of historic structures inevitably requires the constant repair, maintenance and replacement of the structure's components, as those component parts naturally wear out and deteriorate. We have also learned to accept the careful adaptation of historic structures through the addition of modern improvements, such as heating, cooling and fire-suppression systems. In short, most preservation specialists understand that a historic structure is a

living system, which must be allowed to adapt to change through time in order to survive. We have learned to accept this inevitable replacement and adaptation process, as a means of preserving both the building's significance and its useful life.

The field of railway preservation is struggling with some of the same questions. In railway preservation, we are dealing with structures and equipment which were designed and built to operate. Their purpose was to work and to produce. As a natural consequence of that purpose, railway structures and equipment slowly wore out. As this happened, equipment was repaired, parts were replaced and equipment was adapted with modern improvements, all for the purpose of extending the equipment's active life.

What happens to working systems such as these when they are taken out of service and when they can no longer work? What happens to a producing system when it can no longer produce? Does it retain its significance and purpose, or does it become nothing more than a physical symbol of something that no longer exists?

The significance of operating systems

I would like to suggest that the significance of an operating engineering system (ie, a locomotive) is in three parts: how it evolved, what it produced and its relationship to people.

The first part of this significance is widely understood and appreciated. A key part of the significance of a working engineering system is in how it evolved: how it was designed and built, and why it was designed and built that way. That is pure technological history, and we all agree that the best examples of the evolution of locomotive design should be carefully recorded and preserved. We all do that, as part of our standard museum work.

A second and primary part of the significance of an engineering system is the product or service which it produced. In other words, it is the output of the system – not the system itself – which is of primary importance. In particular, understanding the impact which that output had upon society is the key to fully understanding the system's history and significance.

Let me digress in order to illustrate my point. At Lowell National Historic Park, Massachusetts, the National Park Service has carefully preserved a portion of the historic Lowell Mill complex. Architectural historians who visit Lowell get excited about the buildings. Civil engineers love the intricate canal system which powered the mills. Technological historians study the looms which manufactured the cloth. (There are, by the way, as many different types of looms as there are locomotives, and there are small groups of visitors with unusual behaviour patterns whom we fondly call loomfans.) In short, Lowell National Historic Park has commemorated and is preserving an operating engineering system, comprising individual components such as buildings, canals and looms.

But the real key to understanding the significance and impact of the Lowell Mill complex upon the course of American history is knowing that it is not the mills, the canals or the looms that are really important, no matter how interesting they may be. Rather, it is the product of the mills which is important, for it was the product which had a tremendous impact upon American history. That product was cheap cotton cloth, and the ramifications of the availability of cheap cotton cloth upon American history and culture are almost endless. The mass production of textiles had an immediate economic impact upon clothing manufacturing, just as the availability of cheap store-bought clothing had a tremendous economic impact upon American society. Long-term social impacts of the mill system included the birth of America's industrial working class, the immigration and peopling of New England, the beginnings of ethnic strife and class stratification and the growth of labour unions. The Lowell Mills even had a direct political influence upon the great slavery debate in the US, for the mills' voracious appetite for cotton was partially responsible for prolonging the slavery system of the south.

In summary, the real significance of Lowell is its part in the transformation of the US from an agrarian to an industrial society. Lowell is much more than buildings, canals or looms. Understanding and interpreting the significance of the Lowell Mills is much more than understanding how the looms operated, what they looked like or knowing the difference between a single and a double-spindle loom.

In railway preservation, I fear, we have the tendency to let ourselves get caught up in the romantic allure of the locomotive itself. We have the tendency to concentrate on wheel types, to glorify our collections of locomotives (our looms?) and to overlook the larger significance of railway history.

What is that significance? In the half-century between the Civil War and World War One, one of the greatest phenomena in world history took place, as the US evolved from a sleepy agricultural nation into the world's greatest industrial power. Railroads had a predominant role in that evolution. No one has stated it better than William Withuhn, Curator of Transportation for the Smithsonian Institution:

During the nineteenth and early part of the twentieth century, the US was transformed from a vast, thinly populated, agrarian country into the most powerful industrial nation on earth. Of all American institutions in that story, the railroad played a role that I feel can be called decisive. The railroad became a tool of change ... and a presence so influential and so pervasive that today we usually take its effects for granted. For more than a century, the railroad – as a technology and as a social institution – reached into every corner of life, affecting every part of society ...

The history of the railroads is more than old technology or old industrial ways of life, even though those are important ... in our nation's explosive change from the early 1800s right up to today, the railroad laid much of the path – and it laid more than tracks. It laid down cultural patterns which are a central part of the American experience.[2]

I will never be as eloquent as Bill Withuhn, but I believe that the primary significance of railroad history is its product – cheap transportation – and the overwhelming impact which cheap transportation had upon our industrial revolution and the development of the US.

The third area of significance of engineering systems is their human context, which can only be fully understood through the relationship between man and the machine. There is a collective relationship between railroads and society, which we have already discussed. We hope to interpret that relationship in our museum by illustrating the economic, social and political impacts of railroading upon American history and culture.

There is also an individual, one-to-one relationship between the engineering system and its operator, which we feel must be interpreted in order to provide a real understanding of railroad history. This is the relationship which allowed individual labour to harness the awesome power of the machine and put it to use. We hope to interpret this relationship through our operating railroad museum, which will allow visitors to observe our locomotives and cars being overhauled, maintained, serviced and operated by our sweaty, dirty mechanics, much as they used to be.

The consumption of historic fabric

However, if we are going to use our structures as functioning buildings, and if we are going to operate our locomotives and cars to provide public understanding of the operating engineering system called a railroad, then questions arise concerning the consumption of original fabric. This is another question being debated by the railway preservation community today. It is also a question being carefully considered by the National Park Service, since we consider ourselves to be the leading historic preservation agency in the US. We asked ourselves several questions concerning our structures and our equipment:

- how much of the fabric is original?
- how much was changed during its working life?
- what was its original purpose?
- what is our purpose in preservation?

If our purpose is only technological history, then the answer is easy: we should return the piece to a selected period in time, and freeze it. But, at least at Steamtown National Historic Site, that is not our entire purpose. Again, allow me to digress to provide another illustration.

Independence Hall in Philadelphia is a 'working architectural system' which has been adapted for use through time. Without the addition of modern improvements such as electricity, heat, ventilation, fire suppression and security alarms, we would not be able to preserve Independence Hall. We would not be able to keep it alive and functioning, and the public would not be able to visit it. Without the continual replacement of bricks, mortar, shingles, wood and plaster, the building would crumble, the public would be deprived and a significant structure in American history would be lost.

We do not even consider 'freezing in time' our architectural treasures such as Independence Hall. We carefully overhaul, repair and maintain them so that they can both retain their historical significance and adapt through time as living structures. No one can tell how much of the original fabric of Independence Hall still exists, because it really does not matter. What is truly important is that Independence Hall is able to retain its function as a significant structure in American history.

Similarly, I contend that we should not attempt to 'freeze in time' all of our operating engineering systems. Some should be frozen in order to preserve the significant features of their technological significance; others should be allowed to adapt to change through time in order to retain their operating functions and significance.

A typical steam locomotive, through its 30-plus years of service, was continually adapted in order to extend its useful life. A typical locomotive lived through the replacement of drive wheels, wheel sets, bearings, spring sets, drive rods, rod bushings, boiler jackets, boiler tubes, flues, gauges, brakes, brake riggings, brake lines, couplers, staybolts, smokeboxes, vale bushings, stoker engines, washout plugs, cylinders, cylinder saddles, etc, etc. Some had replacement main frames, and most had major overhauls, adaptations and improvements, to extend their useful life. Few people would dare to tell you, with any degree of assurance, how much original fabric a typical steam locomotive has left.

And if you think that is bad, take a look at the future. A tour of the Conrail locomotive shops in Altoona, Pennsylvania, to see how a modern railroad maintains and overhauls diesel locomotives with their interchangeable parts will quickly convince you that if any 'original' part returns to its 'original' locomotive at the end of a major overhaul, it does so purely by chance. Does this mean that in the year 2050 no diesel locomotives operating today will be considered significant due to the loss of 'original' fabric? I suspect not.

In short, when we are dealing with an operating engineering system (a locomotive) which has parts that move and work, then we are dealing with a system that will have parts which wear out, break and need replacement. And we are dealing with a system that was designed and intended to be systematically adapted and improved in order to extend its productive life, from the day it left the erecting shop to the day it was finally retired. The only alternative to this continual change and adaptation is to take the system out of service, to freeze it in time and to lose a portion of its overall significance.

The Steamtown solution

The Steamtown solution is to treat our buildings, our collection and our people as components that work together to interpret a designed and engineered operating system called a railroad. When we can bring visitors in to see classified maintenance through the adaptive use of our historic locomotive shop, when we can bring them in to see running repairs through the adaptive use of our historic roundhouse and when we can let them experience the railroad through the adaptive use of our historic locomotives and cars, then in National Park Service terms we have accomplished our objectives. By using our resources as functioning tools of interpretation, we will fulfil our Congressional mission of providing understanding of the tremendous impact which steam railroading had upon the history and development of the US. And we will also fulfil the National Park Service mission of preserving operating engineering systems for the education and enjoyment of this and future generations.

With an operating railroad museum, we are convinced that we can provide this understanding through the involvement of all five senses: sight, sound, smell, taste and touch. And we hope to stimulate the all-important sixth sense, human emotion, without which there can be no true understanding.

We realise that the Steamtown solution is not for everyone. It is a solution specifically crafted for Steamtown National Historic Site, based upon the state and nature of the historic resources we were given to work with, the highest and best use of those resources and our public mission.

Notes and references

1   US Department of the Interior, National Park Service, *The Secretary of the Interior's Standards for Rehabilitation and Guidelines for Rehabilitating Historic Buildings* (Washington, DC: Government Printing Office, 1983)

2   William Withuhn (testimony presented to the House Subcommittee on National Parks, Forest, and Public Lands, 21 October 1991)

The Strasburg Rail Road, Lancaster County, Pennsylvania

Linn Moedinger

This paper provides a brief history of the Strasburg Rail Road from its rebirth in 1958, illustrates some of the problems we encountered in bringing the line back to life and explains how we have attempted to solve them.

The Strasburg was chartered on 9 June 1832 and although its early history is still unclear we know that it was in operation by the 1850s. It was built as a standard gauge plus railroad: 4 ft 9 inch gauge. We still have some of the original track gauges and occasionally someone gets them confused, so we have tried to set aside the historic track gauges or only use them on curves! The railroad was 4½ miles long and ran from the centre of the small town of Strasburg to Leaman Place outside Paradise, another small town and a junction with the Pennsylvania Railroad (which is now Amtrak). The purpose of the railroad was to connect Strasburg with the main line railroad and to serve the farming community because essentially farming was the only industry in the area. It performed that function quite well for many years, using second-hand steam locomotives until 1926 when steam locomotion was abandoned on the Strasburg Rail Road, probably one of the earliest railroads to abandon steam. Steam was replaced by the only brand new locomotive the railroad ever owned, a 20 ton petrol-mechanical 0-4-0 Plymouth shunter. The Plymouth operated continuously until the 1950s when the need for the railroad was dwindling because more of the freight was going by road. In 1957 the decision was taken to abandon the railroad, and petitions for abandonment were filed with Pennsylvania's Public Utility Commission. In an effort to save the railroad, a group of rail enthusiasts, spearheaded by Don Hallock, sought support from a number of local business people, including Henry Long, a local industrialist. Long, in particular, gave some financial legitimacy to the enterprise, and eventually 24 people were persuaded to buy at least one share of stock each in order to purchase the railroad. Since each share of stock cost $465 the price scared many people away, but the opportunity to be a vice president convinced the 24 stock holders. They elected Henry Long as the sole president as he contributed the most money; he was a total rail enthusiast, a 'foamer', as we call them. Don Hallock still corresponds with people using some of the old stationery which lists all the vice presidents and the titles they gave themselves down the left-hand side of the page; the stationery was much more impressive than the railroad!

Why preserve the Strasburg Rail Road?

Quite simply, the 24 stockholders wanted to play trains. They were tired of playing with miniature steam or model trains and here was an opportunity to buy, own and operate a standard gauge railroad complete with a locomotive, a box car and a track maintenance car. There was never any consideration of railway preservation; the entire endeavour was wholly self-indulgent. Carrying people was never really considered because the stockholders believed that they could make the railroad cover its costs by hauling freight. There was still some freight business; they were connected to a mill at Strasburg and there was some demand for hauling lumber, coal and grain. They felt that if nobody was paid they could make it work.

The first problem for the new owners was that the main road crossing in Strasburg had been tarred over, so that the train could only run half a mile from the mill and then had to stop. The owners, therefore, pulled the track maintenance car across the road, between the traffic, creating grooves in the tarmac, and the main line of the Strasburg Rail Road was open once more for maintenance to start. The main work was to reinstate a proper level crossing and to excavate and repair the 4½ miles of weed-grown track. There was a one-man track gang, Ben Klein, who became Curator at the Railroad Museum of Pennsylvania in Strasburg. He used to single-handedly replace railroad sleepers in the evenings. As a child, I remember watching him, and he was very impressive, because he could replace three or four sleepers in an evening. The taking out was mostly shovel work, but he still had to carry the second-hand sleepers over his shoulder, put them in place and spike them up by himself. A lot of weed removal work was also undertaken. Henry Long's company built a weed machine which I distinctly remember as a large contraption pushed along by the track maintenance car. It had a large rotary wire brush to remove the weeds, but unfortunately it swept the rotten sleepers away too; it was abandoned after a couple of days.

Quite soon it was decided to get the Plymouth shunter going and to run the entire length of the railroad with it. The locomotive blazed up to the road crossing at speed and ploughed into the tarmac on the theory that if the track car could go across, the Plymouth might just make deeper grooves; it did and ground to a halt. The highway department had to remove the tarmac before the level crossing could be re-instated and the railroad could begin to haul freight. In the evenings, if the Strasburg was notified of a freight car at the main line interchange, a crew would be called together, sometimes consisting of quite a few shareholders. They would make a collection to raise enough money for fuel, put it in the Plymouth and then set off.

A little later the first passenger car arrived. The shareholders took the opportunity to buy the passenger car because it cost only one dollar, was complete with seats and was constructed of wood (it was a Reading car). They had already had some success in hauling people on small flat cars fixed up with old bus seats; people seemed to enjoy the ride. These early rides were free. When the Reading passenger car was made operable, the shareholders found, to their surprise, that people wanted to ride on it and were prepared to pay. People still came out to Strasburg to ride in increasingly large numbers.

The railroad was purchased in 1957. In 1959 two more passenger cars were acquired and passenger business rapidly began to eclipse freight. By 1960, the existing terminal, a lumber yard beside the mill in Strasburg was no longer adequate and a new, larger terminal was built. Essentially, the rest of the history of the Strasburg railway is more of the same; more people came to ride the train, more equipment was acquired, especially more steam locomotives, and the railway prospered far beyond the dreams or, indeed, the intentions of the president and his 23 vice presidents.

Why is the Strasburg Rail Road so successful?

There are three primary reasons for the success of the Strasburg Rail Road: location, timing and the Amish – not necessarily in that order. The location is ideal. It is centrally located in a large metropolitan area: New York, Philadelphia, Baltimore and Washington are all within driving distance. The timing was impeccable and the railroad takes no credit for that whatsoever! The preservation of the railroad started at precisely the time the tourist industry began to grow in Lancaster County and the railroad was the only significant attraction in the town of Strasburg. People heard of the county, came to visit, then heard of the railroad and subsequently came to visit that, so as people were discovering Lancaster County they were also discovering the Strasburg Rail Road.

The principal reason for the railroad's continuing success is the Amish people. The main reason people visit Lancaster County is to see the Amish people living their traditional lifestyle. The Strasburg railroad goes right through the Amish farm land, and so it is an excellent way to see Amish farms, without being hindered by traffic jams and false Amish-style tourist traps. The railroad avoids all of this and once tourists board the train, they see nothing but farm land and, depending on the season of the year, they may also see the Amish out farming. There is no more peaceful a sight than watching six mules pulling an Amish plough and listening to the jingling of the harnesses. People even get used to the smell of the place!

There are some secondary reasons for the success of the railroad. Steam locomotion is one, what I call 'the wooden passenger car experience' is another and a third is consistent quality. The railroad discovered very early on that the public identifies with the steam locomotive, and I believe that the appeal of the steam locomotive will be timeless. The wooden cars that the railroad operates are relatively unusual in the US and are probably some of the best there are; the railroad was fortunate in acquiring them at time when there were still a fair number available. To ride in such elaborate cars is a very special experience because, typically, the majority of the cars are fitted out better than most people's living rooms, even though the cars are only standard class.

The quality of the visitor experience is not only in the comfort of the cars but also their visual appeal. Dependability is also extremely important; if people make a specific trip to the Strasburg Rail Road because they want to ride behind a steam locomotive, they will be very disappointed if there is not one waiting for them. The railroad runs 2000 trains a year, and only missed two last year. If a railroad is dependable the public will come back, as is demonstrated by the high level of repeat business at the Strasburg Rail Road.

The theme and philosophy of the Strasburg Rail Road which are outlined above date from when the railroad started. From the arrival of No 31, the first steam locomotive, and from the first time it travelled up and down the railroad (followed by a Pennsylvania Railroad track crew to repair the track behind it) on Labour Day 1960, the theme was adopted: Old-Time Steam Railroading. We have retained the theme to this day, but the implementation of it has changed somewhat because the public has become more sophisticated and demanding. In 1960 you could pile 100 visitors on a coach which seated 72 people and they would be content; today, if you did, that they would be annoyed and demand a refund.

We had originally envisioned the railroad as a small-town 'wooden axle pike' – just a broken-down branch line operation on which the shareholders could play trains. When you transport half a million people a year, however, this idea evaporates. Whether we want to be small-time, old-time railroading or not, when there are 2000 people standing on the platform we have to respond in a professional way. The number of people attracted to the railroad has dictated our theme and our philosophy of operation. Some of the constraints on the execution of that philosophy are dictated by the requirements of our visitors. Although some things can be hidden or disguised, others, such as parking requirements, are more obvious: a parking lot cannot be hidden unless it is put underground. Providing toilets, too, is difficult for such large numbers; we used to have original station toilets but these have had to be upgraded. We also have to bear in mind public liability and we have become somewhat over-cautious, because we do appear to attract a certain number of people who seem set on injuring themselves. We are a 'for profit' business; every penny has to come through the ticket window or from shop sales, and this limits our scope and the speed with which we can advance. We are also controlled by stockholder preferences and some-

times the stockholders can suggest totally impractical ideas with which we have to try to comply.

Regulatory requirements are a further challenge, notably on environmental issues; we are dealing with matters such as smoke abatement and have recently been told that we are ahead of most companies of our size. We have operational regulatory requirements established by the Federal Railroad Administration; occupational constraints, especially in safety matters, as employees are no longer considered expendable as they were in the steam era; and, of course, public requirements such as disabled access. We have to address questions such as to what degree the structure of an historic car should be altered to accommodate disabled passengers.

In the early days the limited means of the Strasburg Rail Road dictated the type of equipment we operated. Basically, if it was old, cheap and available we purchased it. In the middle years we focused a little more on what was appropriate, not just on whether it was cheap and available. Today we are actually disposing of equipment because we cannot maintain it if it is not in line with our operating philosophy. Fortunately, with the State Railroad Museum immediately across the road from our Strasburg station we do not really have the need for static displays. In fact, we complement one another; we run the trains, they interpret and display railroad equipment.

Our relationship with the Pennsylvania Railroad Museum is particularly important in helping us to resolve the conflict between operation and preservation. Once the old-time steam theme was adopted, we put passenger cars in service as quickly and cheaply as possible because we had a rapid increase in patronage. The conflict came when we tried to maintain this equipment; it was not put together in a maintainable fashion. It was not consistent with our philosophy to upgrade the equipment, so the solution was to rebuild and repair our vehicles to a level that allowed an affordable maintenance schedule, to discard unnecessary equipment, but to retain the historic appearance of the railroad. We have also had to staff the operation for the number of visitors we attract, a staffing requirement very different in scale from that envisaged by the original 24 stockholders. The solutions so far have shown favourable results; perhaps time alone will judge whether we have adopted the correct solutions. All we can say at present is that the Strasburg Rail

Road is a very popular visitor attraction in a tourist area, providing a steam-era experience in the countryside that, thanks to the Amish, is itself in a sort of time-warp.

The Ravenglass & Eskdale Railway and its museum

Peter van Zeller

The Ravenglass & Eskdale (R&ER) is a 15 inch gauge railway in the English Lake District. Despite being the smallest practical size for both passenger and freight operation, the R&ER is a line which has looked worldwide before introducing new technology and passing that experience on to other railways – including British Rail. It is now primarily a tourist operation but the railway has a very complex history that can only be adequately explained to visitors through museum display techniques. Starting from a temporary exhibition to celebrate the R&ER passenger centenary in 1976, we were among the first preserved railways in the UK to introduce a conventional museum to complement timetabled service operations. We are delighted that we have just been recommended for registration with the Museums & Galleries Commission.

'La'al Ratty', as the line is affectionately known, looks like something from a toy train set. With its one-third scale locos, it is Thomas the Tank Engine come true for most of the people who ride on it. However, the railway has a long and interesting engineering background and several historic locos. The *River Irt* was built in 1894 (in its original form as *Muriel*) and the *River Esk* in 1923. They operate on a steeply graded 6¾ mile route which was originally the trackbed of a 3 ft gauge railway laid to carry iron ore in 1875. Little of this earlier line survives, save for the alignment, the loco shed at Ravenglass and the station building at Irton Road.

The route is quite dramatic as it clings to the foothills of the Scafells, England's highest mountains. Starting from Ravenglass on the Cumbrian Coast, it first climbs along the valley of the River Mite, then crosses into Eskdale to terminate at Dalegarth. There are steep drops alongside the track. The government railway inspector who came to consider whether the original 3 ft gauge mineral line was suitable for carrying passengers, was not impressed with the works: 'I don't recollect having seen anywhere where the masonry was of such indifferent quality.'[1]

Along the route the original dry-stone wall embankments are still exposed in various places, even though they were supposed to have been widened and covered in spoil to consolidate them before passengers could be carried. The line was obliged to conform with legislation including the 1889 Regulation of Railways Act which required the use of continuous automatic brakes. The two locomotives were fitted with Westinghouse air compressors but, with that delightful lack of standardisation common to many narrow-gauge railways, one engine, *Devon*, had a compressor on the right-hand side, while the other, *Nab Gill*, had one on the left.

The 3 ft gauge line was in receivership within months of opening to passengers and the line became a local joke. One station was an upturned boat but trains stopped anywhere that passengers required. The iron ore mines were soon worked out, though granite and domestic coal traffic continued. Although tourists to the 'English Alps' brought considerable business in the summers, arrears of maintenance finally brought about the closure of the railway to passengers in November 1908. A new Act of Parliament authorised electrification but 'Owd Ratty', the old railway, only ran spasmodically for goods until 30 April 1913. That would have been the end of the Ravenglass & Eskdale story had it not been for some early miniature railway enthusiasts.

Small-gauge railways had long been used for promotional purposes. In 1854 Commodore Perry created a favourable impression of Western technology in Japan after he allowed officials to ride and drive a 22 inch gauge 4-4-0 locomotive. In Britain a contemporary machine, *Pearl*, was built by Peter Brotherhood for demonstration on a 15 inch gauge line,[2] and this became the standard advocated by Sir Arthur Heywood. Heywood laid an extensive railway at his estate, Duffield Bank near Derby, from the 1870s. Alas, there was little commercial or military interest in Heywood's minimum gauge theories and the Duffield Bank line remained a family affair operated by his children and only open to visitors on special occasions.

Meanwhile in the US 15 inch gauge lines built by the Cagney Brothers were successfully operated at exhibitions and amusement parks. They exported their miniature American locomotives all over the world and examples ran on several sites in the UK at the turn of the century. Their success inspired Wenman Bassett-Lowke, whose company promoted the model railway hobby, to build and operate 15 inch gauge miniature locomotives of British appearance. Bassett-Lowke and his colleagues found the derelict line at Ravenglass during 1915 and, under the unlikely circumstances of World War One, leased the line, regauged the track to 15 inches and began to run a proper daily train service. Everything the valley needed, including the Royal Mail, travelled in or out on the small trains.

After it was converted to 15 inch gauge, the R&ER was effectively a preserved railway in embryo. All the characteristics of a preserved railway that we now recognise, such as using a redundant trackbed, bringing in old rolling stock and operating with volunteer enthusiast labour, came together at Ravenglass 35 years before the revival of the Tal-y-llyn Railway started the new wave of railway preservation.

The reopening of granite quarries along the line in the 1920s stimulated another important development: practical 15 inch gauge locomotive power. Neither the true scale models or the Heywood locos were suitable for intensive service on severe gradients. Henry Greenly designed the 2-8-2 *River Esk* to a one-third scale outline for the quarter scale track. It was built at the Davey, Paxman works in Colchester, where diesel engines are built for British Rail's high speed trains, and it still has the original running gear. This led to many similar size locos being built in Germany to provide transport at major expositions, which still run in Dresden, Leipzig, Vienna and Delhi, while in the UK Paxman built locos for the Romney, Hythe & Dymchurch Railway.

Further changes at Ravenglass reflected the need to operate a commercial railway service. Internal combustion engined locos were introduced and a 4 ft 8½ inch standard-gauge line was laid to the granite quarry crushing plant, its track interlaced with the 15 inch gauge. The miniature steam locomotives continued to attract tourists from all over the north of England. However, after World War Two the granite quarries closed, passenger traffic declined and finally the railway was put up for sale. In the absence of a purchaser it was offered for auction in 1960.

The railway was saved by enthusiasts again, who set up the company which now operates the line, along with an associated preservation society. The whole route had to be rebuilt from the trackbed upwards. There had been piecemeal relaying during the 1920s, but there were long lengths of regauged 3 ft rail *in situ* including some original wrought-iron rails of 1874. New hardwood sleepers and 35 lb/yd rail have now been laid throughout concluding with a golden spike driven by the great grandson of Sir Arthur Heywood.

Station areas have also been rebuilt. Ravenglass has new sheds for stock storage and workshops, while redundant British Rail structures like the awning from Millom on platform two and the cast-iron columns from Whitehaven (Bransty) on platform one are linked by the footbridge from Coniston. It is a pastiche of an historic railway station but it was attractive enough to gain an award in the Restored Stations competition and it is practical in giving passengers shelter and masking otherwise basic buildings.

As well as this extensive work on infrastructure, we have had to renew and rebuild rolling stock to carry the number of visitors needed to generate the income to stay in operation (260,169 journeys were made in 1993). The majority of new coaches are lightweight aluminium-roofed vehicles with large windows or open sides. Most popular in reasonable weather conditions, however, are wooden bogie open coaches little changed from those built by Heywood. Redundant examples of early goods and passenger vehicles are kept restored and displayed as part of the museum collection.

Keeping historic locomotives in operation presents the same dilemmas common to every preserved railway. Bushes and other worn components need to be replaced and required safety features such as air brake compressors need to be added. This is precisely what happened when such machines worked in commercial service. *River Irt*, built in 1894, is now using its third boiler on the original chassis. *River Esk* is 70 years old and has been rebuilt piecemeal on the original mainframes. However, the steam locomotives still remain in daily operation, unlike the old internal combustion quarry locomotives which are now museum exhibits because parts such as clutches and carburettors are now virtually unobtainable.

As traffic has grown tenfold, new motive power has been acquired. In 1966 the model-making firm of Clarkson of York completed the *River Mite* which was transported to Ravenglass by traction engine – a great publicity coup at the time. Subsequently the railway's own workshops have rebuilt old locomotives and built completely new ones for the R&ER and other lines. In 1990 and 1992 two steam locomotives based on the 2-6-2 *Northern Rock* design were completed for a leisure park at Shuzen-ji in Japan, thus continuing the long UK tradition of building steam locomotives for export!

The 15 inch gauge is now an international standard and we have had visiting locos from the UK, US and Australia. In California the 15 inch Redwood Valley Railway has scale 3 ft gauge locos, rolling stock and buildings reminiscent of nineteenth-century US practice. In Tasmania the Bushmills Railway operates a 15 inch gauge scale reproduction of the first 2 ft gauge Beyer Garratt loco used on the island and now on display at the National Railway Museum, York. Both these railways are giving their visitors an entertaining yet relevant historic experience which would not be otherwise possible.

We have looked worldwide in conducting experiments which are of interest in the field of railway operation. One locomotive was fitted with a steam supply to the ashpan to provide a gas producer combustion system like that perfected in Argentina by Dante Porta and in South Africa by David Wardale. Even on a tiny locomotive like *River Esk* the combustion effect is exactly the same as on the much larger 3 ft 6 inch gauge South African machines, proving that we can, if necessary, use poor quality coal.

Full signalling interlocked with pointwork was installed at Ravenglass because we are obliged to comply with general railway legislation although we are a small-gauge line. However, having studied the 760 mm gauge Zillertalbahn in Austria, and the radio links used on German and Dutch secondary railways, we use a radio train dispatching system. Locomotives are fitted with a portable VHF transmitter, allowing each driver to communicate directly with the line controller. From an historic point of view, this modern technology has allowed us to keep the rest of the railway free from fixed signalling. By comparison the Tal-y-llyn Railway was a quiet line that has been transformed since preservation. Once we had paved the way with the Department of Transport for radio control, British Rail secondary lines in Wales, Scotland and East Anglia have developed the system and are now worked by a computerised version, although if the computers go down, they revert to our basic voice system.

The R&ER has been a relatively technologically advanced and innovative railway at the cost of its historical roots. Our response to criticism of this policy is that we are an operating railway that must attract and carry passengers to survive. We must comply with past and present legislation, and as a result of these pressures the railway has changed dramatically during its life. It could not readily have been preserved at any particular period; it was forced to evolve and will continue to do so. Yet through our museum we are able to safeguard redundant equipment, bring out its significance for the passenger and generally enhance the visitor experience, saying 'this isn't just a joy ride, it's a heritage train journey'.

In the museum we can illustrate such things as the small scale of our first 15 inch gauge locomotives compared to a full-size mock-up of a 3 ft gauge locomotive. The speed and scale of destruction of the original 3 ft was remarkable: after a couple of years so little was left that reputable railway historians were referring to the line as having a gauge of 2 ft 9 inches! Even when a full history of the line was written in the 1960s, the matter was in doubt until an original sleeper was dug up, sections of rail put on it and the gauge measured. We have acquired wheelsets from the 3 ft gauge Isle of Man Railways to create a replica wagon, and intend to retain the surviving 20 per cent of an original 1876 coach and rebuild the missing 80 per cent of the vehicle.

Photomontages back displays of artefacts to form displays of the winding house that let wagons down an incline from the Nab Gill iron mine to the 3 ft gauge terminus at Boot and the original station at Ravenglass. Here visitors sit in a restored Heywood coach with a 15 inch gauge wagon and track, dwarfed by a section of 3 ft gauge coach, to watch a video account of the line's history. Large diorama models show the otherwise hard-to-appreciate scale of the iron mines, the Beckfoot granite quarries and the Murthwaite crushing plant. These former eyesores are now gently returning to nature; their restoration to the visual appearance they had when they were active would not be acceptable in a National Park.

An important exhibit is the Bassett-Lowke locomotive *Synolda* of 1912. It was built for the private Sand Hutton Railway 20 miles from York and was rescued in scrap condition from Belle Vue Zoo in Manchester in 1978. Painted in the builder's livery, it represents its sister locomotive *Sans Pareil* which began the 15 inch gauge services at Ravenglass in

1915. *Synolda* was restored and is kept in working order for special events such as the 75th anniversary of the reopening.

A current museum project is to re-create a Heywood locomotive with some original parts and castings from original patterns. The original 0-4-0 *Katie* was built in 1896; the re-creation will be on static display in 1994, while it is hoped that it will be operational for its centenary two years later. It has as much of the original as *River Esk* and already illustrates better than any photos how different the scale of the Heywood and Bassett-Lowke locos were. The actual operation of *Synolda* has given a clear insight into the problems of operating such undersized machines, while as a fundraising venture, *Katie* was pushed up the line much as the original needed to be!

We are explaining to our visitors a long and complex history. Without continued operation, the only relic would be a grassy trackbed with sleeper depressions, like the abandoned sections to the mines in Eskdale, which we are signing to form a RailTrail. But the ride is itself an historic experience. Passengers can travel behind *River Esk* in open coaches over the same route in virtually the same conditions as they could when the locomotive was new 70 years ago. The trains wind along the fellside stopping for water where the 3 ft gauge trains stopped 125 years ago. Even if we cannot restore the line to any particular period in its existence, we aspire to show the continuous and continuing development of the railway through our museum activities, through promoting the journey as a 'smuts and cinders in the hair' travel experience and through our varied day-to-day operations.

There are qualities in the operation of a railway – the sights, sounds and smells, the disciplines, the overcoming of problems from slipping on greasy rails, shunting, to struggling with a clinkered fire – that cannot be experienced or understood from a static museum exhibit. The best audio-visual display of a steam locomotive in action is the locomotive in action. Yet there are practical, curatorial and financial reasons why most museums cannot offer these activities with historic full-size equipment on a daily basis. A small-gauge operating railway can provide an economic, practical, unobtrusive and intrinsically attractive visitor experience and transport link for museums, outdoor festivals and expositions.

Notes and references

1   Board of Trade report on the Ravenglass & Eskdale Railway, 29 June 1876, in Davies, W J K, *The Ravenglass & Eskdale Railway* (Newton Abbot: David and Charles, 1968), p164

2   Mosley, D, and van Zeller, P, *Fifteen Inch Gauge Railways - Their History, Equipment and Operation* (Newton Abbot: David and Charles, 1986)

The American experience: railway preservation in the US

Walter P Gray III

'The American experience' offers a look at one key dimension of railroad preservation in the US: the formal railroad museum. The task of this brief introduction is to set and furnish the stage for the papers which follow, and because it is essentially impossible to provide anything like a comprehensive overview of a national preservation effort in a few pages, I must caution that the furnishings will be well chosen but somewhat sparse.

Railroad preservation in the US is the product of work by the railroads, antiquarians, enthusiasts working together in groups or as individuals and, most recently, government. Some consider it to be an organised movement; others see it as the consequence of 10,000 individual acts which are only vaguely related. All agree it is an avocational field that is gradually becoming professionalised and is in search of unifying values.

Preservation is a human activity, and it is appropriate to begin with the human and historical elements of the field. Interest in railroad history was originally the province of economists and the early proponents of America's ideology of technological superiority. Railroads were the key national industry, and it was easier to support notions of progress if there were a few examples available to show where we began. Railroads themselves, most famously the Baltimore & Ohio (B&O), exhibited early equipment to validate their claims for positions of primacy and to turn heritage to competitive advantage.

Engineers and antiquarians began to shape railroad preservation decisions in the 1890s. Several locomotives, a few cars and considerable amounts of documentary material found their way into general museums and historical society collections because they were old. Other items were saved as part of mechanical-engineering study collections. Organised clubs of railroad enthusiasts were established in New England after World War One, with an emphasis on riding trains, photography and the collecting of ephemera, photographs and engineering materials. By the late 1930s some individuals and local groups had begun to collect appreciable numbers of locomotives and items of rolling stock,

an activity which accelerated through the 1950s and continues today.

The overwhelming majority of people involved in railroad history and preservation are avocationalists, 'railfans', who tend to be drawn to the subject for emotional (or at least non-rational) reasons. These are the volunteers and members who are the foundation of most preservation activities. But interest in railroads does not necessarily translate into efforts to preserve them. Compare the numbers of model railroaders with railroad preservationists: *Model Railroader* magazine has a paid monthly circulation of 224,700; *Trains*, America's largest circulation general-interest railroad publication, comes in at 107,000; and *Locomotive & Railway Preservation* sells 13,300 issues every other month. The closer one approaches matters of actual preservation, the smaller the audience.

Kevin Keefe, editor of *Trains*, believes there are no more than 150,000 people in the US with a defined avocational interest in full-size railroads. Recognising that only a portion of this group is inclined toward preservation and the historical aspects of railroading – let us be very generous and say 100,000 – it becomes evident that America's national railroad preservation efforts are conducted by a very small number of people.

Railroad preservation is difficult to define or quantify, and is manifested in an endless variety of ways. It is obviously much more complex than just keeping obsolete locomotives, but until quite recently 'railroad preservation' was understood to mean the saving of steam locomotives, electric streetcars and odd pieces of rolling stock. Serious concern for the preservation of the railroad built environment – railroads themselves and lesser elements such as stations, shops and other facilities – began to develop in the 1950s with the decline of intercity passenger train services and the abandonment of many lines, and reached national consciousness in 1963 with the loss of New York City's Pennsylvania Station. Other activities commonly included under the banner of preservation are the operation of tourist railroads, the collecting of small artefacts (objects which are not locomotives or cars), paper items, photographs, the development of research collections, book publishing and model railroading. These all touch aspects of railroad preservation. Some of these objects, like collections of photographs and those endless notebooks filled with locomotive numbers, are self-created by enthusiasts and have become objects of preservation in their own right.

The emphasis on locomotives, particularly steam locomotives, does allow some interesting, if imprecise, quantification. In 1920 there were about 64,000 steam locomotives in the US. More than 26,000 were in service in 1950, but rather fewer than 1500 exist today, of which approximately 175 are operable at any given moment. The overwhelming majority of the survivors were not formally 'preserved' in museum settings, but were installed in city parks and playgrounds during the 1950s as the jungle-gyms of the Industrial Revolution or as nostalgic park sculptures. Many have since been scrapped, passed to museums or placed back in service by preservationists. The interesting statistic is that of these 1500 pieces, only four dozen pre-date 1880. Certainly much of this is attributable to the fact that far greater numbers of locomotives were built after 1880, and that many of these more modern machines were of designs suitable for service until the end of steam, but I believe it helps demonstrate that formal railroad preservation is a relatively recent phenomenon.

The Stephenson-built *John Bull* of 1831 is generally recognised as the first intentionally preserved locomotive in the US, having achieved status as a relic as early as 1858. Celebration of the US centennial in 1876 prompted the dusting off and repair of other ancient specimens. Most subsequent world's fairs and railroad expositions included railroad-sponsored exhibitions of historic equipment. This resulted in the permanent preservation of several items and an awareness that these old machines had historic value. The earliest locomotives in the B&O Railroad Museum's collection were set aside in 1893. The California State Railroad Museum's oldest specimen is an 1862 4-4-0 restored and preserved in 1899. Many other well-known mid-nineteenth-century locomotives found their way into museum collections or at least safe corners of roundhouses about 1900: some other examples are the Cumberland Valley No 13 at the turn of the century, *Reuben Wells* and *Oregon Pony* in 1904, *William Crooks* about 1907 and *C P Huntington* in 1915. About half the surviving pre-1880 pieces achieved preserved status in the hands of railroads between 1893 and 1917, and another 10 were saved by private parties. The balance, plus most of the remaining post-1880 locomotives, were preserved by the active efforts of enthusiasts after about 1937 or were retired to private individuals, parks or railroad museums in the 1950s.

And what is a railroad museum? In the US there is no agreed standard for what constitutes a railroad museum, and each place that identifies itself as one differs from every other, sometimes in significant ways.

A look through the pages of the current *Steam Passenger Directory*, the most complete listing of museums, tourist railroads and other historical/preservation facilities, indicates the difficulty of defining the field. The entry for the US includes 284 properties, with each identified as being a museum, ride, display or some combination of these elements. Within this group are 204 places that describe themselves as rides, 118 as museums and 78 as displays. The museum category includes 11 'model railroad museums' and 20 general history, technology, children's and transportation museums that happen to have railroad holdings. This leaves about 87 railroad museums, some little more than preserved depots with a caboose parked outside, and others with extensive formal museum facilities. Returning to the figure of 100,000 enthusiasts inclined toward preservation, this translates into something like 1140 members per museum. This sounds about right as an average: my museum, the California State Railroad Museum, larger than most, has about 3000 members and active supporters.

Extending this analysis a little further, only about one-third of these 87 museums have paid full-time staff, and nearly half of all full-time railroad museum employees in the US work at Baltimore, Strasburg, Scranton or Sacramento. Although the figure is an estimate, I believe the entire national railroad preservation workforce is about 200 full-time and another 350 part-time employees in museums, plus perhaps 800 who work for tourist railroads, and several thousand active volunteers. But I digress.

The *Directory* does not fully reflect the overall scale of efforts to preserve railroad objects, of course. Missing from the listing are about 500 locomotives in parks and fairgrounds around the nation, plus nearly 1000 depot buildings no longer in railroad ownership. It is arguable whether all of these are 'preserved' or merely not yet scrapped.

Irrespective of what these railroad museums are, almost all represent one of four combinations of origin and operation. The earliest organised efforts to preserve railroad equipment were undertaken by the railroads themselves, although these efforts were very limited. Other collections were assembled by railroad enthusiasts working individually or in organised groups. A few general museums sought railroad specimens for their collections, and government-sponsored museums have come into existence within the last two decades. Today most of these collections, irrespective of origin, are in museums operated either as private, non-profit corporations, or as governmental (public) entities. There are very few for-profit museum collections (although numerous commercial tourist railroads have displays of old equipment in their grounds, often of deceased locomotives withdrawn from service due to deterioration), and the railroad-operated museum is nearly extinct.

These combine to give us four common formats for creation and operation: private-private, private-public, railroad-private and railroad-public. The most numerous are private, enthusiast-run railroad and trolley museums, the leading example being the Illinois Railway Museum at Union. A private collection assembled by railroad enthusiasts is the basis of my public museum, while the public Railroad Museum of Pennsylvania has its origins as a railroad collection. The B&O Railroad Museum was founded as a railroad collection and is today operated as a private, non-profit institution.

Other factors help to shape the field. American railroads are private companies with varying degrees of sensitivity to the concerns of preservation; they have, in the main, never recognised any obligation to undertake preservation. Indeed, many railroad companies, now defunct, were quite poor in their later years. Poverty is the great preserver, and a few of these lines passed their operating properties wholesale into museum collections.

Nevada's fabled Virginia & Truckee Railroad is the best known of these. Other railroads like the East Broad Top in Pennsylvania died, but did not disappear, surviving in suspended animation with facilities, locomotives and rolling stock intact.

Because railroads are not nationalised or co-ordinated in any way of value to preservation interests, it has been extremely difficult to collect railroad equipment systematically. Chance, opportunity and the quirky preferences of railfan collectors have done much more to define what is in museums today than actual planning. And we had no one like Dai Woodham and no place like his scrapyard in Barry in Wales to serve as a buffer between the technological changes experienced by the industry and the preservation movement's ability to absorb the resultant obsolete equipment.

Railroad preservation at the level of the American railroad museum is largely avocational, segmented both geographically and by means of propulsion (steam, electric and diesel), and to a degree by era. The emphasis is still on the age of steam and the steam locomotive but with a growing recognition that railroading did not disappear with the departure of 4-8-4s and 4-8-8-2s, and that contemporary equipment and the contextual aspects of the built environment also require preservation. The more formal museums have made substantial investments in plant and exhibition facilities, and are moving into the mainstream of the museum movement. The 1990s have brought the first serious call for national co-ordination, and the entire field is wrestling with difficult problems of funding, mission and public service. Railroad preservation in the US is still very much in the early stages of development.

The following papers concern three of the four most intensively developed formal railroad museums in the US: the Railroad Museum of Pennsylvania, the California State Railroad Museum, and the B&O Railroad Museum. The fourth of this exclusive group, Steamtown, was the subject of John Latschar's paper.

The Railroad Museum of Pennsylvania

Robert Emerson

The Railroad Museum of Pennsylvania is a state-owned and operated museum of railroad history and technology, with responsibilities to collect, preserve and interpret objects related to the railroad industry in Pennsylvania to the broadest possible audience. The museum is located in Strasburg, a small community in rural Lancaster County, Pennsylvania. Immediately adjacent to the museum is the Strasburg Rail Road, one of America's most successful and popular steam-powered tourist railroads.

Located on a 14-acre site, the museum facilities consist of an entrance building filled with orientation exhibits, a meeting room, a museum shop, a second-floor temporary exhibitions gallery, a library, an archive and support facilities. Behind this structure, a 45,000 sq ft locomotive and rail car exhibition hall serves as the museum's main attraction. Spanning four tracks and five pedestrian platforms, the hall exhibits 20 locomotives and passenger cars, many from the nineteenth century. Curved tracks and platforms provide an interesting perspective for the display of short trains. An overhead walkway gives visitors a view of the collection from above, and an inspection pit beneath an 1888 freight locomotive allows public viewing from below.

Along the platforms and in several trackside alcoves supporting exhibits tell the human side of the railroad industry in Pennsylvania. Here, stories of engineering achievements, pride in craft, labour, immigration, racial discrimination and working conditions on Pennsylvania's railroads are told through the display of artefacts, graphics and photographs.

Outside, roughly two-thirds of the museum's vehicular collections are stored in a fenced yard area. One of the yard's highlights is an operating turntable which is used to position a number of items in the collections on radial tracks around the table. Visitors particularly enjoy touring the yard, since many of the twentieth-century locomotives and cars most familiar to the general public are stored there. Additionally, the yard provides a more contextual environment for the collection than a modern, more formal museum setting.

The museum's unique collection of vehicular artefacts is its greatest strength. At the core of this collection is an assemblage of historic locomotives and rail cars of the Pennsylvania Railroad (PRR). Of supreme value is the motive power collection which illustrates standard locomotive development on the PRR from the 1880s to 1935, arguably the railroad's period of greatest prosperity and influence. Most of the major classes of steam locomotives developed by or for the PRR over a 50-year period are collected in one location for public viewing.

Although the PRR is the primary focus of the museum's collections, other railroads and railroad suppliers operating in the state are also represented; examples of these objects include the *Tahoe*, built by the Baldwin Locomotive Works of Philadelphia in 1875, and locomotives and cars used by the state's anthracite hauling railroads and by Pittsburgh area steel works lines.

To support the vehicular collections, the museum has assembled approximately 100,000 smaller objects used to build and operate the state's railroads. Archival collections consist of 300,000 photographs and negatives including the negative collection of the Baldwin Locomotive Works and a library of 7000 volumes.

The museum had its beginnings in 1963 when the state legislature authorised the creation of an institution to 'preserve significant artefacts appropriate to the history of railroading in the state and to present through exhibits the highlights of that history ...'. In reality, the authorisation of the Railroad Museum was part of a broader effort to preserve the state's vanishing industrial history. The creation of the Railroad Museum of Pennsylvania was concurrent with the establishment of a lumber museum, an anthracite coal museum complex, an agricultural museum, an iron furnace museum and an historic site at Drake's Oil Well. As a state-owned site, the museum is administered by the Pennsylvania Historical and Museum Commission (PHMC), a state agency founded in 1913 with responsibility for the operation of 60 historic sites, the state archives, the Historic Preservation Program and numerous support services.

In 1965, after a two-year study, a museum site was selected at Strasburg, Lancaster County. The site selection was controversial, since several Pennsylvania communities were vying actively for the museum. Strasburg's attributes included an already thriving steam tourist railroad, a location in a heavily visited tourist area and access to the Strasburg Rail Road's mechanical skills and facilities.

One of the most powerful justifications for the creation of a state railroad museum was to provide a permanent home for the historical collection of the PRR, some 25 locomotives and cars stored in the small central Pennsylvania community of Northumberland. By the early 1960s the PRR collection had been established for a number of years, tracing its history back to 1938 when the PRR initiated a search for vintage locomotives and cars for display at the New York World's Fair of 1939-40.

In August 1938 the PRR's Superintendent of Motive Power was directed to seek out any 'old' locomotives of PRR heritage. The oldest located was former No 1187, a 'Consolidation' type built in 1888 and sold in 1911. No 1187 was obtained from its owners in an exchange for a more modern shunting locomotive. The relic was sent to Altoona for restoration.

Concurrently, six late nineteenth-century passenger cars were assembled from maintenance trains or rescued from tool shed service and restored. Other scattered relics such as the *John Bull* locomotive (1832), a combination car of 1855 and a conjectural replica of the *John Stevens* (1939) were also assembled for the display. The railroad exhibit illustrated the technological progress railroads had made in their 110-year history, their contribution to 'American Civilisation' and their readiness to meet the nation's future transportation needs.

When the World's Fair closed in 1940 most of the vintage equipment was moved to Northumberland, where the collection continued to grow over the next 25 years. In all, some 25 'relics' were gathered by the late 1950s. During the early 1960s the financial burden of maintaining the historical collection and the deterioration of its condition led the PRR to investigate its future. Several museums were considered to be potential recipients, including the newly authorised Railroad Museum of Pennsylvania and the National Museum of Transportation

in St Louis. Responding to pleas from the PRR, historians and influential railroad enthusiasts, the Commonwealth of Pennsylvania created the Railroad Museum of Pennsylvania in 1963. By 1969 construction of a $1.8 million facility was well under way and the rolling stock in the PRR collection was moved from Northumberland to Strasburg. Bowing to pressure from state leaders and influential private citizens, the Penn Central Corporation (PRR's successor) agreed to keep the collection together and sent the remainder to Strasburg on long-term loan to the PHMC. Since the museum building was not yet under construction, the collection was displayed temporarily on the Strasburg Rail Road.

When the museum was opened in 1975, it was the first major building in the US designed specifically to house a railroad museum. The museum had barely opened to the public when the core of the collection was threatened. The Penn Central Corporation had filed for bankruptcy and sale of the PRR collection as a corporate asset became a real possibility. To protect the collection, the PHMC had it listed on the National Register of Historic Places and sought to exchange ownership of the collection for certain of the Penn Central's state tax debts. To make such an arrangement legal, special legislation was required, and in the final hours of the 1979 legislative session, the special bill was signed into law and the collection became state property.

Thus far, the first stage of the museum's development efforts had been concentrated on establishing, constructing and opening the museum and upon acquiring and securing a world-class collection of artefacts and research materials. By the early 1980s, however, retrenchment in state government and the political and economic climate in the US brought an end to the state's ability to run an ever-growing museum programme. From this time onward, tax-based operating budgets shrank or remained stagnant.

At this time the museum had two overwhelming needs. Firstly, action had to be taken to stabilise and restore the deteriorating outdoor collections; and secondly, interpretative displays and programmes had to be developed to attract broader audiences and convince the public of the cultural benefits of railroad preservation.

As state support was so limited, entrepreneurial methods had to be used to fund restoration, displays and education initiatives. Since state operating funds were fixed at about $300,00 per year (enough to pay basic operating expenses), a support organisation known as the Friends of the Railroad Museum was founded to provide money and volunteers for restoration, education, displays, research, publications and a variety of other projects. By 1992 the museum's operating budget had grown to over $1 million, thanks to fund-raising and grants.

Together the PHMC and the Friends of the Railroad Museum embarked on capital fund-raising which generated $2.6 million for an expansion of the exhibition hall (now under construction). This expansion will house and exhibit an additional 26 locomotives and cars. In all 90,000 sq ft of space will be available for thematic displays which blend the technological, social and cultural histories of Pennsylvania's railroad industry.

Another initiative of the 1980s was the implementation of a broad programme of public education. Continuing on-site and outreach programmes are used to inform the public and stimulate interest in railroad history and the cultural importance of railroad preservation. On-site programmes include special children's activities, interpretative walking tours of the outdoor museum yard, first-person interpretation, demonstrations of railroad-related

skills, live steam demonstrations and an annual schedule of special events. Recently a children's centre where young people take part in hands-on activities to learn about railroad history in Pennsylvania has been opened.

Off-site, travelling slide and video programmes keep community organisations abreast of the museum's development and needs. Community and constitutional leaders are kept involved through advisory committees and visits by museum staff and volunteers, and special leadership awareness receptions are held at the museum.

For the future, the museum has a 20-year development plan which calls for the construction of a restoration workshop facility, an expansion of the library and archives, and development of the outdoor yard area. The plan also outlines a phased display programme and a schedule of major restoration projects. (Plate 1)

Concurrently we must continue to broaden the museum's audience. In a nation of cultural diversity, railroad museums still tend to attract white, middle-aged males in disproportionate numbers. Activities must be developed to reflect a greater cultural diversity and appeal to new audiences.

Walter Gray has asked that each of us address the question: 'How does my museum exemplify the

Plate 1. Illustration of master site development concept at the Railroad Museum of Pennsylvania

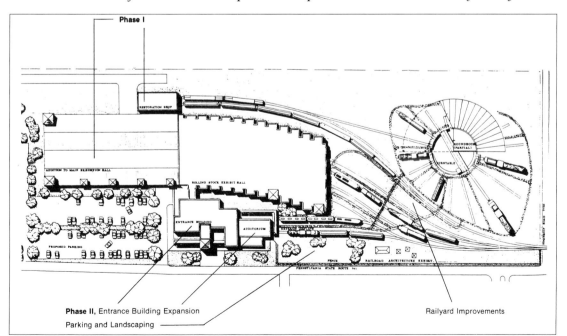

189

American railway preservation movement?'. The Railroad Museum of Pennsylvania can be characterised as a large, well-established, state-sponsored museum with an extensive and distinctive collection. It shares many things in common with other American railroad preservation projects and it possesses a few unusual features as well.

I would like to cite several unusual features on the understanding that they are not necessarily unique to this museum. The California State Railroad Museum, the Baltimore & Ohio Railroad Museum and the Railroad Museum of Pennsylvania are located at the more intensively developed end of the railroad museum spectrum, and I am reviewing the broad panorama of American rail preservation organisations in general, not just these three institutions.

The Railroad Museum of Pennsylvania is the beneficiary of a fairly rational and ambitious corporate preservation policy. Most railroads did not preserve so ambitiously. The early involvement of the state of Pennsylvania established the museum before the PRR collection was scattered. In the early 1960s state commitment to railroad preservation on a scale like this was unique. With a nearby, but distinct, tourist railroad, the Museum's need to operate steam-era equipment is kept to a minimum, allowing concentration on issues of preservation, exhibition and human interpretation. The museum may also draw on the outstanding mechanical expertise of the Strasburg Rail Road's staff.

Our location in the midst of a highly popular tourist region makes the Museum very popular. Our gate receipts exceed basic operating costs, which is particularly unusual for government-operated museums. As part of a large public history agency, we are able to draw upon the professional expertise of curators, conservators, historians, risk managers and others. Thus we can use state system resources to develop such things as mission statements, collections policies, facility-use agreements, operational standards and general management planning. Many of these key elements are missing from a number of sister institutions, although there is a growing trend towards developing these tools.

I would also like to cite the museum's typical features. Much of the collection is stored outdoors, posing a continual maintenance and preservation problem. There is a recognised need to shelter the collection and to improve research and document conservation and restoration-related activities.

Like most preservation organisations, we have a small but dedicated staff whose time is spread too thinly. We depend heavily on volunteers, who provide about 50 per cent of the total staff hours employed on museum projects. There is a growing realisation in the American railroad preservation movement as a whole that education and outreach are key components of institutional survival and development. This realisation accompanies a shift in focus from a rail-orientated programme to one of educating and stimulating the general public.

The California State Railroad Museum

Stephen E Drew

The California State Railroad Museum has been described as North America's finest interpretative railroad museum. In a little less than 20 years, it has become a benchmark by which other similar North American railroad museums are measured. I will in this paper provide a brief overview of the museum, followed by a discussion of some of the distinguishing elements of our efforts at railroad preservation in the US.

The museum

The California State Railroad Museum is located in historic Sacramento, the capital city of the state of California, and the western terminus of the first transcontinental railroad in the US. Metropolitan Sacramento consists of a little over one million residents situated in a rich agricultural area known as California's Central Valley. The museum is situated in Old Sacramento – a restored historic district occupying eight square blocks – located at the point where the city had its beginnings as the furthest navigable inland port on the Sacramento River and the jumping-off point for the gold fields of California in 1849.

The California State Railroad Museum was created because of the need to preserve and interpret a significant collection of locomotives and cars. The collection was begun in 1937 when the newly organised Pacific Coast Chapter of the Railway & Locomotive Historical Society acquired the historic 1875 Baldwin Virginia & Truckee Railroad shunting locomotive No 21, the *J W Bowker,* from the Hobart Estate near Truckee, California. Between 1937 and 1969 the Chapter amassed a collection of 33 locomotives and cars which would become the nucleus of the California State Railroad Museum's collection. Frustrated by unsuccessful attempts to develop their own museum in the San Francisco Bay area, the Chapter began donating their collection in 1969 to the state of California, specifically the Department of Parks and Recreation, for the new California State Railroad Museum at Sacramento. With the receipt of the first dozen pieces of equipment in August 1969, the state of California found itself in the railroad museum business.

Lacking competent in-house expertise, the state invited nation-wide competition among architectural and interpretative design firms; selected for the initial project development were architects Spencer Associates of Palo Alto, California, and interpretative planners Barry Howard Associates of New York. Following close consultation with the California Department of Parks and Recreation, the railroad industry, the Pacific Coast Chapter and historians and consultants, the master plan for the California State Railroad Museum emerged in 1973. A credit to the multidisciplinary planning effort, the plan still serves as a working document, guiding the development of the final phase of the museum today. Of seven components envisioned in the 1973 master plan, only the final phase – the Museum of Railroad Technology – remains to be completed.

The first completed phase of the museum was the Central Pacific Railroad passenger station, which was erected on its original site, the western terminus of the transcontinental railroad. Reconstructed to its 1876 appearance, the passenger station is a veritable 'house museum' featuring a fully furnished station waiting room, a separate waiting room set aside for women and children, a crowded baggage room, telegraphers' and agents' offices and the popular Silver Palace eating stand. Out on the station platform under gas lights are several nineteenth-century steam locomotives and cars. Opened in July 1976, the passenger station was a *ballon d'essai* testing the public's interest in a state railroad museum; fortunately, the number of visitors exceeded expectations and the success of the station helped pave the way for funding additional phases of the museum's development.

The second phase of the museum was the reconstructed Big Four and Dingley Spice Mill buildings. Completed in 1980, the structures house the Huntington, Hopkins & Company hardware store which was operated for decades by two of the legendary 'Big Four' promoters of early Central Pacific Railroad fame. Next door is the Stanford gallery which hosts a diversity of exhibits. Upstairs in the Big Four building are the museum's general offices, the re-created Central Pacific directors' board room and the museum's extensive public research library. Opened in 1981, the library houses more than one million catalogued photographic images, several hundred thousand drawings, extensive railroad company and trade materials, and the Railway & Locomotive Historical Society collection formerly located at Harvard University. The museum library is America's largest facility devoted exclusively to railroad history.

The third and by far the most ambitious phase of the museum to date is the 100,000 sq ft Museum of Railroad History which opened in May 1981. Inside are 21 restored locomotives and cars dating from the 1860s to the 1950s. More than 40 interpretative exhibits present the political, social, cultural and economic impact of railroads and railroading in California and the west – both the good and not so good – from the 1850s to the present. A gala nine-day railroad celebration entitled 'Railfair Sacramento 1981' marked the opening of the Museum of Railroad History; a larger 10th anniversary celebration, 'Railfair '91', is a continuing source of favourable international publicity. We were very pleased that locomotives from the National Railway Museum at York were present in Sacramento for both of these major US railroad celebrations.

The fourth phase of the project involved the acquisition of a 17-mile railroad line running south from the museum grounds along the Sacramento River and beyond the city of Sacramento into rich agricultural lands. In 1984 the museum began running regular steam-powered excursion trains over the northern three-mile portion of what was originally the Southern Pacific's Sacramento Southern Railroad. Planning is under way to extend this service beyond the current destination of Baths station to the small communities of Freeport and Hood, 16 miles south of Sacramento, where Sacramento Southern trains may one day connect with steamboats on the Sacramento River.

The last of three reconstructed or restored historic Central Pacific buildings was completed in 1986 with the re-creation of the 1876 Central Pacific Railroad freight depot. This serves as the terminus for the museum's popular steam excursion trains operating on summer weekends from April until Labour Day, and off-season from October until May on the first full weekend of each month.

The final phase of the museum, named the Museum of Railroad Technology, is rapidly approaching completion. This complex will fulfil the museum's 1973 master plan. The 114,000 sq ft Technology Museum will be located on a site approximately nine blocks south of Old Sacramento, a scheduled station stop along the route of our steam excursion trains. The new facility will include a restoration and maintenance workshop open to the public, our reference collection of stored locomotives and cars and some 40,000 sq ft of formal interpretative galleries devoted to the 'nuts and bolts' of railroad motive power, rolling-stock design, rolling-stock capacity, railroad systems and operations, preservation and railroads today and tomorrow. We have completed site selection, architectural designs and development for the $31.1 million project and are on the threshold of embarking on working drawings within the next few months; opening day might be as early as the summer of 1998 if all goes according to plan.

In July 1992 the museum acquired responsibility for the management of the Railtown 1897 State Historic Park, the 26-acre Jamestown roundhouse and workshop complex with 40 locomotives and cars situated approximately two hours east of Sacramento on California's historic Sierra Railroad.

Today more than 500,000 visitors annually enjoy the California State Railroad Museum. Changing exhibits and progressive programming – including living history, the annual national railway preservation symposium and the US national handcar races – bring the institution to life and provide new reasons for visitors to return to the museum. Operated by the California Department of Parks and Recreation, the California State Railroad Museum has become one of the 'crown jewels' of the California Park Service.

Following this brief overview of the museum, I intend to review some of the philosophies or guiding principles which distinguish the California State Railroad Museum from most other railroad museums in North America.

The museum's approach

First, and foremost, the California State Railroad Museum is an interpretative railroad museum. The museum is consciously *not* another graveyard for old iron, steel and wood relics exhibited in adapted barns or on a myriad of parallel tracks. When we acquire a new artefact, we do not immediately rush to get it on display; we work hard not to be merely a museum with a display of 'things'. What is an interpretative railroad museum? For the Museum of Railroad History, for example, we have selected some 40 interpretative themes which cover the whole gamut of the history of railroading in the state from the 1850s to the present: topics include Theodore Judah, the Big Four, building the transcontinental railroad, railroad architecture, railroads and agriculture, railroads and industry, railroad folklore, railroads and the movies, passenger travel, dinner in the diner, the myth and symbol of the steam locomotive, to name only a few. We have assigned space within the museum for each of these interpretative themes and have drawn on the full-size locomotive and car collection and on smaller three-dimensional and documentary materials to reinforce the story-line. If emulation is any measure of success, then it is of note that members of the museum staff have subsequently drafted interpretative plans for many other railroad museums and historic railroad sites throughout North America.

The California State Railroad Museum is one of the few railroad museums in the US which is located on significant 'historic soil', not simply on a convenient site somewhere that happened to be available. Old Sacramento is the birthplace of railroading in California; it is the logical centre for the state's railroad museum. The first railroad in California ran from what is now the museum grounds in Sacramento to the town of Folsom in 1855. Ground was broken here in 1863 for the start of construction on the western leg of the transcontinental railroad. The largest railroad industrial plant west of the Mississippi River has been located at Sacramento since the 1860s on property which directly adjoins the museum.

We have placed a high priority on accuracy and credibility in our major railroad equipment restorations. Our philosophy has placed a high value on the sanctity of the artefact – erring on the side of cautious restoration and conservation as opposed to injudicious, wholesale reconstruction. Our philosophy is to approach restoration projects with no preconceived ideas as to what appearance the piece must be restored. We have adopted a cautious, analytical approach which places a high value on reliable documentation gleaned from the artefact. This is of great importance when it becomes apparent how little documentation survives for most of the museum's artefacts and it becomes paramount when contemplating the myriad changes and alterations which a piece of operating railroad equipment endures in 50 to 60 years of service. It is like the proverbial case of great-grandfather's axe which has come down through four generations virtually untouched and intact – except for two new handles and three new heads. We have found that even though a piece of equipment may approach the condition of an old chicken coop with only termites 'holding hands' to keep it together, with tools such as industrial archaeology, a good mechanical understanding of process, materials and practice and careful piece-by-piece analysis, the bulk of the information needed to restore a locomotive or car accurately is usually still to be found in the artefact. Firmly rooted in scholarship, we have fought hard to eliminate long-standing traditions of painting historic engines to resemble what an old locomotive 'might' have looked like! Some specific illustrations may be helpful.

In 1967 the Railway & Locomotive Historical Society, Pacific Coast Chapter invested $13,081 to spruce up their Virginia & Truckee locomotive No 3, *Empire*, in order to depict its 'old-timey' appearance on the Virginia & Truckee. The 2-6-0 was presented to the state in 1969 and there were hard feelings amongst the Chapter when we sought their permission to re-restore the rare Baldwin mogul to a more authentic appearance. The resulting product is soundly based on physical documentation, scholarship and a close understanding of Baldwin practice, materials and technology. Undoing $13,081 of restoration work was a tough pill for the Chapter to swallow, but the restoration yielded a spectacular, accurate presentation of what was once a common product of the Baldwin locomotive works in the 1870s but is now the oldest and best-preserved standard-gauge Baldwin mogul in North America today.

For decades the first steam locomotive of the Central Pacific Railroad, the *Gov Stanford,* was on prominent exhibition in the rotunda of the Stanford University Museum. The 1862 Norris engine was exhibited for nearly 20 years in a fictional presentation resulting from the donation of a dozen different cans of brightly coloured paint from the local Acme paint store. The locomotive was gaily painted to resemble someone's idea of what an old engine might have looked like. After it was acquired by the California State Railroad Museum, there was strong opposition to our suggestion that the colour scheme was less than accurate and and that the 4-4-0 should be returned to its appearance in 1899 when it was last worked on by Southern Pacific Railroad in their Sacramento workshops. The *Gov Stanford* was a revered relic which decades of alumni only recognised and knew in its garish appearance. Fortunately, cooler heads and scholarship prevailed. The resultant restoration of the *Gov Stanford* by the California State Railroad Museum in 1980 and 1981 produced a proud new namesake for Stanford University and the return of the rare Richard Norris & Son locomotive to a deep Victorian black finish, complete with white side-walled tyres and silver-gilt lettering. Last operated in January 1895, the *Gov Stanford* is exhibited today in a 10,000 sq ft diorama, just a few hundred feet from where it was first off-loaded, assembled and operated in November 1863 along the banks of the Sacramento River.

Rightly or wrongly, we have chosen a specific documented date, photograph and/or occasion as a fixed point for each one of our major restorations – as opposed to choosing a broad era or 'general' restoration period. Our 1873 V&T No 12 *Genoa*, for example, is accurately restored to its well-documented appearance in April 1902, when the Virginia & Truckee workshops completed a significant rebuilding of the wood-burning 4-4-0. The diminutive 1863 *C P Huntington* has been returned to its November 1914 appearance when it was first displayed as the corporate symbol – old No 1 – of the Southern Pacific Railroad. We had sufficient data to permit an earlier restoration appearance but this would have literally 'thrown the baby out with the bath water' and yielded a complete reconstruction rather than the sensitive restoration of North America's only surviving standard-gauge 4-2-4. This philosophy of restoration to a specific documentable date has subsequently been successfully adopted in the restoration of locomotives and cars at other state-funded museums, most notably in Kansas and in Nevada.

A further underlying premise is that all restoration work must be documented and reversible. Wherever possible, materials are matched without compromise: if it was oak, we use oak; if it was mahogany, we use mahogany. If it requires full rather than nominal dimension wood members, we will use them. Even if the restoration is purely cosmetic, nothing is done to preclude further restoration or a complete return to operating condition at a later date. All work, decisions (right or wrong), findings, drawings, photographs and reports are compiled and are available to the public in our library, leaving the requisite paper trail for our successors to be able to see what we did, why we did it, our processes, opportunities and constraints.

Finally, we have a strong commitment to truth in labelling and presentation. We have shelved more than one restoration project when it became apparent that there was insufficient data to support an accurate restoration. Truth in labelling caused us severe friction with one major donor when we declined to exhibit an otherwise wonderful Pullman-style car with the inappropriate name 'PULLMAN' painted in 12-inch high letters on the letterboard. Ultimately the donor reluctantly agreed to allow us to repaint the car to its appropriate Canadian livery with 'CANADIAN NATIONAL' on the letterboard. We have chosen to display the car in a gently rocking simulation of travel through the night aboard a heavyweight sleeping car – a much broader interpretation than that of a 'Pullman' car – and, to date, no visitor has objected to it.

Fortunately our commitment to historically accurate presentations and truth in labelling prevailed again after a major donor balked, initially refusing to allow us to exhibit a classic 4-4-0 in anything other than the fictitious *Jupiter* paint scheme in which a railroad had lavishly repainted the engine.

In general our philosophy has been to err on the side of quality, not quantity. We would rather do a few projects to high standards than attempt scores of projects with mediocre results. We believe visitors know and appreciate quality. Our goal is not to be the biggest but the finest. Our mission is not to be all things to all people but rather to be a high-quality museum geared to an enthusiastic generalist public. Our continuing acquisitions are made very cautiously against stated priorities in our collection policy. We build on our collection strengths.

We have set a high standard for ourselves with our existing facilities. The challenge ahead of us is not just to meet but to exceed our current standards of quality and innovation in restoration, interpretation and programming. We are leaders in the albeit embryonic discipline of railway preservation in the US. We look forward to measuring the success of our efforts against the standards of international railway preservation forums in the future.

B&O Railroad Museum, Baltimore, Maryland

John P Hankey

The Baltimore & Ohio Railroad (B&O) was the pioneer US railroad; it can trace its roots to the Stockton & Darlington and the Liverpool & Manchester railways in England. In the east we like think of the New York Central as the 'route of modernism'; traditionally, the B&O railroad was the 'route of anachronism'. The B&O Museum is a very new institution with a very old collection in a very old place. It has faced every difficulty, issue, limitation and problem that everyone concerned with railways has faced since the beginning of railroad preservation. We feel, however, that the museum has unparalleled opportunities. We have the ability to re-invent ourselves at what is proving to be a turning point in the museum's history. We can look back over the past 100 years of railway preservation and learn from everyone else's mistakes, pick the best of what we have all done in the past 30 to 40 years of railroad preservation and do our part to take the B&O Railroad Museum to a higher level.

The B&O Railroad was part of a complex of large-scale social, technological and political changes in the US. It was neither the first railroad in the country, nor the largest, nor the best. It was, I think, the most special. It set the standard for railroad development in the US; it reached the Ohio river in 1853, opening up what to we easterners is still 'the West', past the first stretch of mountains. It is important to remember that Charles Carroll, the only surviving signatory to the Declaration of Independence, was a backer and promoter and turner of the first spade of earth for the B&O. The B&O was quick to recognise its role in history. In 1853 it sponsored the creation of one of the first railroad history books in the US: *A History and Description of the Baltimore & Ohio Railroad*. In 1869 the B&O participated in the formation of the myth of the *Tom Thumb*, Peter Cooper's first locomotive in America. In 1876 the B&O exhibited some of its ancient and revered locomotives at the US centennial celebrations. The B&O took part in a series of expositions, centennials and sesquicentennials, hawking its role as a developer of the US. Joseph G Pangborn, a Kansas City newspaper man and promoter, joined the B&O as the country's first public relations agent, and he never let the facts get in the way of a good story. Perhaps by making virtue of necessity he decided that he would market the B&O by promoting its history: 'the historic B&O', 'the picturesque B&O'.

The B&O evolved a corporate culture of history in the late nineteenth century. It was not the fastest railroad and it had the most roundabout route and the slowest trains, but it sold scenery. Pangborn's work manifested itself in a series of historic re-creations which culminated in 1893 with a massive railroad history exhibit at the World's Columbian Exposition in Chicago, celebrating the 400th anniversary of the discovery of America. It was there that Pangborn gathered, replicated, stole and appropriated locomotives and many other railway items, large and small, from all over the US, Canada and Great Britain. While the rest of the fair was concerned with the theme of 'The future and modernism', the B&O resolutely turned through 180 degrees and spoke of history. It can be argued that the years 1893-94 were the high point of the railroad in the US. On the horizon were the automobile and the aeroplane. The Columbian Exposition came at the zenith of the railroad, and the B&O was celebrating its role as the mother of American railroads.

The Exposition closed in 1894 and the exhibits remained in Chicago as part of Marshall Field's Columbian Museum. By 1903 Field had grown tired of technology – he really wanted to create a natural history museum – and he gave the entire railroad collection back to the B&O. The material was subsequently exhibited at the 1904 World's Fair in St Louis and then put into storage. In 1927, the B&O's centennial, the railroad company (by this time even more conscious of its role in history and its place in the railroad industry) dragged the material out of storage and did what we would consider today to be unthinkable: reboilered all the old locomotives, jazzed things up and renamed them. They fiddled with the collection so much that many of the items are replicas, not original locomotives. However, the company put on a stupendous birthday party for the centennial, based in large part on the pattern adopted for the centenary of the English Stockton & Darlington railway in 1925. One and a half million people went to Baltimore to join the birthday party for five weeks in October 1927. It was the B&O's intention to maintain the Baltimore site, the buildings, tracks and collections, as a railroad museum. At about the same time, the Deutsches Museum was developing in Munich, Germany, and the US National Museum was talking seriously about a museum of technology. There was a great interest in large-scale history and technology presentation in the US and in Europe but in Baltimore at least, the Great Depression stopped progress. Then in 1935 a tropical storm swept through Maryland, demolished the buildings and damaged some of the collection, and everything was moved to a vacant roundhouse and stored for safety.

There were several points in the life of the B&O's railroad collection at which it could have been lost, and indeed some pieces were lost in the various moves. In the early 1950s US railroads enjoyed a brief, though temporary, burst of prosperity. In 1953 the B&O no longer required the car repair workshops in a roundhouse building at Mt Clare in Baltimore. The public relations department, which by this time had control of the historic railway collection, saw its opportunity, moved in and on 2 July 1953 the Baltimore & Ohio Transportation Museum opened. In 1958 the museum closed. It re-opened in 1964, but closed again in 1974, this time for renovation. The B&O had been taken over, in 1962, by the Chesapeake & Ohio Railroad which gave the B&O a stronger financial base, and led ultimately to the creation of the Chessie System in 1972, which meant that money was available to celebrate the sesquicentennial of the B&O in 1977. The Chessie System took its responsibilities very seriously and there was talk of setting up a separate, non-profit-making foundation to run the museum. In the meantime, in the mid-1970s, there was a major investment programme to renovate the buildings, improve the displays and make new acquisitions. Despite the physical improvements, however, the museum's mission was unclear, its finances uncertain and its role in the railroad industry complicated and ambiguous. This did not, however, prevent the celebration of the B&Q's sesquicentennial in 1977.

In 1980 the Chessie System merged with another railroad holding company to form CSX Corpora-tion. CSX had little corporate interest in railroad history but was determined to safeguard the collec-tion. Like other railroads, however, they sought to relieve themselves of the responsibility of managing and running a museum. It was decided to create a foundation to manage the museum and its collec-tion as a stand-alone institution, which took close to five years to bring about but was done correctly. Once established, the museum, working in parallel with CSX, underwent an unsuccessful attempt to hire an executive director and build a staff. The railroad did not quite know how to hire a museum professional and no museum professional with any sense would have come to the museum as it was then. The museum lacked a plan, policies, or the procedures to execute them had they existed. The CSX administration could not even tell the candi-dates for the directorial post what the yearly elec-tricity bill was. They had no idea what kind of staff the museum needed and were not even sure of the boundaries of the property. As a result, CSX and the new museum hired the Baltimore City Life Museum to come in on a management contract. They provided expertise and leadership, and di-rected the institution towards becoming a museum. The result was the creation of the museum's first full-time professional staff.

The period from 1987-92 was fraught with difficulties and dangers but the museum now has an experienced professional director, a forward plan and the opportunity, with some help from CSX, for a significant expansion. As I wrote at the beginning of this paper, the museum is at a turning point which offers unparalleled opportunities. The ques-tion now is: what will the B&O Museum become? We have plans and ideas and a two-tier time hori-zon. For us, long-term planning is both meeting the next payroll obligation and looking out to see what is coming at us on the horizon and how we are going to celebrate the 200th anniversary of the B&O railroad in 2027. We like to operate with parallel realities.

Our first challenge has been to understand the site inherited from CSX and formally handed over in 1989. It is an historic site, the birthplace of American railroads. Somewhere in the vicinity of the museum car park is the spot where carpenters put down the first sleepers for the first track of the first main line railroad in the US in the autumn of 1828. That is the beginning of the railroad industry in our country. Here, too, were established the first railway workshops at Mt Clare. Further study of the site convinced us that we needed not just the 11 acres which the museum buildings occupied, but another 25 to 30 acres west along the first mile of the first railroad between Mt Clare and the still-surviving Carollton Viaduct. This site, very close to downtown Baltimore, was to CSX an industrial development area. To the city it was urban waste-land. To us it was even more fascinating because the southern boundary was an eighteenth-century southern Maryland industrial plantation. All sorts of early colonial issues such as tobacco, slaves, wheat and milling could be interpreted along the extended site which also encompassed the spot where the B&O placed its 'first stone' – an icon in itself. The acquisition of this extended site, which is now a reality, offers wonderful possibilities to the develop-ing museum.

A second category of assets is the existing build-ings. They include the remains of the Mt Clare station which dates from 1851 – another icon in railroading – and the extraordinary car repair work-shops of 1884, built as a great roundhouse 240 ft across and 123 ft high. The roundhouse design was clearly influenced by the Crystal Palace and other wonders of Victorian architecture. The complex also includes a very plain 1884 workshop/store-house which now houses the museum's libraries, interpretative displays and offices. Another large building on the site and the most recent gift to the museum from CSX is a former repair and mainte-nance workshop, built in 1869. It gives the museum another several hundred thousand square feet of covered space but at a cost of several million dol-lars because it brings with it all the problems of large-scale industrial buildings: asbestos, lead paint and a crumbling infrastructure.

The collection is the third category of assets inherited by the newly constituted museum. It is a wonderful collection of nineteenth- and twentieth-century items, many from the B&O railroad, the C&O, the Western Maryland; all are part of the 'family' of railroad companies that ultimately consti-tuted the CSX. The earliest items are locomotives from the 1830s and the most recent are items that are being taken out of service today and sent to the museum instead of the scrapyard. We have, for instance, the first streamlined diesel locomotive in the US, and hope to acquire one of the last. What surprised us at the time of the conveyance and valuation of the collection was that the total figure was less than $20 million. It is a pittance compared with the historical value we associate with machines

and objects like this, but useful in persuading the CSX Corporation that the collection was worthy of preservation.

Finally, in this catalogue of what we feel we can categorise as assets, is interpretation: the body of ideas and approaches, the ways in which we deal with history and mediate that history to various publics. We needed to resolve how we were going to interpret and present our collections, so we convened a committee and made a plan. We de-cided initially to allow access to items to let people get up close and see things. The museum's style of exhibition had been the traditional railroad 'interest-ing stuff in cases'; there were many cases with no interpretation at all. A case might contain a brake-beam; the label would read 'a brake-beam'. It was left it to the visitor to work out what a brake-beam was, and why it was important to an understanding of American history.

A priority was to restore locomotive operation to the site – to make the museum a 'living history' site, even if the operation was confined to one small diesel locomotive. A second task was to repair the track on the site, which goes hand-in-hand with locomotive operation. Then a core of volunteers had to be trained. The museum currently has about 150 highly active and very skilled volunteers, many of them with railroad experience, who help us with everything from train operations to building conser-vation.

The mere existence of the museum as a reinvigorated and functioning entity posed all sorts of opportunities. The first which presented itself was the recovery to the museum of a large modern steam locomotive from a shopping centre building a quarter of a mile away. The locomotive had been placed there as the result of an arrangement be-tween the CSX and a land-developer some years previously. It was hauled out at a cost of $100,000 provided by the developer. One does not generally face this kind of object-retrieval problem quite so soon in a museum development programme.

The next opportunity was to begin restoring equipment to operation for the 1991 Railfair in Sacramento, celebrating the 10th anniversary of our colleague institution in California. We sent two replica locomotives, Peter Cooper's *Tom Thumb* and the 1837 Norris locomotive *Lafayette*, to represent the B&O Railroad museum. In another case, a railway enthusiast group working with us decided they would like to see one of our modern diesel electric locomotives work. They provided the

manpower and the money, the museum provided
the project supervision and in a few months we
made it happen. Also, we were able to host a visit
by a large, modern steam locomotive which brought
visitors in from miles away. It also brought the
environmental protection agency and the fire department; we learned then to call them before we lit
a locomotive fire in future.

Using what little political power we had, we
started running main line excursion trains with state
commuter operation equipment and CSX crews to
destinations such as Harpers Ferry, Williamsburg
and Philadelphia; these have been a great success.
On the occasion of the retirement of Hays Watkins,
Chairman of CSX and father of the 'new' B&O
Museum, we solicited a grant from CSX and used
it create a museum library. We have worked very
hard to make more of our objects accessible to
more people and to try to engender a sense of
participation in the museum displays. We continue
to experiment, to train volunteers and generally to
be on the cutting edge of living history as well as
of academic and museum practice. This has led
to the bringing of some of the objects out into
daylight for the first time in 30 years; it has been
amazingly effective and has enhanced the museum's
reputation.

In our interpretation we have begun to deal with
issues which the museum had previously avoided.
A passenger car had been represented by the C&O

Railway as a car with a smoking compartment. In
fact it is a Jim Crow car with segregated accommodation for black passengers. After 40 years of
ducking the issue we are finally acknowledging that
the vehicle is an important object of social history
which can be used to talk about race relations in the
early twentieth-century US. The social history
context of the museum is an important one. The
museum exists in an urban context, not in a corn-
field or in an artificially created environment. This
historic site, the beginning of the B&O Railroad, is
now in downtown Baltimore city with all of the
issues and problems that arise in a poor and deprived neighbourhood. The museum must be
truthful in its interpretation, but it must also be a
force for positive social good and must work with
its local communities and try to involve them.

The future offers the museum a series of opportunities within the framework of a comprehensive
re-interpretation and exhibition plan which has
been prepared. Work has started to return the
historic site to what it once was and that is what
makes the B&O Museum different and special. We
are not trying to represent the whole of railroad
history but just the story of one railroad in one
place through a very distinct span of time. The
museum is searching for something approaching
truth – not a representation but a reality – and is not
the reality of railroading what we are all trying to
represent?

The heritage of the working railway: the work of the Railway Heritage Trust

L J Soane

Introduction

After 1825, when the first public railway between Stockton and Darlington was opened, followed in 1830 by that between Liverpool and Manchester, the railway network rapidly spread throughout the UK until, by the latter half of the century, most of the system had been built – by hand and horse power.

Investors, hoping to get rich quickly, floated railways in fiercely competitive rivalry, so that lines spread to remote rural areas and a proliferation of routes was produced which benefitted passengers, but on which freight traffic was always likely to be sparse.

The provision of facilities for railway operation led to the construction of 9000 stations and 60,000 bridges which, with 1000 tunnels, warehouses, construction and maintenance sheds for locomotives and rolling stock, hotels, signal boxes and numerous other buildings and structures, provided the basis of the railway heritage of today.

Many of the original buildings and structures are well over 100 years old – some more than 160 years – and are still in constant use. This is a reflection of good design and construction by famous engineers, architects and contractors of the day, such as the Stephensons (George and Robert), I K Brunel, the Cubitts, Digby-Wyatt, William Tite, G T Andrews and others, whose burning ambition to create the best in a dynamic new industry has left the UK with a uniquely rich railway heritage.

The enormous range of buildings and structures so built was inherited by British Railways (BR) (established in 1948) when the former private railways were nationalised and merged into one undertaking.

The first railway stations were generally in keeping with the local architecture and would not have looked out of place in the high street of any small country town. Modest in size, using local materials and styles, they were plainly adaptations of existing building types, with speed and economy of construction being a major consideration in their design. There were a few notable exceptions, where neo-classical, Gothic or even Moorish style buildings were intended either to reassure nervous passengers or to impress prospective investors. Thus variations of the country estate 'Gate-keeper's Lodge' or 'Cottage Orné' style served for small stations, where the design of buildings used on the large estates through which the railway passed was frequently adopted, as, for instance, Woburn Sands on the Duke of Bedford's estate at Woburn Abbey. Larger stations were first cousins of the toll road coaching inns, and early locomotive sheds were seen as 'stables for the Iron Horse'.

The second half of the nineteenth century and

Plate 1. Cannon Street station: tower after restoration. (British Railways Board)

the early years of the twentieth was a period of tremendous traffic growth for the railways, and by 1914 they had reached a pre-eminent position. During this time their power and prestige was expressed in the many ambitious buildings and structures which were needed to handle the ever-increasing business. The decline in railways since then is reflected in, for example, the reduction in bridges from 60,000 to 52,000 and stations from 9000 to today's 2550. Many of the bridges are on closed lines but are still owned by BR.

This railway heritage is vast, reflecting the all-embracing influence of the railways on Victorian and Edwardian society. I have already referred to various types of railway buildings in BR's portfolio, but, in addition, BR acquired several historical oddities through land purchase. These include such items as a fourteenth-century refectory pulpit in Shrewsbury, a medieval bridge at Ware, several sections of both the Antonine and Hadrian's roman walls, an Anglo-Saxon cemetery west of Ramsgate station, a Georgian mansion near Watford and the site of a Roman governor's palace at Cannon Street.

Plate 2. Paddington station: roof repairs. (John Byrne)

Plate 3. Bristol Temple Meads station: roof repairs (David Hume & Associates)

Formation of the Railway Heritage Trust

In the 1950s and 1960s – the Beeching era – many of the lines and routes which had not already died a commercial death were axed and old buildings were seen as an embarrassment when trying to present a modern railway image. Demolition of the old was often seen as the means of creating a 'new look' railway and many grandiose stations were cleared away, to be replaced by smaller ones designed for present-day usage and clearly indicating that horse and steam power were relics of the past.

After World War Two the poor condition and demolition of many fine buildings, such as country houses, town halls, theatres and railway stations, generated an interest in conservation. This was reflected by government action in creating lists of buildings of architectural or historic interest, in scheduling ancient monuments and in creating conservation areas and areas of special scientific interest. The grade of listing given to a building – ranging from the highest, Grade I, through Grade II* to Grade II – is used as a guide for prioritising

the award of grants by the Trust. Rising public interest in conservation, and pressure by government to complete the listing process, which had dragged on for 20 years, led to a massive increase in the number of BR buildings listed. In 1985 the total was 630 and this has now risen to 1256 – a 100 per cent increase in eight years. BR, publicly criticised for the poor maintenance of its listed buildings, caused an outcry when the 1838 Doric 'Arch' at Euston – the gateway to the Midlands via the London & Birmingham Railway – was demolished to make way for the new Euston Station. To counter this adverse publicity, BR offered to set up an independent Trust whose aims were:

To conserve and enhance Britain's railway heritage and to encourage the widest public enjoyment of it; in pursuit of this aim to secure for the public benefit the preservation, restoration, improvement, enhancement and maintenance

Plate 4. Great Malvern station: column capitals. (British Railways Board)

Plate 5. Aylesford station: after repairs. (British Railways Board)

of buildings, features and objects of historical and industrial interest built for or used by the railways throughout the United Kingdom.

Encouraged by support given from environmental groups for the formation of the independent Trust, BR offered funding of £1 million for the first year, to be used for the conservation of BR's historic buildings. Initially only BR's operational structures were to benefit but it was soon apparent that non-operational buildings should also be covered by the Trust and the BR Property Board offered a further £200,000 for this purpose.

Under an enthusiastic chairman, Sir William McAlpine, and with three other kindred spirits, the Railway Heritage Trust (RHT) Board was set up on 1 April 1985. It is supported by a staff of three. A key role of the RHT is to act as a catalyst be-

tween BR, the BR Property Board and other interested parties in attracting funds for heritage-related schemes which conserve BR's listed buildings and structures.

To advise and assist the RHT Board, a panel of advisors was appointed, drawn from all parts of the country, whose members had an interest in the work of the RHT and were experts in their own fields: the membership includes architects, journalists, academics, politicians, historians and archaeologists. They are the eyes, ears and sounding boards for railway heritage issues and are encouraged to alert the RHT to any building or structure observed in the course of their travels to be in need of attention. This has enabled the RHT to advise BR of such reports and encourage action by offering grants.

A measure of the success of this approach is that

Plate 6. Ribblehead viaduct. (British Railways Board)

in eight years 344 schemes have received RHT grants from the £9.6 million provided by BR, but a further £8.2 million has been attracted to the work from other interested parties. For BR, the benefits are a concentration of effort and funds (£17.8 million) on selected projects supported by the RHT and external parties, the genuine enthusiasm of local staff who gain an improved working environment, the opportunity to market an attractive historic but restored railway (tourists are particularly impressed) and increased competitiveness in the transport world of car, coach and air travel. Complaints and criticism concerning BR's care for its heritage have reduced dramatically – many of its former critics are now members of the RHT's advisory panel – and BR's positive approach has been held up as an example to other organisations.

Among parties who provide support are local authorities, whose communities frequently identify with 'their' station and are prepared to assist with station garden schemes or even with maintaining and cleaning the fabric. To gain local interest is a good way of overcoming vandalism and graffiti which so often despoil the environment. Many organisations are prepared to assist in such work, on a voluntary basis, and a competitive spirit can be engendered this way. As previously indicated, railway buildings are often of outstanding design, workmanship and grandeur and may be the dominant structure in a town or village. When restored, they give a sense of civic pride and are a tourist attraction. Instead of disused structures and buildings being seen by BR as dilapidated eyesores, managers and staff now envisage new uses and life for them – again with potential benefit to revenue.

The RHT's role as a catalyst and pump-primer in

the sale or lease of disused viaducts has enabled the BR Property Board to dispose of several such major properties by setting up a local trust or other responsible organisation to take over future maintenance. The resulting restoration is beneficial to the local environment, and footpaths and cycleways can be established, or other uses found.

The future

The task ahead can best be illustrated by the progress to date. In the eight years of the RHT's existence, 344 conservation schemes have been carried out involving only 28 per cent of BR's total of 1256 listed buildings and structures. Against the background of the continuing ageing of assets and an increase in the numbers of buildings listed, there should be no diminution of determination to maintain, or even increase, the rate of progress so far achieved. The forthcoming privatisation of BR is, however, a matter for concern and it is for the government to determine how and by whom the future of the railway heritage is to be safeguarded; a decision is awaited.

Collecting for the future in partnership with Dutch Railways

Paul van Vlijmen

Introduction

If it were possible for us to know which objects would be valuable to museums in the future, we could all become rich. In the art world, possible future developments are often the subject of speculation. We have all heard of art dealers backing up-and-coming artists by buying all their work and then launching the collection, with a lot of fuss, as the discovery of the century. If private collectors and museums share this opinion, the artist is home and dry; the museums and collectors can proudly show their latest acquisition to visitors and relations and the art dealer can count his money. However, this kind of collecting really collects the future itself whereas I would like to talk about collecting *for* the future – collecting the kinds of objects we feel should be preserved for later generations. In other words, we would like to be ahead of future developments. If we preserve things now, we can always change our minds about them later!

Collecting in the past

Around the middle of the last century there was hardly any commitment to singling out and preserving material evidence of human technological achievement. This was not true for human expressions of a more cultural nature: collections of paintings and cabinets full of curios existed as early as the seventeenth century and many of our present-day museums have sprung from such collections. However, artefacts which bear witness to the development of the Industrial Revolution were much harder to come by – at least in the Netherlands.

One of the very first steam engines in the Netherlands, *De Arend*, was built by Michael Longridge at Bedlington and was introduced in 1839 on the Amsterdam to Haarlem line. It proved very satisfactory. Together with its sister engines, it ensured that the railways in the Netherlands became a success. In 1857, following 18 years of loyal service, *De Arend* was taken out of use and subsequently scrapped – a fate it shared with numerous other 'firstborns' all over the world. 'Such a pity', we now cry. 'Of all the engines, why was that one lost to mankind?'. We are aware, however, that the grounds for writing off and discarding this and later rolling stock were, in themselves, perfectly understandable. The companies were trying to operate the railways as efficiently as possible and this did not allow for old-fashioned and technically obsolete locomotives. Some figures will support this view: from 1839 to 1958, some 2430 steam engines operated in the Netherlands. Only nine remain in the Dutch Railway Museum; of these, the *De Arend* we have is a 1938 replica. Fortunately, several other steam engines were preserved by various museum lines, but the figures show just how efficient the railways were in destroying the physical evidence of their historical development.

For a long time, the Dutch Railway Museum's policy in terms of collecting rolling stock was rather passive. This was due partly to insufficient exhibition space in the museum's previous accommodation, and for a while this was also the case in the present building. It was also due partly to enthusiastic scrapping by Dutch Railways, especially of steam engines and carriages, causing the museum to miss opportunities on several occasions.

Den Hollander, Chairman of the Board of Dutch Railways from 1946 to 1958, deserves the credit for giving the Dutch Railway Museum a home of its own at the former Maliebaan station. It was also Den Hollander who energetically engaged in modernising and electrifying the Dutch railways after World War Two. Holland was the first country to replace steam traction in its entirety by electric and diesel-electric traction. Towards the end of the steam era, employees at depots, who were keeping back steam locomotives, were reproved: steam was a thing of the past. The idea that the locomotives 'might be good for the Railway Museum' was brushed aside and the engines were scrapped. In 1958 Den Hollander personally handed over the last of the steam engines used by Dutch Railways, a 4-6-0 numbered 3737, to the museum.

Paul van Vlijmen

Rolling stock in the Dutch Railway Museum

In terms of collecting rolling stock, times have changed dramatically in recent years. Thanks to Dutch Railways, the Dutch Railway Museum is now in the fortunate position of being able to carry out an active acquisitions policy, which I will discuss later in this paper.

The Dutch Railway Museum is an independent foundation, governed by a supervisory board consisting of seven members. The Chairman and three of the members hold high positions within Dutch Railways. It has so happened in the past that the Chairman of Dutch Railways was simultaneously Chairman of the supervisory board. The other members of the board represent the museum world and Utrecht City and County Councils. The number of representatives of the Railways indicates that, in terms of management, the museum has very close ties with the national railway company.

In the past, the supervisory board's involvement in the acquisitions policy was modest. The collection was based on the private collection of the museum's first director and during its first few years lacked any rolling stock whatsoever. It was not until the 1930s that the first trams entered the museum, and the first steam locomotives came later still. Although these were not on display, due to the shortage of space, they were at least preserved elsewhere. The collection of paintings, prints, models and railway curios has nevertheless always been sizeable and interesting, and the museum benefitted from that rich collection in 1989 when new and enlarged displays were created. But let me confine myself to rolling stock.

The core of the collection now consists of 10 steam locomotives, a 1908 electric motorcar, a 1927 electric twin-carriage train, a 1934 diesel-electric triple-carriage train and four carriages. In addition, an electric locomotive, a diesel-electric single unit, two buffet cars, shunters, and goods and service equipment are on display. The museum also owns a fairly representative collection of town trams; examples of main line horse, steam and electric trams are also included in the collection. The trams in particular were, in part, taken into the collection as a result of personal preference at a time when hardly any other institutions or museums wished to take on this kind of object; the Railway Museum offered a safe haven for such stock.

There are, however, large gaps in the collection, especially in the area of railways. The steel carriages introduced in the Netherlands between the World Wars are missing; from two major railway companies, not a single engine has survived (a very beautiful specimen was scrapped in 1957); light railway engines are missing; only two front compartments which were sawn off from carriages and displayed in the museum are available to represent early rolling stock. Royal rolling stock is absent altogether. The only remnants of the many splendid royal carriages are a wrought-iron rear gate and a royal water closet. Other than that, we have only photographs and drawings.

Museum of Public Transport or ... Railway Museum?

Notwithstanding the gaps in the collection, at the end of the 1970s the plan was hatched for the Dutch Railway Museum to evolve into a museum of public transport. It was from that perspective that buses were acquired. (They have recently been sold.) Moreover, initiatives to start up local transport museums elsewhere in the country were virtually non-existent at the time. Cities which had their own public transport networks were occupied with matters more pressing than the need to celebrate their history.

The government, at that time a significant co-subsidiser of the museum, was rather attracted to the notion of a museum of public transport. It was even prepared to take on financial responsibility for running the museum, but a long-term condition was imposed; the museum had to be refurbished and modernised. The government could not afford to do this, but another catalyst for change was emerging.

By now it was 1986. The celebration of 150 years of railways in the Netherlands, to be held in 1989, was approaching. Dutch Railways, having kept a very low profile with regard to the museum for many years, presented an ambitious plan for the celebration of the anniversary. An entirely refurbished museum was to occupy a prominent position in the plan.

As well as the pending refurbishment, the now greatly expanded body of museum employees were to be involved in drafting a development plan for the museum. This plan, made possible through financial support from Utrecht City Council, was to form the basis for the further development and expansion of the museum. During the many workshops devoted to drawing up a plan it became apparent that the Railway Museum's strength lay in its current identity and its acknowledged status as a railway museum and not its plans to become a museum of public transport for which no money was available.

The lack of funding caused the government to reconsider its former decision to bear financial responsibility for the museum. Negotiations were held with Dutch Railways to enable the government's obligations to subsidise the museum to be bought out. This resulted in the government paying a lump sum, the interest on which covered the original subsidy, leaving Dutch Railways as the only subsidiser and partner. In turn, this made the decision-making process much easier and faster, especially with regard to refurbishing the museum. Dutch Railways guaranteed the cost of building and refurbishing and also released funds for the renovation of the electric twin-carriage train which was to operate a service between the museum and the grounds where the jubilee celebrations were to be held. In August 1988 the museum partly closed, to reopen as-new in June 1989.

Preservation and management of the collection

'As-new' hardly applied to the rolling stock. The condition of a large part of the collection was found to be deteriorating rapidly. The worry was allayed in part as, against the odds, several local transport museums were opening and these turned to the Railway Museum to acquire tramway stock on loan. Requests were not made in vain as the Railway Museum's policy now focused on the railways and the intention was to dispose of the town trams and keep only a sample collection of intercity trams. Part of the tram collection was, therefore, offered on long-term loan and was professionally maintained or restored elsewhere.

The hour was dark indeed but dawn was nigh. The large backlog which the Railway Museum experienced in maintaining and preserving its collection was shared by many museums and archives. The government sounded the alarm and, in 1991, developed the 'Deltaplan for the Preservation of Culture'. The plan enables museums and archives to obtain a 40 per cent subsidy towards the cost of catching up with any backlog in collection preservation and management. The Railway Museum jumped at the opportunity. A report on the backlog of collection maintenance was produced at

top speed and was then translated into a plan of action and a budget. The costs involved amounted to approximately £1,300,000 sterling, about $2 million. The budget was submitted to Dutch Railways, together with a request that they consider paying 60 per cent of the costs, with the remaining 40 per cent to be contributed by the government. Dutch Railways, having always previously distributed attention and money to the museum in dribs and drabs, proved to be open to the unique opportunity of this large-scale catching-up manoeuvre. The requested amount was transferred by return and the execution of the three-year preservation plan began.

The work is now in progress. Virtually all contracts were allocated to the principal workshops of Dutch Railways, where there appears to be a great commitment to the Railway Museum. Employees are very keen to collaborate over the renovation and preservation of the museum's stock. At times slight disappointment is noticeable when it becomes apparent that the preservation plan aims only to maintain and preserve the stock, this being one of the government's conditions. I have to answer in the negative the question: 'Will it ever run again?'. Transport museums are not unfamiliar with the issue of 'operating' as opposed to 'static' display but, quite apart from the curatorial debate, the Railway Museum faces an additional problem: the museum does not own or control any of its own track and is in the middle of a residential area so that even to run a tiny diesel locomotive causes all kinds of environmental problems.

Implementing the preservation plan has made it possible to restore fully the rolling stock in the existing collection. The Railway Museum will therefore soon have a collection in excellent condition, allowing it to face the future with confidence.

Towards a new collecting policy

The passive collecting policy mentioned earlier has now become active. The collaboration with Dutch Railways has led to the development, in consultation with the Dutch Railways Stock and Workshops Department, of a so-called reservation plan. The plan comprises three parts:

- an inventory and description of the stock already included in the collection
- stock reserved and kept for the museum by Dutch Railways

- stock to be added to the collection at some point in the future

The reservation plan also covers the criteria to be met by locomotives, multiple units, carriages and so on for inclusion in the Railway Museum's collection. These criteria are:

- the individual item of stock must be representative of a whole series which had a significant role in the operation of railways in the Netherlands
- the individual item of stock must represent and demonstrate the technical development of rolling stock on the railways
- the individual item of stock must be important to the Dutch Railway Museum as part of a well-balanced collection

Using these criteria, it was decided, for example, not to add a 1300-series electric locomotive to the collection, as neither its appearance nor its technical principles differ significantly from the 1100-series locomotive already held by the museum. Of the Stock '64 trains, an electric twin-carriage train will be saved complete, whereas the diesel version will only be represented by an engine housing. Some room, however, has been allowed for the inclusion of atypical items in the collection, but these must be of special interest and be able to play a role in education and/or tourism and recreation.

One important point agreed is that, in time, Dutch Railways will hand over all items of stock free of charge to the Railway Museum. But that is not all: each year, Dutch Railways will make available a sum of some £60,000 sterling, approximately $90,000, for the upgrading of any obsolete stock to museum display standard. To deal with the current and future museum stock, Dutch Railways has also appointed a contact who is to act as co-ordinator between Dutch Railways and the Railway Museum. The co-ordinator will handle orders, arrange transport, assist in tracking down drawings and spare parts, and give advice.

Although the museum and Dutch Railways work closely together, differences of opinion, especially about rolling stock, do occur. An example is the first 1000-series electric locomotive, partly developed in the Netherlands. This particular locomotive class, of which 10 ten were built and put to use towards the end of the 1940s, did not prove very successful. Although initially intended for fast passenger trains, after a few years the locomotives were used only for goods trains and even in this field remained troublesome. The class was taken out of use in the 1980s. One was rescued from the scrapyard by a group of private individuals and the museum has had this engine on loan for the past few years. Unfortunately, Dutch Railways resents this as the locomotives were unsatisfactory and proved to be a liability. The museum takes a different approach, however: these were the first Dutch electric locomotives and they are, therefore, significant, both historically and in terms of technological development. In addition, the locomotive on display has a distinctive appearance: its large, exposed driving wheels bear a resemblance to those of a steam locomotive and are interesting to the general public.

Another bone of contention concerns the operation of steam locomotives. Within Dutch Railways, some are of the opinion that steam should no longer be associated with a modern company. Preserved and museum railways in the Netherlands which do run steam locomotives are not associated with Dutch Railways and own their own lines. To operate a steam locomotive, the Railway Museum would need the co-operation of Dutch Railways and thus far that co-operation has not been forthcoming.

The mutual approval of the reservation plan by Dutch Railways and the Dutch Railway Museum is of great significance for the future and relieves some of the worry inherent in collecting present-day material. I like to think that, throughout the world, there are not likely to be many museums which have already established which items to include in their collections in 35 years' time. As an incidental extra, the reservation plan also serves as a catalogue of rolling stock, both now and for the years to come.

Logistical problems

Even in the short term, however, the guaranteed influx of new museum material is already taking its toll on the display capacity inside the museum. Expanding a collection is wonderful, and eminently desirable, but it brings the problem of housing all the material. This issue, too, is being discussed with Dutch Railways. The museum attaches great importance to the availability of a museum train shed for storage and for temporary exhibitions. The ideal solution would lie in saving and using an historic shed. The museum train shed currently in use for storage will probably disappear before too long, resulting in yet another problem: well-preserved and restored stock but nowhere to put it.

Although the partnership with Dutch Railways has intensified over the past few years, it should not be taken for granted. Both partners should regularly discuss how to help strengthen each other's position. The Railway Museum enjoys its role as a shop window for Dutch Railways; it is able to show the public brand new stock before it has even been adopted for use. A short-term plan is to create a large new model railway which will illustrate railway development in the Netherlands in the twenty-first century. Conversely, Dutch Railways are demonstrating an involvement with their own history by giving the museum coverage in promotions, magazine articles and at various special events. Furthermore, Dutch Railways is aware that, in the mind of the public, the Dutch Railway Museum belongs to Dutch Railways and that places a certain obligation on them to maintain the quality and standard of the museum displays. By devoting much time to nurturing relationships with Dutch Railways, the museum hopes to be able to sustain the excellent relations that currently exist.

The museum's ability to collect for the future, in partnership with Dutch Railways, would seem to be secure, as this paper explains. It goes almost without saying, however, that the Dutch Railway Museum concerns itself with far more than collecting rolling stock. The grounds contain uncovered platforms; there is a signal box and a yard; and

there are steam engines that need to be moved periodically. At some point in the future the museum would like to cover the platforms; to give the yard a new pair of points; and to draw up a shunting schedule to allow seven steam engines to be moved. All of these matters require close co-operation with Dutch Railways and in future there may be a charge for some services. Dutch Railways already provides much for the museum completely free of charge, particularly with regard to rolling stock, but they are forced to charge the costs incurred for additions and amendments to the museum buildings and track layout, for transporting some museum objects and for other services. Splitting the company up into independent business and service units is likely to result in charges for services and is a development with which the museum must come to terms.

Even though Dutch Railways' relationship with the Railway Museum will become more business-like in the future, the museum views its future with confidence. Over the years, the Dutch Railway Museum has fostered much goodwill inside the 'parent company' which will prove to be invaluable. The museum can count on the sympathy of many of the departments in Dutch Railways. Employees like being able, or being allowed, to help the museum. The reverse is also true: the museum will do everything in its power to support the company. In this manner, we can demonstrate true co-operation and a true partnership, for now *and* for the future.

A philosophy of display

Alfred Gottwaldt

If we look into the future and all our plans are realised, the Berlin Museum for Transport and Technology ('Museum für Verkehr und Technik') will cover more than 35,000 sq m of exhibition space. I explained in my earlier paper that the museum's first Director planned a comprehensive series of display galleries, not only of the classic means of transport, such as road, water, rail and air, but also of communications such as printing, telephones, radio, film and computers, and of technical hardware such as heavy industry, electricity, crafts, scientific instruments and household technology. At present, only one quarter of this programme has become a reality.

The museum is located beside and on the site of the old Anhalter railway depot. Its nucleus was opened on 14 December 1983 in a turn-of-the-century brick building. Here all museum departments had (and some still have) only small 'showroom facilities' which offer a glimpse into the vast collections still awaiting public display. A new building, the Traffic Hall ('Verkehrshalle'), was added in 1985 and offers a little more space for an holistic presentation.

In 1985 the government of Berlin allowed the museum to reconstruct three adjacent buildings: two locomotive roundhouses with turntables, plus a spacious administrative building between them. (Plate 1) They were opened to the public in 1987 and 1988 respectively, thus giving the museum an exhibition space of 10,000 sq m. Overall construction costs have so far reached about 85 million marks.

The museum location as part of a railway landscape and the use of former railway workshops as an exhibition hall paved the way for the decision to choose the museum's railway collection as the first department to be comprehensively displayed. There are other building projects (eg, for air and water transport) in preparation, in a new, functional design.

There are various railway museums and a number of technical museums in Germany. The general idea of the Berlin museum is to show technical objects as an integral part of the nation's political and social history. Some older museums only cover technological developments whereas we wanted to demonstrate the interdependencies between railways and society. The exhibition was planned for everybody (men, women, children) with a general interest in history, not simply for the expert.

Therefore, our philosophy of display is different from others in three main aspects: it has a clear chronological structure; it deliberately addresses a number of political issues; and it dares to display

Plate 1. A plan of the general layout of the museum showing the two roundhouses used for displaying locomotives.

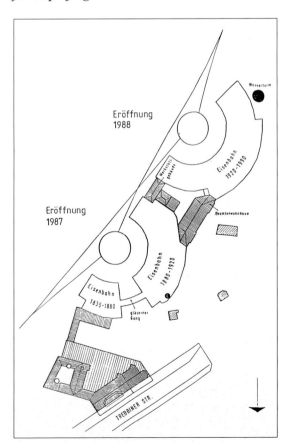

some objects in 'as-received' condition without any trace of restoration.

In the draft concept for the exhibition, set out as early as 1982, there was a proposal to display all objects (large or small, locomotives or train tickets) in date order. This is common to many museums in other fields, but not to most transport museums, which tend to display their objects by type. We did not want to have separate rooms for locomotives, carriages, uniforms, architectural objects, etc. As the roundhouses contain 21 and 19 tracks respectively, we have chosen a system of 'one idea per track', thus presenting one leading railway vehicle on each track with associated smaller objects around it. (Plate 2)

Since the locomotive roundhouse is our best single exhibit, we had to think about its history. It was built in 1874, enlarged several times, but not used after 1952. Before we started work on the site in 1985 it had become a ruin and plants had grown over the collapsed brick and steel structures. It was decided to leave three tracks of the roundhouse in this state, showing how quickly nature returns when man gives up maintenance work. (Plate 3) Visitors often ask why we have 'spoiled' the building and why we have 'wasted' those tracks, but we consider this question in itself to be the answer.

Three more tracks in the first roundhouse were given to a metalwork and railway engineering workshop which is integrated with the exhibition allowing visitors to look in through large windows. Thus there were just 33 tracks left in the two roundhouses for the actual museum displays.

As the museum had inherited many objects from earlier collections, these, and our plans to buy in other objects, had to be woven into the final scheme, in which we had to adapt our concepts to the available space. The exhibition display was divided into 33 'stations' covering the years from 1800 to the present. Each 'station' was given a code consisting of a year and a short phrase of historical significance which also appears in the hall, in the catalogue and elsewhere. It was important to give the phrases both a technical and an historical sense. Sometimes this effect is created by combining a well-known year from German history with a fact from railway history, such as '1871: Bismarck and the railways' or '1914: to war by rail'. Others are more technological, such as '1933: motoring and electrification'. Of course, 1933 was also the year when the Nazi Party took power in Germany. The visitor is expected to see this association and perhaps to question it rather than accept it at first

Plate 2. Interior of one of the museum roundhouses showing locomotives from 1843-1860.

Plate 3. The ruins of the former Anhalter station about 1925. Three tracks were left overrun by nature.

glance. This is particularly important when dark chapters of German history are being covered, such as '1899: our colonial railways', '1940: railway and swastika' or '1943: railways to Auschwitz'. Obviously these 'stations' stimulated a lot of discussion both with the public and with colleagues. Critics point out that this approach is political, not neutral: I entirely agree!

Since no other technical museum in Germany does so, I believe that it is very important to show a typical railway box car which might have been used for the deportation of Jewish people during the War. (Plate 4) We also show a streamlined electrical locomotive decorated with an imperial eagle and swastika, but the impression which might be created is changed by displaying some everyday German documents behind iron bars in front of it. We do not want our visitors to look without questioning and to pass on to another display.

A museum can only display a choice from history. We do not intend to give answers to all the questions we raise, but we want to encourage our visitors to take these questions seriously and to go to the museum library to seek more information.

There is a catalogue containing a description of all the objects displayed in the halls. The catalogue is deliberately object-based and not the 'book about railway history written by museum people' one usually finds.

A number of printed boards in the exhibition try to explain our aims to the visitor and also to the guides or warders in the area. They refer in particular to our idea of showing what age means to an object. I cannot discuss in full the different approaches there are to restoration and repair, to reconstruction and refurbishing. In Berlin we have decided to have a 'case-by-case' policy for restoration. This means that all objects that go to the workshop – primarily locomotives and other vehicles – are carefully examined beforehand. What evidence does an object give if it is left in the condition in which it arrived? What story do we want to tell from and with the object? What historical traces are we destroying when we restore and repaint it in the way most transport museums do?

What we are trying to do, after much debate and with many doubts, is to translate a concept of restoration across from the fine arts to technical

Plate 4 (above). A German railway freight box car, typical of those used to deport Jews during World War Two, displayed at the museum since 1988. Plate 5 (below). A locomotive as received at the museum from a scrap yard and intended for display in that condition.

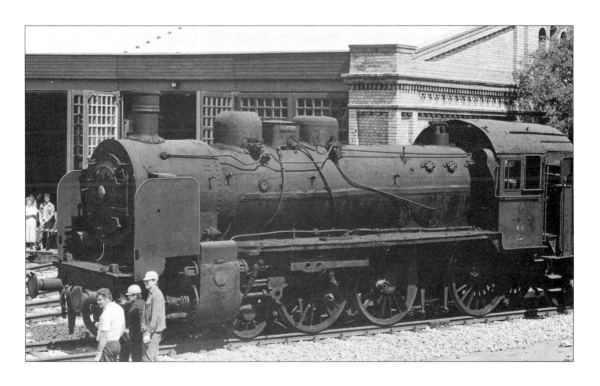

artefacts, to apply the Unesco code and to conserve rather than restore our objects. Some of the locomotives we display are rusty and greasy with broken glass in the cab windows, but they are genuine, they are 'real' and they are ardently discussed by our visitors. (Plate 5) Do we want more?

I will end this paper with some provocative questions. Would we rewind an Egyptian mummy with modern fabric to give it the immaculate appearance it must once have had? Of course not. Why then should we apply polyurethane paint to metal sheets from 1880? If we know the proper recipe for 1880 paint should we mix 'old' paint and use it? What is the idea behind exhibits that look as if they have just left the factory? Do technical objects embody an engineer's idea only, or do these objects live a life of change and development which is worth telling and keeping visible? Perhaps there is no one answer but it is good to know that the museum's visitors understand something of what we are doing and are themselves asking questions!

A commentary on restoration, conservation and the National Railway Museum collection

Dieter Hopkin

The National Railway Museum (NRM) in York is responsible for railway artefacts of national and international importance. What we, as curators, have to recognise is that the material evidence we are dealing with in our collections is the product of collecting and restoration practice spanning 130 years. To provide a commentary on the conservation and restoration of the collections it is, I believe, necessary to adopt an historical museological approach. It is only through this approach that we will be able to understand and interpret many objects in the collections: why they were collected, in what condition they were received and what their subsequent museum history has been. In particular, a study of the locomotive and rolling stock collections shows different trends, fashions and approaches which have affected both the physical appearance of the preserved objects and our perception of them.

In continental Europe the first railway museums developed to display railway artefacts in the late nineteenth century, but in Britain the emphasis was on saving major pieces of railway engineering, primarily locomotives, which were laid aside for preservation from the 1860s. By this time, locomotives built during the first three decades of the nineteenth century had ended their working lives and there was a recognition of the historical significance of some of the pioneer developments which had helped to create the 'Railway Revolution'. Two participants in the Liverpool & Manchester Railway's (L&MR) Rainhill Trials of 1829 were amongst the first locomotives to be selected for preservation. Stephenson's *Rocket*, in a much rebuilt and very dilapidated form, was presented to what was to become the Science Museum collection in 1862. By 1865 *Rocket* had been joined by another Rainhill contender, *Sans Pareil*, and by Hedley's *Puffing Billy* of 1813. Before they were presented for display, these locomotives were 'restored' by their owners.[1]

An examination of *Rocket* shows inaccuracies which were introduced as part of the restoration process. These included a new chimney, copper exhaust pipes, stays, an iron firebox, wooden connecting rods and curved spoke trailing wheels. In the 1920s E A Forward of the Science Museum undertook a re-assessment of *Rocket*, removed some of the inaccurately restored parts and substituted a chimney more compatible with the locomotive in its rebuilt form.[2]

Today the remains of *Rocket* can be seen as an icon of the early railway age, an iron dinosaur crafted by a venerated engineer. The similarity between its black-patinated and fragile remains and those of fossilised dinosaurs in the Science Museum's neighbour, the Natural History Museum, may strike even the casual observer. *Rocket, Sans Pareil,* and *Puffing Billy* at the Science Museum, as *Agenoria* at the NRM, stand as venerated relics which remain largely in 'as-received condition'. It is almost inconceivable to consider even a cosmetic restoration of *Rocket* to its later rebuilt form and inappropriate to contemplate building back the remains to approximate to their 1829 appearance. This latter interpretative goal has instead been achieved through the manufacture of accurate reproductions of the prototype locomotive. To many museum visitors a reproduction is far more accessible and understandable than the remains of the original whose bare bones communicate confusing messages, especially since its current appearance does not relate to the public perception of the icon which is universally recognised as Stephenson's *Rocket*.[3]

During the last quarter of the nineteenth century other early locomotives were laid aside for preservation by Britain's private railway operating companies. The most common form of presentation was not in a museum but mounted on a plinth at some public railway location. Thus Stephenson's Stockton & Darlington Railway (S&DR) 0-4-0 *Locomotion No 1* was placed on a pedestal outside North Road Station, Darlington in 1857 and his 0-4-0 Killingworth colliery locomotive *Billy* was displayed on Newcastle High Level Bridge in 1881. Of necessity, such display, open to the elements, involved a degree of initial restoration and continued cosmetic repair. When this was not provided, the exhibit inevitably deteriorated to destruction, as was the fate of an Eastern Counties Railway Bury 2-2-0 passenger locomotive which, for many years, stood on a pedestal outside Stratford works until scrapped in 1870.[4] How is the present-day curator to interpret the significance of such displays? Were they for public edification, were they monuments to entrepreneurial endeavour or were they intended as examples of engineering sculpture? That they were displayed as part of the working railway environment perhaps implies that they were considered to be part of a continuing tradition and not segregated museum specimens. The reasons for their retention must have influenced the nature and methods of their restoration and must be examined as carefully as the physical remains.

Locomotion is a good example of the varied life experienced by a locomotive which has been preserved for 135 years. After its working life was over it was initially displayed at Darlington North Road for 18 years until overhauled to operating condition for the S&DR's 50th anniversary celebrations in 1875. Fifty years later it was again repaired to take an active part in the centenary celebrations of 1925, albeit on that occasion powered by a concealed internal combustion engine. Subsequently it spent many years on a plinth under the roof of Bank Top station, Darlington, with Hackworth's 0-6-0 *Derwent*. The gradual deterioration of both locomotives in this environment led to their overhaul at Darlington locomotive works in the 1960s. Only in 1975 did *Locomotion* find a place in a museum. Today *Locomotion* is on loan from the NRM to Darlington Railway Centre and Museum and receives only superficial conservation in the form of dusting and cleaning. Only a very detailed and careful examination would identify what parts originate from the S&DR and what are the product of at least four different major restorations.

It is clear from this example that the history of a railway object since the end of its railway operating period is important: a point frequently overlooked by many railway historians for whom the story of the object ends on the date of its withdrawal from the operating fleet. A full understanding of the material evidence contained in the objects' 'in-built archive' can only be achieved through a detailed knowledge of its preservation or museum history which will have been, in many cases, longer than its operating life. A simple example of this can be found in Furness Railway No 3, a Bury 0-4-0 of 1846 which is now part of the National Railway Collection and on display in the NRM's Great Hall.

In 1900 the locomotive was restored and displayed in an enormous iron and glass case at Barrow-in-Furness station. The case was destroyed during a World War Two bombing raid, the locomotive was damaged by shrapnel and still bears the scars today.[5] To attempt to repair the holes caused by the shrapnel would be to distort or corrupt the history of the locomotive.

Hostile enemy action was not the only threat to the preservation of historic railway material in the late nineteenth and early twentieth centuries. In the absence, at that time, of any national museum of railways in Britain, the saving of, and subsequent care for, railway relics was largely dependent on a benign railway management. One incident shows that without a sustained management interest in preservation, railway collections could suffer catastrophically. In 1906 C J Churchward CME of the Great Western Railway (GWR) ordered the destruction of the two surviving GWR broad gauge locomotives: *North Star*, a 2-2-2 of 1837, and Gooch's *Lord of the Isles*, a 4-2-2 of the 'Iron Duke' class. Both locomotives had been housed in the so-called 'works museum' at Swindon for a number of years.[6] Churchward's action is the radical alternative to preservation – wilful destruction – and there are other examples which serve to illustrate that for some important objects the state of preservation was only transitory. Britain's National Railway Collection has been made poorer by such events. Some parts of *North Star* were saved in 1906 and incorporated in a reproduction of the locomotive built in 1925. Perhaps the history of *North Star* should be regarded as two stories, that of the locomotive until 1906 and that of the reproduction from 1925, linked by a few surviving relics. Tim Bryan, in his book *North Star: A Tale of Two Locomotives*, takes this approach.[7] A point of debate arising from this case is the stage at which the amount of surviving material evidence is so small in relation to the re-created object that the vestigial real object becomes a reproduction. Is *North Star* as it stands today a heavily restored original or a reproduction incorporating original parts?

In Britain in the late nineteenth and the first half of the twentieth century, the mainstream of activity in the preservation of historically significant railway material lay with the railway companies themselves and the material was almost invariably not in formal museums. During the inter-War era all four principal private railway companies laid aside rolling stock, relics and records for preservation. A sense of history was seen as a useful tool in developing a company's corporate identity and had considerable publicity value. The centenary celebrations for the S&DR in 1925 and the L&MR in 1930 gave the railways an opportunity to parade their preserved veteran vehicles alongside their latest locomotives and rolling stock. Most of the veterans were restored in some way by being overhauled in the works to operating condition or repainted to an earlier livery. It was often the locomotive works paintshops, made semi-redundant by changed working practices, which were designated as unofficial museums, and it was here that preserved vehicles were repainted and cared for.

Only one of the railway companies, the London & North Eastern Railway (LNER) established a formal museum to house its collections. Opened in 1927, the Railway Museum in Queen Street, York, housed many of the LNER's locomotives which had been brought together for the 1925 centenary celebrations. The museum owed much to the efforts of the company's publicity department and the influence of the Chief Mechanical Engineer of the LNER, H N Gresley.

Gresley's enthusiasm was largely responsible for securing for preservation and restoring Stirling's 8 ft single 4-2-2 No 1 and the pioneer British Atlantic *Henry Oakley*. Why Gresley undertook such projects is a matter for speculation but it may have been as much about providing a suitable memorial for Stirling and Ivatt, his engineering predecessors on the Great Northern Railway (GNR), as preserving the objects *per se*. The Queen Street Museum labels featured not only text about the locomotive but also a large illustration of the engineer who designed it. Historic locomotives were presented as the great works of great engineers.

An engineer-centred approach influenced the restoration philosophy adopted for locomotives; in general, they were altered in such a way as to represent, as closely as possible, their creator's intentions. In some cases this meant building back to an 'as-built' form using engineering drawings as evidence but in others merely repainting. The restoration of the GNR No 1, for instance, was to represent its earliest form. It received some cosmetic changes and was coupled, inaccurately, to a Sturrock tender of suitably antique appearance. It remains so restored today, despite the fact that the NRM acquired a GNR tender for the locomotive in the 1960s which, with the correction of the cosmetic changes of the earlier restoration, would allow

the locomotive to be more accurately displayed. However, with the passage of time the inaccurate early restoration appears to have obtained a dubious sanctity which inhibits us as curators today from undertaking an historical reassessment and re-restoration. We have to face questions such as: if the two tenders are exchanged, what should be the fate of the surplus one which is itself of historical interest?

A further example of a restoration intended to reflect the work of an engineer is provided by the preservation of the former London, Brighton & South Coast Railway (LB&SCR) 0-4-2 *Gladstone* by the Stephenson Locomotive Society in 1927. It was selected as 'the unique achievement of a unique engineer whose influence ... can still be noted at the present time'.[8] It is significant that the membership of the Society, the majority of whom had an interest in pre-grouping railways of the southeast, should select this locomotive and have it built back in 1927 to its LB&SCR appearance, complete with Stroudley's improved engine-green livery and various dummy fittings including a wooden chimney.

To summarise; during the inter-War period the preservation and restoration of historic railway material was an *ad hoc* affair greatly dependent on the influence of senior managers and local initiatives in the one official and the many unofficial museums. Most preservation involved restoration, ranging from radical rebuilding to cosmetic repainting in order to re-create an object's previous, usually 'as-built', identity. Historic locomotives undergoing 'preservation' were treated by the railway workshops no differently from when they were overhauled during their working lives.

Following the nationalisation of the railways in 1948 there was a first attempt to put the preservation of historic railway material within a rational framework. The British Transport Commission *Relics and Records* report of 1951 set out a plan for existing and future collections and a framework for museum organisation.[9] One of the most important features was the appointment of a curator of historical relics, John Scholes, formerly of the Castle Museum, York, who pioneered the development of transport museum practice in Britain. Scholes was largely responsible for the selection and restoration of a very large part of what is now the National Railway Collection during his 20 years as curator to the British Transport Commission and British Railways. His work was assisted by a consultative

Dieter Hopkin

panel of railway historians and enthusiasts, including many who saw the highlight of Britain's railway past as the colourful era of the many private railway companies which existed before 1923.[10]

Scholes recognised that he was working in a new field:

Soon after my appointment in 1951 ... I realised that little professional consideration had been given to the restoration of public transport vehicles. The work that had been done on actual vehicles lacked thorough organised research, was based too much on guesswork and with no consideration as to the true reason for preservation, which surely must be the main criterion for all restoration.

Scholes had a clear view that a locomotive in his collection was preserved 'as a milestone in the development of the steam engine'. He stated that 'its original basic mechanical design is its prime feature and therefore the aim is for restoration "as-built".' Scholes and his railway colleagues were responsible for building back many locomotives currently in the National Railway Collection. He accepted 'that restoration generally destroys most of the original because of the necessity to repair the ravages of age and decay' and held the view that, while an object

may end its operational life in quite a different style and function to that when first produced for work. To preserve such an item in this state is meaningless and is merely keeping a hotchpotch of modifications which have been incorporated to keep it in service.[11]

Based on this strong belief, Scholes researched and had restored a number of locomotives and carriages in the collection. All were done in railway workshops and involved the replacement of major parts, substantial rebuilding and reconstruction. The examples of the South East & Chatham Railway (SE&CR) 4-4-0 No 737 and the record-breaking LNER 4-6-2 *Mallard* clearly show the radical and costly nature of some of this work. The restoration of *Mallard* in 1965 cost in the region of £10,000.[12]

In the face of modern conservation and curatorial theory and practices, Scholes' views seem extraordinary and untenable. Our view today would be that building back to re-create an engineering landmark invalidates the subsequent history and importance of a machine. Many locomotives were modified or rebuilt in service to be better machines with greater technical interest than when they were 'as-built'. For example, the superheated GNR large boilered Atlantic No 251 is of more interest technically than

in its 'as-built' unsuperheated form because it was in this condition that it put up such a high standard of performance. The inclusion of a superheater made little difference to the locomotive's appearance, but in restoring GNR No 251 to its 'original form' and removing the superheater, it has lost a significant element of its history as a working machine.[13] Furthermore, in deciding that an object's significance lies only in its importance as an engineering landmark many other strands of economic, industrial and social interpretation are inhibited, if not precluded, and the wider significance of the object is effectively denied.

The documentation of many of the restorations undertaken on Scholes' behalf by the railway workshops is sadly lacking; there is not even a basic photographic record in a number of cases. Because of this it can be difficult for the curator or researcher to distinguish between the original object and the restoration. Scholes was interested in the original appearance of the vehicles and a great deal of effort and money was put into re-creating the appearance of locomotives in their pre-grouping splendour. Great importance was placed on the cosmetic appearance of exhibits within the British Transport Commission (BTC) collection, and the finishing touch to a Scholes restoration was an immaculately applied colourful livery with elaborate lining. Liveries were important, but there was a tendency in producing the 'exhibition finish' to alter further the public perception of the locomotive from a machine to an art object or an engineering sculpture. While such a treatment of the exhibits in the BTC museums at York, Clapham and Swindon produced visually attractive objects, their surface finish might today be seen as an obstacle to any deeper understanding of the machine and its wider significance.

Under Scholes' regime, a number of items of rolling stock in the National Railway Collection were restored to operating condition for enthusiast and publicity trains in the 1950s and 1960s. Some were removed from museum displays at York and Clapham and were overhauled for use, which inevitably meant further alterations to meet operating requirements.[14]

In 1975, when the National Railway Museum was established in York, it became responsible for many objects which had been materially altered by the restorer's hand. It also inherited a practice of restoring vehicles for operational use. Restoration and operation feature strongly in the first years of

218

the NRM's history when there was a desire to show the NRM as a 'living museum' through demonstrating vehicles, especially steam locomotives, in action. It was also felt that the NRM should play a major role in the 150th anniversary celebrations for the opening of the S&DR in 1975 and the L&MR in 1980, and much of the curatorial effort of the museum was put into restoring vehicles for operation in these two historic pageants.

There are no clear, published statements of the NRM's policy on restoration or conservation, and while some excellent work has been carried out, the theory behind it has not always been sound. In the past the NRM generally followed the practices of Scholes and built back exhibits or rebuilt them for operational reasons. The NRM's parent body at the time, the Science Museum, had not itself been in a position to provide a strong theoretical lead as virtually all of its large railway objects had been restored by their previous owners before being placed on display in the *Land Transport* gallery at South Kensington. Without a strong museological base, the NRM has, inevitably, been drawn along by the main current in its subject area, the independent railway preservation movement, and the museum has not been in a strong position to lead the way in developing theoretical frameworks or in providing practical exemplars. The museum has suffered from a dearth of debate on the ethics of conservation and restoration which reflects the lack of any developed transport museology in Britain.

Much of the NRM's policy for the restoration of vehicles has, in the past, been directed at restoration for operation and not at programmes for conservation. Many of the steam locomotives in the collection have been operated by the NRM or by organisations which have had the locomotives on loan. In other cases the emphasis has been placed on re-painting locomotives to give them an historic livery. As a result, the NRM has no steam locomotives in its collection which have been left in 'as-received' condition – an interesting contrast to the policy outlined by Alfred Gottwald in his paper. In Gottwald's museum in Berlin, many locomotives *are* left in their 'as-received' condition and placed on display in that form.

I do not wish the observations in this paper to be taken as an argument against restoration, but as a case for carefully considered and researched restoration where it is appropriate. I do not believe it should be an automatic assumption that a newly acquired vehicle must be instantly returned back to some previous identity and brought to a gleaming exhibition finish. There are many ethical points to be taken into account when assessing a vehicle for restoration including its current state, a detailed knowledge of the history of the vehicle and a careful assessment of the degree of restoration which may be appropriate and how that will enhance the interpretation of the vehicle. In some cases the decision will be made to restore and in others simply to arrest the deterioration. Whatever is done requires careful documentation to enhance the understanding of the object. In some cases the result may be a hybrid mix of conservation and restoration which can be used to advantage in explaining the complex history of the vehicle. For example, the East Coast Joint Stock Brake 3rd carriage No 12 which is displayed at the NRM is an important representative of the late nineteenth-century development of corridor and gangway lavatory stock. Its exterior had been restored by British Railways in 1952 and, after a period of neglect, it was re-restored externally by the NRM to its 1893 condition in 1986, but the interior was left with its existing late-LNER (ie, 1940s) upholstery.[15] A similar hybrid approach has been taken with the London South Western Railway (LSWR) Tri-composite carriage which has an LSWR restored exterior and an Southern Railway interior.

While some restorations in part or in full at the NRM have been carried out with considerable care and expertise to produce attractive exhibits, the recording of many of the projects is incomplete and the ethical or theoretical base for the work has not always been clear. In a number of cases, treatment of vehicles has followed the Scholes' approach of building back while in other cases a less active, more conservation-minded regime has been adopted. The conservation practices adopted for railway vehicles have, however, been developed in isolation, away from the main strands of museum object and building conservation theory and practice.

It is perhaps time for the NRM to take stock and to re-examine its historical collections and its policies towards them. This will involve consideration of the material evidence provided by each object, its significance in the collection, its interpretative value and the prospects for its long-term care. It may be that the emphasis in these hard financial times has to shift from costly restoration and re-restoration programmes to policies aimed at providing adequate storage for the collections so that as far as possible they do not deteriorate from their 'as-received' condition. Our aim should be perhaps to arrest the decline of a number of objects currently at risk.

At the same time, as curators, we need to have a more thorough knowledge of the objects in our care so that we can interpret them more effectively. We need to understand what they actually represent through detailed study and retrospective documentation. We need to come to terms with some of the inconsistencies in our predecessors' policies and clarify our own approaches. We need to learn from the object's 'in-built' archive. We must ask ourselves why we apparently do not question the almost automatic restoration of a twentieth-century steam locomotive but would not contemplate even a cosmetic restoration of *Rocket* or any other of the early icons? Can age alone be the justification?

It is, I believe, time for a reassessment of many of the major objects in the National Railway Collection. A place in the collection implies that the object is recognised as having significance in itself, and can convey complex historical messages. The fabric, the material evidence, is important and should be conserved as representative of past railway practices. An object on entering the museum collection is the product of those events and practices which have shaped it since its day of manufacture. On entering the museum the object does not physically change but its status has changed. Until it enters the museum it is the product of its original user, the railway industry, and any subsequent changes through restoration, conservation or use are part of a totally different process. As this paper explains, very few of the major large objects in the NRM can truly be said to be in the condition in which the railway used them. Many have been built back or restored and are almost more the products of the museum industry than of the railway industry they are supposed to represent. Restoration at its most extreme can be seen as rewriting history. The argument may be raised that restoration and repair for operation simply continues the practice of the operating railways. However, this argument, on the 'grandfather's axe' logic that nothing is original so we can continue replacing *ad infinitum*, ignores the fundamental change in status of an object when it ends its working life and enters the museum. Future scholars and historians will have a far harder task than ourselves in understanding our collections if we do not take stock of the past and review our current practice.

In reviewing restoration and conservation in the National Railway Collection I have to conclude that the NRM's inheritance is largely one of restoration with little emphasis on conservation and documentary recording. The museum should perhaps shift its emphasis to conservation and to a greater understanding of the objects and consideration of the complex interpretative messages which they can be used to communicate. Railway vehicles are not simply the products of great engineers but of craftsmen; they were built to do jobs as part of a complex railway industry; they have human, economic, industrial and historical significance. Any conservation/restoration regime should not destroy the evidence which allows an object to communicate these complex messages.

The NRM needs to develop an approach to its collections which embodies a conservation ethic reflecting best current practice. In the future it can have a unique role to play in caring for and interpreting its collections. The emphasis should continue to shift from wholesale restoration to careful conservation with a greater emphasis on retaining or recording the material evidence of our collections. The NRM also has a leading part to play in setting standards for and providing guidance in the area of the preservation of railway collections. It is in a unique position, in Britain, as a major state-funded institution devoted to one transport subject area. A simple code of best practice for conservation and care would be a valuable aid in ensuring that important material evidence is not lost in restoration. Such a code might be initially applied to the care of the National Railway Collection at the NRM and elsewhere but could be more widely adapted by all involved in the permanent preservation of important railway material. In providing such guidance the museum would play a decisive part in ensuring the long-term survival of the significant collections which represent Britain's railway heritage.

Notes and references

1 Forward, E D, *Railway Locomotives and Rolling Stock* (London: HMSO, 1948), II: *Descriptive Catalogue*

2 Reed, B, 'The *Rocket*', in Reed, B (ed), *Locomotives in Profile* (Windsor: Profile Publications, 1971), I, pp149-72

3 Casserley, H C, *Preserved Locomotives* (Shepperton: Ian Allan, 1980), 5th edn, p11

4 Barker, R, 'Lost preserved railway rolling stock', *Transport History*, 9 (1978), pp100-9

5 Nock, O S, *Historical Steam Locomotives* (London: A & C Black, 1959), p15

6 Barker, R, 'Lost preserved railway rolling stock', p101

7 Bryan, T, *North Star: A Tale of Two Locomotives* (Swindon: Thamesdown, 1989)

8 Quoted in Simpson, G, 'Saving a loco – 1927 style', *Steam Railway*, 1, 13 (1981), pp40-42

9 British Transport Commission, *The Preservation of Relics and Records* (London: British Transport Commission, 1951)

10 Skeat, W O, 'The consultative panel and the transport museums', *Journal of the Stephenson Locomotive Society*, 42 (1966), pp263-73

11 Scholes, J H, 'Restoration – that is the question: an expert's reflection on the practical problems of preservation', *Railway Magazine*, 112 (1966), pp558-60

12 Scholes, J H, 'Industrial archaeology: preservation, the cost and who pays', *Museums Journal*, 66 (1967), pp250-52

13 Nock, O S, *Historical Steam Locomotives*, p112

14 4079, 'BR did it too', *Trains Illustrated, Steam Alive*, 1, 1 (1979), pp48, 52

15 Hoole, K, *The Illustrated History of East Coast Joint Stock* (Sparkford: Oxford Publishing Company, 1993), p83

A future for the railway?

Stephen Joseph

This paper looks briefly at the possible future of the railway as a transport system and the place of a railway system in present-day transport planning and society.

I grew up in north London where the North London Railway was under threat of closure at the time when I was using it to get to school. I had a real interest in both saving the railway from being closed and, as an embryonic historian, in finding out about how it had influenced the development of north London, especially the suburbs. There was also, at that time, a proposal to build an urban motorway through the area, so transport was an important political issue – and it still is an important political issue in London, as it is in almost any other major city in the world.

It seems to me now that railway closures, in north London or wherever, ought to be behind us because the environment for railways has never been better. This is because the growth in road traffic and the environmental problems it creates are bringing a form of railway renaissance. It is not a return to the railway of the past, it is a move ahead to looking at the success of current railway developments and their potential. If we consider issues such as carbon dioxide emissions and other traffic-generated pollutants, we can establish that pollution from road traffic is bringing both immediate local health problems, such as a reduction in air quality, and global climate problems. Road traffic in every country is now increasingly being seen as the key obstacle to the various environmental targets that every country is setting itself: clean air, the preservation of natural habitats and so on. The traditional reaction of governments to traffic growth has been to project and plan to provide for increased traffic flows in the future. It has been estimated in Britain that if the past 30 years of traffic are extrapolated into the future, traffic will grow by up to 142 per cent, to the level where Britain will have more cars than California, and to accommodate that will need a road from London to Edinburgh 257 lanes wide. (It is not surprising that Transport 2000 suspects that there are civil servants somewhere planning for a 257-lane motorway from London to Edinburgh.) In practice it is clear that there is a limit to the amount of extra road traffic that can be accommodated; we cannot build our way out of congestion. In Britain the Confederation of British Industry estimates the cost of congestion to be £15 billion a year or so. In a sense, the old enemies of the railways, roads and road traffic, are drowning in their own excess, and additional road building is self-defeating.

Railways, which were once seen as a dying technology, only for museums, are now perceived as a new technology providing new solutions. As so often happens, public opinion has come full circle; environmentalists in the last century opposed railways, and literary giants like Wordsworth and John Ruskin railed against the destruction of landscapes. Similar vituperation is now directed at new roads because of the way they destroy wildlife and natural habitats. There have been confrontations and there have been successes and failures in trying to maintain a balance between traffic needs and environmental imperatives.

Transport 2000 is the proof of this, and is an interesting organisation in its own right. It has been in existence for 20 years as an alliance of environmentalists and railway interests. It is partly funded by British Rail, by the railway unions and the railway manufacturing industry, with other funding coming from non-profit groups and local councils. Transport 2000 is funded by rail interests but makes a case for rail that is independent; it is linked with the National Association of Rail Passengers in the US. It is also linked to similar groups in other countries such as Germany, Canada and Australia. These other groups are all slightly different and none of them is made up of quite the same mix as Transport 2000.

Railways are only part of the area that we cover. We do work on roads and road traffic; we are pro walking, cycling and buses as well as rail; and we argue not just for quantitative changes but for improvements in the quality of life. We are actively pursuing the rail versus road debate and the impact of transport policies (or lack of policies) on local communities.

I think it is now the case that similar arguments are being accepted worldwide. The road lobby is starting to be questioned because of the problems that road building and increased traffic have caused. Increasingly, government policy makers are choosing to subsidise railways and people are now seeing the benefits of that spending. In Britain the government is starting to focus on the real cost of motoring and the subsidies that go to cars.

There is a cultural change taking place that can be compared to the cultural change that has occurred about smoking and drink driving – both once socially acceptable. The expression 'one for the road' is never heard these days. In the same way there is a cultural change taking place in attitudes to cars. Chuck Berry sang 'Driving along in my automobile' in the 1960s but nowadays one is more likely to hear songs about delays on the M25, as demonstrated by Chris Rea's song 'Road to hell'. The film *Who Framed Roger Rabbit?* enshrined in myth General Motors' practice of buying up and shutting down all of Los Angeles' tram lines. There is a wonderful line in that film where Bob Hoskins' character jumps on the back of a tram and some kids say, 'Hey, Mister, haven't you got a car?'; he replies, 'Why should I have a car? Los Angeles has the finest public transport anywhere in the world.' That was Los Angeles in 1947 but today Americans find such a comment farcical. Though these instances are merely straws in the wind they reflect a cultural change necessary if public transport is to be favoured over the private car.

Cultural change can both presage and encourage policy change; we have seen in the US the Inter-Service Transport Efficiency Act and the Clean Air Act promoting a return to public transport. In Europe we have seen moves to promote public transport too, and in Britain we have seen reforms of transport grants and planning legislation which encourage public-transport-friendly development. We have seen European countries, such as The Netherlands, set targets for road traffic. In order to help meet targets for the reduction of road traffic growth, the Dutch railways aim to double passenger and freight traffic over 20 years. Whether that is going to be achieved is a different question, but at least the target is there. Railways are only part of the Dutch plan, and success requires a package of measures. In Britain York is a good example of a city that has put together a package of measures including Park and Ride, bus lanes, parking policy, pedestrian and cycle lanes as well as support for the railways.

The railways are part of a transport renaissance which is not just concerned with developments that attract media attention such as the TGV. The renaissance is also about urban rapid transit and the new light rail systems that are being built in cities across the developed world. I have been talking recently to a small company in Birmingham, precisely the sort of company that developed the railway revolution in the first place, which has come up with what it calls 'People Mover'. This is a low-cost flywheel-driven city distributor system which can be laid down on the streets, without having to dig them up, and is rail-based. It is a development that would be of particular help to developing countries. It is a new type of rail development and shows the flexibility and adaptability that railways can have.

The rail renaissance is not, however, unconditional. Governments want increasing control over railway finance and direction. This leads to another trend towards the privatisation and commercialisation of railways which is evident worldwide. This is partly ideological but it is also partly a response to railway pressures. In Europe large state subsidies have been given to railways, and governments realise that they need to make the railways accountable. State-owned railways have been seen as unresponsive to customers – freight and passengers – and there is seen to be a need to inject private marketing skills into the system and for competition to stimulate cross-border traffic in Europe. Railway development needs increased access to private funding and there is a need to reduce railway labour costs. All of these are producing pressures to change some of the very basic things that we have taken for granted about railways.

In particular there is now a trend to separate track from trains. The old certainty of the unity between track and train operations is now being questioned. The Swedish now have a separate track authority and train-operating companies. The EC is following suit and Britain is now heading in that direction too. The Swedish situation has been driven at least in part by the need to get rail and road on a comparable basis so that 'rail track' can be accounted for in the same way as 'road track'.

The idea of open access to the railway track has also been revived from the very early stages of the railways when they were developed as common carriers. In those days the technology to 'manage' open access that we have nowadays was not available, but these are areas that have never been tested before.

Then there is privatisation itself – selling off and separating the state from the operation of the railways. Most systems, even the Japanese railways, still have substantial public control built into the railways because as we have seen there are direct public interests in having a good rail system. The state, then, is still very important; there is a contrast between attitudes to the railways in Britain and in much of the rest of Europe where they are seen as part of the state and a public service. Perhaps this is due to the military role the railways played in France and Germany as compared to the lack of a military role in Britain. This resulted in less state involvement in railways in Britain than in roads in the 1920s and 1930s.

Britain does not have a national rail plan. This perhaps follows the example of other Anglo-Saxon countries such as Canada, where railways have been seen as something separate from the state, as opposed to roads which are of national interest. Approaches to rail privatisation differ widely. In Germany, for instance, there will be an office of rail policy within the federal government, just as there is in the federal government in Washington. In Britain there is no policy, investment and planning framework. The British rail privatisation involves separation of track and train, franchising and competition; no other country is trying this, and progress here will probably be watched very closely. Informed observers are, at present, pessimistic about what privatisation, in the form adopted by the British government, means for railways in this country. It seems to be very much an ideological process rather than something which is built on the railway itself. It has driven the people who actually benefit, use and value railways to become involved

in the debate about the railway future. One of the things Transport 2000 has done is to set up a coalition called 'PLATFORM for better rail services' which brings together disability groups, women's groups and all sorts of rural organisations which rely on railways to voice their concerns about the value of a good rail service. This seems to me to be perhaps the most valuable thing to have come out of the British privatisation of the railways; people have been able to discuss how important railways still are for communities in this country. I think that privatisation elsewhere will have the same result.

It seems to me, leaving the British process aside, that what we are seeing is a synthesis. On the one hand, the US states are moving towards more state involvement to meet clean air targets, to take advantage of the Inter-Service Transport Efficiency Act and to set priorities and objectives of transport policy retaining some private involvement but increasing state involvement too. California is one example. On the other hand, the Europeans are moving away from the state model but nevertheless retain national planning and investment agencies and encourage local government to use railways to meet policy objectives.

There will still be a lot of railways running in the future. There will still be occasions for people to meet and discuss railway history because there will still be plenty of railway history to discuss. My only worry is that there may not be so much of it in Britain, and that Britain will be left out even with the Channel Tunnel, because of the peculiarly British approach to privatisation and to railways which is not really shared by the rest of Europe. I hope I am wrong about Britain's peculiarly local problems; I am sure I am right about the long-term future for the railway as an environmentally friendly and cost-effective mode of public transport.

Summary

Rob Shorland-Ball

In 1910 W Gordon, writing of railways in the UK, noted that:

... we are all concerned with railways. There is no-one living in Great Britain who does not come into contact, somehow, somewhere, with the enormous power and organization of our railways in the aggregate. Concerning a force so potent in our national and business life, it is surely wise and helpful that we should know far more than most of us do ....[1]

It is one of our tasks in museums, as authors and as teachers to illustrate 'the enormous power and organisation of our railways'. Museums have traditionally sought to illustrate the history of their particular subject or subjects but the vividness of the illustration and its capacity to educate depend on the imagination and the pre-existing knowledge of the visitor.

I remember the first time I saw George Stephenson's *Locomotion* – the steam locomotive which opened the Stockton & Darlington Railway. It was on a plinth at Bank Top station, Darlington – a mounted museum object. I forget the exact wording of the label but it ran something like this:

Locomotion No 1 (1825)
Stockton & Darlington Railway
An 0-4-0 with a wrought-iron single straight-flue boiler. The two vertical cylinders are part sunk in the boiler. The pistons of both cylinders are connected by crossheads and rods to two crank pins, one in each opposite wheel and working in unison, the one ninety degrees in advance of the other.
There are two eduction pipes transverse with the engine, joined by two longitudinal pipes, with branches and elbows to correspond, joining through the circumferential line of the chimney, to allow of a circular opening to the full bore, or sectional area of the pipes.

There was probably a mention at the end of the label of George Stephenson and the opening of the line but, even for me, an interested young person, the magic had gone long before I reached the 'full bore' of the eduction pipes. And, with the magic gone, I was unable to appreciate the role of *Locomotion* in the transformation of Britain's industrial and social life.

Several years later I read a copy of L T C Rolt's life of George and Robert Stephenson. He quotes from the diaries of Edward Pease, the Quaker progenitor of the railway, who in turn reports the experience of Robert Metcalf, a worker on the Stockton & Darlington Railway at the time *Locomotion* No 1 was delivered to the line:

No 1 came to Heighton Lane by road/we had to get her on the way/when we got her on the way we pump water into her/we sent John Taylor for a lantern and candle to Acliffe/when we done that I thought I would have my pipe/it was a very warm day though it been back end of the year/I took me pipe glass and let me pipe/I thought to myself I would try to put fire to Jimmy ockam/it blaaze away well/the fire going rapidly/lantern and candle was to no use so No 1's fire was put to her on line by the pour of the sun

As Rolt adds:

There is surely some symbolic significance in this little piece of humble and quite spontaneous ritual by which the sun's heat kindled fire in the belly of the first locomotive in the world to move on a public line of railway ....[2]

That little vignette gave the railway a human connection for me. The magic was rekindled. My interest not only in *Locomotion* but in the wider themes of the Industrial Revolution became more vivid.

Finally, a few years later, I saw the replica *Locomotion* moving under its own steam at the Stockton & Darlington 150th celebrations in 1975 and then subsequently at Beamish Museum. I saw that extraordinary motion-work on top of the boiler, described in such incomprehensible detail on the locomotive label at Bank Top station. I saw it see-sawing up and down as *Locomotion* lumbered along and in truth history *seemed* to 'come alive'. Not because I believed I was seeing history before me – this was, after all, a replica locomotive – but because the successive stimuli triggered my imagination and enhanced my appreciation of the original object and my understanding (and enjoyment) of the working replica. Now I began to understand the technical language of the original Bank Top label. And now the several dimensions of *Locomotion*'s magic – mechanical, human and historical – all came together in a meaningful way. I was able to begin to appreciate this locomotive and its significance in the context of its time.

There is, however, a danger for museums or, indeed, preserved railways, in trying to create history or even in trying to interpret history in the museum context. I remember at my previous museum in Suffolk – a 70-acre open-air site museum concerned with rural life – that I was rather pleased with a steam threshing demonstration which we had set up. The museum's steam traction engine was chuffing away splendidly and we were putting museum-grown, reaper/binder-cut wheat through the threshing machine. We were not in period costume but we had, I felt, achieved a reasonable re-creation of an Edwardian farm operation and our visitors were obviously interested. As the engine driver I had a fairly easy time and I had the opportunity to talk to people. An old man, nodding at the steam engine, said to me: 'We used to hate they buggers.' I knew he had looked after working horses when he worked at a local farm and I supposed it was the fact that the engine had supplanted the horses that he disliked. It was, however, the change from hand work to machine work that he had experienced and resented. He explained that a traction engine never tired; it was still working hard 12 hours or more after it had started. Men and animals tired but the steam engine continued – a remorseless taskmaster, hour after hour. Suddenly our demonstration of steam threshing became – to my inner eye – very different from the rather pleasant, nostalgic re-creation our visitors were enjoying. We had created 'nice' history. I am reminded of that experience whenever there is a danger of nostalgia replacing truth in interpretation. We must avoid becoming 'deferential museums' presenting an image of history that is coloured by our own preconceptions and superimposing simplistic constructs on events that owe more to the vagaries of the chaos theory than to economic determinism.

I believe the papers read in the symposium and published here have explored a variety of constructs and given us much to reflect on – particularly if we are preparing new exhibitions, writing or lecturing on railway history or using our knowledge of railway history to illuminate other work which we or others are undertaking.

From the proceedings I would like to draw out one or two threads which may colour the fabric of the publication.

Jim Ward's introductory paper noted that 'Our fundamental problem is that railroads appeal to us on several levels and the most obvious, the real world of physical things, is often not the most important.' It is the power and energy the railroads released in the human psyche (and, of course, that *was* released *by* that psyche) that is at the heart of our concerns. The symposium and these proceedings are an attempt to discover and delineate the common roots and to understand the separate branches of the railway in society. Ward suggested:

Our only charge is to make sense of the railways' realities, to suggest how important they are to the world as a whole and to invite that world to come and see for itself. Ultimately, it does not matter through what prism we view the industry – visual, textual, artistic or mechanical – because all our approaches are equally legitimate.

An indisputable 'common root' is the very fabric of the railway itself in the UK. Gordon Biddle's paper ranged from the extraordinary – the Causey Arch of *c*1726 (at its time the widest single-span masonry arch in the world) – to the necessary – a cast-iron urinal. Biddle noted that:

... railway building was regarded as a national undertaking from which the country at large would benefit. The profit motive was accompanied by enormous self-confidence in engineering works on an unprecedented scale which, it was believed, would last for ever.

In a stimulating and thought-provoking commentary on Biddle's paper, John Hankey offered an American perspective on the built railway heritage. Hankey commented that:

It matters not whether this built railway heritage is preserved in a museum, worked as a preservation activity, part of the present operating system or privately owned ... The commonplace and the disposable are often where the most interesting conclusions manifest themselves ... In fact, I would like to blur or perhaps obliterate as many boundaries as I can, for they have little meaning for the ideas to follow.

There followed fascinating and contrasting views and observations on railway structures in Berlin, at the Horseshoe Curve in Pennsylvania and on the early Baltimore & Ohio (B&O) Railroad in Maryland. In a real blurring of international boundaries we move from the ruins of great railway stations in Berlin to the sweep of the Pennsylvania Railroad's Horseshoe Curve near Altoona and to Herb Harwood's fascinating glimpse of the discovery of the little B&O station building at Duffields, West Virginia, '... vacant, neglected and obscured with trees, bushes and vines ...'. It was valuable too that Peter Barton from Altoona reminded us of the human dimension which created the structures that we were discussing:

The museum has taken on the task of telling the story of American workers engaged in work of mythical stature, in conceiving, building and running the transportation system that transformed a nation ....

John White developed both the human theme and the significance of mechanical engineering development in a review of early railway locomotive practice, teasing out the common roots and the separate branches. His title, 'Old debts and new visions', suggested another view of the process of change and refinement which we can recognise throughout the history of locomotive and rolling stock development. 'Old debts' to the British inheritance, were, as he said, 'gradually paid off with new visions' from the US and around the world.

Philip Atkins continued the same theme but this time from a British rather than an American perspective. He reviewed the physical survivors from the early years and exposed the curious serendipity which preserved *Agenoria*, a technical anachronism even when it was built, and destroyed several seminal objects like Daniel Gooch's *Lord of the Isles*. Lars Karlsson pursued the idea of the old debts and new visions in his study of the British locomotive in Sweden.

Jack Simmons introduced his paper with some sentences written by Charles E Lee which are so apposite to our deliberations that they are worth quoting again in full:

... [there is an] ever-increasing tendency to make the fundamental mistake of recording a fact as if it were an isolated phenomenon, without considering it in true perspective in relation to the social and economic conditions prevailing ... Railways came into general use in the first half of the last century because of the increasing need for the transport of heavy concentrated loads along fixed routes, often with gradients unsuited to canals; not because they had just been invented. The urge to develop the steam locomotive was provided by the high cost of

horse feed during the Napoleonic wars ... When invention does not coincide with real need, it usually languishes.

Lee's purpose in writing in this way, Simmons told us, was:

to draw attention to the difference between an item of news and what has come to be called background material. News tends to be recorded, and indexed, while attendant conditions do not.

Simmons continued:

There was nothing strikingly original in the remarks just quoted. What *is* striking is to see how often they are disregarded, almost 50 years after they first came out in print. The economic historians, of course, have not disregarded them. From Sir John Clapham onwards some have made it their business to attend carefully to the part the railways played in shaping the British economy. But I am speaking here, as Lee was too, of those who have written specifically about railways, of the history of companies, their mechanical equipment and the services of trains they provided.

The chief explanation of the failure to look enough at the development of railways 'in relation to the social and economic conditions prevailing' at the time is that those who have set themselves to write about it have concentrated their minds too much on recording what happened, and when, and not enough on answering the question 'why?'.

Often, the answer to the question 'why?':

will be found by looking carefully at the condition of the country or the district in which the railways were growing up; not at its social and economic condition alone, but at its political, cultural and moral condition too.

I have quoted at length from the introduction to Simmons' paper because his comments are central to this symposium. I make no apology, then, for one further quotation:

The British railways ... were instruments of private profit. But their work completely transcended that original purpose. They quickly became, and then they remained for the best part of a century, the huge instrument on which the greater part of the inland transport system turned. The full extent of the debt that the country owed to its railways has never been computed; some parts of it will always remain hidden from us now. I hope this paper has done a little to stimulate and encourage further exploration.

Wise words, and a useful introduction to two different aspects of that exploration. First, a study of the practice of urban promotion by American railroads from Roger Grant which concluded that 'it was the railroad that left the most indelible mark upon the national map'.

Second, a description by Patrick Greene of the archaeology of the world's oldest railway station building, the 1830 warehouse at Liverpool Road station in Manchester. The paper was of particular interest because Greene, an archaeologist himself, demonstrated the use of archaeological techniques to unravel the functions of the building and its method of operation. It is sobering to note that although the building is only 160 years old we lack any detailed knowledge of how such an important piece of the railway's operating infrastructure actually worked. And every year which passes means that elements of the railway landscape which seem so familiar are not only becoming unfamiliar but are being forgotten – a reminder, if we need it, that we must record the mundane and the everyday as well as the unusual and the spectacular.

As befits his discipline, Allan Patmore, a geographer, provided a synoptic view of the relationship of the railway to the physical landscape, of the distinctive landscape of the railway itself and of the impact of the railway on the landscape of settlement, illustrated by a case study of the Victorian resort and spa of Harrogate.

Much of the symposium, and these proceedings, was concerned with preservation and interpretation. Three short papers reviewed railway preservation in the UK and are followed by a series of substantive studies of museum developments in Lucerne, in Utrecht and at Steamtown in Scranton, Pennsylvania, which dwell on the problems of interpretation.

Kilian Elsasser described the philosophy informing his work on the creation of a new gallery at the Swiss Transport Museum. He used the word 'edutainment' to reflect the combination of education and entertainment which is the hallmark of all good displays.

Paul van Vlijmen from the Dutch Railway Museum, and himself, interestingly, from a fine-art, not a technical background, described the development and the recent renovation of his museum in Utrecht. He explained that, in carrying out the renovation, the aim was:

... to create a [design which would be as] surprising, clear, unusual and 'timeless' as possible, and one which would

endure for decades both visually and technically. The presentation of the collection was guided by three 'A's: namely, amazement, awe and admiration.

At the symposium the discussion which followed the papers provided a useful commentary from the floor about the planning of the interface between what museum professionals wanted of a museum, what the visitor wanted and what museum professionals wanted the visitor to want. After hearing about museum interpretation it seemed logical, when planning the symposium programme, to visit a preserved railway. The staff of the Keighley and Worth Valley Railway in West Yorkshire made the symposium delegates very welcome and gave their own perspective on preserving and interpreting the railway heritage. Their description of the railway ran as follows:

The epitome of a volunteer-run railway. A thriving branch-line which serves six stations (most of them gas-lit), which is host to an extensive and varied collection of locomotives and where everything continues to provide the atmosphere of the days of the steam railway.

The perennial transport museum debate on operation or display was taken up in John Latschar's paper. Latschar is the Superintendent of the National Historic Site which is under development on part of the Delaware, Lackawanna and Western railroad yards in Scranton, Pennsylvania. The site includes a number of railroad buildings and came to the National Park Service with a heterogeneous collection of locomotives and rolling stock. Latschar explained and justified the decision to treat both buildings and vehicles not as static historical objects but as functioning pieces of equipment within a designed rail-yard system. The vehicles are 'typical working locomotives and cars that hauled the freight, delivered the mail, provided passenger service and connected America'. For Steamtown the value of the collection of buildings and vehicles is in what it did, not what it looked like.

Latschar develops his argument with an observation which I think is worth repeating and reflecting on:

The National Park Service [which is the leading historic preservation agency in the USA] ... brought a slightly different viewpoint of railway preservation to Steamtown. To us, [the Service] railway preservation is a relatively recent offshoot of the overall field of historic preservation. We do not consider railway preservation to be a field unto itself. Over the past few years there has been a lot of worthy debate taking place within the railway preservation community concerning the need to adopt standard preservation criteria. We would like to suggest that many of the criteria and standards which have been accepted in the general field of historic preservation are directly applicable to railway preservation, and should be considered during this debate.

In applying to railway preservation the criteria and standards evolved by the Park Service into a coherent philosophy for the care of historical structures and objects one can find ways of resolving some of the debates considered in the symposium and reflected in the published papers. I quote again from Latschar's paper:

... the significance of an engineering system [like the railway] is the product or service which it produced. In other words, it is the output of the system – not the system itself – which is of primary importance. In particular, understanding the impact which that output had upon society is the key to fully understanding the system's history and significance ... when we are dealing with an operating engineering system [a locomotive] which has parts that move and work, then we are dealing with a system that will have parts which wear out, break and need replacement ... with an operating railroad museum, we are convinced that we can provide this understanding through the involvement of all five senses: sight, sound, smell, taste and touch. And we hope to stimulate the all-important sixth sense, human emotion, without which there can be no true understanding.

Walter Gray, Director of the California State Railroad Museum reflected in his paper on the present position of railroad preservation in the US, noting that:

Railroad preservation ... is largely avocational [and] segmented both geographically and by means of propulsion (steam, electric and diesel), and to a degree by era. The emphasis is still on the age of steam [but] with a growing recognition ... that contemporary equipment and the contextual aspects of the built environment also require preservation.

The three short papers that followed, from Strasburg, Sacramento and Baltimore, admirably showed how much is being achieved.

The penultimate papers were concerned with preserving the past and collecting for the future. Leslie Soane, Director of the (UK) Railway Heritage Trust, provided a blueprint for assisting the preservation of an inheritance of more than 150 years of infrastructure by a nationalised, unified railway system. The catalyst for the creation of the Railway Heritage Trust was a disaster – not a new situation for government-sponsored initiatives affecting the railway, as Jack Simmons' paper reminded us. In this instance the disaster was the demolition of the Doric 'Arch' at Euston. The quality of work which has been achieved subsequently in conserving and restoring the historic structures of the operating railway with the support of the Trust was well illustrated by Soane's paper. Whether, once the British railways are privatised, the Trust can continue its valuable work remains a matter for concern.

Paul van Vlijmen, Director of the Netherlands Railway Museum, described the advantages of working with a nationalised railway that has a preservation plan providing a philosophy, criteria and money for the development of the national railway collection. Van Vlijmen noted that 'throughout the world, there are not likely to be many museums which have already established which items to include in their collections in 35 years' time.'

The papers from Hopkins of the NRM and Gottwaldt of Berlin examined two approaches to display and conservation. The different, yet related, approaches they espoused suggested that we must not become victims of pragmatic absolutism. Circumstances alter cases and we must take informed curatorial decisions about the objects in our care reflecting all the factors that may influence our decisions. Knowledge of what others have done – or failed to do – is always useful.

The final paper, given as an after-dinner speech by Stephen Joseph, Director of the UK transport lobby group Transport 2000, concluded the proceedings with a perceptive view of the possible future of the railway as a transport system.

The proceedings show, in a variety of papers, what has been done within the framework of the *Common Roots* and *Separate Branches* of the title. I believe we have been successful in '... weaving the experiences of this unprecedented gathering of railway preservationists into a useful fabric.'

What will be required to make a garment from the fabric?

First, we will build on the networks that have developed as a result of the symposium meeting in York. Second, the published proceedings will form a coherent record of the meeting. I hope that all who read them will promote the proceedings with opinion formers in the variety of disciplines with which we still (especially in the UK) lack formal academic relationships. Third, Bill Withuhn and I have been sketching out the bones of what we intend will become an International Association of Railway Studies (IARAS). With a secretary and a small international committee it will serve as the catalyst for a number of developments and work as a facilitator to help to:

- promote subsequent international symposia
- continue to promote a working partnership of operators, museums and scholars
- bring together academics and specialists in a number of other fields whose work touches on or is touched by the railway
- liaise with other appropriate bodies (such as the Railway Study Association in the UK) to promote links between current railway developments and the history, archaeology, geography and economics of railway systems past and present
- publish papers and perhaps, ultimately, a specialist journal of railway studies carrying papers

of the quality and range produced for the symposium which will benefit from the synergy of juxtaposition in such a journal
- seek funding, by grants and sponsorship, to underwrite publications and symposia and to establish research fellowships attached to appropriate institutions such as major railway museums
- promote the creation of a university Chair of Railway Studies which might combine in an appropriate department both historical and present-day work on railways
- harness the skills, knowledge and enthusiasm of the railway preservation movement to the academic study of the railways and their impact on society, and, where appropriate, serve as an exemplar of good practice
- ask and, in the railways context, try and answer the question 'why?'.

The contact address for IARAS is:

Rob Shorland-Ball, Secretary, IARAS, c/o National Railway Museum, Leeman Road, York YO2 4XJ, UK.

Notes and references

1   Gordon, W, *Our Home Railways* (London: Ian Allan, 1962), 2nd edn

2   Rolt, L T C, *George and Robert Stephenson* (London: Longman, 1960)

Index

This index includes personal and company names, place names and names of railways and locomotives. Page numbers in italics denote illustrations.